Encyclopedia of Public Health

Encyclopedia of Public Health

Principles, People, and Programs

VOLUME 2: M–Z

SALLY KUYKENDALL, EDITOR

GREENWOOD™

An Imprint of ABC-CLIO, LLC
Santa Barbara, California • Denver, Colorado

Library of Congress Cataloging in Publication Control Number: 2017045280

ISBN: 978-1-61069-982-2 (set)
978-1-4408-4809-4 (vol. 1)
978-1-4408-4810-0 (vol. 2)
978-1-61069-983-9 (ebook)

22 21 20 19 18 1 2 3 4 5

This book is also available as an eBook.

Greenwood
An Imprint of ABC-CLIO, LLC

ABC-CLIO, LLC
130 Cremona Drive, P.O. Box 1911
Santa Barbara, California 93116-1911
www.abc-clio.com

This book is printed on acid-free paper ∞

Manufactured in the United States of America

Contents

Guide to Related Topics

Centers for Medicare and Medicaid Services (CMS)
Community Health Centers (CHCs)
Environmental Protection Agency (EPA)
Food and Drug Administration (FDA)
Health Resources and Services Administration (HRSA)
Indian Health Service (HIS)
National Cancer Institute (NCI)
National Center for Injury Prevention and Control (NCIPC)
National Heart, Lung, and Blood Institute (NHLBI)
National Institute on Drug Abuse (NIDA)
National Institutes of Health (NIH)
State, Local, and Territorial Health Departments
Substance Abuse and Mental Health Services Administration (SAMHSA)
Surgeon General
U.S. Department of Agriculture (USDA)
U.S. Department of Health and Human Services (DHHS)
U.S. Public Health Service (PHS)
World Health Organization (WHO)

Laws and Guidelines

Affordable Care Act (ACA)
Americans with Disabilities Act (ADA)
Belmont Report, The
Emergency Medical Treatment and Labor Act (EMTALA)
Evidence-Based Programs and Practices
False Claims Act (FCA)
Health Insurance Portability and Accountability Act (HIPAA)
Master Settlement Agreement (MSA)
Public Health Law
Social Security Act (SSA)
Stark Law

Major Events in the History of Public Health

Agricultural Safety
Ancient World, Public Health in the
Americans with Disabilities Act (ADA)
Cutter Incident, The
Family Planning
Fluoridation
Food Safety
Greco-Roman Era, Public Health in the
Heart Disease
Infectious Diseases
Master Settlement Agreement (MSA)
Maternal Health
Medicaid
Medicare
Middle Ages, Public Health in the
Modern Era, Public Health in the
Motor Vehicle Safety
Oral Health
Pandemic
Penicillin
Polio
Public Health in the United States, History of
Quarantine
Renaissance, Public Health in the
Social Security Act (SSA)
Tuskegee Syphilis Study
Vaccines

People

Anderson, Elizabeth Milbank (1850–1921)
Baker, Sara Josephine (1873–1945)

Principles

Maternal Health
Medicine
Men's Health
Mental Health
Needs Assessment
Nutrition
Patient Safety
Physical Activity
Population Health
Precaution Adoption Process Model (PAPM)
PRECEDE-PROCEED Planning Model
Prescription Drugs
Prevention
Quarantine
RE-AIM (Reach, Effectiveness, Adoption, Implementation, and Maintenance)
Reciprocal Determinism
Research
Risk-Benefit Analysis
Self-Efficacy
Social Cognitive Theory (SCT)
Social Determinants of Health (SDOH)
Social Ecological Model
Spiritual Health
Transtheoretical Model (TTM)
Veterans' Health
Women's Health

Professional Organizations and Resources

American Journal of Public Health (AJPH)
American Public Health Association (APHA)
Association of Public Health Laboratories (APHL)
Association of State and Territorial Health Officials (ASTHO)
Certified in Public Health (CPH)
Council on Education for Public Health (CEPH)
Degrees in Public Health
Grants
Health and Medicine Division of the National Academies of Sciences, Engineering, and Medicine
National Association of County and City Health Officials (NACCHO)
National Health and Nutrition Examination Survey (NHANES)
Nation's Health, The
Public Health Department Accreditation
Society of Public Health Education (SOPHE)

Programs

Affordable Care Act (ACA)
Centers for Disease Control and Prevention (CDC)
Centers for Medicare and Medicaid Services (CMS)
Community Health Centers (CHCs)
Environmental Protection Agency (EPA)
Evidence-Based Programs and Practices
Family Planning
Fluoridation
Food and Drug Administration (FDA)
Genetics
Global Health
Health and Medicine Division of the National Academies of Sciences, Engineering, and Medicine
Health Resources and Services Administration (HRSA)
Healthy People 2020
Healthy Places
Heart Truth® (Red Dress) Campaign, The
Home Safety

Specialty Areas of Practice

Introduction

Public health encompasses a broad array of programs, principles, and professional disciplines. The field is a multidisciplinary science, drawing from medicine, biology, sociology, management, psychology, political science, communications, marketing, and engineering. Public health works with traditional medical practice to promote health and well-being and to prevent disease and injury. Although the two systems have similar goals, each uses different strategies to achieve the goals. Traditional Western medicine focuses on individuals. Public health focuses on groups of people. Western medicine is reactionary, responding to individual cases of injury or disease. Public health is proactive, identifying at-risk groups and working to stop a problem early, sometimes before the problem starts. Western medicine is treatment oriented. Public health strives for prevention. Although the traditional medical system treats individuals suffering from a health problem, public health intervenes to prevent potential problems. The two systems work together to alleviate human suffering and to promote quality of life.

The public health workforce is composed of diverse professionals who work together through many different agencies and organizations. Common functions are to monitor community health, investigate outbreaks of disease, empower communities, mobilize partnerships, and care for vulnerable populations. Over the past 100 years, public health has realized significant achievements, increasing life span and quality of life. Activities work at the macro-level with policies, regulations, and programs and at the micro-level of influencing individual health behaviors. Public health extends beyond the day-to-day tasks of disease prevention and health promotion. Public health is a frame of mind, a political advocacy, a social movement of advocating for others, especially those who lack the power and resources to secure their own health. Public health professionals work toward a common vision for equitable health and health care in the United States.

The origins of public health trace back to early humans who devised ways to dispose of human waste without contaminating drinking water. As bacteriology and immunology emerged as scientific disciplines, so did the multidisciplinary field of public health. The most commonly recognized definition of public health was penned by Charles-Edward Amory Winslow, founder of the Yale School of Public Health. In 1920, Winslow described the newly emerging public health profession as:

> The science and art of preventing disease, prolonging life, and promoting health and efficiency through organized community efforts for the sanitation of the environment,

> the control of communicable infections, the education of the individual in personal hygiene, the organization of medical and nursing services for the early diagnosis and preventive treatment of disease, and for the development of the social machinery to insure everyone a standard of living adequate for the maintenance of health, so organizing these benefits as to enable every citizen to realize his birthright of health and longevity. (Winslow, 1920, p. 183)

Winslow's definition is timeless. Key points are (1) public health uses systematic investigations and organized knowledge to understand, predict, and intervene in adverse health conditions; (2) public health uses creativity and collaboration to design effective prevention activities; (3) public health encompasses a wide array of topics including sanitation, hygiene, health education, administration of health services, and health policies; and (4) public health is founded in the basic principle of human rights. More recently, the Essential Services Working Group defined the purpose of public health as preventing the spread of disease; promoting safe environments for living, working, and recreating; preventing intentional and unintentional injuries; promoting and encouraging healthy behaviors and mental health; responding to natural and man-made disasters and assisting communities in recovery; and assuring readily accessible, quality health services. In summary, public health practice is a cross-disciplinary field, using science, creativity, and collaboration to promote human health.

Public health professionals firmly believe that physical and mental health is a basic human right, not a choice, not a reward, not a privilege. Toward this vision, public health is a social movement with health equity as the main objective. Just as early man recognized that it was the responsibility of each and every member of the society to safeguard the community well or sources of drinking water, modern man is responsible for the health of others in society. In the landmark document, *The Future of Public Health*, the Institute of Medicine (1988) defined the mission of public health as "the fulfillment of society's interest in assuring the conditions in which people can be healthy" (p. 40). The IOM points to the responsibility of government and society in supporting and promoting health. This concept may seem a little alien to American culture, which embraces the ideals of independence, individualism, and self-determination. The idea that members of a group have responsibility of caring for others in society requires individuals to consider the needs of others before their own. This means that companies cannot dump waste into the ground where toxic chemicals could potentially poison the water of local residents; tobacco companies cannot market addictive and harmful products to children; and bystanders cannot turn away when they hear domestic violence. Public health requires everyone, corporate leaders, businesses, politicians, communities, schools, police, parents, neighbors, and individuals to consider the short- and long-term impact of their own behaviors on others. Social justice requires society to balance benefits and burdens. Members of society who experience burdens due to a particular action deserve benefits, and those who enjoy benefits from a particular action should carry a fair share of the burden.

The precautionary principle is used to set the bar on social responsibility. The precautionary principle states that *if* an action is *believed* to cause harm, even when there is insufficient science to support a biological connection, the burden of proof is on the actor not on the potential victim. In the case of toxic waste, the business is responsible for proving that runoff is not hazardous. The company cannot dump waste until the runoff is deemed safe through rigorous, impartial scientific study. It is not the citizens' responsibility to prove that waste products are causing disease.

The duty of providing public health services rests primarily on state, tribal, local, and territorial health departments. These entities are managed and financed by different sources. The issue of financing is important because microorganisms do not recognize state, county, or city boundaries. Sufficient funding ensures problems are addressed before they escalate out of control. State health departments are funded by the federal government, Medicare, Medicaid, state funds, and monies collected from fines for public health violations. State departments perform epidemiological surveillance, disease screening, laboratory services, treatment, and technical assistance. If there is a major outbreak of tuberculosis, the state health department would investigate, test, and treat. The majority of local public health departments are governed by local government. For example, the San Francisco Department of Public Health is governed by the city of San Francisco through the San Francisco Health Commission. The mayor of San Francisco appoints health commissioners who oversee public health programs, hospitals, home health care, outpatient treatment, disease surveillance, vital records, primary care, dental services, and maternal health services. A few states—Kentucky, Georgia, and Florida—share governance with local authorities. Local health departments are financed through local, state, and federal sources. Public health in U.S. territories of Puerto Rico, Guam, Virgin Islands, American Samoa, and the Commonwealth of Northern Mariana Islands and Freely Associated States of the Republic of Marshall Islands, Federated States of Micronesia, and Republic of Palau is funded through federal grants and cooperative agreements. Tribal health departments operate within the jurisdiction of the tribal nations to serve the health needs of Native Americans.

In general, state, tribal, local, and territorial health departments provide many of the day-to-day functions of public health, such as managing immunization programs; communicable disease screening, surveillance, and treatment; food safety and nutrition education; and inspections of restaurants, schools, and day care centers. Different populations may also present unique geographic, cultural, or economic challenges. For example, the World Health Organization reports that replacing traditional diets of nutrient-dense foods with imported energy-dense foods is causing obesity and other major health problems among Pacific Islanders (WHO, 2010). Thus, public health departments serving Pacific Islanders must focus on the negative effects of acculturation. Federal agencies are responsible for ensuring that state, tribal, local, and territorial governments have the capability to provide needed services. The federal government will only intervene if health threats extend beyond the region, require solutions outside of state or local jurisdiction, or in which states do not have the capacity to act. A man-made or natural disaster, such as major flooding, will prompt action by federal public health agencies.

Beyond assisting in natural or man-made health emergencies, the federal government manages the health of the nation by setting goals, policies, and standards, managing resources and supporting scientific research toward health solutions. Federal agencies responsible for ensuring public health include the Centers for Disease Control and Prevention (CDC), Agency for Healthcare Research and Quality, Environmental Protection Agency, Food and Drug Administration (FDA), Substance Abuse and Mental Health Services Administration (SAMHSA), National Cancer Institute (NCI), National Institute on Alcohol Abuse and Alcoholism (NIAAA), National Institute on Drug Abuse (NIDA), Department of Agriculture (USDA), Office of Minority Health (OMH), and the U.S. Public Health Service Commissioned Corps (USPHSCC). Within the CDC is the Office for State, Tribal, Local, and Territorial Support; Office of Public Health Preparedness and Response; National Institute for Occupational Safety and Health; Center for Global Health; Office of Public Health Scientific Services; Center for Surveillance, Epidemiology, and Laboratory Services; National Center for Health Statistics; Office of Noncommunicable Diseases, Injury, and Environmental Health; National Center for Birth Defects and Developmental Disabilities; National Center for Chronic Disease Prevention and Health Promotion; National Center for Environmental Health; Agency for Toxic Substances and Disease Registry; National Center for Injury Prevention and Control; Office of Infectious Diseases; National Center for Immunization and Respiratory Diseases; National Center for Emerging and Zoonotic Infectious Diseases; and the National Center for HIV, Viral Hepatitis, STD, and TB Prevention. The multiple centers, institutes, and offices within the CDC enable effective and efficient responses to public health threats. Each group provides specialized expertise while still accessing valuable resources from across the network.

Public health services are delivered by individuals of many different backgrounds and skill sets working in for-profit and nonprofit agencies, communities, and all levels of government. The public health workforce is one of the most professionally diverse groups one could envision. Workers include physicians, nurses, nutritionists, health inspectors, occupational health and safety workers, social workers, dentists and dental assistants, emergency responders, health educators, journalists, laboratory workers, X-ray technicians, animal control, veterinarians, researchers, scientists, statisticians, administrators, and policy experts. Each group offers their own distinct professional skills and together, practitioners create a larger system of care. Partnerships with the private sector, civic groups, nongovernmental organizations (NGOs), faith communities, schools, hospitals, community centers, tribal health, law enforcement, transit organizations, and employers develop a network, reaching as many people as possible in as many ways as possible. Each entity contributes in a unique way. In the case of head injuries, the National Operating Committee on Standards for Athletic Equipment (NOCSAE) develops and publishes standards for helmet safety; helmet manufacturers make helmets that meet the standards; parents purchase safety helmets; athletic organizations require players to wear helmets consistently and correctly; and coaches develop maneuvers to avoid high-impact plays (National Center for Injury Prevention and Control, 2015). Creating systems of care, developing policies, providing direct care and education, and advocating for health and safety require many different skills and partnerships.

Over the past century, public health in the United States has emerged as a unique discipline. Major achievements in the control of communicable diseases, oral hygiene, family planning, motor vehicle safety, workplace safety, heart disease prevention, and smoking cessation have extended human life span by approximately 25 years. These achievements were accomplished by many people and groups working together toward the common goal of disease prevention and health promotion.

The *Encyclopedia of Public Health: Principles, People, and Programs* describes selected public health strategies, achievements, and challenges throughout U.S. history. The entries featuring *principles* describe basic and complex concepts, and models and theories that help to guide effective public health practice. These entries provide a deeper understanding and appreciation of the field, the logic behind why public health professionals do what they do. The entries on *programs* present a sample of important, evidence-based interventions, policies, and organizations. There are many, many health education and health promotion programs. Not every program works, and some programs can cause more harm than good. The encyclopedia entries highlight programs that serve as a positive model for other programs. The context of why and how these programs were developed and implemented provides an understanding of the history of public health and best practices for the future. The entries on *people* detail the lives and achievements of social reformers, biologists, microbiologists, medical doctors, nurses, dentists, and other health professionals. The unique contributions of these men and women foster respect for all public health professionals. The stories of these pioneers reveal insightful discoveries, dogged perseverance, and dignity despite racism, gender biases, and professional or scientific challenges. Their stories tell us where public health has been and where public health must go. Their stories encourage emerging professionals to pursue a career in public health, medicine, epidemiology, biostatistics, or research. The field offers so many opportunities and needs people from diverse backgrounds with different skills. Public health belongs to everyone, and everyone belongs in public health.

Sally Kuykendall

Further Reading

American Public Health Association. (n.d.). *What is public health?* Retrieved from http://www.apha.org/~/media/files/pdf/factsheets/whatisph.ashx.

Essential Services Work Group. (n.d.). *Ten essential services: Purpose and practices of public health.* Atlanta: Centers for Disease Control and Prevention. Retrieved from http://www.cdc.gov/stltpublichealth/hop/pdfs/Ten_Essential_Public_Health_Services_2011-09_508.pdf.

Healthy people: The Surgeon General's report on health promotion and disease prevention. (1979). Rockville, MD: Department of Health, Education, and Welfare, Public Health Service, Office of the Assistant Secretary for Health and Surgeon General.

Institute of Medicine. (1988). *The future of public health*. Washington, DC: The National Academies Press.doi:10.17226/1091. Retrieved from http://www.nap.edu/catalog/1091/the-future-of-public-health.

National Center for Injury Prevention and Control. (2015). *HEADS UP to youth sports*. Atlanta: Centers for Disease Control and Prevention. Retrieved from http://www.cdc.gov/headsup/youthsports/index.html.

Office of State, Tribal, Local and Territorial Support, Centers for Disease Control and Prevention. (2013). *United States public health 101*. Retrieved from http://www.cdc.gov/stltpublichealth/docs/usph101.pdf.

Winslow, C. E. A. (1920). The untilled field of public health. *Modern Medicine, 2*, 183–191.

World Health Organization. (2010). Pacific Islanders pay heavy price for abandoning traditional diet. *Bulletin of the World Health Organization, 88*(7), 481–560. Retrieved from http://www.who.int/bulletin/volumes/88/7/10-010710/en.

Chronology

c. 1754 BCE	Code of Hammurabi states laws of Mesopotamia including medical fees
c. 1000 BCE	*Sushruta Samhita* records Indian medical and surgical practices
c. 600 BCE	Early bioterrorism: Assyrians poison enemy wells with rye ergot fungus
c. 460 BCE	Hippocrates proposes that diseases are related to diet, activity, lifestyle, and environment rather than punishment from the gods
c. 300 BCE	*Yellow Emperor's Inner Canon* documents Chinese medical practices
583	Roman Catholic Church isolates people with leprosy
c. 860	*Al-Risalah al-Dhahabiah* (*The Golden Treatise*) records medicine and wellness in Persia (Iran)
1346	Plague extends to Europe initiating the Black Death
1403	Venice establishes the first quarantine station
1431	Joan of Arc is declared a witch and burned at the stake
1492	Christopher Columbus sails to the Caribbean Islands
1520	Cortez exploration unintentionally introduces smallpox to the Aztec
1620	Pilgrims establish Plymouth colony
1628	William Harvey describes the circulatory system
1632	King Charles I licenses The Guinea Company to export African slaves to America
1683	Anton Van Leeuwenhoek visualizes microscopic animals
1754	Indigenous Americans are intentionally infected by blankets from smallpox victims
1775	American Revolutionary War begins
1776	Declaration of Independence

1783	American Revolutionary War ends with an estimated 4,435 U.S. service member deaths; Yellow fever epidemic
1794	Philadelphia establishes the first local board of health
1796	Edward Jenner inoculates James Phipps with cowpox
1798	Marine Hospital Service is founded
1831	Forced removal of Native Americans begins with the Choctaw Nation
1837	Great Plains smallpox epidemic decimates Native American people
1838	Forced removal of the Cherokee Nation results in the Trail of Tears
1842	Edwin Chadwick publishes *The Report on the Sanitary Conditions of the Labouring Population of Great Britain*
1843	Dorothea Dix publishes *Memorial to the Legislature of Massachusetts* documenting the living conditions of mentally ill in Massachusetts
1847	American Medical Association is founded; Ignaz Semmelweis recommends that doctors wash their hands to reduce infections
1848	Women's rights convention held at Seneca Falls, New York
1849	Elizabeth Blackwell is the first female to earn a medical degree from a U.S. college
1850	Lemuel Shattuck releases *Report of the Sanitary Commission of Massachusetts*; Congress passes the Fugitive Slave Act mandating all states to cooperate in the capture and return of suspected slaves
1854	John Snow traces London cholera outbreak to the Broad Street pump; Florence Nightingale establishes the first school of nursing at Saint Thomas's Hospital
1869	Massachusetts establishes the first state board of health
1861	American Civil War begins
1863	President Lincoln signs the Emancipation Proclamation
1865	American Civil War ends with an estimated 498,332 deaths
1871	John Maynard Woodworth is appointed the first supervising surgeon (surgeon general) of the Marine Hospital Service
1876	Alexander Graham Bell invents the telephone; Robert Koch discovers *Bacillus anthracis*

1877 Louis Pasteur proves germ theory

1878 National Quarantine Act

1884 Robert Koch and Friedrich Loeffler propose Koch's postulates, scientific criteria used to determine causal organism of an infectious disease

1885 Karl Benz builds the first gasoline-powered automobile

1886 Labor protests at Haymarket Square escalate to violence and death

1889 Andrew Carnegie publishes *The Gospel of Wealth* encouraging philanthropy; Jane Addams establishes Hull House

1891 Florence Kelley investigates working conditions in the garment industry

1896 London pedestrian Bridget Driscoll is struck and killed by a gasoline-powered automobile, becoming the first recorded motor vehicle fatality; Wilhelm Conrad Roentgen discovers X-ray

1898 Spanish American War begins

1901 Oldsmobile introduces the speedometer

1902 Spanish American War ends with an estimated 2,446 U.S. service member deaths

1904 National Child Labor Committee organized

1906 Upton Sinclair describes the meatpacking industry in *The Jungle*; Meat Inspection Act and the Pure Food and Drugs Act are passed

1907 George Soper traces Oyster Bay typhoid outbreak to cook Mary Mallon

1908 Ford Motor Company produces the Model T; Clifford Beers writes *A Mind That Found Itself* describing his experiences as a mentally ill patient

1909 National Association for the Advancement of Colored People forms

1910 Flexner Report; Alice Hamilton investigates occupation-related diseases

1912 *Titanic* sinks

1913 American Society for the Control of Cancer (American Cancer Society) is founded

1914 World War I begins; Margaret Sanger publishes the birth control pamphlet *Family Limitation*

1917 United States joins allied troops in World War I

1918 Flu pandemic

1919 World War I ends with 116,516 U.S. service member deaths

1923 George Papanicolau creates the Pap smear to detect cervical cancer

1924 Martha May Elliot directs the National Children's Bureau Division of Maternal and Child Health

1928 Alexander Fleming discovers penicillin

1929 Great Depression starts with the stock market crash of October 29, Black Tuesday

1930 Veterans Health Administration (VHA) established

1931 FDR elected president

1932 Tuskegee Syphilis Study started

1933 Widespread amoebic dysentery cases traced to Chicago World's Fair hotel

1934 Midian Othello Bousfield advocates for health needs of African American people

1935 Social Security Act signed into law

1937 The National Safety Council creates a national plan for farm safety

1939 World War II begins

1941 Charles Drew creates blood storage and transfusion techniques; Japan attacks Pearl Harbor

1942 Explosion at the Benxihu Colliery in China kills 1,549 coal mine workers

1945 World War II ends with 405,399 U.S. service member deaths; Grand Rapids, Michigan, becomes the first community with fluoridated water

1946 Centers for Disease Control and Prevention founded; National Mental Health Act

1948 World Health Organization is founded; Donora smog incident occurs; Framingham Heart Study begins

1949	Florence Sabin reorganizes Colorado State Board of Health
1950	Korean War begins
1951	Malaria eradicated in the U.S.
1952	International Planned Parenthood founded
1953	Korean War ends with 54,246 U.S. service member deaths; James Watson and Francis Crick discover the chemical structure of DNA
1954	Richard Doll and Austin Bradford Hill publish landmark study linking smoking to lung cancer among doctors
1955	Vietnam War begins; Jonas Salk creates the polio vaccine; Cutter Incident
1956	Mercury poisoning from industrial wastewater is identified in Minamata, Japan; Min Chiu Li discovers chemotherapy for cancer
1958	Working for Volvo, Nils Bohlin invents the three-point seat belt
1961	Food and Drug Administration approves oral contraceptives
1962	Rachel Carson publishes *Silent Spring*
1964	Civil Rights Act; Surgeon General's report on *Smoking and Health*
1965	Medicare and Medicaid established; Ralph Nader publishes *Unsafe at Any Speed: The Designed-in Dangers of the American Automobile*
1966	Narcotic Addict Rehabilitation Act
1968	First heart transplant surgery
1969	*Time Magazine* reports Cuyahoga River fires
1970	Occupational Safety and Health Act
1971	Ban on tobacco advertisements on television and radio
1972	Tuskegee Syphilis Study terminated
1974	*The Belmont Report*
1975	The Indian Self-Determination and Education Act; Vietnam War ends with 90,220 U.S. service member deaths
1976	Nurses' Health Study commences
1977	Smallpox eradicated

1979	First edition of *Healthy People* published
1981	AIDS epidemic begins in the United States
1983	Amsterdam establishes the first community organized needle exchange program
1984	First seat belt law passed in New York; gas leak in Bhopal, India, kills at least 3,787 people and injures an estimated 558,125
1985	Salmonella in milk from Hillfarm Dairy, Illinois, infects 16,284 people resulting in at least two deaths
1986	Chernobyl nuclear disaster; Emergency Medical Treatment and Labor Act (EMTALA) established
1988	The Institute of Medicine releases *The Future of Public Health*
1990	Desert Storm War begins; Americans with Disabilities Act signed into law; Researchers from the National Institutes of Health use gene therapy to treat Ashanti DeSilva
1991	Desert Storm War ends with 1,948 U.S. service member deaths
1993	*E. coli* in undercooked hamburgers from Jack in the Box infects over 700 people resulting in four deaths
1996	Lead eliminated from U.S. gasoline; Dolly, the first cloned mammal, is born; Port Arthur massacre prompts Australia to outlaw automatic and semiautomatic rifles
1997	WHO declares obesity a global epidemic
1998	Five tobacco companies settle a lawsuit brought by 46 states, five U.S. territories, and the District of Columbia seeking reimbursement for health care costs resulting from smoking
2001	September 11 terrorist attacks; Anthrax attacks on U.S. Senators and news agencies; Global War on Terror begins
2003	Worldwide severe acute respiratory syndrome (SARS) outbreak; Human Genome project completed
2005	London transit bombings; Hurricane Katrina
2007	Virginia Tech shooting
2010	Affordable Care Act passed
2011	Tōhoku earthquake and tsunami; Fukushima Daiichi nuclear disaster

2012	Ebola epidemic in West Africa
2013	Boston Marathon bombing
2015	Emmanuel African Methodist Church shooting
2016	Pulse nightclub shooting

M

MALLON, MARY (1869–1938)

Mary Mallon was born in Ireland and immigrated to the United States in 1883 or 1884. A strong, healthy woman, Mallon sought work in domestic service, advancing from maid to cook. Mallon would have passed unnoticed through history if it were not for epidemiologist and sanitation engineer George Soper. In the winter of 1906–1907, Soper was hired to investigate an outbreak of typhoid in Oyster Bay, New York. Typhoid is caused by the gram-negative bacterium *Salmonella typhi*. The pathogen attacks the heart, brain, and respiratory systems, causing high fever, headache, delirium, abdominal pain, intestinal hemorrhage, inflammation, and in severe cases, death. Typhoid epidemics were not uncommon. They mostly occurred in large, crowded cities, military bases, colleges, and universities. In 1906, New York City recorded 3,467 cases and 639 deaths (Soper, 1939). Many more cases probably went unreported. Doctors and public officials believed that typhoid was caused by polluted water, milk, or sewer gas. Soper suspected human transmission by an asymptomatic carrier. When Mallon refused to provide bodily samples for microscopic analysis, public health authorities imprisoned her. On release, Mallon promised not to work as a cook. However, she soon returned to cooking, including holding a position at a hospital where employees nicknamed her "Typhoid Mary." After evading public health authorities for several years, Mallon surrendered and lived her final years on North Brother Island in New York. She is suspected of infecting at least 51 people.

Mallon presents an interesting case study from several perspectives. From a historical-biological perspective, Mallon was living evidence of asymptomatic human carriers of disease. Tracking her—and the bacterium inside of her—provided public health officials with essential clues regarding how to combat the spread of infectious disease. From a social perspective, Mallon's story is the case of a disadvantaged immigrant worker who did not understand how she could make others sick when she was not sick herself. She is an example of the many people who prepare food in restaurants, hospitals, and hotels across the country and the need for public health education on good handwashing and food preparation practices. From an ethical perspective, Mallon's case raises the question of how much authority public health officials have, specifically, whether they possess the authority to imprison someone who poses a danger to public health.

Little is known of Mallon's childhood or family. She was a very private person, and no family ever visited her during her time on North Brother Island. Mallon first came to the attention of scientific communities in 1907. In the summer of 1906,

Mallon was hired through Mrs. Stricker's employment agency to cook for the family and domestic staff of New York banker Charles Henry Warren. Warren rented a house on Oyster Bay, Long Island, from Mrs. George Thompson. Six of the eleven people in the house came down with typhoid. A number of inconclusive reports were written about this incident, but Thompson realized that mysteries regarding the source of this contagion had to be revealed before the dwelling could be rented again. Thompson hired George Soper, who had gained a reputation as an epidemic fighter. After inspecting the well, the overhead water tank, the cesspool, the privy (outhouse), the food supplies, the bathing facilities, and eventually the sanitary condition of the house next door, Soper concluded that a human carrier might be responsible. The timing of the illnesses coincided with a Sunday when the cook had prepared a special treat of fresh peaches and ice cream. Soper surmised, "I suppose no better way could be found for a cook to cleanse her hands of microbes and infect a family" (Soper, 1939, p. 702).

Soper traced the cook and her employment history through Mrs. Stricker's agency. He found seven typhoid epidemics related to Mallon's employment. Four months into his investigation, Soper learned that Mallon was working as a cook on Park Avenue in New York. He went to her place of employment:

> I had my first talk with Mary in the kitchen of the house. I suppose it was an unusual kind of interview, particularly when the place is taken into consideration. I was as diplomatic as possible, but I had to say I suspected her of making people sick and that I wanted specimens of her urine, feces, and blood.
>
> It did not take Mary long to react to this suggestion. She seized a carving fork and advanced in my direction. I passed rapidly down the long narrow hall, through the iron gate, out through the area and so to the sidewalk. I felt rather lucky to escape. (Soper, 1939, p. 704)

Soper attempted a second intervention with Mallon, confronting her at a rooming house. Mallon denied ever having any symptoms of the illness or causing any cases of typhoid. She again refused to give specimens. When Soper heard that Mallon was leaving the Park Avenue position, he feared another epidemic. He contacted the New York City health department who sent Dr. Josephine Baker to collect the specimens. Mallon refused and Baker returned with two police officers. Mary ran away. After a three-hour manhunt, Mallon was found hiding in a neighbor's outbuilding. Dr. Baker recalled:

> She fought and struggled and cursed. I tried to explain to her that I only wanted the specimens and that then she could go back home. She again refused and I told the policemen to pick her up and put her in the ambulance. This we did and the ride down to the hospital was quite a wild one. (Soper, 1939, p. 706)

Mallon was placed in locked isolation at Willard Parker Hospital. Her fecal specimens contained the typhoid bacteria. For several years, Mallon was forced to stay in a small cottage at the Riverside Hospital on North Brother Island. Mallon sued the city for imprisonment without due process of law. The judge dismissed her case on the grounds that the court was unwilling to take responsibility for releasing her. In 1910, the public health department released her on the condition that she promise to avoid employment undertakings that involved food preparation. Moreover, she was supposed to report to the New York State Department of Health every three months. Mallon did not keep her promise, and for several years, the Department of Health lost track of her.

Soper considered his investigation closed until 1915 when Dr. Edward B. Cragin of the Sloan Hospital for women contacted him. The hospital had an outbreak of 25 cases of typhoid fever. The staff referred to the cook as "Typhoid Mary." Cragin asked Soper to come to the hospital. Soper confirmed that the cook was indeed Mary Mallon. Mallon was sent back to the bungalow on North Brother Island. This time she did not fight. She was older and life had been a struggle. For the next 23 years, Mallon lived in relative isolation on North Brother Island. She trained as a laboratory technician and earned a fair wage. She took occasional trips to the city. On December 25, 1932, a delivery man found Mallon on the floor, paralyzed by a stroke. She was moved to Riverside Hospital and died on November 11, 1938. Bacteriologists and public health officials surmised that Mallon must have gotten a mild case of typhoid fever as a child.

For a number of decades, Mallon would become an object of attention as countless numbers of bacteriologists, public health officials, lawyers, and local magistrates sought to find ways of protecting the individual rights of potential typhoid carriers while they worked at controlling the spread of typhoid. Historian Judith Walzer Leavitt argued that in Mallon's "epic battle with public health officials she won a pyrrhic victory," in that public health theorists learned that in their "subsequent interactions with healthy carriers," they needed to base their actions on both "laboratory findings" and "socially sensitive policies." Historian John Andrew Mendelsohn disagreed with some of Leavitt's interpretations and argued that what public health officials learned was that isolation needed to be the exception and not the rule—typhoid carriers needed to be kept under constant surveillance for reasons of personal hygiene and food handling regulation. Researcher Norman Gibbins noted that "Typhoid Mary's" plight has a great deal to tell us about how to cope with contemporary emergent diseases, including AIDS, Ebola virus, and bovine spongiform encephalopathy.

Marouf A. Hasian Jr. and Sally Kuykendall

See also: Baker, Sara Josephine; Code of Ethics; Epidemic; Food Safety; Handwashing; Infectious Diseases; Quarantine

Further Reading

Byrne, Joseph P. (Ed.). (2008). *Encyclopedia of pestilence, pandemics, and plagues.* Westport, CT: Greenwood.

David, M. Z. (Ed.). (2015). *Infectious diseases: An encyclopedia of causes, effects, and treatments* (3 vols.). Santa Barbara, CA: Greenwood.

Gibbins, L. (1998). Mary Mallon: Disease, denial and detention. *Journal of Biological Education (Society of Biology)*, *32*(2), 127.
Greenwood, V. (2015). The frightening legacy of Typhoid Mary. *Smithsonian*, *45*(11), 1.
Leavitt, J. W. (1992). Typhoid Mary strikes back: Bacteriological theory and practice in early twentieth-century public health. *Isis*, *83*(4), 608–629.
Marineli, F., Tsoucalas, G., Karamanou, M., & Androutsos, G. (2013). Mary Mallon (1869–1938) and the history of typhoid fever. *Annals of Gastroenterology: Quarterly Publication of the Hellenic Society of Gastroenterology*, *26*(2), 132–134.
Soper, G. A. (1939). The curious career of Typhoid Mary. *Bulletin of the New York Academy of Medicine*, *15*(10), 698–712.
Tunc, T. E. (2008). *Mallon, Mary (1869–1938)*. Santa Barbara, CA: ABC-CLIO.

MASTER SETTLEMENT AGREEMENT (MSA)

Between 1987 and 1993, medical expenditures due to smoking increased from $21.9 billion to $50 billion. Over 43 percent of the costs were paid by Medicare, Medicaid, and other federal and state sources (Medical-Care Expenditures Attributable to Cigarette Smoking—United States, 1993, 1994). In 1994, the state of Mississippi filed a lawsuit against the tobacco industry seeking to recover $940 million. Other states quickly followed aiming to recover payments made by Medicaid for patients that had experienced smoking-related illnesses. The Master Settlement Agreement (MSA) was the resolution of the class action lawsuit filed by attorney generals representing 46 states, five U.S. territories, and the District of Columbia against tobacco companies Philip Morris USA, R. J. Reynolds, Brown and Williamson, and Lorillard. During the lawsuit, it was revealed that the tobacco companies were intentionally targeting young people with cigarette advertising. Marketing plans focused on replacing smokers who died with younger smokers, who, once addicted, would purchase cigarettes for 20–40 years.

The MSA dictated that the petitioners could not file any future claims due to unforeseen conditions. Secondly, the monetary judgments awarded would be paid only to the states, territories, and District of Columbia that initiated the lawsuit and that individuals seeking to obtain a financial judgement were prohibited. The "participating manufacturers" were required to make yearly payments compensating the above states for medical costs related to smoking-associated health conditions that were paid by their state-run programs. In addition, criteria were established for a code of conduct, how sales are conducted, the advertisement of tobacco-related products, as well as levying penalties for the failure to adhere to the standards set forth. Although the MSA originally only included five tobacco producers, later other manufacturers decided to participate and agreed to follow the original terms of the agreement.

The MSA was a way to allow the concerns of the litigants to be addressed without the need for additional taxpayer dollars being spent on a prolonged lawsuit that could have a potentially upsetting outcome. On the side of the manufacturers, they were required to finance a national campaign targeting minors on the dangers of smoking while also making annual payouts to the litigants. This lawsuit only addressed the needs of the respective parties and did not prohibit future class action lawsuits brought about by individuals, labor unions, or private health insurance carriers (The Master Settlement Agreement, 2015).

The yearly payout calculations are completed by an independent auditor who determines the amount to be paid by each "participating manufacturer." Should there ever be a disagreement regarding the amount to be paid the issue would then be assessed by three arbitrators. Payments that are in dispute are held in an interest earning escrow account while the dispute is being resolved. Additionally, a payment of $12.75 billion was determined for the first five years. This amount can be adjusted based on actual cigarette shipments and sales. The health care–related payments will be made indefinitely, although the base payment would see a gradual increase.

Furthermore, the restrictions imposed on cigarette manufacturers are the strictest that have been implemented. These restrictions include targeting minorities, the use of animated characters (cartoons), giving out complimentary samples, advertising products if it is not within the location of a sales office, offering trademarked apparel and merchandise, and petitioning the legislature for the benefit of the tobacco industry. The MSA is an ongoing settlement contract, making it the largest civil resolution in history.

Leapolda Figueroa

See also: Leading Health Indicators; Public Health Law; Truth Campaign, The; *Controversies in Public Health:* Controversy 2

Further Reading

Apollonio, D. E., & Malone, R. E. (2010). The "We Card" Program: Tobacco industry "Youth Smoking Prevention" as industry self-preservation. *American Journal of Public Health, 100*(7), 1188–1201. doi:10.2105/AJPH.2009.169573

Healton, C., & Nelson, K. (2004). Reversal of misfortune. *American Journal of Public Health, 94*(2), 186–191.

The Master Settlement Agreement: An overview. Tobacco Control Legal Consortium. (2015). Retrieved from http://www.publichealthlawcenter.org/sites/default/files/resources/tclc-fs-msa-overview-2015.pdf.

Medical-care expenditures attributable to cigarette smoking—United States, 1993. (1994). *Morbidity and Mortality Weekly Report, 43*(26), 469.

Northridge, M. E. (2005, March). It takes lawyers to deliver health care. *American Journal of Public Health, 95*(3), 376.

Sepe, E., Ling, P. M., & Glantz, S. A. (2002). Smooth moves: Bar and nightclub tobacco promotions that target young adults. *American Journal of Public Health, 92*(3), 414–419.

MATERNAL HEALTH

Maternal health encompasses the health of women before, during, and after childbirth. The experience of pregnancy and childbirth is individual to each mother. For many, it is a time of celebration and personal fulfillment. For others, it is a time of pain, suffering, and ill health. Each year, 65,000 women in the United States experience severe complications related to pregnancy, a condition known as severe maternal morbidity (SMM) (CDC, 2016). Six hundred of these women die due to infections, bleeding, high blood pressure, heart, or other conditions during pregnancy. Internationally, 830 women die every year as a result of complications during pregnancy and childbirth (WHO, 2015). Maternal mortality is higher among women living in rural and poor communities. About 99 percent of deaths occur in developing countries with scarce resources; about half of maternal deaths occur in sub-Saharan Africa and one-third in South Asia. In many cases, complications could be prevented. Public health clinics provide family planning care to men and women of child bearing age, typically aged 15 to 49 years. Caring for both the mother and the baby are crucial to ensure full-term delivery with as few birthing complications as possible and the best start in life.

Historically, maternal health in America can be traced to Native American and European practices, which viewed childbirth as a natural, nonmedical experience. To early Native Americans, childbirth was a spiritual experience. Native women limited activities and followed diets consistent with tribal beliefs. The Cherokee avoided squirrel, raccoon, pheasant, speckled trout, rabbit, and salt during pregnancy. Although some beliefs were superstition—wearing a scarf around the neck was believed to cause strangulation of the umbilical cord—other beliefs are consistent with good health practices. Limiting salt intake reduces risk of high blood pressure, preeclampsia and eclampsia, potentially fatal conditions. Some Native American women went off alone to give birth in a quiet, comfortable place while others gave birth in dwellings specifically constructed for pregnant women. Historians believe that most births were attended by one or more female companions, family members, a doula, or elders of the community (Pearson, n.d.). Notes from the time period suggest that Native American women experienced few complications and returned to normal activity levels soon after childbirth. Pilgrims followed European practices of using female birth attendants. Mrs. Bridget Lee Fuller (d. 1667) is credited with delivering two or three babies on board the *Mayflower* in 1620. However, records show that Mrs. Fuller did not actually sail to America until 1623 when she arrived on the *Anne* (Beal, 2015). Midwives filled a social and religious role, teaching and encouraging young women how to care for themselves and their babies. Midwives were highly respected and in demand. Mrs. Wiat of Dorchester (d. 1705) reportedly attended over a thousand births, and Ruth Barnaby of Boston (1664–1765) practiced for 40 years. As the New World expanded, European midwives were recruited by towns, colonies, and even the Dutch West India Company. In the South, female slaves tended to births of blacks and whites, alike. Lacking formal education, midwives typically learned through hands-on practice. Midwifery was considered a calling. Formal training, apprenticeship, or professional organizing were considered unnecessary because childbirth was seen as a natural process. Medical interventions were thought to be dangerous. This is not to say that childbirth was without danger. Maternal and infant deaths occurred due to bacterial infections, epidemics such as smallpox, and diphtheria, or postpartum bleeding and puerperal fever.

The medicalization of childbirth started in the middle of the 18th century with the development of doctor of medicine as a professional field. Prior to this time, anyone could practice medicine. Working as a doctor did not require a license or professional training. To develop as a profession, doctors needed to define their role and develop formal training schools. Originally, doctors intended to share obstetrical cases with midwives. Midwives would tend to routine cases while doctors tended to more complex deliveries. Midwife training schools were established in New York City and Philadelphia. However, the cost of attending was prohibitive to women, and practicing midwives believed that childbirth was a natural process. Midwives' allegiances were to the individual patient, not an organized profession.

Dr. William Smellie (1697–1793) and Dr. William Hunter (1718–1783) are considered the fathers of obstetrics. The London physicians studied difficult cases and devised procedures for resuscitating stillborn newborns and disentangling strangulating umbilical cords. Since social norms of modesty frowned on males being present during delivery, man-midwives, as they were known, had to make a strong case for wealthy women to seek out recommended procedures. Although Smellie believed that childbirth was a natural process, he also invented forceps to aid delivery. Their experiences, knowledge, procedures, and diagrams were carefully

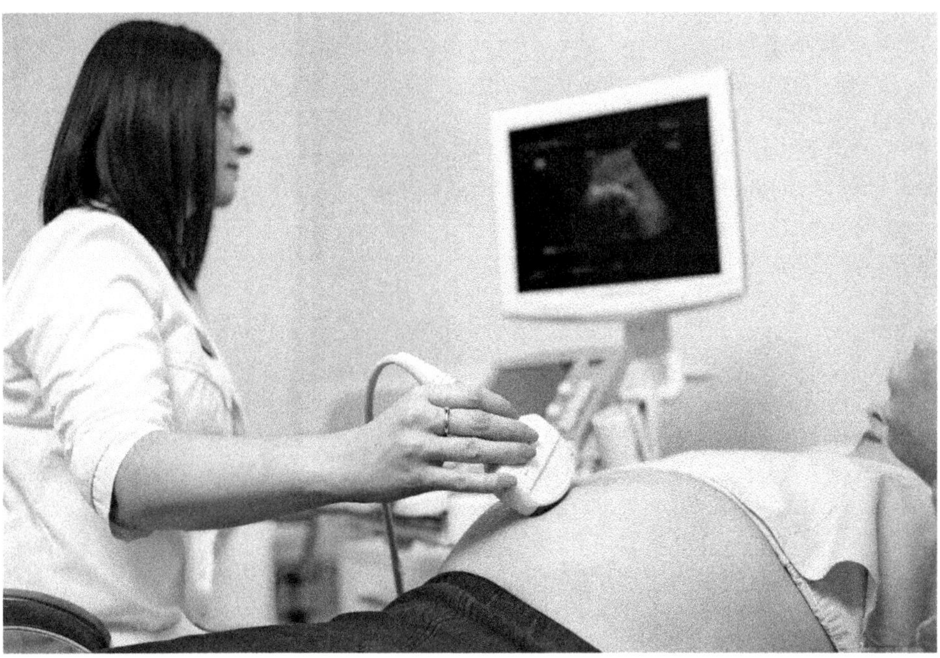

Pregnancy poses special health risks for mother and fetus in that new health problems may emerge or existing health problems are aggravated. (Serhii Bobyk/Dreamstime.com)

documented and widely disseminated. Smellie's book, a *Treatise on the Theory and Practice of Midwifery* (1752), was published in nine editions, translated into French, German, and Dutch, and sold throughout Europe and North America. Although the book is described as "by far the finest obstetric text of the day, and still a treat to read" (Dunn, 1995, p. F77), one New Zealand author questions how Smellie and Hunter accessed their anatomical models. Most scholars assume that the women died of natural causes. In a self-published book, Don Shelton asserts that Smellie and Hunter hired people to murder pregnant women on the streets of London, a practice known as burking. Shelton's claim is based on statistical analysis of the mortality rates during the time period of the studies (Shelton, 2010). It would have been statistically improbable for Smellie and Hunter to gather 30 women in their ninth month of pregnancy other than through burking. Historian Helen King and others refute Shelton's claims, noting that one cadaver could be used for multiple drawings, features may have been enhanced to compensate for body decomposition, or the artist used nonhuman models (King, 2011). Regardless of how Smellie and Hunter obtained their models, history shows that doctors were eager to step into the role of midwives, and in doing so, pregnancy and childbirth were transformed from a natural event to a medical procedure.

Employing both doctors and midwives, public health approaches reproductive health from a biological, spiritual, and social perspective. Maternal care starts before a woman gets pregnant. Family planning is critical. Unintended pregnancies, either *unwanted* or *mistimed*, have serious health implications. Unwanted pregnancies are those where the woman did not intend to get pregnant and does not want the child. With mistimed pregnancies, the mother planned on getting pregnant. Yet, the pregnancy occurred earlier or later than expected. If the mother does not realize that she is pregnant or is in denial, she is less likely to get prenatal care and may continue using alcohol, tobacco, or other teratogens. She may seek an abortion, which puts her at risk for infection, bleeding, and depression. Mistimed pregnancies have slightly better outcomes than unwanted pregnancies. Babies born of unwanted pregnancies are more likely to be low birth weight. Mothers are less likely to breast feed, missing an important opportunity for early nutrition and building immunity. Poor, young, and single females with low self-efficacy, poor communication skills, and questionable support from partners are the least likely to plan pregnancy. Although some families are able to handle the additional stresses of an infant in the household, for many young girls, pregnancy aggravates existing dysfunctions and increases risk of physical or emotional victimization. Public health services focus on reducing unintended pregnancies, spacing children, and limiting family size to ensure better maternal and child health. Family planning services are considered one of the greatest public health achievements of all time. The birth control movement, led by Margaret Sanger (1879) legalized birth control counseling and clinics. Today, public health family planning services prevent 1.3 million unintended pregnancies each year (CDC, 1999). Maternal death rate is down from 608 deaths per 100,000 live births in 1915, when family counseling was illegal, to 12 deaths per

100,000 live births (Hoyert, 2007). National and local organizations, such as Planned Parenthood, offer free family planning services. Future steps are to continue to reduce unintended pregnancies. Currently, 49 percent of pregnancies are unintended, and over half of those pregnancies are expected to result in abortion (Henshaw, 1998).

The Progressive Era brought forth a series of public health movements to both reform and promote maternal and child health care. The Maternity and Infancy Care Act of 1921 provided funding services for mothers and set a foundation for other programs that still exist today. The Special Supplemental Nutrition Program for Women, Infants, and Children (WIC) was established for families on medical leave to ensure a proper diet for children and their caregivers. Other programs include the National Easter Seal Society and the March of Dimes Birth Defects Foundations, which are known for prevention and treatment efforts. The United Nations Population Fund works around the world collaborating with governments and health experts to train workers and improve conditions of reproductive health services to promote an international standard for quality maternal health (UNFPA, 2016).

Maternal care may be separated into preconception, antenatal, pregnancy, and postpartum. Preconception planning is critical to ensure a healthy mother and child. Plans should be realistic, taking into consideration health care, financial, social, and material needs. The United States Department of Agriculture (USDA) calculates that the average national costs for an infant are $16,175 in the first year (USDA, 2016). Under the Family and Medical Leave Act (FMLA), mothers in the United States are eligible for 12 weeks (84 days) of unpaid maternity leave. In comparison to other countries, the United States falls short in supporting new mothers and fathers. Only 12 percent of U.S. workers are eligible for paid family leave, and the disadvantaged are at greatest disadvantage. Twenty-two percent of those in the highest income bracket are eligible for paid leave while only 4 percent of those in the lowest income bracket are eligible (Bureau of Labor Statistics, 2013). Norway offers 322 days of paid maternity leave. Fathers are eligible for 70 days of paid leave with an additional 26 weeks at 100 percent pay or 36 weeks at 80 percent pay (Citation, 2014). Additionally, many countries offer a children's allowance, a small stipend to be used toward baby clothes, diapers, food, and other supplies. Internationally, there is a move to alleviate the disparity between new maternal leave and paternal leave. Ensuring equal benefits supports the idea of equal responsibility in parenting, which supports healthy childhood development and equality in other aspects of society. The United States can learn much by following the lead of other countries in how they perceive and support young mothers and fathers.

Pregnancy is a high-risk time. New health problems may emerge or existing health problems are aggravated as one body assumes responsibility for nurturing two. During preconception, women should discuss contraception and pregnancy plans with their health care provider, consider screening for genetic diseases, address any chronic illnesses, stop smoking, limit alcohol, and maintain a healthy life style. Being aware of potential problems can prevent or compensate for difficulties. An estimated 10 percent of women of reproductive ages have difficulty getting pregnant. Through careful screening and diagnosis, doctors can identify and treat possible causes of infertility. With an estimated 60 percent of women in the United States overweight or obese, weight gain during pregnancy is increasingly a concern. Recommended weight gain during pregnancy for the woman of normal weight (BMI of 185–24.9) is 25 to 35 pounds. Weight gain is important to ensure healthy fetal development. Too little weight gain and the infant will be small. Small infants have difficulty breastfeeding, which creates other developmental delays. Women who are overweight or obese are limited to gaining 15 to 25 pounds or 11 to 20 pounds, respectively. Too much weight gain creates larger babies, which can cause difficulties in labor and delivery. Also, the mother will have problems losing the weight after the baby is born, increasing her risk for heart disease, diabetes, high blood pressure, stroke, gall bladder disease, and some forms of cancer. Preconception is a good time to connect with health education resources, create a healthy lifestyle, and start practicing pelvic floor muscle training to reduce the risk of urinary or fecal incontinence, a condition that affects 6 to 29 percent of women (Mason, Glenn, Walton, & Appleton, 1999).

Expecting mothers attend regular antenatal visits at doctors' offices or clinics. Visits increase in frequency as they get closer to the anticipated due date. At the first visit, the health professional performs a routine physical exam, screens for chronic or genetic diseases, orders antenatal lab work, prescribes prenatal vitamins, and counsels the mother on diet and activity. Subsequent appointments monitor the weight of mother and baby, progress to date, nutritional status, and connect the parents with antenatal classes to develop birth and postpartum plans. Antenatal appointments are important as many birth complications come with little warning. The major health problems experienced during pregnancy or after delivery are bleeding, infection, high blood pressure, excessive weight gain, gestational diabetes, hyperemesis gravid arum, and depression. Severe bleeding, infections, or high blood pressure leading to eclampsia can result in death. Knowing and monitoring the pregnancy may prevent or alleviate problems. Postnatal care begins within the first 24 hours of delivery. The mother is monitored for bleeding, sepsis, blood pressure, uterine prolapse, and other problems that may have presented during delivery. In addition to mothers, this is a crucial time to monitor breathing, nutrition, and development of the newborn.

Traditionally, women's reproductive health was viewed as falling under social and religious purview. Midwives cared for the mother and baby following natural, holistic practices. With the development of medicine as a professional field of study, birth and death were medicalized. Medicine introduced formal practices, tools, and drugs to support and promote healthy births. Yet, the event that made the biggest impact on maternal health was not having babies or at least not having babies in close succession. As women's rights expanded, so did the use of contraceptives, family planning, and ultimately, improved health for women. Today, maternal care starts preconception and continues throughout the months after birth. Midwives, nurse practitioners, and obstetricians who use a combination of natural and medical techniques are further refining the field. Women are advised to follow a healthy lifestyle of nutritious, balanced diet and physical activity. Although public health has achieved great success in the area of maternal health, we still have a long way to go. Other countries around the world provide better support during the first years of life. Expanding maternity and paternity leaves to support young parents can create a ripple effect influencing other aspects of society.

Christine M. Thomas and Sally Kuykendall

See also: Anderson, Elizabeth Milbank; Baker, Sara Josephine; Birth Defects; Dunham, Ethel Collins; Eliot, Martha May; Ellertson, Charlotte Ehrengard; Family Planning; Infant Mortality; Intimate Partner Violence; Planned Parenthood; Sanger, Margaret Louise Higgins; Women's Health

Further Reading

American College of Nurse Midwives. (2017). Retrieved from http://www.midwife.org/.

Beal, J. (2015). Bridget Lee Fuller: Mayflower myth vs. historic midwife. *Midwifery Today with International Midwife, 115,* 50.

Bureau of Labor Statistics. (2013). *National Compensation Survey, March 2013.* U.S. Department of Labor. Retrieved from http://www.bls.gov/ncs/ebs/benefits/2013/ebbl0052.pdf.

Centers for Disease Control and Prevention (CDC). (1999). Achievements in public health, 1900–1999: Family planning. *Morbidity and Mortality Weekly Report, 48*(47), 1073–1080.

Centers for Disease Control and Prevention (CDC). (2016). *Maternal and infant health.* Retrieved from http://www.cdc.gov/reproductivehealth/maternalinfanthealth/.

Citation. (2014). *Parental employment benefits around the world.* Retrieved from https://www.citation.co.uk/news/parental-employment-benefits-around-the-world.

Dunn, P.M. (1995). Perinatal Lessons from the Past: Dr. William Smelley (1697–1763), the master of British midwifery. *Archives of Disease in Childhood, 72,* pp. F77–F78. Available at: http://www.ncbi.nlm.nih.gov/pmc/articles/PMC2528415/pdf/archdischfn00061-0079.pdf.

Henshaw, S. K. (1998). Unintended pregnancy in the United States. *Family Planning Perspective, 30,* 24.

Hoyert, D. L. (2007). Maternal mortality and related concepts. National Center for Health Statistics. *Vital Health Statistics,* 3(33). Retrieved from http://www.cdc.gov/nchs/data/series/sr_03/sr03_033.pdf.

King, H. (2011). Second opinion: History without historians? Medical history and the Internet. *Social History of Medicine,* 24(2), 212. Retrieved from http://www.academia.edu/643250/History_without_historians_Medical_history_and_the_internet.

Mason, L., Glenn, S., Walton, I., & Appleton C. (1999). The prevalence of stress incontinence during pregnancy and following delivery. *Midwifery,15,* 120.

Pearson, E. H. (n.d.). *Native American customs of childbirth.* National History Education Clearinghouse. Retrieved from http://teachinghistory.org/history-content/ask-a-historian/24097.

Shelton, D. (2010). The emperor's new clothes. *Journal of the Royal Society of Medicine, 103*(2), 46.

UNICEF. (2016). *Maternal and newborn health.* Retrieved from http://www.unicef.org/health/index_maternalhealth.html.

United Nations Population Fund (UNFPA). (2016). *Maternal health.* Retrieved from http://www.unfpa.org/maternal-health.

USDA. (2016). *Cost of raising a child calculator.* Retrieved from http://www.cnpp.usda.gov/tools/CRC_Calculator/default.aspx.

Wertz, R. W., & Wertz, D. C. (2013). Notes on the decline of midwives and the rise of medical obstetricians. In P. Conrad & V. Leiter (Eds.), *The sociology of health & illness: Critical perspectives.* New York: Worth.

World Health Organization (WHO). (2015). *Maternal mortality: Fact sheet no. 348.* Retrieved from http://www.who.int/mediacentre/factsheets/fs348/en/.

MEASLES

Measles, also known as rubeola, is an airborne infectious disease that affects over 20 million people throughout the world and causes over 200,000 deaths each year (Caserta, 2014). Although a measles infection often begins with general symptoms such as fever, coughing, and runny nose, individuals afflicted with measles begin to form a characteristic rash on the face and body as well as small white spots on the inside of the cheeks. Suspected measles infection can then be confirmed through laboratory testing.

Measles, which is typically seen in children, is highly contagious and can spread through coughing and sneezing. Although common in developing countries, measles is a very rare disease in the United States due to the comprehensive system of vaccination that American children undergo, which includes building immunity to the measles virus. The World Health Organization declared measles to be the fifth vaccine-preventable disease to be eradicated from the Americas (World Health Organization, 2016). They attributed this to a comprehensive 22-year effort to implement mass vaccination against measles as part of the measles, mumps, and rubella vaccine. A cost-effectiveness study on measles in Latin America and the Caribbean alone estimates that vaccination will prevent over 3 million measles cases and 16,000 deaths between 2000 and 2020. The success of measles vaccination serves to underline the efficacy and importance of vaccination.

Although measles has been eradicated in the Americas and other areas throughout the world, some countries still face the risk of measles infection due to lack of vaccination. Measles is particularly dangerous because of its high rate of complications such as diarrhea and secondary bacterial infections. Diarrhea from measles can often cause death through severe dehydration and often necessitates the use of medical management to maintain proper hydration levels. In countries like the United States where such medical management and proper nutrition are available, the measles-attributable fatality rate can be as low as 0.3 percent (Perry & Halsey, 2004). In underdeveloped countries, however, where such health care resources are limited and populations suffer from high levels of malnutrition, the measles-attributable fatality rate can reach as high as nearly 30 percent. Therefore, the prognosis of measles in infected patients is often very dependent on external conditions such as health care access and the ability to receive proper hydration, nutrition, and medical care.

The history of measles affecting humanity is an extensive one. In the tenth century, Rhazes, an ancient Persian physician, was one of the first clinicians to systematically describe measles and disseminate that information between the Middle East and Europe. Throughout the following millennium, measles outbreaks affected Europe and other continents on the planet, killing millions of individuals. It is estimated that between the mid-19th century and 2005 alone, measles was responsible for killing over 200 million people throughout the world (Torrey & Yolken, 2005).

Measles has been an endemic disease throughout human history, meaning that many human populations have been chronically exposed to the disease. Throughout this exposure, those populations developed a collective resistance against measles. This occurs when individuals who are unable to survive the illness are eliminated from the population, leaving a population of individuals who show greater ability to survive the measles virus. Additionally, since many of the adults in a population were exposed to measles during their childhood, they developed an immune-based resistance. Therefore, it is primarily the children of these populations who do not have immune-based resistance and are therefore at risk of becoming infected with active measles virus. With the use of vaccination however, these children can become protected through an artificially induced immune resistance, and these vaccinated children can even act as a buffer to protect unvaccinated children from measles infection.

Another fascinating discovery regarding measles, which can be applied to many different human-to-human infectious diseases, is the idea of critical community size. The critical community size is the lowest population size in which an infectious disease can survive indefinitely. Studies regarding a series of measles outbreaks in the 1950s in the United States led to the observation that measles only persisted in communities above a certain size threshold. This observation led to the theory that in communities with populations below the critical community size, there were too few susceptible hosts and too many resistant individuals that measles and other infectious diseases could not continue their transmission and would become extinct. This theory serves to support the importance of vaccination, since the number of resistant individuals can be artificially inflated through vaccination and therefore prevent measles and other infectious diseases from being able to efficiently find susceptible hosts. The idea that there can be a true and full population-wide resistance against an infectious disease has been enabled by the advent of vaccination.

This population-wide resistance to measles, however, played a large role in human history before vaccination, particularly in interactions between civilizations that were resistant and civilizations that were not resistant. When the European explorers and settlers came to the Americas, the indigenous populations had not been exposed to a variety of diseases, including measles. Since they did not exhibit this resistance, and measles was endemic in the Europeans, many indigenous people became infected with the measles virus. The death toll of such infections, which not only included measles but also smallpox, diphtheria, typhoid, and tuberculosis, was staggering and led to the collapse of the indigenous populations in the Americas.

Although clinicians may view measles from the perspective of treating individuals, public health professionals seek to alleviate the burden of measles at a population-wide level. Widespread vaccination is undoubtedly the most effective and crucial strategy for eradicating measles in each country of the world. Logistical challenges in distributing measles vaccines to underdeveloped countries are a barrier, and innovative approaches to vaccine manufacturing, quality control, and distribution are being developed to overcome such challenges. As more governmental and nongovernmental humanitarian funds are poured into global vaccination efforts, the 21st century is likely to include the global eradication of measles.

Shayan Waseh

See also: Epidemic; Global Health; Infant Mortality; Infectious Diseases; Influenza; Vaccines; World Health Organization; *Controversies in Public Health:* Controversy 3

Further Reading

Caserta, M. T. (2014). Measles. *Merck Manual: Professional edition.* Kenilworth, NJ: Merck & Co.

Perry, R. T., & Halsey, N. A. (2004). The clinical significance of measles: A review. *Journal of Infectious Diseases*, *189*(S1), 4–16.

Torrey, E. F., & Yolken, R. H. (2005). Their bugs are worse than their bite. *Washington Post.* Retrieved from http://www.birdflubook.org/a.php?id=40&t=p.

World Health Organization. (2016, September). *Region of the Americas is declared free of measles.* Retrieved from http://www.paho.org/hq/index.php?option=com_content&view=article&id=12528:region-americas-declared-free-measles&Itemid=1926&lang=en.

MEDICAID

Medicaid is a health insurance program for low income people, those who either do not earn enough money or do not have enough resources to cover health care needs. The Medicaid program is administered by the Centers for Medicare and Medicaid Services (CMS), a division of the U.S. Department of Health and Human Services (DHHS). The program was designed to ensure that America's poor population has access to affordable, quality medical services. Medicaid was created on July 30, 1965, when President Lyndon B. Johnson enacted Title XIX of the Social Security Act. The Health Insurance for the Aged (Medicare) Act and Medicaid offered states matched funding to support health care for low income children, their caretaker relatives, people who are blind, and people with certain disabilities. Although states are not required to participate in Medicaid, all states currently do participate. A condition of funding is that the state follows federal Medicaid laws on basic eligibility, scope, and type of services. Otherwise, states can tailor their benefits. This means that Medicaid programs vary from state to state. The CMS monitors systems to ensure adherence to federal guidelines and to prevent fraud.

Over the years Medicare eligibility, services, and requirements have evolved as health and medical needs change. In 1967, Medicare introduced the Early and Periodic Screening, Diagnosis, and Treatment (EPSDT) program. The EPSDT program ensures that children covered by Medicaid receive regular medical screening to assess childhood development and to provide recommended immunizations, health education, and dental care. EPSDT services are critical to early identification and treatment to prevent long-term health problems. The Medicaid and CHIP Payment and Access Commission (MACPAC) estimate that more than 40 million children were eligible for EPSDT in 2014. Yet, less than 60 percent took advantage of these services. In 1981, the federal government implemented freedom of choice waivers. These waivers allow the states to waive certain federal requirements in order to test new programs or services. The federal government also introduced the idea of Disproportionate Share Hospitals (DSHs). Prior to the DSH ruling, patients covered by Medicaid were often turned away from or quickly transferred out of prestigious or wealthy medical institutions. DSH-supported hospitals willing to accept and provide care to a higher proportion of low income patients to receive additional incentives. In 1986, Medicaid was expanded to include infants and pregnant women with income up to 100 percent of the Federal Poverty Level (FPL). The following year, coverage was expanded to mandate coverage for children up to 6 years old and pregnant women who earned up to 133 percent of the FPL. In the 1990s, prescription drug rebate program was created and phased-in coverage for children aged 6 to18. The Affordable Care Act (ACA) expanded Medicaid further and offered subsidies for individuals who are not covered by employer health insurance plans and willing to purchase insurance through the health insurance marketplace. Challenges remain in how to ensure accessible, quality health care within an environment of rising health care costs.

Sally Kuykendall

See also: Affordable Care Act; Centers for Medicare and Medicaid Services; Children's Health; Maternal Health; Medicare; Planned Parenthood; Prescription Drugs; Roosevelt, Franklin Delano; Social Security Act; U.S. Department of Health and Human Services; *Controversies in Public Health:* Controversy 1

Further Reading

Centers for Medicare and Medicaid Services. (2017). Retrieved from https://www.cms.gov/.

Medicaid. (2017). Retrieved from https://www.medicaid.gov/index.html.

Medicaid and CHIP Payment and Access Commission. (2017). Retrieved from https://www.macpac.gov/.

MEDICARE

Medicare is a health insurance program for people with certain disabilities, people with end stage renal disease (ESRD), or people age 65 and older. The Medicare program is administered by the Centers for Medicare and Medicaid Services (CMS), a division of the U.S. Department of Health and Human Services (DHHS). The program was designed to ensure that the U.S. elderly population has access to affordable, quality medical services and does not fall into poverty due to the combination of fixed income and rising medical costs.

After the Great Depression of the 1930s, the United States moved into a period of economic expansion. Contrary to what one would expect, life expectancy *increases* during times of economic recession or depression and *decreases* during times of economic growth. (Experts believe that people are more likely to engage in unhealthy behaviors—smoking, drinking, or lack of exercise—during times of economic boom.) From 1933 to 1936, life expectancy decreased for all groups. Nonwhite

Hungry, unemployed men wait for meals at crime boss Al Capone's charitable soup kitchen in Chicago. President Franklin D. Roosevelt envisioned a system of care for the elderly living on fixed income. On July 30, 1965, President Lyndon B. Johnson enacted The Health Insurance for the Aged (Medicare) Act providing hospital, extended care, and home health care to all Americans age 65 and over. (Social Security Administration)

males lost over six years of average life span (Tapia Granados & Diez Roux, 2009). President Franklin Roosevelt feared the rising costs of medical care for elderly people who were living on fixed incomes. He dreamed of a national system of health insurance. However, he also knew that the American Medical Association opposed the idea, and in order to get the Social Security Act passed, he removed national insurance from Social Security legislation. President Harry S. Truman was more vocal in calling for national health insurance. Many seniors lived in poverty and only about half had health insurance. In 1949, Minnesota senator Hubert Humphrey proposed the first national health care bill entitled Post Hospital Care for the Aged. Humphrey explained, "the moral test of a government is how that government treats those who are in the dawn of life—the children; the twilight of life—the elderly, the shadows of life—the sick, the needy, and the handicapped" (Shalala, 2000, p. 2). Humphrey's Bill did not pass; however, his efforts were continued by President Lyndon B. Johnson. On July 30, 1965, Johnson enacted an amendment to the Social Security Act. The Health Insurance for the Aged (Medicare) Act and Medicaid provided hospital, extended care, and home health care to all Americans age 65 and over. Johnson signed the bill into law at the Truman Library in Independence, Missouri, in the presence of former president Truman. Immediately after signing the legislation, Johnson enrolled Truman as the first Medicare beneficiary. Mrs. Truman was the second. Louisiana senator Russell Long described the bill as "the largest and most significant piece of social legislation ever to pass Congress in the history of our country. It will do more immediate good, for more people, who need the attention of their government, than any other Bill that Congress has ever enacted" (Shalala, 2000, p. 4). More than 19 million people enrolled in Medicare within the following year.

Over time, Medicare has evolved as needs and health services change. In 1972, Medicare eligibility was expanded to include people with disabilities and people with end stage renal disease (ESRD). The following year, Medicare was amended to include coverage by health maintenance organizations (HMOs). In 1977, the Health Care Financing Administration (HCFA) was established to manage the Medicare and Medicaid programs. In 1988, coverage was expanded further to include hospital and skilled nursing facilities, outpatient prescriptions (later repealed), and caps on liability.

Today, Medicare is managed by the Centers for Medicare and Medicaid Services. The program consists of three main parts. Medicare Part A (Hospital Insurance) covers inpatient hospital care, skilled nursing care, hospice care, and some home health care. Part A is financed through taxes paid while working. Medicare Part B (Medical Insurance) covers necessary medical supplies, doctors' services, and outpatient care, such as physical and occupational therapy. Part B is financed through insurance premiums. Medicare prescription drug coverage is an insurance program that covers prescription drug costs. As of 2017, more than 57.6 million people were enrolled in Medicare plans with 25 million people enrolled in Medicare's prescription drug plans (Centers for Medicare and Medicaid Services). The retiring baby-boom generation is expected to push enrollment over 80 million, creating an enormous challenge for the federal government and younger generations.

Sally Kuykendall

See also: Affordable Care Act; Aging; Centers for Medicare and Medicaid Services; Disability; Disability Movement; Medicaid; Prescription Drugs; Roosevelt, Franklin Delano; Social Security Act; U.S. Department of Health and Human Services; *Controversies in Public Health:* Controversy 1

Further Reading

Centers for Medicare and Medicaid Services. (2017). Retrieved from https://www.cms.gov/.

Medicare. (2017). Retrieved from https://www.medicare.gov/.

Shalala, D. (2000). *Remarks by the Hon. Donna E. Shalala, Former U.S. Secretary of Health and Human Services at the 35th Anniversary event, Hubert H. Humphrey Building,* U.S. Department of Health and Human Services, Washington, DC, pp. 2–7. Retrieved from https://www.cms.gov/About-CMS/Agency-Information/History/Downloads/CMS35thAnniversary.pdf.

Tapia Granados, J. A., & Diez Roux, A. V. (2009). Life and death during the Great Depression. *Proceedings of the National Academy of Sciences of the United States of America, 106*(41), 17290–17295. Retrieved from http://doi.org/10.1073/pnas.0904491106.

MEDICINE

Medicine is the science and practice of diagnosing, treating, and preventing disease at the individual level. Medicine is part of public health in that medicine promotes health and prevents disease. The main difference between medicine and public health is that medicine focuses on individual patients and public health focuses on groups of people. The two systems are separate yet related. Community health centers, also known as public health clinics, practice medicine, serving as medical homes for vulnerable populations. Medicine plays an important role in ensuring that some conditions, such as meningitis, do not become an epidemic. On the other hand, individualized medical care requires a high level of expertise and is very expensive. Society struggles to sustain a health care system that primarily depends on individualized medicine. To ensure the best possible care while still maintaining health care costs, experts are seeking optimal ways to integrate medicine and public health services (Committee on Integrating Primary Care and Public Health, 2012).

Medical services are typically provided by a doctor, nurse, dentist, nutritionist, or other licensed health care professional who has completed the education, training, and licensing requirements to practice in the clinical area. Preparation for a professional career in medicine typically requires that students complete courses in the social sciences, natural sciences, and mathematics. Courses in anatomy and physiology are central to understanding normal and abnormal functions of the human body and to advance to caring for patients. Training also includes time in supervised clinical practice where the student gains hands-on experience in interacting with patients (and diseases), learning clinical routines and observing experienced professionals. After basic training, the health professional may specialize in a certain type of medicine. Medical specialties are often categorized by body system (cardiology, neurology, or endocrinology), patient type (pediatrics, adolescent health, or geriatrics), or disease (trauma, oncology, or HIV/AIDS). All medical professionals work under a code of ethics requiring honesty, integrity, professionalism, and respect for others. The code of ethics promotes trust between patient and provider.

Under the medical model, care is individualized to the patient. For example, if individuals develop symptoms of difficulty breathing, they can go to a doctor's office or clinic where they are assessed, examined, and interviewed. The doctor, physician assistant (PA), or nurse practitioner (NP) gathers information on symptoms, past medical history, family history, and recent exposures. The health care professional orders diagnostic tests, such as lung function tests, allergy testing, chest X-ray, or electrocardiogram. Based on the physical exam and test results, the medical provider rules out certain diseases and makes a possible diagnosis. If the patient is diagnosed with asthma, the caregiver would prescribe medicine for long-term asthma control and quick relief in emergencies. Together, the patient and health care provider develop a personal asthma action plan that includes how to use the prescribed treatment, how to recognize and avoid asthma triggers, and how to use tools, such as a peak flow meter to monitor the treatment plan. The health care provider follows up regularly with the patient to ensure effective asthma control. Each phase of care (diagnosis, treatment, and prevention of reoccurrences) is individualized to the patient. Medicine works in parallel to public health preventing further exacerbation of disease and promoting health.

Unfortunately, the current system of medical care is reactionary, expensive, and fragmented. In 2007, the American Academy of Family Physicians (AAFP), American Academy of Pediatrics (AAP), American College of Physicians (ACP), and American Osteopathic Association (AOA) developed the Joint Principles of the Patient-Centered Medical Home (PC-MH). Under the PC-MH model, each person has a medical home, a place where he or she can get comprehensive medical services. Each patient has a personal physician who monitors the patient's health and progress. The person can go to the medical home for acute medical care, chronic disease care, wellness, and health promotion services. The system is oriented toward caring for the whole person across all health care systems, clinics, hospitals, rehabilitation units, and community-based services. Advantages of the PC-MH model are that the patient can access uninterrupted, comprehensive, culturally competent medical care, and the care can be coordinated through a central archive of medical records (AAFP, AAP, ACP, & AOA, 2007). The PC-MH system mimics the national health services of other countries. Challenges exist in how to secure and coordinate such a complex system of care for so many people.

The main difference between medical care and public health is that medicine focuses on individual treatment whereas public health focuses on groups of people. Neither system is superior to the other. Both systems work together to prevent disease and promote health. The next steps are to find ways to integrate medicine and public health in order to ensure the best possible care with minimal public and personal expenses.

Sally Kuykendall

See also: American Medical Association; Community Health Centers; Greco-Roman Era, Public Health in the; Health; Health and Medicine Division of the National Academies of Sciences, Engineering, and Medicine; Hippocrates; Renaissance, Public Health in the

Further Reading

AAFP, AAP, ACP, & AOA. (2007). *Joint principles of the PCMH.* Retrieved from http://www.aafp.org/dam/AAFP/documents/practice_management/pcmh/initiatives/PCMHJoint.pdf.

Committee on Integrating Primary Care and Public Health. (2012). *Primary care and public health: Exploring integration to improve population health.* Washington, DC: National Academies Press.

National Heart, Lung and Blood Institute. (2014). *What is asthma?* Retrieved from https://www.nhlbi.nih.gov/health/health-topics/topics/asthma.

MENINGITIS

Meningitis is an acute inflammation of the membranes—called the meninges—that surrounds and protects the central nervous system (CNS). The inflammation is primarily caused by bacterial or viral infection and may also be caused by head injury, cancer, or certain drugs. Meningitis outbreaks are serious public health emergencies. Invasion of the host and reproduction of the infectious organism can progress rapidly, within hours, and fatality rates can be as high as 10 to 15 percent. Twenty-percent of those who recover suffer from long-term disabilities, such as memory impairment, hearing and vision loss, or learning difficulties (Centers for Disease Control and Prevention, 2016). Incidence rates vary by location and type. Bacterial meningitis affects approximately 4,000 people, and viral meningitis affects approximately 1 in every 10,000 people in the United States where rates have been on the decline (Thigpen, Whitney, Messonnier, Zell, Lynfield, & Hadler, 2011). Other areas of the world, such as northern Africa, Brazil, and India, are more susceptible to recurrent outbreaks. Although anyone may contract meningitis, infants, the elderly, and people with compromised immune systems are more susceptible. Severity varies based on many factors, including the strain and dosage of microorganism, host immunity, and access to effective treatment. Meningitis outbreaks require a carefully planned, coordinated approach by public health staff, the local community, and medical professionals. As soon as a case is identified, public health epidemiologists identify the mechanism and source of infection. Health departments alert local schools and community centers. Information on means of transmission, symptoms, and prevention is disseminated through newsletters, news reports, social media, television, and radio. The overall goal during an outbreak is to ensure early identification and prevention so that those who are affected will seek treatment and those who are at risk will get vaccinated.

Throughout history, meningitis has raised curiosity and spurred medical progress. The earliest case is found in the mummy of Pharaoh Amenemope (1300–1075 BCE) on display in the Museum of Egyptian Antiquities in Cairo, Egypt. Examination of the remains reveals that this Egyptian ruler probably died from meningitis. The earliest documentation of symptoms is attributed to the ancient Greek physician and Father of Western Medicine, Hippocrates (c. 460 BCE–c. 375 BCE). Hippocrates studied and documented many different ailments and symptoms. His detailed descriptions of seizures, aphasia, paralysis, and fever spurred him to openly refute the common belief that neurological disorders were caused by evil spirits possessing the body. This knowledge meant that care and treatment of people with neurological problems transferred from religious leaders, who attempted to rid the body of evil spirits through harmful, aggressive means to medical practitioners, who used carative therapies. In 1768, the Scottish physician Robert Whytt identified a specific type of meningitis, tuberculosis meningitis. The relationship between microorganism and disease was not identified until the 19th century. The movement of one early and severe epidemic of meningitis can be found in a description from Switzerland in 1805 with others following in the United States, Europe, and Africa soon after. In 1884, a Russian physician described the common symptoms of meningitis, and in 1891 a new and effective diagnostic tool, the lumbar puncture, was devised. Lumbar puncture collects a sample of cerebral spinal fluid (CSF) from the spinal column, which allows the organism to be identified and correct treatment administered. By the early 20th century specific viral strains were identified as sources of infection leading to meningitis and the first vaccines were created. When penicillin was discovered in 1944, it became an effective treatment for bacterial meningitis.

The CNS is composed of the brain and spinal cord, which are surrounded by a series of membranes called the meninges. The meninges consist of three layers: the dura mater, the arachnoid mater, and the pia mater. The primary function of the meningeal layers is to protect the CNS. The meninges contain the cerebral spinal fluid (CSF), the liquid that bathes and sustains the CNS. The fluid is located within the space between the arachnoid and pia mater, known as the subarachnoid space, and supplies mechanical and immunological support for the CNS. Meningitis is most often caused by an infection of the CSF resulting in inflammation of the meninges and producing potential damage to the CNS.

Meningitis symptoms vary depending on age group and type of infection. In adults, many symptoms are shared regardless of their source and can arise within

24 hours of contraction. Common symptoms include severe headache, fever, vomiting, stiffness in the neck, altered mental status, and sensitivity to light and noise. In a particular type of bacterial meningitis, there may be an accompanying rash. In small children and infants, obvious symptoms can be difficult to determine but may include irritability, altered feeding patterns, and vomiting. Often, infants with meningitis can present with an enlarged fontanelle, the soft spot on the skull, or poor reflex responses.

Bacterial meningitis may be highly contagious and cause severe symptoms and long-term complications. The most common sources of bacterial meningitis in the United States are *Haemophilus influenza, Listeria monocytogenes, Streptococcus pneumoniae,* and *Neisseria meningitidis,* which affect different age groups with varying frequency. The bacteria that cause meningitis are typically not spread in the air but by the exchange of fluids from the throat and respiratory tract. Bacterial meningitis, specifically the *Neisseria meningitidis* strain, can easily spread in communal living settings such as college dormitories and military barracks.

Viral meningitis typically produces less severe symptoms than bacterial meningitis and is the most common type contracted. Although contact with an infected individual may spread the virus, it does not mean that the newly infected individual will contract meningitis as a result. Viruses that may produce meningitis include herpes, mumps, non-polio enteroviruses, influenza, measles, arboviruses, and *Lymphocytic choriomeningitis.* Adults usually recover from viral meningitis within 10 days if they are otherwise healthy.

Fungal meningitis is a relatively rare condition and is not spread as easily as bacterial or viral infections. Although anyone is susceptible to contracting fungal meningitis, it is typically contracted by individuals with compromised immune systems and spreads through soil contaminated with infected fecal matter whereby fungal spores are inhaled and spread to the CNS. The most commons types of fungal meningitis are caused by *Cryptococcus, Histoplasma, Blastomyces,* and *Coccidioides.*

Parasitic meningitis, otherwise known as primary amebic meningoencephalitis (PAM), is a rare, noncontagious condition that is fatal if contracted. PAM is caused by *Naegleria fowleri* entering an individual through the nasal passage and infecting the CNS, causing death within 12 days. It is found around the world but only in freshwater such as lakes, rivers, geothermal sources, and poorly maintained swimming areas. Meningitis can also result from noninfectious sources but produce the same set of symptoms. Noninfectious meningitis is not contagious, and its sources include traumatic head injury, cancer, complications following surgery, and *systemic lupus erythematosus.*

Meningitis is typically diagnosed by the presence of elevated inflammatory signals and/or infectious agents in blood or CSF collected from the patient. Other means of diagnosis are based on rectal or naso-oropharyngeal swabs or stool samples. Identifying the exact source of infection is crucial to effective treatment, and bacteria can be cultured to identify their specific strain and viruses identified by analyzing their DNA for the presence of specific genes. Bacterial meningitis can be treated effectively with appropriate antibiotics, particularly if treatment starts soon after the initial infection. The recovery rate following antibiotic treatment is high, though long-term effects may include brain damage and impaired hearing. No direct treatment exists for viral meningitis, but the infection typically subsides in 7 to 10 days, after which most infected individuals recover. Depending of the severity of inflammation, long-term complications following treatment may still persist and include seizures, hydrocephalus, hearing loss, and brain damage. Fungal meningitis is typically treated with antifungal drugs that can be delivered intravenously. Despite successfully being able to treat *Naegleria fowleri* in the laboratory, the source of parasitic meningitis, treatment has been unsuccessful in infected individuals. Vaccines exist for many strains of meningitis-causing bacteria but not for the most common sources of viral, fungal, or parasitic meningitis. Corticosteroids may be administered to help decrease the likelihood of complications from the meningeal inflammation that results from infection.

Meningitis is a frightening and deadly disease that spreads rapidly among people who are in close contact with others. When an outbreak emerges, public health professionals must move quickly to identify the causal organism, sources of the outbreak, individuals who need early treatment, and to prevent continued transmission. People who contract the disease require intensive monitoring, treatment, and medical support to prevent long-term complications. The most effective way to control meningitis is through prevention. Following recommended vaccination schedules, maintaining a healthy immune system through good nutrition, adequate sleep, avoiding direct or indirect tobacco smoke, and good hygiene and handwashing are the best ways to prevent and limit transmission.

Simon Waldbaum

See also: Antibiotic Resistance; Epidemic; Epidemiology; Handwashing; Infectious Diseases; Influenza; Penicillin; Prevention; Vaccines

Further Reading

Centers for Disease Control and Prevention. (2016). *Information for healthcare professionals about adolescent vaccines.* Retrieved from http://www.cdc.gov/vaccines/who/teens/downloads/hcp-factsheet.pdf.

Harrison, L. H., Trotter, C. L., & Ramsay, M. E. (2009). Global epidemiology of meningococcal disease. *Vaccine*, *27*, B51–B63.

Rosenstein, N. E., Perkins, B. A., Stephens, D. S., Lefkowitz, L., Cartter, M. L., Danila, R., et al. (1999). The changing epidemiology of meningococcal disease in the United States, 1992–1996. *Journal of Infectious Diseases*, *180*, 1894–1901.

Rosenstein, N. E., Perkins, B. A., Stephens, D. S., Popovic, T., & Hughes, J. M. (2001). Meningococcal disease. *New England Journal of Medicine*, *344*, 1378–1388.

Thigpen, M. C., Whitney, C. G., Messonnier, N. E., Zell, E. R., Lynfield, R., Hadler, J. L., et al. (2011). Bacterial meningitis in the United States, 1998–2007. *New England Journal of Medicine*, *364*, 2016–2025.

Yoder, J. S., Eddy, B. A., Visvesvara, G. S., Capewell, L., & Beach, M. J. (2010). The epidemiology of primary amoebic meningoencephalitis in the USA, 1962–2008. *Epidemiology Infections*, *138*, 968–975.

MEN'S HEALTH

Men's health is a branch of public health that aims to promote men's physical, mental, and social well-being and to prevent or treat diseases or conditions that uniquely affect males. In terms of health promotion, men's health encompasses educating males on physical and emotional wellness, how to care for their body, and how to prevent injuries and diseases. With respect to prevention and treatment, men's health focuses on diseases or conditions that are more common, more serious, or specific only to men, exhibit different risk factors or symptoms among men, or require different treatments (Rich & Roe, 2002). Examples of such diseases include impotence (erectile dysfunction), heart disease, prostate and testicular cancer, genitourinary disorders, or male pattern baldness. As a group, men are a special population with unique health challenges. Males suffer from heart disease, cancer, unintentional injuries, stroke, chronic respiratory disease, diabetes, suicide, and chronic liver diseases at greater rates than females. On average, men die five to eight years earlier than women. Gender disparities exist because men are more likely to engage in risky behaviors or work in dangerous jobs and less likely to participate in regular health care screening and preventive practices. In addition to addressing pathophysiological and physiological conditions, men's health explores the unique psychosocial experiences of males in society with respect to prevention, treatment, and coping with illness. Men's health is a developing field with enormous opportunities for further investigation and specialty practice.

Men suffer higher rates of both acute and chronic diseases than women. Men are 1.5 times more likely to die from heart disease, cancer, and respiratory diseases (Centers for Disease Control and Prevention [CDC], 2015). Men are two times more likely to die of heart disease. The majority of sudden cardiac events (70–89 percent) occur among men (CDC, 2015). Prostate cancer is the most frequently diagnosed cancer among men, accounting for 185,000 cases and 29,000 deaths annually (Wilkins & Savoye, 2009). Colorectal cancer affects 71,099 men and causes 27,230 male deaths annually. Many of these health problems can be prevented through healthy eating, regular physical activity, maintaining a healthy weight, controlling stress, not smoking, and avoiding excessive alcohol consumption. Regular prostate specific antigen (PSA) screening and physical examination can detect and treat prostate problems early. Regular colorectal examinations can detect abnormal growths in the colon or rectum and eliminate polyps that lead to colorectal cancer.

Despite opportunities in health promotion and disease prevention, men are less likely to visit health care providers for screening or care. Men have higher rates of cigarette smoking, alcohol, and substance abuse and are more likely to suffer motor vehicle crashes, homicide, or on-the-job injuries (Barua, 2009; Shmerling, 2016; White & Holmes, 2006). Men are 25 percent less likely to visit a health care provider and 40 percent less likely to undergo preventive screening (Murray-Law, 2011). Researchers believe that there are multiple factors that create reluctance to visit a health care provider. Men do not have to access medical care for birth control or for fatherhood, as women do. Hence they do not have the opportunity to develop a habit of health promotion in adolescence or early adulthood. In American culture, traditional male traits encouraging the suppression of emotion, promotion of aggression, or increased risk-taking may also inhibit health-seeking behaviors (Murray-Law, 2011; Oliffe et al., 2010).

Men present a unique population for public health practice. Socially, men participate in many high-risk behaviors, yet are less likely to engage in regular medical screenings. Research in men's health is developing slowly. There are many opportunities in this field, such as considering the impact of class, culture, or socioeconomic status on male health. To protect this population, public health is challenged to find new ways to increase and support healthy behaviors.

Godyson Orji

See also: Cancer; Chronic Illness; Health; Health Disparities; *Healthy People 2020*; Human Immunodeficiency Virus and Acquired Immune Deficiency Syndrome; Leading Health Indicators; Lesbian, Gay, Bisexual, and Transgender Health; Tuskegee Syphilis Study; Women's Health; Wynder, Ernst Ludwig; *Controversies in Public Health:* Controversy 2

Further Reading

Barua, K. (2009). Why men die earlier than women: 56. *Journal of Men's Health*, 6(3), 241–241. doi:10.1016/j.jomh.2009.08.054

Centers for Disease Control and Prevention (CDC). (2015). *Leading causes of death in males United States, 2013*. Retrieved from https://www.cdc.gov/healthequity/lcod/men/2013/index.htmMurray-Law, B. (2011). Why do men die earlier? *Monitor on Psychology*, 42(6), 58–63. Retrieved from http://www.apa.org/monitor/2011/06/men-die.aspx.

National Center for Health Statistics (NCHS). (2016). *Health, United States, 2015: With special feature on racial and ethnic health disparities*. Hyattsville, MD. Retrieved from https://www.cdc.gov/nchs/data/hus/hus15.pdf#053.

Oliffe, J. L., Robertson, S., Frank, B., McCreary, D. R., Tremblay, G., & Goldenberg, S. L. (2010). Men's health in Canada: A 2010 update. *Journal of Men's Health*, 7(3), 189–192. doi:10.1016/j.jomh.2010.07.001

Rich, J., & Roe, M. (2002). *A poor man's plight: Uncovering the disparity in men's health*. Retrieved from http://health-equity.pitt.edu/38/.

Shmerling, R. H. (2016). *Why men often die earlier than women*. Boston: Harvard Health. Retrieved from http://www.health.harvard.edu/blog/why-men-often-die-earlier-than-women-201602199137.

White, A., & Holmes, M. (2006). Patterns of mortality across 44 countries among men and women aged 15–44 years. *Journal of Men's Health & Gender*, 3(2), 139–151.

Wilkins, D., & Savoye, E. (2009). Men's health around the world: A review of progress and policy across 11 countries. *European Men's Health Forum (EMHF)*. Retrieved from http://www.emhf.org/wp-content/uploads/2013/12/EMHFreport_globalmenshealthLR.pdf.

MENTAL HEALTH

Many public health issues are related to mental health or mental illness. Promoting positive mental health is integral to reducing addictions and violence and to helping people live healthy, fulfilling lives. The World Health Organization (WHO) defines good mental health as "a state of well-being in which the individual realizes his or her own abilities, can cope with the normal stresses of life, can work productively and fruitfully, and is able to make a contribution to his or her community" (WHO, 2013, p. 6). Although mental health is a concern for all age groups, adolescence is a critical period in developing lifelong attitudes and practices. For all age groups and particularly adolescents, good mental health includes four aspects: (1) a positive identity, (2) the ability to manage thoughts and emotions, (3) the ability to build social relationships, and (4) the aptitude to learn and to acquire an education.

A positive self-identity is made up of values, those intangible elements of personality that are behaviorally expressed on a regular basis. The Search Institute (SI), a nonprofit foundation focused on helping communities raise children and adolescents into happy, healthy adults, has conducted more than 80,000 surveys in order to identify values associated with good mental health. They include integrity, honesty, responsibility, restraint, power, self-esteem, purpose, and optimism (SI, 2006).

Integrity is a matter of adhering to what is right even when no one is looking. Honesty means telling the truth, even about mistakes, accidents, or having done something wrong. Responsibility is about holding yourself accountable for what you say and do, and not blaming others. Restraint is the ability to hold back impulses and assess a situation completely before speaking or acting. Power refers to exerting influence on those things in life you can control—such as what you say and do—and not trying to control what you cannot, such as what others say and do. Good self-esteem is about liking yourself. Adolescents who practice and develop those aspects about themselves that they like enjoy good mental health. This includes addressing weaknesses. Having a purpose or meaning in life is associated with well-being among all age groups (Steger et al., 2009, pp. 43–52). People whose purpose is to help others, such as by correcting social ills (inequality, hunger, or poverty), are mentally healthier than those who are only out for themselves (SI, 2006). Optimism is having a positive future perspective that ultimately things will turn out alright. Optimism is about trying, even if you fail.

Stress is inherent in life's every change and challenge. Without stress there is boredom. With too much stress we feel overwhelmed. Learning how to manage stress entails predicting it, preparing for it through rehearsal or seeking support, and—after the stress passes—recovering through rest and relaxation.

A main source of stress are the expectations held about how things should turn out. Unrealistically high expectations of others, oneself, and life in general typically lead to disappointment. Adolescents who check their self-expectations with parents or trusted adults to ensure they are high but realistic have better mental health than those who do not (SI, 2006).

The wise use of time is an essential stress management technique associated with good mental health. Time spent planning and making decisions is a good investment. Adolescents who read, engage in creative or artistic pursuits, organized sports, or volunteer in their community for three or more hours per week generally enjoy good mental health, as compared to those who do not (SI, 2006). The same holds true for participating in religious or spiritual pursuits; but the mental health benefit is achieved with just one hour per week or more.

During adolescence, one of the best uses of time is to initiate and develop healthy relationships. However, those who limit time spent "just hanging out" to two or fewer nights per week tend to be happier than adolescents who "do nothing" three or more nights per week (SI, 2006).

Humans are the most social species on the plant, as evidenced by the length of time human children remain connected to their caregivers, and our reliance on social networks to work, play, and love. Social support is one of the main factors in mental well-being (Morgan et al., 2008). Using your network to problem solve or get reassurance promotes good mental health (SI, 2006). But simply having a strong support network—even if you do not use it—is protective of mental health.

The WHO (2013) identifies safety, stability, and nurturance as key aspects of healthy relationships. These features are important in family relationships, as well as with teachers, coaches, or friends' parents, who may be supportive. These adults may serve as one-time advisers or as role models. Same-age peers who model prosocial (as opposed to antisocial) behaviors also contribute to good mental health (SI, 2006). One 2017 study identified 55 ways to foster and deepen healthy relationships, such as talking out problems together and sharing things you admire (Roehlkepartain et al., 2017). Key aspects that lead to their development include empathy. Empathy is one social skill that is associated with increased life satisfaction (SI, 2006). Empathy is about understanding where another person is coming from both logically and emotionally. Two negative aspects of social relationships include conflict and pressure. Conflict and disagreements are an occasional part of relationships. Being able to problem solve and negotiate in order to resolve conflicts peacefully is associated with greater life satisfaction (SI, 2006). Threats of violence or intimidation have no place in a healthy relationship.

Another form of social conflict is feeling pressured to do something that you do not believe in. When this pressure comes from others of a similar age or status it is known as peer pressure. Being able to resist social pressure is associated with mental well-being (SI, 2006). Believing that others who love and respect you would never pressure you into doing something you did not believe in can help you stand your ground.

Most adolescents spend a large portion of their time in school. Education is associated with long-term mental health. Graduating high school and immediately pursuing college increases the likelihood of graduating with a bachelor's degree (Radford et al., 2010). Delaying by one year reduces your chances by 20 percent; waiting two years between high school and college, your chances drop by 68 percent. High school and college students whose parents are involved in schooling have better mental health than those without it (SI, 2006). Parents may be able to help maintain motivation to do well in school, such as by setting up rewards for outstanding performance, or withholding certain incentives when performance is inadequate. Communicating expectations, such as expectations for school performance, can result in positive mental health (SI, 2006).

David J. Reynolds

See also: Beers, Clifford Whittingham; Behavioral Health; Mental Illness; National Institutes of Health; Spiritual Health; Substance Abuse and Mental Health Services Administration; Veterans' Health; Violence; World Health Organization; *Controversies in Public Health:* Controversy 2

Further Reading

Morgan, A., Currie, C., Due, P., Gabhain, S. N., Rasmussen, M., Samdal, O., and Smith, R., (2008). Mental well-being in school-aged children in Europe: Associations with social cohesion and socioeconomic circumstances. In A. Mathieson & T. Koller (Eds.), *Social cohesion for mental well-being among adolescents*. Copenhagen, Denmark: World Health Organization Regional Office for Europe. Retrieved from http://www.euro.who.int/__data/assets/pdf_file/0005/84623/E91921.pdf.

Radford, A. W., Berkner, L., Wheeless, S. C., & Shepherd, B. (2010). *Persistence and attainment of 2003–04 beginning postsecondary students: After 6 years* (NCES Publication No. 2011-151). Retrieved June 27, 2017, from http://nces.ed.gov/pubs2011/2011151.pdf.

Roehlkepartain, E. C., Pekel, K., Syvertsen, A. K., Sethi, J., Sullivan, T. K., & Scales, P. C. (2017). *Relationships first: Creating connections that help young people thrive*. Minneapolis: Search Institute. Retrieved July 2, 2017, from http://page.search-institute.org/relationships-first-020217a?submission=233714421.

Search Institute. (2006). *40 developmental assets for adolescents (ages 12–18)*. Minneapolis: Author. Retrieved June 27, 2017, from www.search-institute.org.

Steger, M. F., Oishi, S., & Kashdan, T. B. (2009). Meaning in life across the life span: Levels and correlates of meaning in life from emerging adulthood to older adulthood. *The Journal of Positive Psychology, 4*(1), 43–52.

World Health Organization. (2013). *Mental Health Action Plan 2013–2020*. Geneva: WHO Press. Retrieved June 25, 2017, from www.who.int.

MENTAL ILLNESS

Mental illness is defined as "collectively all diagnosable mental disorders" or "health conditions that are characterized by alterations in thinking, mood, or behavior associated with distress and/or impaired functioning" (Department of Health and Human Services, 1999). One in five U.S. adults, 43.8 million individuals, experience some type of mental illness each year (National Institutes of Mental Health [NIMH], n.d.). Individuals with mental illness are at increased risk of other chronic medical problems and die approximately 25 years earlier than other people. Unfortunately, the health needs of the mentally ill are not being met. Only 41 percent of adults with mental illness and 63 percent of adults with serious mental illness receive mental health services (Center for Behavioral Health Statistics and Quality, 2015). Public health agencies, such as the NIMH, Substance Abuse and Mental Health Services Administration (SAMHSA), local, state, and territorial health departments, and community-based organizations, are working to reduce the stigma of mental illness and to provide effective, accessible, evidence-based treatments and programs within communities.

Mental illnesses are defined by the *Diagnostic and Statistical Manual* (*DSM*), currently in the fifth edition of publication. The manual divides mental illnesses into discrete categories, outlines diagnostic criteria, and provides inclusion and exclusion criteria for each diagnosis. Major categories are schizophrenia spectrum and other psychotic disorders, anxiety disorders, and depressive disorders. Schizophrenia is arguably one of the most devastating illnesses affecting about 1 percent of the population. Schizophrenia presents as a wide range of symptoms. Hallmark features are hallucinations, delusions, and disorganization in thought and behavior. Anxiety disorders are characterized by excessive or unrealistic worry, which may be related to specific tasks, events, objects, or rituals. About 10 percent of the U.S. population suffers from an anxiety disorder. Depressive disorders are characterized by a period of chronic sadness associated with changes in energy, sleep, weight, or attention. Almost 10 percent of the American population suffers from some mood disorder. Major depression affects 7 percent of the adult population and 12.5 percent of adolescents. Major depression is twice as common in adult females as in adult males and four times more common in adolescent females as in adolescent males. Of those with severe depressive symptoms, 43 percent report difficulties in work, home, and social activities (Pratt & Brody, 2014). Of those with severe symptoms, only 35 percent report contact with a mental health worker in the past year. Depression has a significant association with medical problems. Those with depression are more likely to have heart disease, obesity, alcoholism, smoking, and other mental health problems such as anxiety disorders, substance use disorders, and eating disorders. Depression is also associated with lower workplace productivity and greater absenteeism, resulting in unemployment. The economic burden for depression, including workplace costs and the costs of medical and psychiatric services, was estimated to be $210.5 billion in 2010.

Many adult mental illnesses begin in childhood. Half of all cases of mental illness begin by age 14 and 75 percent by age 24. About 1 out of every 10 minors meet criteria for a serious emotional disturbance, which is defined as a mental health problem that interferes with the child's ability to function socially, academically, or emotionally (Pratt & Brody, 2014). As in the adult population, depression and anxiety are most prevalent. Mental illnesses have important implications on long-term health and wellness. Thirty-seven percent of students with a mental health condition drop out of school (Center for Behavioral Health Statistics and Quality, 2015). This represents the highest dropout rate of any disability group. Seventy percent of youth in state and local juvenile justice systems have a mental illness (NIMH, n.d.). Unfortunately, as with adults, many children with mental health problems do not receive mental health care. Only 50 percent of children with mental health disorders received treatment for their disorder within the past year. Suicide is the third leading cause of death for people aged 10–24 and the second leading cause of death for people aged 15–24. If you know someone who is struggling with life-threatening mental illness, the National Suicide Prevention Lifeline (1-800-273-8255) is available 24 hours a day, seven days a week for assistance.

Mental illnesses are categorized as serious when they substantially interfere or limit one or more major life activity, such as self-care, personal relationships, or workplace functioning. Serious mental illness affects 4.1 percent of the adult population—roughly 1 in 25 adults, or 10 million individuals—in a given year (National Institutes of Mental Health, n.d.). Mental illness occurs frequently in conjunction with substance use issues. Of 20.2 million Americans with substance use issues, 50.5 percent—10.2 million adults—had a co-occurring mental illness (Center for Behavioral Health Statistics and Quality, 2015).

Social and cultural factors interact with mental illness. The relationship between homelessness and mental health problems is well documented. For example, 26 percent of homeless adults staying in shelters live with serious mental illness (Center for Behavioral Health Statistics and Quality, 2015). An estimated one out of two homeless adults in shelters have a severe mental illness or substance use disorder. Individuals within the criminal justice system are also disproportionately more likely to have mental health problems. Studies estimate that 20 percent of state prisoners and 21 percent of local jail prisoners have a recent history of a mental health condition (Glaze & James, 2006). Individuals of different races are at different risk for having a mental illness. For example, 16.3 percent of Hispanic adults, 19.3 percent of white adults, 18.6 percent of black adults, and 28.3 percent of American Indian/Native Alaskan adults live with a mental health condition (NIMH, n.d.).

Mental illnesses are treatable diseases of the brain. Current evidence suggests that the combination of psychotherapy and medication management is most effective in controlling symptoms of mental illness. Cognitive behavioral therapy has been shown to be effective in treating depression, anxiety disorders, eating disorders, post-traumatic stress disorder (PTSD), and schizophrenia. Dialectical behavioral therapy has been shown to be effective in the treatment of borderline personality disorder. If psychotherapy alone does not adequately treat symptoms, medication management may be indicated. For major depressive disorder (MDD), antidepressants are the class of medication shown to be most effective. Selective serotonin reuptake inhibitors (SSRIs) are the first line antidepressant. If symptoms of depression are severe and refractory to pharmacologic treatment, brain stimulation interventions

Dior Vargas attends her weekly counseling session to manage major depressive disorder. Vargas founded the People of Color & Mental Illness Photo Project deconstructing stigmas of mental illness. (Shaul Schwarz, Verbatim/Getty Images for Be Vocal)

such as electroconvulsive therapy may be indicated. Some anxiety disorders may also be treated by antidepressant, as well as anxiolytics, another class of medications that includes benzodiazepines. Schizophrenia is treated by a class of medication called antipsychotics, which itself is subdivided into typical antipsychotics and atypical antipsychotics. Bipolar disorder is predominantly treated with lithium and/or anticonvulsant medication (Sadock, Sadock, Sadock, & Ruiz, 2015).

One of the largest barriers to treatment is the stigma of mental illness. Although much has been done to reduce the stigma through education and public service announcements, attitudes that blame the victim continue to severely inhibit treatment seeking.

Prevention efforts focus on promoting mental health. Mental health is "a state of well-being in which the individual realizes his or her own abilities, can cope with the normal stresses of life, can work productively and fruitfully, and is able to make a contribution to his or her community" (World Health Organization, 2016). Mental health maximizes mental assets rather than disability. Generally, the notion of well-being includes the presence of positive moods and emotions (like happiness and contentment), the absence of negative emotions (like depression and anxiety), and a sense of life satisfaction and fulfillment. There are no absolute determinants. For example, paid employment is important for accessing resources and developing meaning and purpose. Income has a positive effect among people of lower socioeconomic levels and lessens for those of higher incomes. Generally, well-being is closely associated with and dependent on good health, positive relationships, and availability and access to basic resources like food, shelter, and income. Positive emotions are more closely associated with having supportive and healthy social relationships.

Mental illnesses are extremely common among Americans. Many people suffer from depression or anxiety. And while mental illnesses are treatable, many people do not recognize the symptoms or neglect to seek treatment. Current public health efforts focus on reducing the stigma of mental illness in order to facilitate early diagnosis and treatment. Friends, family members, and coworkers are critical in supporting people with mental illness in seeking treatment.

Timur Suhail-Sindhu, Maria DiGiorgio McColgan, and Sally Kuykendall

See also: Addictions; Adverse Childhood Experiences; Beers, Clifford Whittingham; Behavioral Health; Child Maltreatment; Children's Health; Dix, Dorothea Lynde; Eating Disorders; Intimate Partner Violence; Men's Health; Mental Health; Substance Abuse and Mental Health Services Administration; Syringe Service Programs; Veterans' Health; Violence; Women's Health

Further Reading

Center for Behavioral Health Statistics and Quality. (2015). *Behavioral health trends in the United States: Results from the 2014 National Survey on drug use and health* (HHS Publication no. SMA 15-4927). Retrieved from https://www.samhsa.gov/data/sites/default/files/NSDUH-FRR1-2014/NSDUH-FRR1-2014.pdf.

Department of Health and Human Services. (1999). *Mental health: A report of the Surgeon General.* Rockville, MD: U.S. Department of Health and Human Services; Substance Abuse and Mental Health Services Administration, Center for Mental Health Services, National Institutes of Health, National Institute of Mental Health. Retrieved from https://profiles.nlm.nih.gov/ps/retrieve/ResourceMetadata/NNBBHS.

Glaze, L. E., & James, D. J. (2006). *Mental health problems of prison and jail inmates.* Bureau of Justice Statistics Special Report. Washington, DC: U.S. Department of Justice, Office of Justice. Retrieved from https://www.bjs.gov/content/pub/pdf/mhppji.pdf.

Goffman, E. (1963). *Stigma: Notes on the management of spoiled identity.* Englewood Cliffs, NJ: Prentice Hall.

National Alliance for Mental Illness. Retrieved from https://www.nami.org.

National Institutes of Mental Health. (n.d.). *Statistics.* Retrieved from https://www.nimh.nih.gov/health/statistics/index.shtml.

Pratt, L. A., & Brody, D. J. (2014). Depression in the U.S. household population, 2009–2012. NCHS data brief, no 172. Hyattsville, MD: National Center for Health Statistics. Retrieved from https://www.cdc.gov/nchs/data/databriefs/db172.pdf.

Sadock, B. J., Sadock, B. J., Sadock, V. A., & Ruiz, P. (2015). Kaplan & Sadocks synopsis of psychiatry: Behavioral sciences/clinical psychiatry. Philadelphia: Lippincott Williams & Wilkins.

World Health Organization. (2016). *Mental health: Strengthening our response.* Fact sheet. Geneva: WHO. Retrieved from http://www.who.int/mediacentre/factsheets/fs220/en.

MIDDLE AGES, PUBLIC HEALTH IN THE (500–1500 CE)

The Middle Ages spanned the era between the Fall of the Roman Empire and the beginning of the Renaissance. Corruption, abuse, and civil insurrection gradually eroded the power of the Roman Empire. The Western Roman Empire entered the Dark Ages, a period marked by ignorance, chaos, conflicts over power, famine, and disease. The Eastern Roman or Byzantine Empire thrived under Emperor Constantine I. With Constantinople serving as the center, Spain, North Africa, Eastern Europe, and the Middle East enjoyed great economic and military power. The most common health problems during this era were cholera, typhoid, typhus, bubonic plagues, dysentery, malnutrition, and injuries. Many people never survived past childhood. The average life span was about 30 years old. Public health problems were caused by the large population movements of war and trade. Although the period was a terrible time for population health, the hardships ultimately created the foundations for early, organized systems of care.

During the early Middle Ages, health care was primarily administered by older women who learned the art of healing from earlier generations and by hands on experience. Members of the Crafte of the Wise also worshipped the gods, goddesses, and priestesses that predated Christianity. These peasant healers practiced midwifery and used herbs, spells, incantations, and charms to treat the ill or disabled. Their pagan rituals included dances, feasts, sexual intercourse, and animal sacrifices. The power and respect earned through healing combined with salacious pagan rituals were a threat to the emerging Christian church. In an effort to gain followers and to become the one, true religion, the church labeled the healers as deviants possessed by the devil. Anyone who healed and was pagan, peasant, or female was killed or driven into secrecy. A cottage industry grew around witch-hunting. The church and state persecuted and executed thousands of female healers. Christian priests and wealthy patrons who practiced a combination of Christianity and paganism were let off with a warning or a few Hail Marys (Campbell, 1978). The emerging medical profession was complicit in the mass executions. Witch hunts forced peasants to seek care from physicians while also diverting attention from the popular and ineffective medical practices of the day, bloodletting and leeches. The suppression of female healers helped to legitimize medicine as a patriarchal profession and institutions of higher learning as the main source of medical knowledge. Early on, these early medical doctors separated into two guilds, one for medicine and one for surgery. Physicians formed the Apothecary Guild and surgeons formed the Barber's Guild.

The church collected and secured Greek and Roman medicine albeit through a theological lens. Medicine was considered inferior to religion. Disease and healing were explained by theological rationalization. Sickness was deemed a punishment for sin or a test of faith. Human medicine, diet, herbs, surgery, or bleeding could be used, but heavenly medicine of prayers, exorcism, relics, and incantations was preferred. The church monopolized medicine, education, philosophy, and art. Greek temples were transformed into churches. Monasteries housed libraries and herbal gardens, eventually becoming centers of education and health care. Priests translated Greek medical texts into Latin, merging medicine and morality. Few medieval medical texts survive because parchment was valuable and reusable and medicine was perceived as less important in comparison to religion. Charity and mercy for the poor existed alongside the ascetic lives of monks and priests. Over time, medical institutions and hospitals emerged from the Christian monasteries. Consistent with church teachings, women were excluded from academic medical institutions.

Starting in 1275, pack ice shifted from the Arctic region into the North Atlantic, creating the Little Ice Age and the Great Famine of 1315–1322. Low temperatures shortened the growing seasons. Heavy rains flooded and damaged crops. Widespread famine caused malnutrition, disease, cannibalism, infanticide, and death. The story of Hansel and Gretel, two children abandoned by their parents and captured by a cannibalistic witch, originated from this time period. Millions of people died. Structural poverty became deeply ingrained in British society. Approximately 60 percent of families were exempt from paying taxes due to poverty (Dyer, 2012). The English government established several laws during the mid to late 14th century that formed the foundation of community care. The first law restricted begging to those who were unable to work. The able-bodied were required to work. With mandatory work requirements, local towns and villages implemented laws to prevent local residents from demanding higher wages. Townspeople could not work outside of the village during harvest season. Subsequent laws required that beggars return to the community where they were born or best known and that the community care for them. Hospitals and almshouses developed to care for the poor, elderly, disabled, orphans, widows, and ill. These institutions relied on charity and were often located on main roads where travelers might stop and donate resources. Although the wealthy were constantly reminded of their responsibility to the poor, there is little evidence that poor relief was sufficient to meet the needs of the large population of poor. Local governments tried to establish long-term support through taxes, parish collections, and estate planning. However, communities also trimmed their expenses by kicking out those whom they deemed not worthy of poor relief. These early systems of community relief were the foundation of government-organized health care.

One of the most devastating health events of human history occurred during the Middle Ages. The Black Death pandemic of 1346–1353 killed one-third to one-half of the world's population, an estimated 100 million people. The plague came in waves, starting in Asia and spreading along the Silk Road and into the Middle East and Europe. The causal pathogen, *Yersinia pestis*, was carried by fleas on rats living on merchant ships. As the ships sailed along trade routes, they carried the rats with plague-infested fleas. The disease was transmitted from harbors and ports inland. The thatched countryside roofs attracted rodents and insects. Few areas were left unscathed. The bubonic plague is a particularly horrific disease. Bacteria enter the skin through a flea bite. The body attempts to fight the infection with swollen lymph nodes, fever, and chills. Within a few days, the victim experiences headache, seizures, and muscle cramps. As the body succumbs to the infection, organs begin to fail. The victim vomits blood. Extremities and skin decay. Death occurs within 10 days. Priest-physicians using heavenly medicine hastened the spread by bringing people together in prayer and religious services. Physicians who practiced human medicine did better, advising the patients to rest and creating unintentional isolation. The plague permanently impacted social structures and economies in Western Europe. So many peasants died that there was a shortage of workers. The poor who survived could negotiate higher wages, thereby improving their quality of life and social status.

The Middle Ages were a challenging time for public health. The medical advances of the ancient Greeks and Romans were dismissed and disregarded due to politics and arrogance. The knowledge that had been transmitted between generations of female lay healers was vilified and extinguished. Mankind struggled with war, deadly epidemics and pandemics, poverty, and famine. The darkness of the Middle Ages stands in sharp contrast to the illuminating philosophies and discoveries of the Greco-Roman period and the Renaissance. Unfortunately, some of the misguided values continue today. Diseases, such as AIDS, are perceived by some as punishment for sin. Victims of violence, substance abusers, smokers, and people who are obese are too frequently blamed for their health problems. Victim blaming undermines public health efforts. People suffering from a stigmatized health problem are less likely to seek treatment. Service agencies have to work harder for funding. The second carryover from the Middle Ages is the representation of groups that support women's health as evil and harmful. Planned Parenthood provides numerous services to women and is the ongoing target of vilifying accusations. The Middle Ages left a lasting impression of ideas, values, and perceptions, some good, some harmful.

Sally Kuykendall

See also: Ancient World, Public Health in the; Epidemic; Greco-Roman Era, Public Health in the; Infectious Diseases; Quarantine; Smallpox

Further Reading

Brodsky, P. L. (2006). Childbirth: A journey through time. *International Journal of Childbirth Education*, *21*(3), 10–15.

Campbell. M.-A. (1978). Labeling and oppression: Witchcraft in medieval Europe. *Mid-American Review of Sociology*, *3*(2), 55–82.

Dyer, C. (2012). Poverty and its relief in Late Medieval England. *Past & Present*, *216*(1), 41–78.

Lippi, D. (2012). Witchcraft, medicine and society in Early Modern Europe. *Archives of the History & Philosophy of Medicine*, *75*(1), 68–73.

Magner, L. (1992). *A history of medicine.* New York: Marcel Dekker.

Minkowski, W. L. (1992). Women healers of the Middle Ages: Selected aspects of their history. *American Journal of Public Health*, *82*(2), 288–295.

Rosen, G. (1993). *A history of public health* (Expanded ed.). Baltimore: The Johns Hopkins University Press.

MODERN ERA, PUBLIC HEALTH IN THE

The modern practice of public health encourages and organizes states, communities, and individuals in order to promote human health by means of certain practices, such as education, sanitation, and improved medical infrastructure. The creation of a national, coordinated system of public health from the often haphazard arrangement of individual charity, religious devotion, or private business that were prevalent in the Early Modern Era was assisted by the birth of the modern nation state, where administrative powers broadened following the French Revolution (1789–1799), as well as advances in medical science such as bacteriology and epidemiology.

The proliferation of hospitals funded at public expense and often supporting a school of medical students was the setting for the transition to modern practices of public health. This process was aided by the political and social revolutions that rocked Europe at the end of the 18th century following the French Revolution. The older system of religious charity and aristocratic patronage that had been the primary means of supporting public health initiatives in previous centuries was swept aside by the egalitarian, secular leanings of revolutionary governments. In their place, at least in theory, a system of state funded and guided medical institutions would radiate from a central organization situated in the national capital, which was better equipped to efficiently administer medical aid and alleviate disease in the furthest corners of nation and empire in a timely manner. In practice, this lofty plan took a full century or more to be developed in some countries.

Epidemic diseases such as yellow fever or cholera were opposed with many of the same practices available to health professionals in previous centuries, such as quarantine or a "cordon sanitaire." However, as doctors determined that diseases were transmitted by germs and bacteria rather than *miasmas* ("bad air") as previously thought, the development of preventative medicine gained a greater appreciation among public health officials. The development of a vaccine for smallpox by Edward Jenner (1749–1823) in the last decade of the 18th century led to a newfound confidence in the power of preventative measures to eradicate various diseases. The new governments of Europe determined to apply their centralized apparatus to the dissemination of these new vaccines and medical techniques through education or legal compulsion.

The epidemic of cholera that struck Europe in the 1830s also shook the confidence of medical professionals in the ability of medicines alone to prevent disease. As displaced agrarian populations flooded European cities in search of work during the Industrial Revolution, poor living conditions among the urban poor underlined the importance of sanitation and public hygiene in public health. Sir Edwin Chadwick in Great Britain and François-Vincent Raspail in France determined that access to clean water, efficient waste disposal, and open-air spaces such as parks could improve the health of urban dwellers nearly as effectively as vaccines and medicines. In 1848, Great Britain passed the Public Health Act, which combined once separate administrative bodies in order to efficiently administer sanitation and clean water, and in 1851 vaccination for smallpox became compulsory. These developments resulted in the contemporary fields of urban planning and engineering as prominent contributions to public health initiatives. Notable examples are the fountains erected by Sir Richard Wallace throughout the city of Paris during the 1870s and later.

The cholera epidemics allowed European doctors firsthand experience observing the effects of environment on patients often squeezed into cramped, ad hoc hospitals. The rise of hospitals occurred alongside the birth of the medical laboratory, where researchers could observe, experiment, and develop new approaches to medicine outside of the clinical environment. These laboratories would grow throughout the late 19th and 20th centuries into the major university and pharmaceutical research laboratories of the Modern Era. Although the hospital and the laboratory had much to teach one another, at times they went their separate ways between the "practical" clinical doctor and the "impersonal, objective" researcher. In this way, the clinical applications of medicine lagged at times behind the discoveries of their more sensational research colleagues.

Public health was often allied to the European imperial system, and it reflected the prejudices prevalent in society. The encounter between the European powers and their colonies throughout the world, in particular Africa and Asia, included a dichotomy between the "civilizing mission" of Western medicine, with its desire to better humankind through the eradication of various diseases, and imperialist expansion and power. Developments in bacteriology allowed medical professionals to isolate causes of diseases to particular pathogens. At the turn of the 20th century, British physician Ronald Ross identified the mosquito as the carrier of malaria, while Walter Reed and James Carroll (both physicians in the U.S. Army) found likewise for yellow fever. Advances in sanitation and hygiene, combined with new vaccines and medicines, made a positive contribution to the standard of living in what was called "the third world." The building of the Panama Canal, among other colonial projects, would have been far more costly in manpower without these advances. However, extreme interpretations of eugenics divided populations into "white" hospitals and "native" ones, which caused a crisis of identity for the humanitarian philosophy of medicine as the benevolent healer of all humankind.

According to the theory of epidemiological transition proposed in 1971 by Abdel Omran, as medical advances ensure a higher rate of survival in a population through the control of epidemic disease, the prevalence of infectious diseases in a population is overcome by chronic diseases, such as cancer or heart disease. Throughout the 20th century, public health expanded from merely responding to health emergencies to inculcating preventative measures. These included the chlorination of drinking water in cities, dietary education programs, occupational safety procedures, family planning, and tobacco education. These developments in public health, while increasing the human life span, have led to concern in some quarters for the level of government control in decisions which, they propose, are best left to individual conscience. In part, the development of *Public Health 2.0* in the beginning of the 21st century sought to alleviate these concerns by involving public health professionals and interested individuals by direct communication, such as grassroots activity and social media.

Sean P. Phillips

See also: Ancient World, Public Health in the; Greco-Roman Era, Public Health in the; Middle Ages, Public Health in the; Renaissance, Public Health in the

Further Reading

Berridge, V. (2016). *Public health: A very short introduction*. Oxford, UK: Oxford University Press.

Porter. D. (1998). *Health, civilization, and the state: A history of public health from ancient to modern times*. London and New York: Routledge.

Rosen, G. (1993). *A history of public health* (Expanded ed.). Baltimore: The Johns Hopkins University Press.

MOTOR VEHICLE SAFETY

Motor vehicle crashes (MVCs) are one of the leading causes of death in the United States. Each year, over 30,000 people die and more than 2.5 million people are treated in emergency departments as a result of MVCs. The cost of medical care and lost productivity for MVCs exceed $80 billion per year. Motor vehicle safety is a specialty area within public health policy and practice. Engineers, policy makers, epidemiologists, motor vehicle manufacturers, health educators, pediatricians, hospitals, insurance companies, city planners, public safety, and even restaurant servers all work to enhance car, bicycle, motorcycle, pedestrian, and child passenger safety; promote safety of inexperienced or aging drivers; and prevent impaired or distracted driving. Collaborations in civil engineering, public planning, automobile design and manufacturing, driver education programs, and government regulations have significantly reduced motor vehicle fatalities. Between 1925 and 1997, deaths due to MVCs decreased from 18 per 100 million vehicle miles traveled (VMT) to 1.7 per 100 million VMT (Motor-Vehicle Safety: A 20th Century Public Health Achievement, 1999). Despite progress, MVC death rates in the United States are about two times higher than comparable countries (Centers for Disease Prevention and Control [CDC], 2016). Many more injuries and deaths could be prevented through compliance with seat belt laws, speed limits, proper use of child car or booster seats, strengthening the skills of young drivers, and reducing impaired or distracted driving.

The first recorded motor vehicle fatality occurred in London in 1896 when pedestrian Bridget Driscoll was struck and killed by a gasoline-powered motor vehicle during a demonstration at Crystal Palace. Driving under the influence was first reported in 1904. The *Quarterly Journal of Inebriety* issued the warning:

> We have received a communication containing the history of twenty-five fatal accidents occurring to automobile wagons. Fifteen persons occupying these wagons were killed outright, five more than two days later, and three persons died later. . . . A careful inquiry showed that in nineteen accidents the drivers had used spirits within an hour or more of the disaster. . . . [M]anagement of automobile wagons is far more dangerous for men who drink than for driving of locomotives on steel rails. . . . The precaution of railroad companies to have only total abstainers guide their engines will soon extend to owners and drivers of these new motor wagons. (Crothers, 1904, pp. 308–309)

From early on, car manufacturers worked to protect their customers. In 1901, Oldsmobile introduced the speedometer. General Motors added headlights in 1908. Further safety developments included shatterproof glass, tinted windshields, rear turn signals, seat belts, and air bags.

In 1966, Congress passed the National Traffic and Motor Vehicle Safety Act and the Highway Safety Act. The first National Highway Traffic Safety Administration (NHTSA) director, Dr. William Haddon Jr., was a public health physician. Haddon is credited with introducing driver licensing, regulations on driving under the influence, and motorcycle safety. Under his leadership, car manufacturers developed new features, and road engineers implemented improved lighting, safety barriers, guardrails, roadside signage, and better delineation of curves. Holden's success is attributed to using the agent-host-environment model to identify specific risk factors and to develop interventions for each factor. Under the agent-host-environment model, MVCs are not unavoidable "accidents." It is not an "accident" when someone drinks alcohol, gets behind the steering wheel, and crashes into a telegraph pole. Injury and death are caused by adverse interaction of three factors: the agent, the host, and the environment. The *agent* is the vector or factor that controls the energy. When energy of the force exceeds the body's ability to provide physical protection, injury occurs. In the case of MVCs, the moving motor vehicle is the agent. Potential and type of injury is influenced by the condition of the vehicle, tires, air bags, and speed. The *host* is the driver. Host factors for injury or safe driving are skill, experience, knowledge, and physical and mental condition. The *environment* is the physical and social environment. Physical environment is road and weather conditions, guardrails, and signs. Social environment is opportunities for driver training, traffic laws, and social attitudes toward driving. The advantage of using the agent-host-environment model is that it points to multiple areas for intervention. Using the model, windshields were modified so that they did not become jagged pieces of glass that could sever the carotid artery of the driver or passenger; steering wheels were engineered so that they collapsed on impact rather than causing chest injuries; vehicle doors were strengthened so that doors held passengers in; and safety belts became standard equipment. Holden also took the model one step further by considering precrash, crash, and postcrash factors. Postcrash factors included the integrity of the vehicle's fuel system to withstand impact, emergency medical services (EMS), and rehabilitation systems.

Different motor vehicles have different inherent risk factors. Mopeds and scooters move at slower speeds, which reduces risk of injury. However, drivers have very little skin protection. Even in minor crashes, the rider is likely to experience road burn with embedded gravel and high potential for infection. Trail bikes and motorcycles travel at faster speeds, increasing potential for leg and head injuries. All-terrain vehicles tip over easily, trapping the victim and causing crush injuries. Snowmobile drivers are at risk for neck, face, and head injuries due to low branches. Automobiles provide greater protection for the driver and passengers. However, cars travel at faster speeds, and SUVs have a higher center of gravity, increasing the likelihood of rollover. Motor vehicle manufacturers work to design safe vehicles that protect the occupant and passengers. Interventions include automatic seat belts, full face helmets for motorcyclists, leg protection, bumpers, air bags, and larger, more visible instrument panels. Regular vehicle inspections ensure that safety mechanisms are maintained after purchase and delivery.

Eighty-five percent of crashes are attributed to human error. At the host level, age, skill, physical development, knowledge, fatigue, and mental capacity play a

Collaborations in civil engineering, public planning, automobile design and manufacturing, driver education programs, and government regulations significantly reduced motor vehicle fatalities from 18 per 100 million vehicle miles traveled (VMT) in 1925 to 1.7 per 100 million VMT in 1997. (Anastasia Aleksandrenko/Dreamstime)

role in motor vehicle crashes. The requirement to pass a driving test before attaining a driver's license is an example of a host level intervention. In 1975, the NHTSA created the Fatal Accident Reporting System, now known as the Fatality Analysis Reporting System (FARS). FARS is a national database compiled from police reports, automobile registration files, driver license files, highway department data, hospital records, emergency medical services records, death certificates, and medical examiner and coroner reports. The database contains 127 data points describing the make and model of the vehicle, weather conditions, extent of damage, and driver and passenger characteristics, among other important features to consider. FARS is a valuable source of information helping to identify problems and solutions and evaluate interventions.

Motor vehicle safety is an excellent example of the depth and breadth of public health. As the number of vehicles on the road increased, MVCs have also increased. Car manufacturers, lawmakers, safety and road engineers, and public health educators have carefully and thoughtfully collaborated to improve the safety of drivers, passengers, and pedestrians. Future directions focus on high-risk groups of young drivers, elderly drivers, and reducing driving under the influence.

Alex Black and Sally Kuykendall

See also: Agricultural Safety; Alcohol; Biostatistics; Healthy Places; Injuries; Nader, Ralph; National Center for Injury Prevention and Control; Public Health Law; Risk-Benefit Analysis; Rural Health

Further Reading

Centers for Disease Prevention and Control. (2016). *Motor vehicle safety.* Retrieved from https://www.cdc.gov/motorvehiclesafety/index.html.

Crothers, T. D. (1904). Editorial: Announcement. *The Quarterly Journal of Inebriety, XXVI*(3), 308–309.

Motor-vehicle safety: A 20th century public health achievement. (1999). *Morbidity and Mortality Weekly Report*, *48*(18), 369.

National Highway Traffic Safety Administration. *Road safety.* Retrieved from https://www.nhtsa.gov/road-safety.

Pfizer, Inc. (2006). *Milestones in public health.* New York: Pfizer Global Pharmaceuticals.

Ten Great Public Health Achievements—United States, 1900–1999. (1999). *Journal of the American Medical Association*, *281*(16), 1481.

Waller, P. F. (2002). Challenges in motor vehicle safety. *Annual Review of Public Health*, *23*(1), 93.

N

NADER, RALPH (1934–)

Lawyer and activist Ralph Nader was one of the most influential figures of the twentieth century. He founded and led the consumer rights movement in the United States for nearly four decades and was instrumental in raising awareness and improving the safety of automobiles, workplaces, food, air, and water. Nader helped develop and pass tobacco regulations, the Wholesome Meat Act of 1974, the Occupational Safety and Health Act of 1970, and the Safe Drinking Water Act of 1974. "Naderism" has become synonymous with the use of citizen action to combat business and government practices deemed detrimental to public health and public interest. Many of the issues that Nader selected for improvement went unrecognized until he brought them to the forefront of public interest. Reviled by big business, Nader worked tirelessly to raise awareness of injustices, abuse of power, and corporate greed. In later years, Nader focused on reducing obesity and achieving living wages and universal health care.

Nader was born in Winsted, Connecticut, on February 27, 1934, the son of Lebanese immigrants who instilled in him strong moral and democratic values. After attending Winsted's Gilbert School, Nader enrolled at the Woodrow Wilson School of Public and International Affairs at Princeton University, graduating magna cum laude with a major in government and economics in 1955. He then entered Harvard Law School, where he was editor of the *Harvard Law Record*. Nader became aware of the problem of automobile safety through several experiences. Throughout high school and college he had several friends who were disabled or died by car crash, and he noticed that the driver was often blamed for the crash. During summers, he worked as a cook at Yosemite National Park. Hitchhiking across the country, he was often one of the first people on the scene of a car crash. While in law school, he published his first article on the subject, "American Cars: Designed for Death," in the *Harvard Law Record*. In 1958, Nader earned his law degree with distinction. He spent six months working as an army cook at Fort Dix, New Jersey. During the Korean War (1950–1953), more airmen died in car crashes in the states than through the war. The army investigated ways to prevent deaths due to car crashes. When Nader realized that car crashes were preventable, he was angry. In 1959, he started a small law practice in Hartford, Connecticut. Once again, he was confronted by cases of preventable motor vehicle crashes.

Becoming convinced that he could accomplish little on the local level, Nader moved to Washington, DC, in 1964. As a staff consultant on highway safety to Daniel Moynihan (then assistant secretary of labor for policy planning), Nader compiled a massive report on the subject, which became the best-selling muckraking book *Unsafe at Any Speed: The Designed-in Dangers of the American Automobile* (1965). In it, Nader charged that the automobile companies sacrificed safety for speed and appearance, citing the Chevrolet Corvair as especially unsafe. The book raised concerns regarding the use of reflective materials for dashboards, creating glare and temporarily blinding drivers and manufacturers' failure to provide seat belts and anti-roll bars. More importantly, Nader explains how experts within the industry failed to speak out against corporate greed and dangerous designs:

> There are men in the automobile industry who know both the technical capability and appreciate the moral imperatives. But their timidity and conformity to the rigidities of the corporate bureaucracies have prevailed. When and if the automobile is designed to free millions of human beings from unnecessary mutilation, these men, like their counterparts in universities and government who knew of the suppression of safer automobile development yet remained silent year after year, will look back with shame on the time when common candor was considered courage. (Nader, 2011, p. 256)

General Motors (GM) responded by hiring a detective to uncover damaging material on Nader's private life. The effort not only failed to compromise Nader, but also embarrassed GM president James M. Roche, who had to apologize before a Senate committee. Nader's book led Congress to pass the Traffic and Motor Vehicle Safety Act of 1966, which called on the federal government to set safety standards that must be met by all cars sold in the country.

Directing his attention to other areas involving health and safety, Nader became involved in efforts that helped to bring about the Wholesome Meat Act of 1967 and legislation providing for better safety standards in the construction of natural gas pipelines and underground mining. In 1969, Nader helped establish in Washington, DC, the Center for Study of Responsive Law, which conducted investigations of such federal commissions as the Federal Trade Commission, suspected of being unduly influenced by the very industries it were supposed to be regulating. In 1970, Nader started the Public Interest Research Group (PIRG) to work for consumer and political reform on the community and college campus level. In 1971, he launched Public Citizen, Inc., a consumer lobbying group to counteract the influence of powerful corporate lobbies.

Inspired by Nader's idealism, many young people, who became known as Nader's Raiders, joined his crusades through these and other organizations like the Center for Auto Safety, the National Insurance Consumer Organization, and the Health Research Group. Relying on individual contributions, on foundation grants, and on Nader's earnings as a writer and speaker for funds, these organizations conducted investigations of a wide range of consumer issues, including the environment, nuclear power, health care, freedom of information in government, and tax reform. They also pushed for legislative and judicial remedies for the abuses they uncovered, using class-action suits and other legal tools to achieve their goals.

Nader and his various groups influenced the creation of several new government "watchdog" agencies, including the Occupational Safety and Health Administration, the Environmental Protection Agency, and the Consumer Product Safety Commission. They were also largely responsible for at least eight federal consumer protection laws, among them laws regulating radiation dangers, the use of cyclamates in diet foods, and the use of DDT in the control of insect pests. On the local level, Nader and his associates sparked the establishment of consumer affairs commissions in most major cities and aroused public concern about product safety and value.

Despite their accomplishments, Nader and his associates drew fire for being fanatics and for conducting superficial and slanted research. Moreover, in the conservative climate of the 1980s, Nader's brand of activism seemed doomed to extinction. Nevertheless, he and his associates kept up their crusades on a variety of fronts.

In 1980, Nader resigned as president of Public Citizen, Inc., so that he could devote more time to organizing citizens on the community level. With Ronald Reagan's election to the presidency in 1980, Nader attacked the administration for offering a government that favored business and ignored consumer interests. The following year, a Nader group published a study of the Reagan administration entitled *Reagan's Ruling Class: Portraits of the President's Top One Hundred Officials*. Continuing his critique of corporate influence, Nader in 1986 coauthored *The Big Boys: Power and Position in American Business*, a study of nine powerful chief executive officers of corporations. Two years later, he helped bring about the passage of Proposition 103 in California, a law that lowered some auto insurance costs. The following year, GM announced that air bags would become standard equipment on many 1990 models, something that Nader had fought for during the past decade. Also around this time, Nader used national radio talk shows to forestall a congressional pay hike.

A firm believer in the power of the ordinary citizen to effect change, Nader in the early 1990s set out to make his Connecticut hometown a model democracy. In the presidential election of 1996, Nader, running as the candidate for Green Party USA, received some 580,000 votes, nearly 1 percent of the national total and about 3.5 percent of the total votes cast in California. He ran for president again in 2000, this time garnering 3 percent of the nationwide vote, as well as considerable controversy for siphoning Democratic votes from Vice President Al Gore.

One of the greatest achievements of public health during the 20th century was a 90 percent reduction in motor vehicle deaths (Motor-Vehicle Safety: A 20th Century Public Health Achievement, 1999). Safety belts, head rests, shatter-resistant windshields, and energy-absorbing steering wheels are just a few of the many advances that make vehicles safer for drivers and passengers. Yet, none of these would be possible without Nader's willingness to recognize a problem, reject the status quo, and stand in opposition to those with power and money. As the leader of the consumer movement for a quarter century, Nader remains a living symbol of the importance of individual commitment to social and public health reform.

James M. McPherson, Gary Gerstle, and Sally Kuykendall

See also: Air Pollution; Healthy Places; Injuries; Motor Vehicle Safety; National Center for Injury Prevention and Control; Public Health Law

Further Reading

Bollier, D. (1989). *Citizen action and other big ideas: A history of Ralph Nader and the modern consumer movement.* Washington, DC: Center for Study of Responsive Law.

Buckhorn, R. (1972). *Nader: The people's lawyer* [e-book]. Prentice Hall. Available from Book Review Digest Retrospective: 1903–1982 (H. W. Wilson), Ipswich, MA.

Burt, D. M. (1982). *Abuse of trust: A report on Ralph Nader's network: Capital Legal Foundation.* Washington, DC: Regnery Gateway.

Kaplan, D. A. (2014). Ralph Nader: The *Fortune* interview. *Fortune, 169*(3), 94.

Motor-Vehicle Safety: A 20th Century Public Health Achievement. (1999). *Morbidity and Mortality Weekly Report, 48*(18), 369–374. Retrieved from https://www.cdc.gov/mmwr/preview/mmwrhtml/mm4818a1.htm.

Nader, R. (1965). *Unsafe at any speed: The designed-in dangers of the American automobile.* New York: Grossman.

Nader, R. (2011). Unsafe at any speed: The designed-in dangers of the American automobile. *American Journal of Public Health, 101*(2), 254–256.

Nader, R. (2016). *Breaking through power: It's easier than we think.* San Francisco: City Lights.

Nader, R., & Gordan, J. (1968). Safety on the job. *New Republic, 158*(24), 23–25.

Parry, M. (2011). Ralph Nader: Public health advocate and political agitator. *American Journal of Public Health, 101*(2), 257. doi:10.2105/AJPH.2009.191163

Whiteside, T. (1972). *The investigation of Ralph Nader: General Motors vs. one determined man.* Gettysburg, PA: Arbor House.

NATIONAL ASSOCIATION OF COUNTY AND CITY HEALTH OFFICIALS (NACCHO)

In addition to the day-to-day tasks of immunizations, prenatal care, nutrition education, sexually transmitted disease treatment and prevention, and policies to control urban sprawl, local public health departments and their staff are prepared to deal with a myriad of life-threatening emerging and reemerging health issues. The National Association of County and City Health Officials (NACCHO) is a nonprofit organization serving approximately 1,500 local health departments and 13,000 individual members. Founded in the 1960s, the mission of NACCHO is "to be a leader, partner, catalyst, and voice for local health departments" (NACCHO, 2016). NACCHO supports local health department administrators and practitioners by providing skill-building resources and networking opportunities. Programs include the philanthropic effort, Foundation for the Public's Health, the NACCHO career network, internships, and consulting in performance improvement, process design, workforce development, or technical assistance. The organization adheres to the core values of health equity, excellence in practice, collaboration, respect, integrity, leadership, evidence-based practice, and innovation. NACCHO notes that many health determinants exist within the community, and public health departments are in the ideal position to alleviate community health hazards. By training local public health officials to function as strategists, coalition builders, policy makers, and researchers, NACCHO advances community health. The organization also works to reduce obstacles related to insufficient funding, politics, and the quiet, unassuming, confidential nature of public health practices. To overcome obstacles, NACCHO works to raise public awareness of critical issues in public health and advocate for public health funding and support. The organization is also open to individuals with professional interest in public health.

Sally Kuykendall

See also: Administration, Health; Association of State and Territorial Health Officials; Centers for Disease Control and Prevention; Collaborations; Community Health Centers; State, Local, and Territorial Health Departments

Further Reading

National Association of County and City Health Officials. (2016). Retrieved from http://www.naccho.org/.

NATIONAL CANCER INSTITUTE (NCI)

The National Cancer Institute (NCI) is one of the major institutes within the National Institutes of Health (NIH), which itself is within the U.S. Department of Health and Human Services. The primary purpose of the NCI is to coordinate the federal government's National Cancer Program and to support cancer research and treatment. The NCI uses a variety of approaches to accomplish these goals, including conducting and disseminating research and providing grant funding to basic and clinical cancer research labs at a variety of research institutions.

The funding of the NCI is appropriated by Congress through the traditional federal budget process, which involves the participation of the legislative and executive branches of the federal government. In the 2016 to 2017 year, the budget allocated to the NCI was nearly $5.4 billion; this budget covers many diverse objectives including basic science research, cancer prevention, cancer diagnosis, survivorship support, cancer risk factor research, and more (NCI, 2016). Additionally, the NCI provides financial support for workforce training of students and professionals in order to foster development of the future cancer scientist workforce. The beneficiaries of the workforce support programs that include high school and college students, graduate and doctoral students, and early career scientists. In the 2016 to 2017 year, over 3,600 individuals were supported by this program.

The NCI is also responsible for coordinating the cancer research work of a network of nearly 70 NCI-designated Cancer Centers, which are the universities and research centers at the forefront of NCI-funded cancer research. These 69 NCI-designated Cancer Centers include a spectrum of sites, from basic science laboratories to comprehensive cancer centers. In order to qualify to become an NCI-designated

Cancer Center, institutions must participate in combining laboratory science, population science, and clinical studies in a coordinated and high-quality way (American Cancer Society, 2014). NCI-designated Cancer Centers perform the bulk of the cancer research work that NCI grants are meant to fund. Examples of some of the ongoing research projects carried out by NCI-designated Cancer Centers include research into the biological mechanisms that protect cells against cancer, clinical trials of new or modified cancer medications, and sociological and public health–oriented cancer research.

The history of the NCI, as well as its NCI-designated Cancer Centers, can be traced back nearly three quarters of a century to 1937, when President Franklin D. Roosevelt signed legislation establishing the NCI. It was only about two decades later, in 1955 and 1960, that anticancer drugs began to be tested with NCI funding and that the NCI-designated Cancer Center status was formally established and given to research institutions, respectively.

Another tremendous step in the growth of the scope and work of the NCI came in 1973 when the institute established the Surveillance, Epidemiology, and End Results (SEER) program, which is responsible for collecting population-level data regarding cancer incidence, survivorship, and mortality. SEER collects statistics from a massive cancer registry that covers approximately a quarter of the entire U.S. population. With this information, the SEER database serves to inform public health professionals and researchers about trends in cancer rates. It is in this way that the SEER program has been responsible for some of the most significant epidemiological and sociological cancer research findings in the United States. Some of these research findings include showing the correlation between race and higher mortality in some cancers, such as prostate cancer. Additionally, the SEER program can be used by public health professionals in order to inform initiatives that target particularly cancer-vulnerable populations such as African Americans and Hispanics in order to promote health equity.

Over the decades following the establishment of the SEER program, the NCI has established and participated in a variety of other important programs that serve the cancer-oriented mission. In 1983, the NCI launched the Community Clinical Oncology Program, also known as CCOP, which connects patients of cancer doctors with ongoing clinical trials. In the year 2000, the NCI established the Center to Reduce Cancer Health Disparities (CRCHD), which works to alleviate racial and ethnic disparities in cancer outcomes and health of patients undergoing cancer treatment. In 2005, the NCI worked in conjunction with the National Human Genome Research Institute to establish the widely used Cancer Genome Atlas. The Cancer Genome Atlas allows researchers to access a deep body of knowledge regarding the genomic changes behind cancer etiology. The NCI has evolved approaches and programs to adapt to contemporary challenges in cancer treatment and resource allocations. The institute creates and supports initiatives that range from precision medicine to global cancer medicine, as well as genome-based clinical drug research.

The NCI was created in response to the immense public health challenge of alleviating cancer in the American and world population. Cancer, as the second leading cause of death in the United States, represents a complex disease with many causes, mechanisms of pathology, and harmful effects. Therefore, the coordinated research efforts carried out by and supported through the NCI are essential to better understanding how cancer operates and how to best approach managing and curing cancer. The NCI is at the forefront of cancer research in the United States as well as the entire world, and serves to enable advancements in cancer research in a rich diversity of ways.

Shayan Waseh

See also: Cancer; Environmental Protection Agency; Genetics; Health Communication; Healthy Places; Leading Health Indicators; Men's Health; National Institutes of Health; Nutrition; Prevention; Research; Skin Cancer

Further Reading

American Cancer Society. (2014). *National Cancer Institute Cancer Center program information.* Retrieved from https://www.cancer.org/treatment/finding-and-paying-for-treatment/choosing-your-treatment-team/nci-cancer-center-programs.html.

Mohanty, S., & Bilimoria, K. Y. (2014). Comparing national cancer registries: The national cancer data base (NCDB) and the surveillance, epidemiology, and end results (SEER) program. *Journal of Surgical Oncology*, *109*(7), 629–630.

National Cancer Institute. (2016). *NCI overview.* Retrieved from https://www.cancer.gov/about-nci/overview.

NATIONAL CENTER FOR INJURY PREVENTION AND CONTROL (NCIPC)

In the United States, intentional and unintentional injuries are the leading cause of death for people aged 1 to 44. Beyond the number of people who die each year, many, many more seek treatment in emergency departments, clinics, and doctor offices. Motor vehicle crashes, falls, prescription drug overdoses, gunshot wounds, suicides, and other incidents affect young, working populations, those with the greatest potential to contribute to society. The National Center for Injury Prevention and Control (NCIPC) strives to reduce injuries by identifying, monitoring, and studying injuries, supporting prevention research, and creating and offering evidence-based programs. The NCIPC is a valuable resource for accurate data, quality resources, and evidence-based programs in injury prevention.

WISQARS (Web-based Injury Statistics Query and Reporting System) is the injury center's online database. WISQARS collects injury data from hospitals, national surveys, death certificates, and Census Bureau to provide accurate data on fatal and nonfatal injuries. A chief advantage of WISQARS is that the data are easy to retrieve and many times have already been analyzed and charted for easy visualization in reports or presentations. For example, the NCIPC's *Ten Leading Causes of Death and Injury* charts are helpful in providing background information to audiences. The charts present the most recent national mortality or nonfatal injury data highlighting why injuries are a leading health problem. Alternatively, students, public health practitioners, researchers, and others can use the WISQARS database to search injury-related data. For example, if a student is writing a paper on traumatic brain injuries (TBIs) and wants to know the annual cost of emergency department (ED) visits for TBIs among young people (aged 5–21), the student would enter the search criteria into the database and WISQARS would provide results. In 2010, there were 657,864 emergency department visits for TBIs. Total medical costs were $2,726,495,000 (average = $4,144/ED visit). Loss of work costs totaled $3,276,481,000. Thus, total combined costs for ED visits for TBIs for people aged 5 to 21 years were more than $6 billion. The data may be used to inform audiences, compare age groups, examine trends, or map rates. Providing accurate data allows communities and policy makers to make smart decisions regarding health care needs, policies, and resources.

The NCIPC also acts as a resource, providing information on programs and best practices in injury treatment and prevention. HEADS UP is a series of NCIPC resources designed to educate parents, youth, school personnel, and health care providers on prevention, early detection, and response to brain injuries. The materials provide information on the basics of brain injury, symptoms, recovery, recommendations for safe return to activities, policies, and prevention. STEADI (Stopping Elderly Accidents, Deaths & Injuries) is a training course for health care providers to help identify falls risk among elderly patients, modifiable risk factors, and effective interventions. The PROTECT Initiative is a collaboration of public health organizations, private companies, consumer advocates, and scholars developing ways to keep children safe from unintentional drug overdose. The group investigates and recommends ways to improve medication packaging to prevent unsupervised ingestion by children, create dosing methods, which reduce the potential for parent/caregiver dosing error, and create effective educational campaigns. The NCIPC continues to develop programs and campaigns to reduce specific intentional and unintentional injuries.

The National Center for Injury Prevention and Control is a clearinghouse of information on some of the leading causes of death and disability in the United States. The center provides accurate, unbiased information on issues such as prescription drug overdoses, gun violence, sports-related concussions, falls, motor vehicle safety, and suicide prevention.

Sally Kuykendall

See also: Aging; Agricultural Safety; Centers for Disease Control and Prevention; Child Maltreatment; Elder Maltreatment; Epidemiology; Healthy Places; Home Safety; Infant Mortality; Injuries; Intimate Partner Violence; Motor Vehicle Safety; Prevention; Sports-Related Concussions; Violence

Further Reading

National Center for Injury Prevention and Control. (2017). Retrieved from https://www.cdc.gov/injury/index.html.

NATIONAL HEALTH AND NUTRITION EXAMINATION SURVEY (NHANES)

The National Health and Nutrition Examination Survey (NHANES) investigates the nutrition, health, and physical activity of children and adults in the United States. It is an ongoing program of the National Center for Health Statistics. The NHANES project started in the 1960s, following the National Health Survey Act of 1956—a bill authorizing federal research to study disease, injury, and disability across the nation. Previous methods had become outdated, and the federal government needed better data to identify and quantify health problems in order to plan health programs, promote the health of the nation's workforce, estimate future needs for medical devices and medical care, and suggest what issues need further investigation.

The NHANES project is unique because study teams travel to the area of interest that currently includes up to 15 communities across the United States. The study personnel interview and examine people to learn more about the inhabitants, health behaviors, and health concerns. Each member of the team contributes unique skills. The team consists of bilingual interviewers, a physician, a dentist, medical technicians, nurses, health educators, and phlebotomists. Five thousand people are selected to participate each year, and they are identified based on their ability to represent other people of their age, gender, and racial or ethnic group. Each participant represents approximately 50,000 other people. Study participants are initially interviewed in their home and then undergo a detailed physical examination in a specially designed mobile laboratory. The interviewers ask questions about diet, physical activity, sexual experiences, drug, alcohol, and tobacco use. The clinical examinations gather information on height, weight, blood pressure, bone density, eyesight, kidney function, sexually transmitted diseases, blood tests, and other physiological functions. The NHANES primarily focuses on common health-related behaviors such as substance abuse, physical fitness, and sexual practices, and diseases such as diabetes, anemia, cardiovascular disease, obesity, kidney disease, osteoporosis, respiratory diseases, and sexually transmitted diseases. All information gathered by the interviews and medical staff is confidential. Data are entered into a database with any personal identifiers removed. Researchers who are interested in tracking a specific disease can download and analyze the de-identified data. The NHANES provides valuable information to both the individual participants and public health professionals who work for government, nonprofit, and for-profit organizations. Participants receive the results of their physical exam, dental exam, eye exam, and hearing exam, blood tests, body scan, and lung function tests. The Department of Health and Human Services, among other interested organizations, receives information on emerging health issues and the need for public health policies and programs, and add to our knowledge about the connections between health behaviors and disease.

Many important health milestones developed from NHANES data, such as the growth charts that pediatricians use to compare a child's weight and height to other children of the same age and gender in order to screen for delayed growth or development; policies to remove lead from gasoline, food, and soft drinks; tracking the increase in obesity throughout specific areas of the country; identifying the need for diabetes prevention programs among ethnic minorities; targeting heart disease prevention programs among at-risk groups of people; and developing new ways to measure lung function in order to study asthma. As health concerns evolve, scientists continue to refine the NHANES instrument and procedures. The NHANES program provides valuable insights and opportunities to advance our knowledge of diseases and ways to prevent and treat health issues.

Sally Kuykendall

See also: Children's Health; Community Health; Environmental Health; *Healthy People 2020*; Nutrition; Obesity; Prevention; Research

Further Reading

Centers for Disease Control and Prevention. (2015, August 17). *National health and nutrition examination survey homepage.* Retrieved from http://www.cdc.gov/nchs/nhanes.htm.

Division of Public Health Methods, Office of the Surgeon General, Public Health Service. (1957). The National Health Survey Act. *Public Health Reports, 72*(1), 1–4.

U.S. Department of Health and Human Services. (2014). *National health and nutrition examination survey, 2013–2014.*

NATIONAL HEART, LUNG, AND BLOOD INSTITUTE (NHLBI)

The National Heart, Lung, and Blood Institute (NHLBI) is a federal agency responsible for advancing knowledge of the causes, treatment, and prevention of heart, lung, and blood disorders. The mission of the NHLBI is to provide "global leadership for a research, training, and education program to promote the prevention and treatment of heart, lung, and blood diseases and enhance the health of all individuals so that they can live longer and more fulfilling lives" (NHLBI, 2017). In the United States, cardiovascular disease claims more lives than any other health problem. One in four deaths is due to heart disease (CDC, 2015). In addition to the leading killer, the NHLBI addresses anemia, asbestos-related lung diseases, bone marrow transplants, congenital heart defects, cystic fibrosis, insomnia, Marfan syndrome, pneumonia, sarcoidosis, Von Willebrand disease, and many other medical problems. The NHLBI supports and encourages research into the causes of heart, lung, and blood disorders, translation of research findings into clinical practice, training of specialists in heart, lung, and blood disorders, and education of the general public on recent scientific advancements. Working under the auspices of the National Institutes of Health, the NHLBI collaborates with scientists, physicians, patients, families, and communities to reduce risk of disease and improve quality of life for those living with these diseases. Among the many notable prevention campaigns sponsored by the NHLBI are the *National Wear Red Day* and the *Heart Truth® Campaign*. Recognizing that women will often care for their children, spouses, parents, and friends before taking care of themselves, these campaigns remind women that heart disease is a leading cause of death and women need to take care of themselves. The programs encourage people to wear red on the first Friday in February as a way to raise awareness of heart disease among women. The campaigns have been very successful in reaching busy women.

Insomnia is one example of the many, many health issues that the NHLBI addresses and offers a good example of the NHLBI in action. Sleep deprivation is a public health problem. Chronic sleep insufficiency increases risk of motor vehicle crashes, home and workplace injuries, obesity, heart disease, hypertension, stroke, diabetes, depression, and infections. Socially, people who do not get enough sleep are moody, irritable, forgetful, and make poor decisions. Sleep deprivation impairs academic and job performance and interferes with interpersonal relationships. The American Academy of Sleep Medicine recommends 8 to 10 hours of sleep per 24 hours for adolescents (aged 13–18 years) and 7 or more hours per 24 hours for adults (over 18 years) (Paruthi et al., 2016). When adults are able to sleep without limitation, the average sleep time is 8 to 8.5 hours (Roehrs, Timms, Zwyghuizen-Doorenbos, & Roth, 1989). A nationwide survey shows that one out of three adults reports insufficient sleep on 14 or more of the last 30 days (CDC, 2009). The most common causes of sleep disorders are obstructive sleep apnea, insomnia, restless legs syndrome and periodic limb movements in sleep, narcolepsy, and prescription or over-the-counter drugs, such as caffeine, alcohol, and nicotine. Shift workers and adolescents are at risk due to lifestyle factors that alter the circadian rhythm. Chronic sleep deprivation creates a cumulative sleep debt that increases risk of harmful consequences. *Healthy People 2020* Objective SH-4 aims to "increase the proportion of adults who get sufficient sleep." To improve sleep health, the NHLBI convenes working groups to review and summarize sleep disorder research, identify genetic, pathological, environmental, and cultural and lifestyle factors that disrupt healthy sleep, suggest ways to improve prevention efforts, and translate the science of sleep from research to bedside and community practice. The NHLBI provides materials to health care practitioners on screening and diagnosis of sleep disorders and ways to manage disorders. Treatment addresses the underlying medical or psychological condition and in cases where the underlying condition is unknown or resistant to treatment, behavioral or pharmacological therapy may be used. Behavioral treatment replaces maladaptive behaviors with therapeutic interventions such as relaxation therapy, sleep restriction therapy, stimulus control therapy, or cognitive therapy. Pharmacological treatment consists of hypnotic medications, antidepressants, antihistamines, or melatonin. To prevent sleep disorders and the consequences of sleepiness, the NHLBI recommends educating at-risk populations (young people, shift workers, and people with sleep disorders) on the hazards of sleep deprivation, promoting rumble strips to alert drowsy drivers, delaying high school start times, driver education, safe rest areas for drivers, and interactive curricular materials for teachers and students. The NHLBI maintains a database of sleep education materials with information tailored to selected audiences. The work supported by the NHLBI brings attention to this often unrecognized health issue and prevents numerous motor vehicle crashes.

The NHLBI supports rigorous investigations into the causes, treatment, and prevention of heart, lung, and blood disorders. Through intramural and extramural research, training, and education, the NHLBI works with other agencies, scientists, health care professionals, and community members to determine effective methods for prevention and treatment. As a result, the NHLBI has designed some unusually creative and highly effective prevention campaigns that can influence hard-to-reach audiences.

Sally Kuykendall

See also: Centers for Disease Control and Prevention; Heart Disease; Heart Truth® (Red Dress) Campaign, The; *Healthy People 2020*; Hypertension; National Institutes of Health; Physical Activity; U.S. Department of Health and Human Services

Further Reading

Centers for Disease Control and Prevention (CDC). (2009). Perceived insufficient rest or sleep among adults—United States, 2008. *Morbidity and Mortality Weekly Report, 58*(42), 1175–1179.

Centers for Disease Control and Prevention (CDC). (2015). *Heart disease facts.* Retrieved from https://www.cdc.gov/heartdisease/facts.htm.

National Heart, Lung, and Blood Institute. (2017). Retrieved from https://www.nhlbi.nih.gov/.

Paruthi, S., Brooks, L. J., D'Ambrosio, C., Hall, W. A., Kotagal, S., Lloyd, R. M., & . . . Wise, M. S. (2016). Recommended amount of sleep for pediatric populations: A consensus statement of the American Academy of Sleep Medicine. *Journal of Clinical Sleep Medicine, 12*(6), 785–786. doi:10.5664/jcsm.5866

Roehrs, T., Timms, V., Zwyghuizen-Doorenbos, A., & Roth, T. (1989). Sleep extension in sleepy and alert normals. *Sleep: Journal of Sleep Research & Sleep Medicine, 12*(5), 449–457.

NATIONAL INSTITUTE ON DRUG ABUSE (NIDA)

The National Institute on Drug Abuse (NIDA) conducts and supports research on the causes and consequences of addictive substance use and translates this science into practical advice for policies, programs, and practices in public health. NIDA is 1 of the 27 institutes within the National Institutes of Health (NIH). The NIH is the largest biomedical research agency in the world. The NIH mission is to enhance quality and length of life by improving health and reducing illness and disability. NIDA focuses exclusively on studying the biological, neurological, social, and behavioral mechanisms that promote or inhibit substance use and abuse. NIDA researchers study the brain to determine the effects of illicit drug use. Research findings are translated into evidence-based programs and practices for use in schools, hospitals, outpatient clinics, community, and public health. NIDA provides a wealth of information for students, patients and family members, other researchers, health professionals, and policy makers. Information ranges from safe disposal of unused medicines to opioid abuse to adolescent brain cognitive development.

Following the Protestant values of early colonial America, addictions were originally believed to be a moral flaw. In *An Inquiry into the Effects of Ardent Spirits upon the Human Body and Mind,* professor of medicine of the University of Pennsylvania Dr. Benjamin Rush (1812) presented a continuum of beverages with their associated personality traits, diseases, vices, and consequences. Rush associated water, milk, and "small beer" with health, happiness, and "serenity of mind." Cider, wine, porter, and strong beer in moderation were associated with cheerfulness and nourishment. Grog, bitters, cordials, and gin, brandy, or rum in the morning were associated with idleness, fighting, lying, stealing, burglary, and murder in addition to tremors, vomiting, jaundice, dropsy, epilepsy, depression, palsy, and insanity. Recommended treatments were whipping, immersing the body in cold water, or inducing vomiting, terror, anger, or sweating. Rush reported, "Many hundred drunkards have been cured of their desire for ardent spirits by a practical belief in the doctrines of Christian religion" (Rush, 1812, p. 32). This medical classic shows how the leading doctors promulgated misconceptions about addictions as a moral failing. The fallacies continued throughout the 20th century with America's *War on Drugs* and the *Just Say No* campaign. Misconceptions regarding substance abuse are dangerous because they lead to harmful stereotypes that blame the victim and encourage communities to use treatments that do not actually work. With limited resources in health, it is imperative that addictions are accurately understood and that treatments are based on the science of addiction rather than personal or religious beliefs.

NIDA started in 1935 as a research facility connected to a Public Health Service hospital in Lexington, Kentucky. In 1948, the center became the Addiction Research Center (ARC). ARC researchers achieved several ground-breaking discoveries, such as the use of methadone to treat heroin addiction, mechanisms of drug relapse, the role and function of opioid receptors, use of opioid antagonists to treat heroin overdose, and creating drug profiles to evaluate the potential for addiction of new drugs on the market. Starting in the 1970s, NIDA commenced a regular, large-scale survey of America's high school and middle school students to identify the incidence and prevalence of substance use and abuse. The *Monitoring the Future Survey* allows public health professionals to monitor trends in drug abuse and to identify populations at risk. In addition to understanding what drugs are increasing in popularity, the researchers have noted some unique problems, namely the *honeymoon period* and *generational forgetting* (Johnston et al., 2017). The honeymoon period is the time between when a drug first becomes accessible and information on adverse consequences is widely recognized. For example, methylenedioxypyrovalerone ("bath salts") is a synthetic cathinone offered as a cheap substitute for methamphetamine or cocaine. Promotional advertising spreads quickly through word of mouth before researchers have the opportunity to study short- and long-term effects. With more people trying or using the drug, adverse effects start to become apparent. People using bath salts have committed some very gruesome murders. Synthetic cathinones are addictive and cause anxiety, paranoia, hallucinations, extreme agitation, and violence (NIDA, 2016). Generational forgetting is when younger generations rediscover drugs that were used by older generations and fell out of popularity. Comeback drugs include heroin, LSD, ecstasy, and methamphetamine. NIDA works with numerous audiences to reduce the exploitation of the honeymoon period or generational forgetting. NIDA develops fact sheets on specific drugs, creates curricula for use in schools, offers research-based guides in drug treatment and prevention, and partners with other agencies to promote evidence-based programs and practices in substance abuse prevention.

NIDA is a great resource for people seeking detailed, accurate, and up-to-date information on addictions in general or on a specific drug or type of addiction. *NIDA for Teens* (https://teens.drugabuse.gov/drug-facts) is a library of information featuring the definition, street names, physical and emotional effects, side effects, adverse effects, and risks for particular drugs. The website also features where to turn if you or a friend is in crisis. The National Suicide Prevention Lifeline (1-800-273-TALK) assists those who are struggling with addictions firsthand or with someone they love. The Substance Abuse Treatment Facility Locator (1-800-662-HELP) is a searchable database of substance abuse treatment facilities, mental health centers, health care centers, and physicians. Accurate information is one of the most powerful tools in addressing addictions. NIDA is the best source for accurate information on drug facts.

Sally Kuykendall

See also: Addictions; Alcohol; National Institutes of Health; Prescription Drugs; Substance Abuse and Mental Health Services Administration; Syringe Service Programs; *Controversies in Public Health:* Controversy 2

Further Reading

Johnston, L. D., O'Malley, P. M., Meich, R. A., Bachman, J. G., & Schulenberg, J. E. (2017). *Monitoring the future national survey results on drug use, 1975–2016: Overview, key findings on adolescent drug use.* Ann Arbor: Institute for Social Research, University of Michigan.

NIDA. (2016). *Synthetic cathinones ("bath salts").* Retrieved from https://www.drugabuse.gov/publications/drugfacts/synthetic-cathinones-bath-salts.

NIDA. (2017). Retrieved from https://www.drugabuse.gov/.

Rush, B. (1812). *An inquiry into the effects of ardent spirits upon the human body and mind.* Boston: Manning & Loring. Retrieved from https://archive.org/details/2569027R.nlm.nih.gov.

University of Michigan. (2017). *Monitoring the future.* Retrieved from http://monitoringthefuture.org/.

NATIONAL INSTITUTES OF HEALTH (NIH)

The National Institutes of Health (NIH) is the federal agency responsible for advancing scientific knowledge on the causes, treatment, and prevention of human diseases in order to promote the well-being of the nation. The agency's mission is to "seek fundamental knowledge about the nature and behavior of living systems and the application of that knowledge to enhance health, lengthen life, and reduce illness and disability" (NIH, 2017). Founded in 1887 as part of the Marine Hospital Service, the organization's original purpose was to study pathogenic organisms in order to prevent epidemics. NIH research gradually moved from studying cholera and yellow fever to fungal infections, fluoridation, treatment of bipolar disorder, human retroviruses, Lyme disease, HIV, enzyme deficiencies, HPV vaccine, congenital heart diseases, addictions, Alzheimer's disease, chronic fatigue, and many other behavioral health, mental health, and medical problems. NIH researchers have

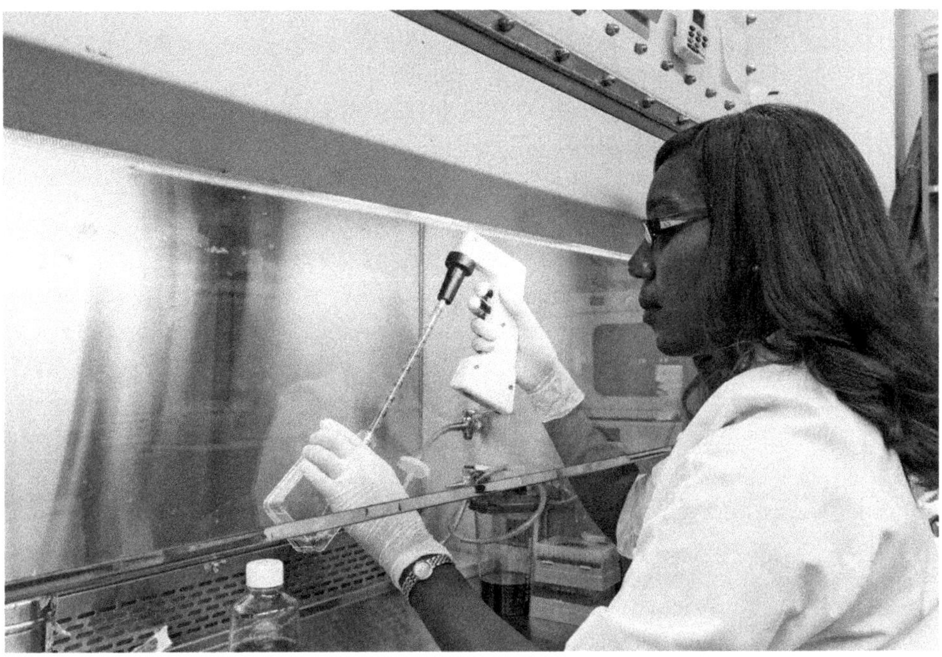

A researcher at the National Institutes of Health (NIH) studying cancer therapy. The NIH is the largest biomedical research agency in the world. NIH researchers hold 88 Nobel Prizes and 195 Lasker Awards for groundbreaking achievements in medicine and human physiology. (David Sone/National Institutes of Health)

earned 88 Nobel Prizes and 195 Lasker Awards. Today, the NIH is the largest biomedical research agency in the world, operating under the U.S. Department of Health and Human Services (DHHS) and managing over $32 billion in research grants each year.

The responsibility to ensure judicious use of taxpayer funds creates challenges. One review of NIH-funded research claimed that NIH grant reviewers preferred cautious, conservative projects that were within the scope of the reviewer's own research interests rather than ground-breaking research (Nicholson & Ioannidis, 2012). The reviewers shied away from studies that could be a financial risk. Other reports suggest that researchers who are good at networking and self-promotion are more likely to attain NIH grant support than other competent scientists. In response to these criticisms, the NIH established a new line of grants for novel, pioneering research. The current goals of the NIH are to foster and support:

1. Scientific collaborations that protect and improve individual and public health.
2. Development of health researchers and biomedical research facilities.
3. Discovery of biomedical knowledge and technology.
4. Scientific integrity, professionalism, accountability, and social responsibility within biomedical research.

Federal support of biomedical research ensures that researchers are free to study challenging diseases and health problems without financial or administrative pressures.

The NIH supports multiple types of health-enhancing research and is especially valuable to scientists studying unusual topics. Pharmaceutical or biomedical agencies will not invest in studying problems that are expected to yield little return on investment. Therefore, researchers studying rare or unusual diseases face obstacles in funding and other stages of the research process. Typically, there is limited information on the disease. Finding other scientists interested in studying the disease may be difficult because journals are hesitant to publish articles with limited reader interest. Locating and enrolling research participants can be challenging. The NIH's Office of Rare Diseases Research (ORDR) supports researchers interested in rare diseases by providing access to resources, dissemination of research, customized literature reviews, lists of advocacy organizations, access to study participants, and funding opportunities. The benefit to studying rare diseases is that study findings can provide common insights that apply to other health issues.

Public health researchers need a source of support that follows ethical guidelines of practice. Researchers and the public cannot and should not depend on businesses to determine what diseases or health issues warrant investigation. The NIH supports a healthy nation by prioritizing research studies and allocating support to promising studies, thus enhancing health promotion in areas of critical need.

Sally Kuykendall

See also: Centers for Disease Control and Prevention; *Healthy People 2020*; National Cancer Institute; National Heart, Lung, and Blood Institute; Public Health in the United States, History of; Research; U.S. Department of Health and Human Services; U.S. Public Health Service; *Controversies in Public Health*: Controversy 1

Further Reading

National Institutes of Health. (2017). Retrieved from https://www.nih.gov.

Nicholson, J. M., & Ioannidis, J. A. (2012). Research grants: Conform and be funded. *Nature*, 492(7427), 34–36. doi:10.1038/492034a

NATION'S HEALTH, THE

The Nation's Health is a newspaper reporting local, state, national, and global news of interest to public health students, professionals, and policy makers. The newspaper is published 10 times per year by the American Public Health Association (APHA). The publication originally developed from a Chicago monthly medical magazine, *Modern Medicine.* Started in 1919, *Modern Medicine* published articles on medical advances, industrial and social health, and health administration. One section, entitled "The Nation's Health," was edited by C. E. A. Winslow and featured information on public health administration and public welfare. In May 1921, *Modern Medicine* changed into *The Nation's Health.* Unlike other professional publications *The Nation's Health* did not publish original research articles and instead focused on explaining how new ideas, science, and laws impact public health and public health practice. In 1927, *The Nation's Health* was once again delegated to status as a section, this time within the *American Journal of Public Health.* In January 1971, *The Nation's Health* became a separate publication following the original intention of providing current news on developments in public health. The first issue contained letters to the editor and articles on Medicaid, cardiovascular diseases, mental illness, nurse-midwifery, a recent epidemic of falls from high places among children, and health of Mexican Americans. Dr. Paul B. Cornely offered his insights into public health with an article entitled "The Hidden Enemies of Health and the American Public Health Association." Cornely reported 1970s concerns as a national addiction to the abundant life, perversion of democracy, pollution of the mind, racism, and the impact of technology on human connections. He offered solutions such as deconstructing consumerism, developing social responsibility, putting humans before technology, and protecting vulnerable populations from abuse and tyranny by an economic oligarchy. With the exception of an epidemic of falls from urban buildings, Cornely's topics and concerns could be headlines in today's public health news! Currently, *The Nation's Health* presents headline news and offers regular sections entitled APHA Advocates, Vital Signs, Journal Watch, APHA in brief, *The Globe*, *The Nation*, state & local, health findings, student focus, book reviews, on-the-job, and classified advertisements. The publication provides information relevant to public health professionals and policy makers in a clear, easy to understand format, a necessary asset in ensuring a professional and qualified workforce.

Sally Kuykendall

See also: American Journal of Public Health; American Public Health Association; Cornely, Paul Bertau; Rosen, George; Winslow, Charles-Edward Amory

Further Reading

American Public Health Association. (2017). Retrieved from https://www.apha.org/.

Cornely, P. B. (1971). The hidden enemies of health and the American Public Health Association. *American Journal of Public Health, 61*(1), 7–18.

Editorial. (1971). The nation's health. *American Journal of Public Health, 61*(1), 1.

The Nation's Health. (2017). Retrieved from http://thenationshealth.aphapublications.org/.

NEEDS ASSESSMENT

A needs assessment is a planned series of actions designed to identify and understand the conditions or resources that are required to achieve ideal wellness of an individual, community, or population of interest. In public health, *need* is a noun (as opposed to a verb), broadly defined as the gap between current health status and desired health status. Put another way, a *need* is an identified concern or problem. The needs assessment aims to understand, in detail, what the gap is and why the problem exists within a specific group. For example, suppose there was an abnormally high prevalence of childhood obesity in one area (current situation). The desired situation would be that all children in that area are within healthy weight range (ideal situation). The *need* is the gap between the current condition, high rates of childhood obesity, and the desirable, healthy weights.

In a sense, the *need* would also be the problem that children in the community are overweight or obese. The objective of the needs assessment would be to understand why children are overweight or obese, what factors contribute to the problem, and the consequences of the disease on the community. In this case, children may have limited areas for recreational activity, a high-fat diet, or concerns for neighborhood safety that may limit outdoor activities. By investigating the behaviors of who has the disease and who doesn't have the disease, public health professionals determine how and why the disease occurs and what needs to be done to stop the disease. Knowing the specific factors that enable the problem allow public health professionals to allocate resources where they will be most effective. A needs assessment does not necessarily focus on one need or disease. A needs assessment can take into account numerous needs at the same time and can help to prioritize those needs, as in cases of impoverished communities that suffer from numerous health problems. In addition to public health, needs assessments are widely used in education, business, government, and marketing.

The practice of performing needs assessments was formally developed in the late 1970s by Roger Kaufman. Considered the "father of needs assessment," Kaufman combined concepts from psychology, sociology, industrial engineering, and mathematics to develop planning strategies for needs assessments. He identified three levels, known as levels of planning. The mega, macro, and micro levels of planning form the foundation and principles for needs assessments performed today (Kaufman, Rojas, & Mayer, 1993). Mega-level planning starts by developing an idealistic vision for society. In an ideal society, all children would have equal opportunities for healthy social, emotional, and physical development, safe places to play, and a nutritious, balanced diet. Macro-level planning looks at the organizational, community, or group or population-based level. The ideal community to prevent childhood obesity would have safe and convenient recreational sites, access to fresh fruits and vegetables to support healthy diet, and quality health education in preschool, elementary, middle, and high schools. Micro-level planning looks at the individual or family level. Factors that support healthy weight are regular physical activity and a diet that is low in refined sugars and fat. Needs assessments can include data collection and planning on all three levels or may address a single level. By envisioning and striving toward the ideal society, community, or individual, the needs assessment becomes proactive rather than reactive.

There are generally three phases to conducting a needs assessment: pre-assessment, assessment, and post-assessment (Witkin & Altschuld, 1995). During the pre-assessment phase, practitioners develop a work group, examine what is already known about the needs in the community, set the purpose and goals for the assessment, and identify methods for conducting the needs assessment. During the pre-assessment phase, secondary data collection methods are used. Secondary data collection is when the public health practitioner obtains information from empirical research studies, literature reviews, policies, and government or agency reports related to the community, population, or problem being assessed. The assessment phase of the needs assessment occurs when the practitioner gathers information directly from individuals and stakeholders within the community specific to the need being addressed. This process is known as primary data collection. Primary data collection includes quantitative methods, qualitative methods, or both. Quantitative data enumerate the problem (number of people impacted) and qualitative data describe the problem (adverse health effects). The most commonly used quantitative method is surveys, which can be mailed, e-mailed, delivered over the phone or online, or administered in person to participants. The most commonly used qualitative methods include in-depth interviews, focus groups, and community observations. In the post-assessment phase of the needs assessment, the practitioner uses the findings from the needs assessment to develop practical strategies to address and improve the need within the community. The findings can be used to inform decisions to reallocate resources within a community or create policies, health education materials, or public health programs and interventions to address the need, ultimately improving the lives of the population in need.

More recently, capacity assessments—also known as assets assessments—are performed at the same time as needs assessments. Capacity assessment is similar to needs assessment in that it is a planned process, but it is different from a needs assessment because the assets of the individual, community, or population are assessed rather than the needs (Gilmore, 2012). Capacities, or assets, are the resources that the individual, community, or population has available and what they are capable of doing. Assets can be utilized to address the problems or needs within a community. For example, in a community with a predominance of a preventable condition, such as obesity, some assets would include hospitals, health care community centers or organizations, and safe parks or other recreational areas. Assets assessments can also inform needs assessments because if there is a resource missing in the community that would help to address the need, then it would be necessary to introduce that resource to the community. For example, if the assets assessments did not identify any recreational centers in that community with a predominance of obesity, then recreational centers would have to be built to provide safe places for physical activity.

Many models are available to help a public health practitioner systematically conduct needs and assets assessments. Commonalities among the models include utilizing a social ecological approach and a general three-phase process (pre-assessment, assessment, post-assessment). One of the most widely used approaches that can be applied to needs assessment is the social ecological approach. This approach is based on the belief that one's health is influenced by many factors, including family and friends, the organizations that exist in their neighborhood, the community in which they live, and the policies that affect them. This allows the public health practitioner to gain a better understanding about the need because it assesses the issue(s) in different ways. An analysis of these factors can collectively describe what is lacking, which can explain why the need exists. For example, in a community with a predominance of obesity, it may be that the individuals within the community do not exercise or eat a balanced diet because they believe it is too hard to exercise, they do not like the taste of healthier foods, and they do not have friends who encourage them to exercise or eat better. There also may be a lack of access to healthy foods and recreational centers in the neighborhood, and there may be many fast food restaurants available. Finally, there may be policies that make nutritious foods, such as vegetables, more expensive than less healthier options, such as candy bars, in the neighborhood. By understanding individual characteristics, the public health practitioner can get a clear picture of the current situation, understand why there is a gap that exists between the current and ideal situations, and advocate reducing obesity within the community.

Noora F. Majid and Nadav Antebi-Gruszka

See also: Collaborations; Community Health; Core Competencies in Public Health; Environmental Health; Evaluation; Evidence-Based Programs and Practices; Health

Education; Intervention; PRECEDE-PROCEED Planning Model; Prevention; Public Health Department Accreditation; Research

Further Reading

Gilmore, G. D. (2012). *Needs and capacity assessment strategies for health education and health promotion*. Burlington, MA: Jones & Bartlett.

Kaufman, R., Rojas, A. M., & Mayer, H. (1993). *Needs assessment: A user's guide*. Englewood Cliffs, NJ: Educational Technology.

Witkin, B. R., & Altschuld, J. W. (1995). *Planning and conducting needs assessments: A practical guide*. Thousand Oaks, CA: Sage.

Your Complete Resource Site on Needs and Needs Assessments. (2008). Retrieved from http://www.needsassessment.org.

NIGHTINGALE, FLORENCE (1820–1910)

Known the world over as the "The Lady with the Lamp," Florence Nightingale rose to fame during the Crimean War (1853–1856) for introducing the first female nurses to military medical facilities. Her determination to provide wounded and sick soldiers with the best possible care brought her to the battlefield, as well as to wartime hospitals. After the war, she convinced the government of Great Britain to reexamine its medical facilities and sanitation procedures for all soldiers. Responsible for transforming nursing from a disreputable practice to a professional career fit for educated and genteel women, Nightingale pioneered professional training for nurses and indelibly shaped the nature of nursing throughout the world.

Born on May 12, 1820, in Florence, Italy (from which she got her name), Florence was the daughter of William Edward and Frances (Smith) Nightingale. The Nightingales were well-educated members of the British upper class. Therefore, Florence and her older sister Parthenope (named after the Greek city in which she was born) lived privileged lives and spent their time on the European continent and in their two homes in England, one in Derbyshire and one in Hampshire. Both girls were educated by their father, who gave them rigorous instruction in several foreign languages, history, philosophy, literature, and mathematics. A charming and beautiful girl, Nightingale was expected to enjoy a successful social life and marry well. Instead, she chose a life of social service, prompted by a general seriousness in her disposition and an incident when she was 17 that convinced her to devote her life to a worthy cause. On February 7, 1837, while in the garden at the family home in Hampshire, Nightingale believed that God spoke to her and told her that she had a great calling in life. Nightingale was mystified as to the exact nature of the calling but began actively seeking ways to answer God's call.

To the dismay of her family, Nightingale turned her attention to nursing. She had always been interested in tending the sick in the country villages near her family's homes, a responsibility that fit well with her genteel status. Professional nursing at this time was nonexistent, and informal nursing was widely regarded as a disreputable profession, not far removed from prostitution. Nightingale's father, therefore, refused her request to study nursing by working in a hospital, although she began visiting hospitals around 1844 to inspect conditions there. Her father suggested instead that she study parliamentary reports dealing with the subject of public health and sanitation, a task that she undertook with energy. Within a few months, she had become an expert on the government's role in these fields. Her interest in public health and sanitation was also encouraged by her neighbor, Sidney Herbert, a prominent politician of the British Liberal Party. Herbert was enthusiastic about all kinds of reform and spent long hours discussing medical reform with Nightingale.

Nightingale's interest in nursing and health remained strong throughout the 1840s. She received her first practical experience nursing at the end of the decade while traveling on the European continent with her friends Charles and Selina Bracebridge. The trio journeyed to Egypt in 1849. On their return in the summer of 1850, they passed through the town of Kaiserwerth, Germany, where the Institution of Protestant Deaconesses gave training to women to tend the sick. Nightingale was fascinated by the school, the first of its kind, and returned the following year to complete the four-month training course. This experience strengthened her resolve to pursue a career in nursing and to make the profession a respectable one for women.

When newspapers reported high death rates due to filth, shoddy care, and lack of supplies, Florence Nightingale organized 38 nurses to care for wounded soldiers of the Crimean War. Despite appalling conditions and hostility from male medical staff, Nightingale's nurses reduced patient mortality rates from 45 percent to 2 percent. (Library of Congress)

In 1853, Nightingale finally overcame the objections of her parents to her chosen career. Her father granted her an independent income of £500 a year and his permission to study nursing. That same year, she accepted her first professional position, as superintendent of the Establishment for Gentlewomen during Illness. In this capacity, Nightingale showed herself well suited to administrative work.

The following year, British society was scandalized by reports of hospital conditions for soldiers fighting in the Crimean War. The reports, written by *London Times* correspondent William Howard

Russell, detailed the filth, shoddy care, and lack of supplies that contributed to a high death rate for wounded and ill soldiers. At the prompting of her old friend Herbert, who was then the British secretary of state, Nightingale organized a brigade of 38 women and traveled to the Crimea to help nurse the soldiers. Departing England on October 21, 1854, Nightingale and her entourage arrived at the military hospital at Scutari, Turkey, on November 5.

The doctors at Scutari greatly resented the presence of the nurses and initially refused to allow them access to the wards. As the casualties from the Battle of Inkerman (fought on the very day of the nurses' arrival) began to pour into the hospital, however, Nightingale and her nurses leaped into action and began providing aid to the wounded. Despite this much-needed help, the all-male staff at the hospital continued to resent Nightingale's presence and worked to undermine her mission throughout her stay in the Crimea.

The challenges for Nightingale were substantial. In addition to the hostility of the medical staff, the conditions in the hospitals were appalling. Russell had not exaggerated the plight of the wounded soldiers; if anything, he had glossed over them. The hospital at Scutari was overcrowded, filthy, disease-ridden, and infested with rats, mice, lice, and other vermin. In addition, most of her nurses were inexperienced, and some behaved poorly. Nightingale was forced to send a few of them home because of drunkenness or improper relations with the soldiers. Although only a few of the nurses behaved in such a manner, news of their misconduct spread quickly and did much to harm the reputation of the fledgling nursing program.

Nevertheless, Nightingale tackled these challenges with vigor. Reportedly on her feet 20 hours a day, she established a laundry and a kitchen, purchased much-needed supplies with funds gathered from a private subscription in England (one of her first purchases was 200 scrub brushes), and brought order and cleanliness to the institution. It was during this period that she earned her famous sobriquet, "The Lady with the Lamp," as she solely and personally attended the soldiers in the wards at night so as not to tempt any of her nurses into indiscretions or promote false rumors of the nurses' conduct. Within a matter of months, these reforms had resulted in a dramatic lowering of the fatality rate among soldiers brought to the hospital; it dropped from roughly 45 percent to 2 percent. For her efforts, Nightingale earned the undying adoration of the wounded soldiers, many of whom viewed her as nothing less than a saint.

With the hospital at Scutari running more smoothly, Nightingale embarked on an expedition to visit other military hospitals in the Crimea in May 1855. Already exhausted from overwork, she contracted what was known as Crimean fever during the trip and became violently ill in Balaclava. Although she recovered sufficiently within a few weeks to return to Scutari and resume her duties there, her health never fully recovered. Nevertheless, she remained in the Crimea until August 1856.

Nightingale's work in the Crimea had been well publicized in Britain, and the country anticipated giving her a warm welcome on her return. Instead, she slipped quietly into the country without fanfare. She could not escape the attentions of a grateful public, however. The sultan of Turkey gave her a diamond bracelet in appreciation for her efforts, while Britain's Queen Victoria sent her a personal letter and a brooch designed by Prince Albert. Even before Nightingale's return from the Crimea, the public had established a fund so that she could establish a nursing school after her return to Britain. Before she could turn her attention to this endeavor, however, she felt compelled to publicize the need for a professional nursing corps in the military and the imperative of medical reform in general. In October 1856, she had a private audience with Queen Victoria, Prince Albert, and Secretary for State Lord Panmure.

Following the interview, Panmure established a royal commission to report on sanitary conditions in the Crimea and asked Nightingale to serve on it. She wrote most of the commission's final report, demanding that the military reevaluate its medical facilities and take steps to improve sanitary conditions among all soldiers, not just the sick or wounded. This report prompted the founding of the Army Medical School shortly thereafter. In 1857, her attention turned to the Indian Rebellion and focused on concern with the general welfare of British soldiers, both at home and abroad. Two years later, she served on another royal commission investigating sanitary conditions in India, which ultimately led to the establishment of a sanitary department in the British government's India office.

By 1860, Nightingale was able to turn her attention back to nursing. The public fund taken up in her behalf during the Crimean War totaled some £45,000 by that point. She used the money to establish a nursing school at St. Thomas' Hospital in London. The first of its kind in the world, the Nightingale School for Nurses sought to train women to undertake nursing as a profession. The school was unique not only for its emphasis on both classroom work and hands-on training but also because it was the only secular institution to undertake this task. The few other nursing schools that existed in the world at this time were all associated with religious orders and functioned as part of established churches. Furthermore, the Nightingale School refused to train nurses just for genteel patients but educated women to work in workhouses and public facilities as well. Nightingale took on all of the administrative work associated with the school, although she had little time to personally teach or supervise her students. Nonetheless, she had a tremendous impact on her graduates, who traveled all over the world and established nursing schools patterned after her own. She also published a book, *Notes on Nursing*, in 1860 that outlined her philosophy and methods. This book was eventually translated into 11 languages and is still widely read throughout the world.

Starting in 1859, a wealthy merchant from Liverpool, William Rathbone, hired nurses to care for the sick and poor people of his district. When he tried to expand health services to other districts, he could not find enough trained nurses. He contacted Nightingale hoping that she would send nurses from the St. Thomas school. Instead, Nightingale suggested that Rathbone open a nurse training school at the Royal Liverpool Infirmary. The Liverpool school was opened to train nurses as district nurses. By 1864, Rathbone had another request. The Liverpool Workhouse

Infirmary housed 1,200 sick poor people. Rathbone wanted Nightingale to use her influence to convince the workhouse administrators that the institution needed a nursing staff and matron (director of nursing). However, Nightingale was focused on sanitation in India. Her attention shifted after the death of a workhouse patient. One newspaper reported that the death was due to "filthiness caused by gross neglect" (Monteiro, 1985, p. 182). Nightingale seized on the opportunity for advocacy. She developed a three-part plan for the nursing care of ailing poor people. The plan included a tax for the Medical Relief Fund, providing finances to care for poor patients. Rathbone's model of district nurses was replicated in other large cities and eventually became the field of public health nursing. Nightingale's vision of the Medical Relief Fund became the United Kingdom's National Health System.

Nightingale's accomplishments are all the more remarkable in that she was physically disabled after 1857. Her fragile health following her bout with Crimean fever could not sustain an active life after her return to England. Instead, she maintained a voluminous correspondence with her many friends and allies in British society and government, thus lobbying effectively on behalf of her causes. From her bed, she managed the affairs of the Nightingale School and promoted several other reform efforts, most of which were related to public health. She remained one of the most revered figures of the Victorian Age and was idolized by much of British society. Near the end of her life, she received two prestigious awards for her work: the Royal Red Cross in 1883 and the Order of Merit in 1907. She was the first woman to receive the latter award. After more than seven decades of public service, Nightingale died in her home at London on August 13, 1910. In her will, she refused the government's offer to bury her in Westminster Abbey with a national funeral. Instead, she was interred near her parents' home in Hampshire.

Sally Kuykendall

See also: Chadwick, Edwin; Dix, Dorothea Lynde; Infectious Diseases; Shattuck, Lemuel

Further Reading

Baly, M. E. (1986). *Florence Nightingale and the nursing legacy.* London: Croom Helm.

Cope, Z. (1958). *Florence Nightingale and the doctors.* Philadelphia: J. B. Lippincott.

Garofalo, M. E., & Fee, E. (2010). Florence Nightingale (1820–1910): Feminism and hospital reform. *American Journal of Public Health, 100*(9), 1588. doi:10.2105/AJPH.2009.188722

Huxley, E. (1975). *Florence Nightingale.* New York: Putnam.

Lynn, M. (2006, January 1). Florence Nightingale as a social reformer: Lynn McDonald describes the lasting impact of Florence Nightingale on improving public health for the poor. *History Today, 56*(1), 9.

Monteiro, L. A. (1985). Florence Nightingale on public health nursing. *American Journal of Public Health, 75*(2), 181.

Smith, F. B. (1982). *Florence Nightingale: Reputation and power.* London: Croom Helm.

NUTRITION

Nutrition is a scientific field encompassing the biology, chemistry, psychology and sociology of food selection, intake, digestion, catabolism, absorption, and excretion. Many of the leading causes of death are related to nutrition. Overweight and obesity, malnutrition, iron-deficiency anemia, hypertension, dyslipidemia, and tooth and gum diseases are just a few diseases directly related to diet. Heart disease, stroke, diabetes, cancer, birth defects, and substance abuse are nutrition-related problems that top the list of public health concerns. The healthy body requires a balanced intake of macronutrients (carbohydrates, proteins, and fats), micronutrients (vitamins and minerals), and water to stay healthy and to resist disease. Carbohydrates, proteins, and fats are macronutrients that provide carbon, oxygen, and hydrogen to the body. These nutrients give the body the energy that it needs to perform basic and advanced functions. Proteins also provide nitrogen for body structures. Micronutrients (vitamins and minerals) provide other essential and nonessential components. Water facilitates biochemical reactions and lubricates organs and systems. To support public health, the U.S. Department of Agriculture (USDA) studies food and recommends optimal levels of macronutrients and micronutrients. Individuals, registered dieticians, nutritionists, and health professionals use these guidelines to prevent and control disease. Government agencies and organizations offer many helpful resources on nutrition. One easy-to-use tool is *MyPlate*. Helping people to understand nutrition and to follow a healthy diet can reduce many of the leading causes of death.

Healthy sources of carbohydrates are fruits, vegetables, and grains. The fruit group consists of any fruit that is fresh, canned, frozen, and dried or 100 percent fruit juice. Fruits are a great source of fiber, potassium, fiber, vitamin C, and folate (folic acid). The vegetable group consists of any vegetable that is raw, cooked, fresh, frozen, canned, and dried/dehydrated or 100 percent vegetable juice. There are five subgroups of vegetables: dark-green, starchy, red and orange, beans and peas, and other vegetables. Vegetables are a good source of potassium, dietary fiber, folate (folic acid), vitamin A, and vitamin C. Fruits and vegetables reduce the risk of heart disease, stroke, certain types of cancers, obesity, and Type 2 diabetes. A diet rich in fruits and vegetables may help maintain healthy weight, lower blood pressure, and prevent kidney stones. Whole and refined grains provide calories, dietary fiber, B vitamins (e.g., thiamin, riboflavin, niacin, and folate), and minerals (e.g., iron, magnesium, and selenium). The difference between whole grains (e.g., whole-wheat flour, cracked wheat, oatmeal, whole cornmeal, and brown rice) and refined grains (white flour, degermed cornmeal, white bread, and white rice) is that the former contains the entire grain kernel (i.e., bran, germ, and endosperm), whereas, the latter no longer has the bran and germ. The USDA recommends at least 50 percent of all grains eaten per day should be whole grains as whole grain is important in maintaining a healthy weight and digestive system, and reducing the risk of heart disease, diabetes, and high blood pressure.

Proteins provide vitamin B (e.g., niacin, thiamin, riboflavin, and B6), vitamin E, iron, zinc, magnesium, and amino acids. Amino acids are the building blocks for body structure, growth, and maintenance. There are 20 different amino acids, 9 essential and 11 nonessential. Each amino acid fulfills a specific function. Essential amino acids must be taken in through the diet because the body cannot manufacture that specific amino acid. It is important that people take in the correct amount and proportion of amino acids. Animal meat, poultry, seafood, eggs, and dairy products are complete sources of protein because they contain all of the nine essential amino acids as well as some nonessential amino acids, in the correct proportions needed for the body. It is unwise to rely on protein supplements because some amino acids displace other amino acids, creating a deficit and impairing with the body's ability to build proteins which rely on that amino acid. Vegetarians use the concept of mutual supplementation, balancing sources of incomplete protein such as beans and rice, hummus (chickpeas and sesame seeds), tofu and broccoli or spinach salad with pine nuts. Although easier to digest than many plant sources of protein, animal sources of protein can be high in saturated fat, which can lead to cardiovascular disease. It is important to select protein sources that are low in saturated fats and cholesterol and to follow the recommended guidelines. Excess protein is not stored by the body. It is converted into body fat. Insufficient protein intake, a problem known as protein energy malnutrition, is a major problem in third world countries where raising animals to eat is prohibitively expensive. Kwashiorkor is a disease that affects children aged 1–4. The term *kwashiorkor* means "rejected one," referring to when a mother must wean her child from breastfeeding because she is due to have a second child. The mother replaces the easily digested and protein-rich breast milk with the local diet, typically one high in starchy vegetables. The classic symptoms of kwashiorkor are lack of energy, and fluid and electrolyte imbalances that cause swelling and bloating, enlarged liver, thinning hair, and skin problems. In countries such as the United States where protein is readily available, protein energy malnutrition is rare and typically due to alcohol or substance abuse, wasting diseases (cancer or AIDS), or living in an abusive household where diet and activities are highly controlled.

The dairy group provides calcium and vitamin D, which help to build strong bones. All foods that are made from milk such as yogurt and cheese as well as calcium-fortified soymilk are part of the dairy food group. Foods that are made from milk that have little to no calcium are not part of the dairy group (e.g., cream cheese, cream, and butter). When making dairy choices, it is recommended to select fat free and low fat foods since fat does not have any nutrients. Calcium is also found in nondairy products such as kale, collard and turnip greens, bok choy, calcium-fortified juices, cereals, breads, rice milk, almond milk, canned fish, soy products, and beans. However, the absorption rate of calcium varies for nondairy foods.

In the United States, many adults take dietary supplements in the form of vitamins, minerals, herbals, botanicals, amino acids, or enzymes. Since a dietary supplement is a supplement, it does not go through the same research and development as prescriptions and over-the-counter drugs. This means that the FDA does not regulate, review, or approve dietary supplements. Pregnant or lactating women, newborns, infants, the elderly, people with AIDS or other wasting diseases, people recovering from severe burns, or people taking medications that interfere with normal body metabolism may need supplements. For the most part, normal, healthy individuals do not require dietary supplements because they can get the macronutrients and micronutrients that they need through eating a balanced diet, which includes a variety of foods. Health care providers can assist individuals in deciding whether dietary supplements are beneficial to their overall health.

There are several tools designed to help people plan and follow a balanced diet. *MyPlate* is a color-coded plate that reminds individuals to eat the correct proportions of the five food groups. A healthy diet is made up of grain (color-coded as orange), protein (purple), vegetables (green), fruits (red), and dairy (blue). The recommended amounts depend on one's age, gender, and level of physical activity. The U.S. Department of Agriculture created a free user-friendly website called Food-A-Pedia. Individuals can look up nutrition information of over 8,000 foods and compare the foods side-by-side to evaluate nutritional values. The USDA (2016, n.d.-c) also created a free website called Food Tracker for people to keep track of their food intake and nutrition goals. There is an option for the users to track their food consumptions over time by signing up for a free account. Users may also personalize their profile to age, gender, level of physical activity, height, and weight. This information helps calculate the user's daily calorie limit.

Food nourishes the body and ensures that cells and organs can function properly. However, too much, too little, or the wrong types of food can lead to malnutrition, chronic illnesses, or premature death. Public health professionals work with individuals, communities, and organizations to ensure that people have sufficient knowledge to select nutritious foods and to access nutritious foods. Nutritionists and health educators continue to improve and refine diet planning tools to ensure that members of the public are able to easily and effectively plan healthy diets.

Susana Leong

See also: Cancer; Diabetes Mellitus; Eating Disorders; Food and Drug Administration; Food Insecurity; Global Health; Heart Disease; Leading Health Indicators; Maternal Health; National Health and Nutrition Examination Survey; Obesity; Physical Activity; Rural Health; School Health; U.S. Department of Agriculture; Women's Health

Further Reading

Energy, food, and you: An interdisciplinary curriculum guide for secondary schools. (1979). [Seattle, Wash.]: State Office of Health Education [1979]. Retrieved from https://babel.hathitrust.org/cgi/pt?id=umn.31951002865703i;view=1up;seq=9.

Sizer, F. S., & Whitney, E. (2008). *Nutrition: Concepts and controversies* (11th ed.). Belmont, CA: Thomson Wadsworth.

The Surgeon General's report on nutrition and health. (1989). Washington, DC: U.S. Department of Health and Human Services, Public Health Service: For sale by the Superintendent of Documents, U.S. G.P.O., 1988 [i.e. 1989].

U.S. Department of Agriculture. (n.d.-a). *Choose MyPlate*. Retrieved July 25, 2016, from http://www.choosemyplate.gov.

U.S. Department of Agriculture. (n.d.-b). *Food-A-Pedia.* Retrieved July 25, 2016, from https://www.supertracker.usda.gov/foodapedia.aspx.

U.S. Department of Agriculture. (n.d.-c). *Food Tracker*. Retrieved July 25, 2016, from https://www.supertracker.usda.gov/foodapedia.aspx.

U.S. Department of Agriculture. (2016). *Smart Nutrition 101*. Retrieved July 25, 2016, from https://www.nutrition.gov/smart-nutrition-101.

U.S. Department of Health and Human Services. (2015). *Antioxidants.* Retrieved July 25, 2016, from https://medlineplus.gov/antioxidants.html.

O

OBESITY

Obesity occurs when the individual consumes more calories than the body needs and excess body fat accumulates. Excess weight damages the body's organ systems leading to chronic health problems. Adults who are overweight or obese are at greater risk for cardiovascular disease, hypertension, Type 2 diabetes, dyslipidemia, stroke, fatty liver disease, gallbladder disease, respiratory illnesses, cancers (breast, colon, gallbladder endometrial, prostate), arthritis, chronic back pain, and infertility. Even moderate overweight or obesity increases the risk of disability and premature death (Office of the Surgeon General, 2001). Children who are overweight or obese suffer from unique problems. As their small bodies struggle to carry additional weight, they are at risk for heart attack, difficulty breathing, and bone and joint problems. Moderately overweight children have elevated low density lipoprotein (LDL) levels, and markedly obese children exhibit increased blood pressures, high triglyceride levels, and reduced high-density lipoprotein (HDL) levels (Reilly et al., 2003). Being overweight and obese as an adolescent is a risk factor for obesity in adulthood. Obese children and adults suffer from social stigmas, anxiety, depression, and binge-eating disorders. The causes of obesity are complex and multifactorial, dependent on genetic, metabolic, cultural, environmental, socioeconomic, and behavioral factors (Tappy, Le, Tran, & Paquot, 2010). In the United States, obesogenic factors include food insecurity, aggressive marketing of junk foods and drinks, and social and cultural traditions (sedentary lifestyle, Western diet, large portion sizes normalized). Obesity is treatable. Long-term weight loss is achieved through a combination of interventions focused on a healthy, low-calorie diet, increased physical activity, and behavior therapy. Public health professionals work with communities, parents, and patients to prevent and address this growing epidemic.

Health professionals use a number of methods to assess obesity. Body mass index (BMI) compares weight relative to height and is calculated using this equation: weight (kilograms) divided by height (meters) squared. In the United States, the average BMI is 26.6 and 26.5 for adult men and women, respectively. Obesity is defined as a BMI of 30.0 kg/m^2 or higher. A BMI of 40.0 kg/m^2 or higher denotes extreme, or morbid obesity (Pi-Sunyer et al., 1998). For children and adolescents, aged 2 to 19, growth occurs at various rates. As a result, BMI is plotted on growth charts and translated into a percentile ranking for children of the same age and gender. If a child's BMI is above the 85th percentile for his or her age, he or she is considered overweight. If a child's BMI is above the 95th percentile, the child is classified as obese. BMI should be used with caution as it can overestimate body fat in individuals who are muscular and can underestimate body fat in people who have lost muscle mass, such as the elderly (Office of the Surgeon General, 2001). An alternative measure of obesity, waist circumference compares abdominal fat content to total body fat content. In comparison to BMI, waist circumference is a stronger predictor of heart disease and diabetes. A waist circumference greater than 35 inches (88 cm) or 40 inches (102 cm) in women and men, respectively, correlates to increased risk of obesity-associated diseases (Pi-Sunyer et al., 1998). Other ways to assess obesity are waist to hip ratio, skinfold thickness, bioelectrical impedance, magnetic resonance imaging, and underwater weighing.

Globally and nationally, obesity is an epidemic. An estimated 66 million American adults are obese, and 74 million adults are overweight (CDC). From 1980 to 2000, the prevalence of obese adults increased from 13 percent to 28 percent in men and from 17 to 26 percent in women, respectively (CDC). During that time, the total prevalence of overweight or obese adults in the United States increased from 56 to 64 percent (CDC). Overweight and obesity are more common in minority groups and individuals with lower socioeconomic status and education level (Pi-Sunyer et al., 1998). Since the 1970s, childhood obesity has more than tripled (Ogden et al., 2016). From 1980 to 2010, the prevalence of obesity increased from 6.5 to 18 percent for children 6–11 years old and 5 to 18.4 percent for adolescents 12 to 19 years old (Ogden et al., 2014). As of 2014, the prevalence of obesity for all American children was 17 percent (Johnson et al., 2014). The prevalence is higher among minority children and children from low income communities (Ogden et al., 2014). Mexican American and non-Hispanic blacks have higher prevalence compared to their non-Hispanic white counterparts (Johnson et al., 2014; Ogden et al., 2010). Annual medical costs attributed to obesity are estimated to be as high as $190 billion, which amounts to approximately 21 percent of all medical spending (Cawley & Meyerhoefer, 2012).

The safest and most effective treatments for obesity are diet and exercise. In the clinical setting, physicians will first rule out or treat any underlying medical causes, such as hypothyroidism or Cushing's syndrome. Patients with high waist circumference or two or more risk factors for obesity-related diseases may be referred for nutritional or behavioral counseling to learn strategies in self-monitoring, contingency planning, cognitive restructuring, problem-solving, and reinforcement. Motivation is key to successful weight loss. Weight reduction goals must be realistic and achievable. An initial goal of 10 percent weight loss (approximately 1-pound loss per week) over the first six months is recommended. After initial weight loss, the body may compensate by lowering energy expenditure. This syndrome may appear as weight gain. Knowing what to expect and when empowers the patient to attain and maintain weight loss goals. Prescription medications, such as those approved by the Food and Drug Administration, can also be used to invoke weight loss, although data to support long-term effects are minimal (Office of the Surgeon General, 2001). As with any medication, the benefit of the drug should outweigh the risks of side effects. Finally, bariatric surgery is an alternative option for extremely obese individuals where medical therapy has failed. Weight loss surgery options of gastric restriction, gastric banding, and gastric-bypass surgery have shown success in appropriate surgical candidates (Pi-Sunyer et al., 1998). As with any surgery, patients must meet eligibility criteria to qualify for surgery. In the pediatric population, weight loss surgery is recommended for obese adolescents who have exhausted all other medical weight loss options and are greatly impacted by their weight. Weight loss surgery is only offered to adolescents who are no longer growing, failed to lose weight within six months of a weight loss treatment program under guidance of a physician, remain drug free, and demonstrate commitment to the lifestyle changes required for the surgery (Hassink, 2014). The good news is that weight loss can successfully reduce risk of heart disease, diabetes, and hypertension (Pi-Sunyer et al., 1998). Carefully planned treatment and follow-up can help individuals maintain a healthy weight. Effective treatments consider long-term weight management.

Obesity is costly to both individuals and society. Obesity is responsible for increased hospitalization, longer hospital stays, decreased life expectancy, and increased mortality. Moreover, obesity is responsible for lost productivity, lost wages, and disability (Office of the Surgeon General, 2001). Medical costs related to obesity have increased and will continue to rise as more people live with multiple chronic illnesses. As with other public health concerns, obesity must be tackled aggressively and effectively. Factors such as income, inaccessibility to healthy foods (food deserts), nutrition education, and motivation hinder weight loss. Given the investments in research and programming to combat the obesity epidemic, it is more important, now than ever before, for the government to garner support and develop partnerships for our nation's future.

Maria DiGiorgio McColgan and Staceyann Smith

See also: Body Mass Index; Diabetes Mellitus; Global Health; Heart Disease; Leading Health Indicators; Maternal Health; National Health and Nutrition Examination Survey; Nutrition; Physical Activity; U.S. Department of Agriculture; Women's Health

Further Reading

Cawley, J., & Meyerhoefer, C. (2012). The medical care costs of obesity: An instrumental variables approach. *Journal of Health Economics*, *31*(1), 219–230.

Centers for Disease Control and Prevention (CDC). National Center for Health Statistics. *National Health and Nutrition Examination Survey.* Retrieved from http://www.cdc.gov/nchs/nhanes/ nhanes_questionnaires.htm.

Finkelstein, E. A., Trogden, J. G., Cohen, J. W., & Dietz, W. (2009). Annual medical spending attributable to obesity: Payer- and service-specific estimates. *Health Affairs*, *38*(5), w822–w831.

Flegal, K. M. (2010). *Changes in terminology for childhood overweight and obesity.* National health statistics reports; no. 25. Hyattsville, MD: National Center for Health Statistics.

Hassink, S. G. (2014). *Pediatric care: Prevention, intervention and treatment strategies for primary care* (2nd ed.). Elk Grove Village, IL: American Academy of Pediatrics.

Johnson, C. L., Dohrmann, S. M., Burt, V. L., & Mohadjer, L. K. (2014). *National health and nutrition examination survey: Sample design, 2011–2014.* National Center for Health Statistics. *Vital Health Statistics, 2*(162).

Office of the Surgeon General. (2001). *The Surgeon General's call to action to prevent and decrease overweight and obesity.* Office of Disease Prevention and Health Promotion, Centers for Disease Control and Prevention, National Institutes of Health. Rockville, MD.

Ogden, C. L., Carroll, M. D., Kit, B. K., & Flegal, K. M. (2014). Prevalence of childhood and adult obesity in the United States, 2011–2012. *Journal of the American Medical Association, 311*(8), 806–814.

Ogden, C. L., Carroll, M. D., Lawman, H. G., et al. (2016). Trends in obesity prevalence among children and adolescents in the United States, 1988–1994 through 2013–2014. *Journal of the American Medical Association, 315,* 2292.

Ogden, C. L., Lamb, M. M., Carroll, M. D., & Flegal, K. M. (2010). Obesity and socioeconomic status in adults: United States, 2005–2008. National Center for Health Statistics Data Brief. Number 51. Retrieved from https://www.cdc.gov/nchs/data/databriefs/db51.pdf.

Pi-Sunyer, X., Becker, D., Bouchard, C., Carleton, R. A., Colditz, G. A., Foreyt, et al. (1998). Clinical guidelines on the identification, evaluation, and treatment of overweight and obesity in adults—The evidence report. *Obesity Research, 6*(Suppl. 2), 51S–209S.

Reilly J. J., Methven, E., McDowell Z, C., Hacking, B., Alexander, D., Stewart, L., & Kelnar, C. J. H. (2003). Health consequences of obesity. *Archives of Disease in Childhood, 88*(9), 748.

Tappy L., Le, K., Tran, C., & Paquot, N. (2010). Fructose and metabolic diseases: New finding, new questions. *Nutrition, 26,* 1044–1049.

U.S. Department of Health and Human Services, Centers for Disease Control and Prevention Division of Nutrition, Physical Activity and Obesity. (2017). *Body mass index (BMI).* Retrieved from http://www.cdc.gov/healthyweight/assessing/bmi/.

ORAL HEALTH

Dental caries is one of the most common diseases, affecting 37 percent of children aged 2 to 8 and 91 percent of adults aged 20 to 64 (CDC/National Center for Health Statistics, 2016). People of low income, low education, minority status, disability, or other chronic illnesses are at greatest risk. Tooth and gum decay can cause pain, inability to chew, taste, or smell food, malnutrition, weight loss, facial disfigurement, speech disorders, and is the leading cause of school absences. Despite the widespread epidemic, oral and craniofacial problems are easily preventable. Good oral hygiene, consisting of regular dental screenings, flossing, brushing, healthy diet, and avoiding tobacco and alcohol, help protect teeth, heart, and overall health. Public water fluoridation decreases dental caries by up to 30 percent, and dental sealants decrease cavities by 60 percent. *Healthy People* objectives are to reduce dental caries among all age groups, increase access to preventive services, including dental sealants and water fluoridation, and build public health infrastructure so that more public health clinics have a dental professional with cross-training in public health.

To avoid tooth and gum disease, the American Dental Association (2016) and the American Heart Association (AHA, 2013) recommend maintaining good oral health. Gum disease is an infection of the tissues that support the teeth. Both the ADA (2016) and AHA (2013) state that visiting the dentist regularly, eating a balanced diet, limiting snacks between meals, brushing twice a day, and flossing daily are important in preventing tooth decay and cavities. Seeing a dentist regularly for a dental cleaning and examination along with education on good oral hygiene can help prevent most dental diseases (ADA, 2016). The recommendation from dental professionals is to have your teeth cleaned professionally every six months (USDHHS, 2016). This is important, even if individuals are brushing and flossing regularly, because a dentist is able to help remove plaque that individuals are not able to remove with brushing and flossing alone and provide fluoride treatment (USDHHS, 2016). During a routine dental exam, the dentist may take X-rays to catch potential problems in the early stages. This prevents the problem from becoming more serious and also expensive to fix in the future. In addition to regular routine visits, the dentist will check for symptoms, which may include pain in a tooth for no particular reason or pain that is caused by food, beverages, brushing, or flossing. Instead of waiting for the next scheduled appointment, it is important to call a dentist if one is feeling sensitivity to hot and cold foods and/or drinks. The longer a problem remains untreated, the more difficult it is to repair.

The foods we eat can also enhance oral health. Dairy products such as milk and yogurt strengthen teeth since they are full of calcium, a mineral that forms the hard

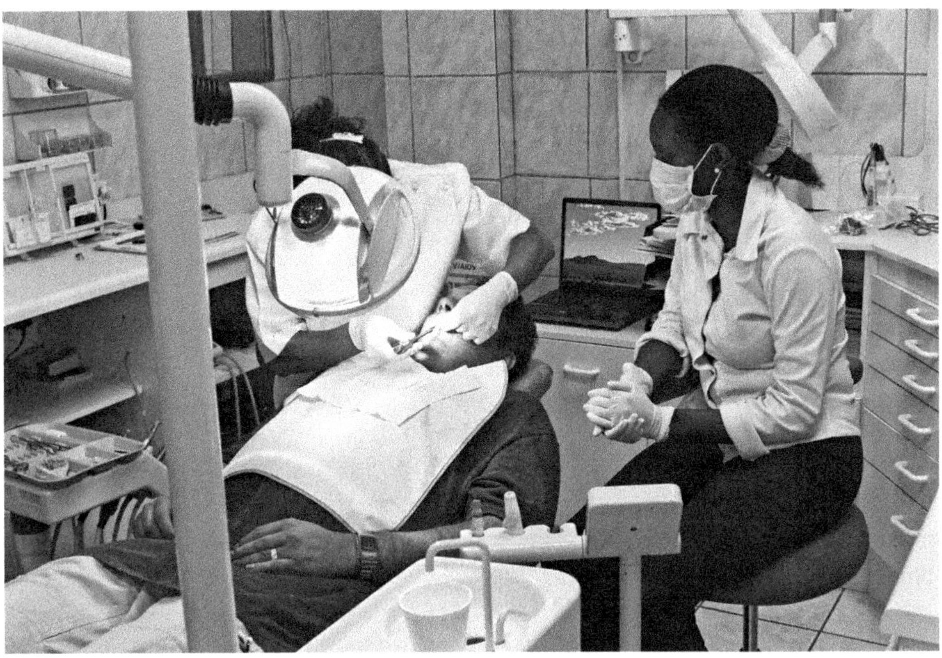

A dentist screens her patient for tooth or gum diseases. Oral problems are easily preventable with a healthy diet, regular dental checkups, flossing, and brushing. (iStockphoto.com)

enamel protecting the teeth (ADA, 2016). Lean proteins, such as chicken and fish, help rebuild tooth enamel. Fruits and vegetables have high water content, so they are helpful when it comes to washing away acids, bacteria, and food particles in one's mouth. Another way to reduce one's risk for tooth decay is by chewing nuts. Chewing nuts helps stimulate saliva production, reducing tooth-destroying acids. Foods to avoid are hard, sticky candies or acidic beverages such as lemon water (ADA, 2016). Coffee and tea with added sugar can cause dry mouth and dehydration, as do alcoholic drinks. Crunchy foods such as chips are high in carbohydrates. Easily trapped between teeth, the carbohydrates turn into sugar, attacking tooth enamel.

Water is best in helping the human body to stay hydrated, distributing nutrients, getting rid of waste, keeping your skin healthy, and aiding in the movements of your muscle (ADA, 2016). Sport drinks and energy drinks are not good for the teeth as they have a lot of added sugar. When an individual drinks soda or juice with meals, cavity-causing bacteria from the leftover food stuck to the teeth will come in contact with the sugar and will produce acid to wear out the teeth. Drinking water with one's meals lowers the chance of the cavity-causing bacteria eating the unwanted sugar. The acids that are in one's mouth are diluted by the water, which aids in keeping one's teeth cavity-free. The fluoridated tap water from the kitchen sink helps make one's teeth stronger because the fluoride is resistant to acid attack. As of 2012, approximately 75 percent of individuals in the United States had access to fluoridated water from their kitchen sinks.

In order to keep one's teeth cavity-free, it is important for individuals to brush their teeth for two minutes when they wake up in the morning and before they go to sleep. The American Dental Association recommends flossing at least once a day. Flossing helps remove plaque, prevent gum disease, and prevent cavities in hard to reach areas. Toothbrushes should be replaced every three to four months or after experiencing a cold (USDHHS, 2016). If you brush your teeth with a worn-out toothbrush, the toothbrush will not clean the teeth as well. Some research studies have shown that an electric toothbrush is able to clean teeth better than manual toothbrushes (USDHHS, 2016). Your dentist can recommend what kind of toothbrush is best and areas to concentrate on while brushing. In addition to caring for teeth with brushing, flossing and regular dental checkups, athletes should take additional precautions, wearing mouth guards during activities with high risk of injury. According to the AHA (2013), researchers have noted an association between several heart conditions and oral health. More studies are being done to gather data on a possible connection.

Approximately 108 million Americans do not have dental insurance (U.S. Department of Health and Human Services [USDHHS], 2014). Medicare does not cover checkups, cleanings, and fillings, as it only covers dental services that are related to certain medical conditions or treatments. The National Institute of Dental and Craniofacial Research's website (NIDCR) provides information for the public on where to find low-cost dental care near where they live. If anyone has questions about where to find dental care near where they live, there is a toll free number at 1-866-232-4528, and you can also e-mail them at nidcinfo@mail.nih.gov for more information. Some options for low-cost dental care are dental schools and dental hygiene schools (http://www.ada.org/en/coda/find-a-program/search-dental-programs); community health centers (http://www.hrsa.gov/index.html); Medicaid state-run programs (https://www.medicaid.gov); and Medicare for individuals 65 and older and for individuals who are under 65 with specific disabilities (https://www.medicare.gov/coverage/dental-services.html).

Fewer people are suffering from gum and tooth decay due to advancements in dentistry, health education, fluoridated water sources, and good personal hygiene. From a policy perspective, advancements are fairly inexpensive and cost effective. Community-wide water fluoridation costs $0.11 to $4.92 per person per year (for equipment, maintenance, and monitoring) and saves $5.49 to $93.19 per person per year (in treatment and other costs) with larger communities benefiting the most. On the downside, we have seen an increase in the number of preschool children suffering from tooth decay, and more education is needed to prevent baby bottle tooth decay. School-based dental sealant programs, where a thin layer of plastic is applied to the tooth as a protective barrier, can provide easily accessible dental services, protect the teeth of those who are at greatest risk, and promote lifelong oral hygiene habits.

Susana Leong

See also: Dean, Henry Trendley; Fluoridation; Health Belief Model; Nutrition

Further Reading

American Dental Association (ADA). (2016). *Mouth healthy.* Retrieved from http://www.mouthhealthy.org.

American Heart Association (AHA). (2013). *Dental health and heart disease.* Retrieved from http://www.heart.org/HEARTORG/HealthyLiving/Dental-Health-and-Heart-Health_UCM_459358_Article.jsp.

CDC/National Center for Health Statistics. (2016). *Oral and dental health.* Retrieved from http://www.cdc.gov/nchs/fastats/dental.htm.

Centers for Disease Control and Prevention (CDC). (2016). *Division of oral health.* Retrieved from http://www.cdc.gov/oralhealth.

Guide to Community Preventive Services. (2016). *Preventing dental caries: Community water fluoridation.* Retrieved from https://www.thecommunityguide.org/findings/dental-caries-cavities-community-water-fluoridation.

National Institute of Dental and Craniofacial Research. (2016). *Finding low-cost dental care.* Retrieved from http://www.nidcr.nih.gov/oralhealth/PopularPublications/FindingLowCostDentalCare.

U.S. Department of Health and Human Services. (2014). *Oral health.* Retrieved from http://www.hrsa.gov/publichealth/clinical/oralhealth.

U.S. Department of Health and Human Services. (2016). *Dental care: Adults.* Retrieved from https://medlineplus.gov/ency/article/001957.htm.

P

PANDEMIC

The word *pandemic* is a combination of two Greek words *pan*, meaning "all," and *demos*, meaning "people or population." Pandemic is defined as a rapid, widespread outbreak of any infectious disease(s), affecting multiple human populations across geographical countries and continents at a particular point in time. Examples of infectious disease pandemics are the 2009 H1N1, human immunodeficiency virus (HIV) and acquired immune deficiency syndrome (AIDS), and the 2013 to 2015 Ebola virus. According to the World Health Organization (WHO), the 2009 H1N1 pandemic was a worldwide infectious disease that caused 18,138 deaths across 74 countries, mostly in America, Asia, and Europe continents (2010). The HIV/AIDS pandemic has caused the death of 35 million people globally, with 36.7 million people currently living with HIV across the world (Joint United Nations Program on HIV/AIDS [UNAIDS], 2017; WHO, 2016). A 2016 Ebola virus report by the WHO identified 28,657 suspected cases and 11,325 deaths affecting people from Sierra Leone, Liberia, Guinea, Senegal, Nigeria, Mali, United Kingdom, Italy, Spain, and the United States (Piot, Muyembe, & Edmunds, 2014).

Pandemic is an epidemic of a worldwide spread or a global infectious disease outbreak. The World Health Organization (2014) identified past and present epidemic outbreaks that equate to pandemic or epidemic with the capabilities of become globally pandemic. The WHO (2014) identification includes:

- *Airborne diseases:* influenza (seasonal, pandemic, avian), severe acute respiratory syndrome (SARS), Middle East respiratory syndrome coronavirus (MERS-CoV)
- *Vector-borne diseases:* yellow fever, chikungunya, Zika virus, West Nile fever
- *Waterborne diseases:* cholera, shigellosis, typhoid fever
- *Rodent-borne diseases:* plague, leptospirosis, Hantavirus, Lassa fever, rickettsia (murine typhus)
- *Hemorrhagic fevers:* Ebola virus disease, Marburg virus disease, Crimean-Congo hemorrhagic fever, Rift Valley fever
- *Other zoonotic diseases:* Nipah virus infection, Hendra virus infection

Pandemics may affect susceptible and vulnerable populations of any age, gender, race, or geographical regions or continents. Initial impact is typically realized within 6 to 12 weeks. Further spread beyond 12 weeks depends on the causes and strength of the pathogen. Otherwise, mitigation can be very effective toward control and minimizing the number of deaths. Climatic factors such as prevailing winds transporting aerosol particles and migration of infected people, animals, or insects make it difficult to control a pandemic. Uncontrolled pandemic poses challenges to regional and global economies, strains available resources (medical supplies, vaccine, antiviral medications, medical facilities, hospital beds, and medical staff), and threatens human resources through illness and death. Government officials may contain the outbreak through travel restrictions, trade restrictions, border closures, or business restrictions. Vaccinations may be recommended in cases where there are known causes.

Classifications or Phases

Prior to the 2009 H1N1 outbreak pandemics were not classified. The WHO (2009) pandemic alert levels are:

- *Phase 1:* "No viruses circulating among animals have been reported to cause infections in humans."
- *Phase 2:* "An animal influenza virus circulating among domesticated or wild animals is known to have caused infection in humans, and is therefore considered a potential pandemic threat."
- *Phase 3:* "An animal or human-animal influenza reassortant virus has caused sporadic cases or small clusters of disease in people, but has not resulted in human-to-human transmission sufficient to sustain community-level outbreaks."
- *Phase 4:* "Characterized by verified human-to-human transmission of an animal or human-animal influenza reassortant virus able to cause 'community-level outbreaks.' The ability to cause sustained disease outbreaks in a community marks a significant upwards shift in the risk for a pandemic."
- *Phase 5:* "Characterized by human-to-human spread of the virus into at least two countries in one WHO region."
- *Phase 6:* "The pandemic phase, is characterized by community level outbreaks in at least one other country in a different WHO region in addition to the criteria defined in Phase 5. Designation of this phase will indicate that a global pandemic is under way."

The pandemic alert levels are used to guide the activities toward management and control of potential or actual disease outbreaks. The classifications provide the benchmark for assessing disease outbreaks and spread within a population. A limitation of the classification system is that the first three phases are often unrecognized, and the pathogen may achieve widespread circulation before official detection.

During Phases 1 to 3, public health agencies work to prevent and control pandemics by encouraging timely vaccinations among at-risk populations, establishing clinical guidelines on treatment and quarantine, educating the public on personal hygiene, proper handwashing, and social distancing (isolation, quarantine, and cancellation of public gatherings including school closures), and supporting health professionals in the use of personal protective equipment (PPE). These phases serve as an important precursor to preparedness with the goal of reducing morbidity and mortality, planning the roles of medical staff and stakeholders, allocating scarce health resources, and surveillance to control local epidemics from becoming global pandemics. Phase 4 poses significant risk of spreading to neighboring regions or other countries. During Phase 4, public health agencies refine surveillance operations, reduce risk among the vulnerable populations, and coordinate and communicate with various stakeholders. Phase 5 and Phase 6 are very high pandemic alert levels with planned mitigation such as implementing containment measures and deployment of vaccine. During Phases 5 and 6, part of the mitigation goals to reduce risk includes mobilization of resources to reduce the societal and economic impact of the affected countries, provision of pharmaceutical interventions through the various levels of the health system, and recovery. By following the WHO guidelines, local, regional, and global public health systems protect limited health resources and ensure effective response to potential pandemic threats.

Godyson Orji

See also: Centers for Disease Control and Prevention; Epidemic; Epidemiology; Global Health; Immigrant Health; Influenza; Middle Ages, Public Health in the; Vaccines; World Health Organization; Zombie Preparedness; *Controversies in Public Health:* Controversy 3; Controversy 5

Further Reading

Joint United Nations Program on HIV/AIDS (UNAIDS). (2017). *UNAIDS data 2017.* Retrieved from http://www.unaids.org/sites/default/files/media_asset/20170720_Data_book_2017_en.pdf.

Piot, P., Muyembe, J. J., & Edmunds, W. J. (2014). Ebola in West Africa: From disease outbreak to humanitarian crisis. *The Lancet Infectious Diseases, 14*(11), 1034–1035. Retrieved fromhttp://dx.doi.org/10.1016/S1473-3099(14)70956-9.

World Health Organization (WHO). (2009). *Current WHO phase of pandemic alert for pandemic (H1N1) 2009.* Retrieved from http://www.who.int/csr/disease/swineflu/phase/en/.

World Health Organization (WHO). (2010). Pandemic (H1N1) 2009–update 103. Retrieved from http://www.who.int/csr/don/2010_06_04/en/.

World Health Organization (WHO). (2014). Pandemic and epidemic diseases (PED). Retrieved from www.who.int/csr/disease/WHO_PED_flyer_2014.PDF.

World Health Organization (WHO). (2016). *Global health observatory (GHO) data HIV/AIDS.* Retrieved from http://www.who.int/gho/hiv/en/.

PASTEUR, LOUIS (1822–1895)

French chemist Louis Pasteur is known as the Father of Microbiology for his landmark discoveries in the germ theory of disease, vaccinations, and safe methods of food preservation. His experiments in bacteriology and immunology provided valuable information that helped to significantly reduce mortality due to infectious diseases in the 20th century.

Pasteur was born on December 27, 1822, in Dôle, France, to Jeanne-Etiennette (Roqui) and Jean-Joseph Pasteur. The son of a tanner, Pasteur was not particularly studious. He enjoyed drawing and intended to study art. In 1840, he earned his bachelor of letters degree at the Collège Royal de Besançon. He worked as a tutor at the college while taking science courses and eventually earning a general degree in science. In 1842, Pasteur studied for his master of science degree at the École Normale Supérieure in Paris. In 1849, he was appointed acting professor of chemistry at the University of Strasbourg. From 1854 to 1857 he was professor of chemistry and dean of sciences at the University of Lille, eventually returning to the École Normale Supérieure as administrator and director of scientific studies. In 1867 the Sorbonne appointed him professor of chemistry.

From his early work on crystals, such as those of tartaric acid (a product in the fermentation of grapes), Pasteur proceeded to examine the process of fermentation itself, a topic that would provide him with important background information and methods for his later research on contagious diseases. Yeast had been thought to be a chemical structure that served as a catalyst in the conversion of sugar into alcohol, but Pasteur discovered that yeast was organic matter, feeding on sugar and thus producing alcohol. When wine soured, it simply indicated the presence of the "wrong" kind of microorganisms. Pasteur conducted numerous experiments to prove his point, also examining the souring of milk. Pasteur's discoveries raised the question of how microorganisms got into the wine. At the time, scientists believed in spontaneous generation; microorganisms could come into existence without parental organisms. Pasteur disproved spontaneous generation by demonstrating that nothing would happen with a fermentable fluid when surrounded by sterile air. As soon as regular air was brought in contact with the substance, microorganisms began to develop. Hence, he concluded that air contains spores of microbes.

The next step for Pasteur was to examine the problem of contagious diseases that seemed to spread through direct or indirect contact. The question was whether microorganisms could possibly cause these as well. There had been germ theories of disease for a long time, yet they could not be proven until Pasteur's day. Pasteur was aware of these theories, and in 1857 he became convinced that microorganisms might also be responsible for infectious diseases. Though at first it was only a theoretical concept, in the mid-1860s Pasteur began to work on an actual problem: he was asked to examine a deadly disease of the silkworm, which threatened to ruin the silk industry in France. By the late 1860s Pasteur had identified two different silkworm diseases and the microbes that were responsible for them. Although in the middle of his investigation Pasteur suffered a stroke that left the left half of his body permanently paralyzed, he continued to work.

Pasteur's findings did not have an immediate effect, as many physicians did not think that a link existed between the ailments of the silkworm and those of human beings. In 1876 and 1877, however, Pasteur showed that microorganisms were the cause for anthrax disease in animals and human beings. At about the same time, Robert Koch came to the same conclusion. In 1877 Pasteur published a study on anthrax, a paper that became a significant document in supporting the germ theory of disease. Pasteur applied the methods he had used in his experiments with fermentation to prove that anthrax bacteria spread the disease. These experiments showed that no matter how often an infected substance was passed from animal to animal, anthrax bacteria continued to multiply and thus remained potentially as deadly as in the blood of the first infected animal.

Louis Pasteur creates a vaccine against the highly fatal bacterium anthrax. (Library of Congress)

Once he had established the germ theory of disease, Pasteur wondered what could be done to protect human beings and animals from deadly infectious diseases. He thus became interested in the concept of vaccination that had first been applied by the English physician Edward Jenner. Pasteur realized that a germ can change and consequently can actually be used as a vaccine. He first experimented with the problem of fowl cholera in chickens and found that some cultures of microorganisms did not cause the disease and instead made chickens resistant against virulent cultures in the future. Pasteur became convinced that it would be possible to produce vaccine in the laboratory. He proceeded to create a vaccine against anthrax, the effectiveness of which he demonstrated in a well-publicized demonstration in 1881. However, his antirabies treatment is usually cited as Pasteur's greatest triumph. In July 1885 he successfully treated the first human being, Joseph Meister, a boy suffering from rabid dog bites.

Pasteur's own microbiological research center, the Pasteur Institute, was inaugurated in Paris in 1888. Even before the opening of the institute, Pasteur had many students who would make important contributions to microbiology. Pasteur believed that many factors, other than microorganisms, effect the course of infectious illnesses, such as the hereditary constitution of a patient, nutritional state, emotional equilibrium, season of the year, and climate.

Pasteur died on September 28, 1895, in Marnes-la-Coquette, France. Today the Pasteur Institute is a private nonprofit foundation with about 20 establishments on five different continents. Research is focused on fighting infectious viral, bacterial, and parasitic diseases such as AIDS.

Anja Becker and Sally Kuykendall

See also: Bioterrorism; Emergency Preparedness and Response; Food Safety; Infectious Diseases; Jenner, Edward; Koch, Heinrich Hermann Robert; Sabin, Florence Rena; Vaccines

Further Reading

Achievements in public health, 1900–1999: Control of infectious diseases. (1999). *Morbidity and Mortality Weekly Report*, *48*(29), 621–629. Retrieved from https://www.cdc.gov/mmwr/preview/mmwrhtml/mm4829a1.htm.

Debré, P. (1998). *Louis Pasteur.* Baltimore: Johns Hopkins University Press.

Dubos, R. (1988). *Pasteur and modern science.* Madison, WI: Science Tech.

Geison, G. L. (1995). *The private science of Louis Pasteur.* Princeton, NJ: Princeton University Press.

PATIENT SAFETY

Patient safety is a field of health care that focuses on the prevention of adverse effects or events suffered by patients because of health care intervention. Examples of adverse events include medication errors, surgery on the wrong body part, iatrogenic infections, patient falls, or impersonation of hospital staff to commit a crime. In 1999, the Institute of Medicine issued the landmark report, *To Err Is Human.* The report noted that approximately 100,000 patients die each year due to lapses in patient safety. The Institute of Medicine challenged the health care industry to reduce the number of iatrogenic incidents and deaths. Over the next 10 years, health care systems undertook risk management efforts to reverse the alarming statistics. Despite the efforts, data suggest that there has been no real improvement. The upward trend continues. Death due to iatrogenic events is one the leading causes of mortality in the United States. In addition to deaths, there are numerous other health care–related events resulting in injury or disability. The actual number of incidents is difficult to measure. Occurrences are not always reported as a medical event or error. The reasons for such errors are complex and multifactorial. Everyone has a role in making health care safe, including the providers, the health care team, and the patient. As consumers of health care, it is important for patients to know and practice strategies to enhance patient safety.

The patient is the hub of the health care spokes of a wheel that need to work together to assure patient safety. Patients should be engaged, actively involved, and informed of their health care concerns, recommended treatment, and medications. Patients and families that understand their care and the reasons for treatment more readily identify potential errors and play a significant role in avoiding events. Anticipating the possibility that an event may occur, and taking steps to avoid problems, is the role that all participants in health care, including the patient, need to pursue to manage the risks that are associated with health care. A proactive role by the patient and family will help to decrease risk. Patients should take part in discussions and decisions regarding the care that is needed. Engaged and involved patients become better health care consumers by seeking information about illnesses or conditions that affect them. Asking questions of physicians and their assistants, as well as the health care team, helps patients to have a better understanding of their diagnosis and treatment. The patient may consider obtaining a second opinion to reassure best possible treatment options are being considered. Health care consumers should pay attention to care and treatment; if something does not seem right, bring it to the attention of the care team. Health care consumers should keep track of their medical history by maintaining a log or journal of important medical issues as well as dates of treatments and initiation of medications. The journal should include medical conditions, illnesses, immunizations, allergies, and hospitalizations. A responsibility of the health care consumer is to prepare for physician appointments by writing down questions regarding health problems, change in medicines, medical tests, surgery, or treatment options. During the actual appointment with the physician, refer to the list and ask pertinent questions. Take notes and if there is something not understood, request a further explanation. Clarify with the physician when follow-up care is needed if the medical symptoms should continue.

The physician should be informed of things that may affect treatment, including previous conditions, reactions to medications and treatments, and allergies and religious beliefs that could impact the care provided (e.g., administration of blood products). Decreasing risks for patient safety continue following the physician appointment. The health care consumer should follow physician instructions by obtaining prescriptions and scheduling tests, lab work, and follow-up appointments. Medications should be taken exactly as prescribed. When tests and studies are completed, make sure the results are obtained. The patient should not assume that "No news is good news." If there is no communication regarding test results, contact the physician to verify the test results.

Medication events are usually preventable, but can occur when medication is not taken as prescribed. Lack of communication, illegible handwriting, and not fully understanding the purpose of the medication or how to take it are risk factors that can result in errors. These events can occur at the time the medication is prescribed by the physician, dispensed by the pharmacist or at time of administration, and can result in risks for health care consumers. Prevention measures include scrutiny and observation of medications and instructions. The best prevention measure is to ask questions, especially if something does not seem correct. Inform the physician of every medication that is being taken, including over-the-counter medications, vitamins, and herbal supplements. A current list of all medications should be maintained and kept in a wallet or purse to have it readily available for physician visits or emergencies.

Health care consumers can also play a role in inpatient medication safety. The hospital staff and providers should be informed of all medications that are being taken by the consumer, including over-the-counter medications, vitamins, and herbal supplements. Lists of allergies should include those related to food, Latex, and intravenous dye as well as the reactions that occur when consumed or contact occurs. The consumer should have an identification band on at all times that should be verified by all staff prior to administration of medications, lab work, tests, and treatments. The verification should be completed before initiation of medications. If the medication does not appear to be correct, question if it is correct before taking the medication. The transition from inpatient status to home at time of discharge can cause discrepancies and potential medication events. Before leaving the hospital, there should be a review of the medications that were taken prior to admission and the ones that are to be taken when returning home. The review should include the time the medication was last taken and when the next dose will be due. If a medication that was taken prior to admission is not discussed at time of discharge, question if it is to be resumed at home. Question any concerns and follow instructions for medications at home.

Health care acquired infections are ones that occur while being treated for a health-related diagnosis, and an infection occurs while under treatment. Infections can occur in hospitals, outpatient clinics, dialysis centers, and long-term care facilities. Prevention is the key to decrease the risk of infection. Frequent handwashing by health care staff, patients, and visitors is very important as a preventive measure. Take antibiotics as directed and for as long as requested by the physician. Preparation for surgery includes infection preventive measures. Patients are usually required to wash with an antibacterial soap prior to surgery and to use an antibacterial ointment in the nares of the nose. Patients play a key role in preventing infections by following the preventive measures required before surgery.

There are times surgery is needed to correct a medical problem. Preventive safety measures need to be followed by patients and health care professionals to decrease the risk of a surgical event or occurrence. Each physician, nurse, and health care staff that comes in contact with the patient prior to and during surgery will ask the patient to state his or her name, date of birth, and to confirm surgical procedure to be completed. The patient needs to answer the questions each time. This is a safety measure and not meant to be an annoyance or inconvenience. Surgical sites should be marked by the physician to assure that the correct side is verified by all staff involved with the procedure. At any time that the patient has a concern about the procedure, questions should be asked.

In 2002, The Joint Commission, the accrediting body for health care facilities, established the Speak Up program. S-P-E-A-K-U-P for Patient Safety encourages health consumers to recognize the need to be engaged and involved with their care. The acronym encourages patients to ask questions and to voice their concerns, to pay attention to care received, and to be knowledgeable about their illness and medications. When in doubt, patients should speak up and ask questions, without hesitation.

Health care organizations are focused on patient safety and assuring that preventive measures are in place to decrease the risk of harm or injury. All members of the health care team and the patient have a responsibility for patient safety. Engaged patients are informed patients. Understanding patient safety practices is the first step to navigating the health care system safely.

Kristie Lowery

See also: American Medical Association; Antibiotic Resistance; Emergency Medical Treatment and Labor Act; Handwashing; Health Information Management; Health Insurance Portability and Accountability Act; Infectious Diseases; Prescription Drugs; *Controversies in Public Health:* Controversy 1; Controversy 2

Further Reading

Centers for Disease Control and Prevention (CDC). (2014). *Patient safety: What you can do to be a safe patient.* Retrieved from http://www.cdc.gov/HAI/patientSafety/patient-safety.html.

The Joint Commission. (2002). *Speak Up initiatives.* Retrieved from http://www.jointcommission.org/speakup.aspx.

Kohn, L. T., Corrigan, J., & Donaldson, M. S. (2000). *To err is human: Building a safer health system.* Washington, DC: National Academy Press.

PENICILLIN

Antibiotics, particularly penicillin, are one of the most important public health advances of all time. Penicillin was the first known antibiotic, and before it was discovered, infectious diseases were the leading cause of death around the world.

Penicillin is an antibiotic that falls under the group called B-lactams. This grouping is based on its chemical structure, which contains a B-lactam ring. Penicillin binds to proteins contained within certain bacteria, triggering impairment of the bacteria's cell wall. This impairment causes the cell to die off, inhibiting the growth of the bacteria. Penicillin is considered "bactericidal" since it kills the cells, as opposed to slowing them down. It is available as penicillin V and penicillin G. Penicillin G is available as penicillin G sodium, penicillin G benzathine, and penicillin G potassium, based on variations in its chemical structure. Penicillin V is available as penicillin V potassium with a unique ability to uphold stability in an acidic environment. Penicillin G is administered intravenously (IV) or intramuscularly (IM) but is not stable in an acidic environment; therefore, if administered orally penicillin G becomes ineffective. In contrast, penicillin V potassium has the ability to be administered orally and finds success in an acidic environment, holding up against gastric acid found within the stomach, and is therefore available as an oral tablet and oral liquid.

Penicillin is dosed in units with an average dose of penicillin G, ranging from 300,000 units to 4 million units on an every 6- to 8-hour basis. For the venereal disease syphilis, penicillin G is given as a large injection and for a multitude of infections. Penicillin V is administered in tablets and oral solution—the average dose ranging from 250 mg (400,000 units) to 500 mg (800,000 units) every 6 to 8 hours from 7 to 20 days (National Library of Medicine, 2015a).

Penicillin was discovered in London (1928) by Alexander Fleming—a researcher who focused on the characteristic properties of the blood and its ability to fight against bacteria. While conducting another study, Fleming discovered a mold that was growing due to contamination in one of his laboratory dishes. He realized the mold was destroying staphylococci bacteria. When viewing areas of the mold, a ring was seen around each area of mold that was free of any staphylococci. With this discovery, Fleming disbanded his other experiments and focused his energy on identifying this mold for its potential affects to fight infectious diseases. Fleming isolated the mold and was able to identify its properties conclusive with *Penicillium notatum*. Hence, the name Penicillium converted to penicillin. Although there was still much to investigate, Fleming published his findings in 1929, indicating the potential use of penicillin in treating certain infectious diseases (Wennergren & Lagercrantz, 2007).

Fleming's experiments failed clinical attempts with penicillin, but he continued to seek its use. He found penicillin to be unstable and sought out additional ways to concentrate the strains. In 1940, Ernst B. Chain and Sir William Dunn successfully purified penicillin crude extract. Chain, who was a chemist, and Dunn, a pathologist, had been working in similar experimental areas as Fleming. Chain and Dunn discovered Fleming's 1929 publication and continued their investigation in mice, showing increased survival rates among mice that had been infected with streptococci. With results published in 1940 in *The Lancet*, studies were then initiated in human trials, and Fleming came back to the forefront with his research. After successful treatment of one of Fleming's dear friends via the use of penicillin, London news flurried with announcements of this groundbreaking finding (Wennergren & Lagercrantz, 2007).

Earning the Nobel Prize in Medicine in 1945, acknowledgment was made to Sir Alexander Fleming, Dr. Ernst B. Chain, and Sir Howard Flory. Penicillin became available during World War II to help treat wounds stricken by infection and to aid in the treatment of venereal disease and postwar recovery. Government officials coordinated the distribution of penicillin to military soldiers and finally to public distribution in March 1945 (Quinn, 2013).

Penicillin is prescribed for infections produced by gram positive bacteria, including streptococcus, staphylococcus aureus, and pneumococcus. These bacteria can cause infections including the skin and surrounding tissue, upper respiratory tract, pneumonia, wounds, and meningitis, Lyme disease, and syphilis, to name a few. One of the biggest challenges experienced with penicillin is with allergic reactions and bacterial resistance. Allergic reaction to penicillin occurs in approximately

8 percent of people in the United States whereby alternative antibiotics must be used. Allergic reactions can range from nonsevere to rare, but fatal, hypersensitivities. Penicillin allergies can be difficult to assess since many allergic reactions, when retested, may not present themselves again. These are called "unverified" penicillin allergies, and it is difficult to know if these reactions would occur again if administered the antibiotic. In the case of allergic reactions, many individuals are then switched to a class of antibiotics called cephalosporins or nonpenicillin beta-lactams (Macy, 2014).

Bacterial resistance is another huge obstacle with broad range antibiotic use and bacteria, which have mutated throughout the years. Cells that once died off when in contact with penicillin have now evolved against protein binding. Bacteria have developed the activity to work around B-lactam, and it is the B-lactam component that has provided such past success for penicillin. Bacteria have now started to produce something called B-lactamase—what researchers call drug resistant—due to changes in penicillin-binding proteins (PBPs) (Zervosen et al., 2012). B-lactamase produced by current bacteria breaks down the B-lactam ring of the penicillin, rendering it ineffective. Current bacteria also have altered their cell wall, changing their protein structure that was once an effective binding site for penicillin. Penicillin remains highly dependent on cellular proteins to bind to the cell, alter the cell wall, and produce death of the cell. As drug-resistant PBPs develop, the efficacy of penicillin continues to change (Macheboeuf et al., 2006).

Toxicity can occur with penicillin, which causes toxic effects to the liver, kidneys, and other organs. It is affected only against bacterial infections and should not be administered for viral infections. Although a person may feel better after the first few doses of penicillin, it is very important to continue with the full prescribed regimen of treatment. If the full length of treatment is interrupted, effectiveness can be decreased and bacterial resistance increased. The most common side effects seen with penicillin include nausea, vomiting, diarrhea, and gastrointestinal upset. Therefore penicillin is best taken one hour before meals or 45 minutes after meals to maintain absorption yet decrease gastrointestinal side effects. Ampicillin and amoxicillin are close cousins to penicillin with variations to their structure, allowing for, in some cases, better efficacy in ridding the body of certain bacteria (National Library of Medicine, 2015b).

Antibiotics have created a large breakthrough in the treatment of bacterial infections. With its discovery in 1928, penicillin has provided substantial treatment to numerous bacterial infections, creating the path for all current antibiotics on the market today. Penicillin continues to remain a large part of public policy, continuing to enhance the collaboration of scientific research. Penicillin mold strains continue to be used in the development of new antibiotics, new bacterial strain identification, and continued research regarding dosing, administration, and chemical stability of antibiotics. Although many pharmaceutical companies have decreased their research of antibiotics, penicillin still remains as one of the most widely studied chemical entities (Quinn, 2013). Drug resistance still remains as one of the major drawbacks to penicillin and continues to be heavily studied by chemists. Even though pharmaceutical manufacturers have decreased marketing of new penicillin-based antibiotics, PBPs remain a focus of researchers to decrease continued resistance and increase efficacy in the continued effort to cure infectious diseases (Macheboeuf et al., 2006).

Eileen L. Sullivan

See also: Antibiotic Resistance; Handwashing; Infectious Diseases; Prescription Drugs; Prevention; *Controversies in Public Health:* Controversy 2

Further Reading

Kardos, N., & Demain, A. L. (2011, November). Penicillin: The medicine with the greatest impact on therapeutic outcomes. *Applied Microbiology and Biotechnology*, *92*(4), 677–687.

Macheboeuf, P., Contreras-Martel, C., Job, V., Dideberg, O., & Dessen, A. (2006, September). Penicillin binding proteins: Key players in bacterial cell cycle and drug resistance processes. *FEMS Microbiology Reviews*, *30*(5), 673–691.

Macy, E. (2014, November). Penicillin and beta-lactam allergy: Epidemiology and diagnosis. *Current Allergy and Asthma Reports*, *14*(11), 476.

National Library of Medicine. (2015a). *Penicillin g and v.* Retrieved from http://livertox.nih.gov/PenicillinGandPenicillinV.htm.

National Library of Medicine. (2015b). *USP penicillin v potassium.* Retrieved from http://dailymed.nlm.nih.gov/dialymed/fda/fdaDrugXsl.

Quinn, R. (2013, March). Rethinking antibiotic research and development: World War II and the penicillin collaborative. *American Journal of Public Health*, *103*(3), 426–434.

Wennergren, G., & Langercrantz, H. (2007, January). One sometimes finds what one is not looking for (Sir Alexander Fleming): The most important medical discovery of the 20th century. *Acta Paediatrica (Oslo, Norway, 1992)*, *96*(1), 141–144.

Zervosen, A., Sauvage, E., Frère, J.-M., Charlier, P., & Luxen, A. (2012). Development of new drugs for an old target: The penicillin binding proteins. *Molecules (Basel, Switzerland)*, *17*(11), 12478–12505.

PHYSICAL ACTIVITY

Physical activity is any bodily movement that works muscles and requires more energy than resting (Brehm, 2014; National Heart, Lung, and Blood Institute [NHLBI], 2016). Some examples of physical activity are walking, running, dancing, and gardening. Physical activity is not the same as exercise. Exercise is a type of physical activity that is planned and structured, done with the intention of improving fitness and/or sport performance (Brehm, 2014; NHLBI, 2016). Some examples of exercise are weightlifting, taking a group exercise class, and playing on a sports team.

Physical inactivity has been classified as the fourth leading risk factor for mortality, causing over 3 million deaths around the world (WHO, 2010). Regular physical activity helps improve overall health and fitness, and reduces the risk for many chronic diseases (ODPHP, 2008). For example, being physically active lowers the risk of heart disease, stroke, Type 2 diabetes, depression, and some cancers. Adequate levels of physical activity also improve bone health and help control weight (ODPHP, 2008; WHO, 2010). In addition, people who are physically active tend to live longer (ODPHP, 2008).

Released in 2008 by the United States Department of Health and Human Services, the *Physical Activity Guidelines for Americans* provide evidence-based guidance to help Americans aged six and older understand how to improve their health through physical activity (ODPHP, 2008). This resource, the first publication of physical activity national guidelines, serves as the primary voice of the U.S. government's guidance on physical activity for Americans. The guidelines focus on three types of physical activity: aerobic, muscle strengthening, and bone strengthening.

Aerobic activities are those in which people move their large muscles rhythmically for a sustained period. Some examples of aerobic activity are running, bicycling, swimming, and dancing. Aerobic activities make a person's heart and cardiovascular system stronger by making the heart beat more rapidly to meet the demands of the activity. Aerobic activities can be done with light, moderate, or vigorous intensity. It is recommended that most physical activity be moderate or vigorous intensity,

Regular physical activity strengthens bones and muscles, including the heart muscle. (Kaspicreative/iStockphoto.com)

although light activity is better than no activity at all. Light-intensity activities are everyday activities that do not require very much effort, such as walking slowly or doing the dishes. During moderate-intensity activities, the heart will beat faster than usual and breathing will be harder than usual. The "talk test" is an easy way to assess intensity; people doing moderate-intensity activities can usually talk, but not sing, while doing the activity. During vigorous-intensity activity, when the heart beats much faster and breathing is much harder than usual, people generally are not able to say more than a few words without pausing for a breath. Although the intensity level of an activity varies depending on the person (e.g., gardening may be more difficult for some people than others), different activities have been classified as moderate or vigorous based on the amount of energy that the body tends to use while doing the activity. For example, moderate activity examples are bicycling slower than 10 miles per hour and brisk walking; vigorous activity examples are bicycling 10 miles per hour or faster, jogging, and running (NHLBI, 2016; ODPHP, 2008).

Muscle-strengthening activities increase bone strength, improve muscular fitness, and help maintain muscle mass by making muscles do more work than they are used to doing. Examples of muscle-strengthening activities include carrying heavy loads, lifting weights, or activities that use body weight as resistance (e.g., push-ups or pull-ups) (ODPHP, 2008).

Bone-strengthening activities promote bone growth and strength by placing a force on the bones, often through impact with the ground. Bone-strengthening activities can be aerobic and/or muscle strengthening. Some examples are running, jumping rope, playing basketball, and playing tennis (ODPHP, 2008).

For children and adolescents, the 2008 guidelines recommend engaging in at least one hour of physical activity each day. The guidelines also state that it is important to encourage youth to participate in activities that are enjoyable and age-appropriate, and offer variety. Most of the hour should be either moderate or vigorous activity, and vigorous activity should be included at least three days per week. In addition, youth should complete a muscle-strengthening and a bone-strengthening activity at least three days of the week.

For adults, the guidelines recommend engaging in at least 150 minutes per week of moderate or 75 minutes per week of vigorous aerobic physical activity. Adults also should participate in muscle-strengthening activities (involving all major muscle groups) on at least two days per week. In addition to specific guidelines for children and adults, the ODPHP also puts forth messages and guidelines for older adults, pregnant and postpartum women, adults with disabilities, and people with chronic health conditions (ODPHP, 2008).

The guidelines state that some physical activity is better than none, and that people who participate in any amount of activity gain some health benefits. In general, the benefits of physical activity outweigh the risks. Heart problems, for example, are rarely a result of physical activity; in most cases, physical activity–related heart problems happen to people who have existing heart conditions (NHLBI, 2016).

Despite the clear guidelines and scientific data that support the benefits of physical activity, many Americans do not get enough physical activity. Studies have shown that only about 20 percent of adults and 30 percent of high school students meet the physical activity guidelines put forth by the Office of Disease Prevention and Health Promotion (CDC, 2014). Rates of activity and inactivity vary geographically and demographically. Americans living in the South are more likely to be inactive compared to those living in other regions of the country. Lower physical activity levels have been observed among minority groups and those with lower socioeconomic status. More white adults (23 percent) meet the physical activity guidelines than black adults (18 percent) and Hispanic adults (16 percent). Adults with more education are more likely to meet the activity guidelines than adults with less education. Finally, men (54 percent) are more likely than women (46 percent) to meet the guidelines (CDC, 2014).

Physical inactivity is an important public health issue, requiring consideration from policy makers, educators, practitioners, researchers, and public health professionals, all of whom play a role in people's understanding of and ability to carry out physical activity guidelines. Although the 2008 *Physical Activity Guidelines for Americans* provide an authoritative voice on physical activity and health, disparities in and levels of physical activity suggest that there is more to be done. The ODPHP is currently working with the CDC, the National Institutes of Health, and the President's Council on Fitness, Sports, and Nutrition to develop a second edition of the physical activity guidelines, estimated to be released in 2018. The second edition is expected to build on the first, with the addition of information about federal physical activity and education programs. Recommendations to improve people's activity levels include (1) encouraging funding of research that will lead to a more comprehensive understanding of how to measure, monitor, and improve physical activity levels; (2) creating or modifying environments that facilitate walking or bicycling (e.g., safer sidewalks, crosswalks, and bike lanes); and (3) supporting the development of physical activity policy, including school policies that focus on physical activity (CDC, 2014; WHO, 2010). Following these suggestions may help to address the gap that currently exists between the physical activity recommendations and the reported physical activity levels.

Elizabeth Y. Barnett

See also: Body Mass Index; Diabetes Mellitus; Healthy Places; Heart Disease; Heart Truth® (Red Dress) Campaign, The; Hypertension; Leading Health Indicators; Nutrition; Obesity; PRECEDE-PROCEED Planning Model; Prevention; Social Determinants of Health; Social Ecological Model

Further Reading

Brehm, B. A. (Ed.). (2014). *Psychology of health and fitness*. Philadelphia: F. A. Davis.

Centers for Disease Control and Prevention (CDC). (2014). *Facts about physical activity.* Retrieved from https://www.cdc.gov/physicalactivity/data/facts.htm.

National Heart, Lung, and Blood Institute. (2016). *Physical activity and your heart.* Retrieved from https://www.nhlbi.nih.gov/health/health-topics/topics/phys.

Office of Disease Prevention and Health Promotion (ODPHP). (2008). *2008 Physical activity guidelines for Americans summary.* Retrieved from http://www.health.gov/paguidelines/guidelines/summary.aspx.

World Health Organization (WHO). (2010). *Global recommendations on physical activity for health.* Geneva: Author.

PLANNED PARENTHOOD

Planned Parenthood Federation of America, Inc. (Planned Parenthood) is a non-profit organization that provides sexual and reproductive health care to men and women. The organization provides 5 million services, regardless of sexual orientation, gender identity and expression, or ability to pay (Planned Parenthood 2015–2016 Annual Report, 2017). In the United States, 2.4 million men, women, and young adults utilized a Planned Parenthood facility in 2015. The majority (85 percent) of those who accessed services at Planned Parenthood were 20 years or older, with 11 percent of the population served being men (Planned Parenthood 2015–2016 Annual Report, 2017). Services include low-cost sexual, reproductive, and preventative health care, comprehensive sex education, and advocacy. Programs are designed to advance health equity and reproductive justice and to address the societal barriers that inhibit women's reproductive autonomy (Stevens, 2017, p. 8; "What Is Planned Parenthood's Mission Statement?" 2017).

History

The origins of Planned Parenthood date back a century ago. Margaret Sanger and her sister, Ethel Byrne, established the first birth control clinic on October 16, 1916, in Brooklyn, New York. Sanger was later jailed for sharing information on birth control, catapulting her to the forefront of the reproductive rights movement. The history of Planned Parenthood is not only rooted in Sanger's relentless fight for access to birth control and family planning, but also in her controversial beliefs in eugenics (a doctrine that supports forced or planned breeding and sterilization) (Burke & Castaneda, 2007). Sanger's nuanced relationship with the eugenics movement was strategically used to develop a language that legitimized birth control, moving the conversation away from social welfare and into the realm of science (Ordover, 2003, p. 138). Despite her belief that all women are entitled to sexual and reproductive autonomy, Sanger's legacy is tainted with the development of class and disability-based eugenics doctrine and the endorsement of race-based surgical experimentation. Planned Parenthood openly addresses this aspect of their founder's convoluted beliefs in order to create an inclusive discourse that elevates reproductive justice for all women today (Ordover, 2003).

Through the leadership of the current president, Cecil Richards, Planned Parenthood provides a wide array of services at more than 600 active health care centers nationwide (Planned Parenthood 2015–2016 Annual Report, 2017). These services include reproductive and sexual health care, preventative services, LGBT services, abortion services, men and women's general services, and patient education such as cancer screening and birthing classes ("Our Services," 2017). In 2015, Planned Parenthood, along with their 56 governed affiliates, provided health care services to 2.4 million people Planned Parenthood 2015–2016 Annual Report, 2017). Of those services provided, 45 percent were STI testing and treatment, 30 percent were contraception services, 14 percent were other women's health services, 7 percent were cancer screenings, 3 percent were abortion services, and the remaining 1 percent defined as other services (Planned Parenthood 2015–2016 Annual Report, 2017). As the largest provider of sex education in the United States—reaching schools, communities, incarcerated populations, and faith-based entities through various programs provided by the organization—Planned Parenthood is also spearheading the movement for comprehensive sex education. This is most evident in the middle school program, *Get Real: Sex Education That Works*, an age appropriate school-based program with interactive family activities recently placed on the U.S. Department of Health and Human Services list of evidence-based sex education programs in 2015 ("Get Real," 2015).

Planned Parenthood also provides interactive online tools such as the *Online Health Services (OHS) Program*, which gives users easy access to contraceptives, as well as medication for urinary tract infections; *Consent 10*, an online video series that takes an in depth look into consent; as well as their app, *Spot On*, a period tracker that helps women predict their menstrual cycle, locate clinics nearby, and provides tips from Planned Parenthood providers. Planned Parenthood was recently showcased at the Sun Dance Festival and won a People's Choice Award for their documentary fiction, *Across the Line*, a virtual reality that walks the viewer through the eyes of a patient seeking abortion services. Through global partnerships, Planned Parenthood works with 12 countries that foster 230,000 mobile sites for reproductive education and services worldwide (Planned Parenthood 2015–2016 Annual Report," 2017). More recently, Planned Parenthood engaged religious leaders as critical community stakeholders in Burkina Faso by educating them on the importance of sexual and reproductive health to promote culturally relevant ideals around the value of family and community.

Despite these positive impacts, Planned Parenthood faces many obstacles. With opposition from conservative right-wing, anti-choice politicians, Congress recently voted to block over $200 million in Title X funding to Planned Parenthood and any facility that provides abortion services (Desjardins, 2017). Additionally, 24 states have attempted to remove Planned Parenthood health centers and restrict their ability to participate in the Title X program or be refunded by Medicaid. Extremists have also used deadly force. A more recent case took place in a Colorado Springs center in November 2015 where a gunman entered a facility and killed three innocent people. Finally, recent allegations claiming that Planned Parenthood sold fetal tissue in an anti–Planned Parenthood documentary was recently discredited and the documentary's creators charged with 17 felonies in the state of California (Karimi, 2017). Despite false allegations, political opposition, and physical attacks, Planned Parenthood continues to fight back, filing suits against the removal of health facilities that block access to services and challenging states that have falsely claimed the organization profited from fetal tissue donation.

Planned Parenthood continues to create new opportunities to support the sexual and reproductive health of women, men, and youth both here and abroad. Presently, Planned Parenthood is looking to design more comprehensive health care through the expansion of services to the trans community as well as men. By sponsoring partnerships such as Trust Black Women and Latino Community Investment Grants, Planned Parenthood's future work involves amplifying the voices of women of color as they work closely with leaders and organizations to elevate the reproductive justice agenda and increase service use in black and brown communities.

Additionally, Planned Parenthoods around the country are working more closely with youth through young adult community programs such as *PPFA's Generation (PPGen)* and *Planned Parenthood Action Fund's Generation Action (PPGenAction)* to increase advocacy across generations. Both programs are campus groups across the United States, designed to enhance reproductive health and freedom by combating abortion stigma; addressing sexual assault on campuses; creating and advocating for innovative reproductive health legislation; and enhancing inclusivity regardless of race, sexual orientation, expression, and identity. The organization seeks to advance reproductive health by supporting an average of 70 research studies a year on topics ranging from contraception to the HPV vaccination (Planned Parenthood 2015–2016 Annual Report, 2017).

It is estimated that one in five women will use services at Planned Parenthood in her life (Planned Parenthood 2015–2016 Annual Report, 2017). For many, this organization is the only health care provider who can support vulnerable women in their time of need. For others, Planned Parenthood is a staple in their community known to provide care and services founded on respect and patient autonomy. Whether in support of or against Planned Parenthood, it must be acknowledged as fact that the defunding of this organization will result in the loss of more than 1.5 million people having access to health care and preventative services (Planned Parenthood 2015–2016 Annual Report, 2017). This not only includes safe and legal abortion services but access to routine screenings and care that support and sustain healthy communities worldwide. The acknowledgment of this fundamental fact herein lies the truth behind Planned Parenthood's tenacity and their relentless fight to provide access to services that sustain reproductive self-determination—no matter what.

Tenille J. Torres

See also: Family Planning; Maternal Health; Sanger, Margaret Louise Higgins; Women's Health

Further Reading

Burke, C. S., & Castaneda, C. J. (2007). The public and private history of eugenics: An introduction. *The Public Historian*, 29(3), 5–17. Retrieved from https://doi.org/10.1525/tph.2007.29.3.5.

Desjardins, L. (2017, March 30). *Why the Senate voted to block funding for Planned Parenthood and other abortion providers.* Retrieved from http://www.pbs.org/newshour/updates/senate-vote-block-abortion-funding-affects-planned-parenthood/.

"Get real: Comprehensive sex education that works" joins list of evidence-based programs from U.S. Department of Health and Human Services. (2015, February 5). Retrieved from https://www.plannedparenthood.org/planned-parenthood-massachusetts/newsroom/get-real-comprehensive-sex-education-that-works-joins-list-of-evidence-based-programs-from-us-department-of-health-and-human-ser.

Karimi, F. (2017, March 29). *Planned Parenthood: Anti-abortion activists behind secret videos charged—CNNPolitics.com.* Retrieved August 2, 2017, from http://www.cnn.com/2017/03/29/politics/planned-parenthood-video-charges/index.html.

Margaret Sanger—Our founder. (n.d.). Retrieved from https://www.plannedparenthood.org/uploads/filer_public/b5/d4/b5d47c32-89f2-45d9-b28c-243cb85f3f55/sanger_fact_sheet_oct_2016.pdf.

Ordover, N. (Ed.). (2003). Margaret Sanger and the eugenic compact. In *American Eugenics* (NED–New ed., pp. 137–158). Minneapolis: University of Minnesota Press. Retrieved from http://www.jstor.org/stable/10.5749/j.ctttt7tz.19.

Our services, affordable healthcare & sex education. (2017). Retrieved from https://www.plannedparenthood.org/get-care/our-services.

Planned Parenthood 2015–2016 annual report. (2017). Retrieved from https://www.plannedparenthood.org/uploads/filer_public/18/40/1840b04b-55d3-4c00-959d-11817023ffc8/20170526_annualreport_p02_singles.pdf.

Planned Parenthood at a glance. (2017). Retrieved from https://www.plannedparenthood.org/about-us/who-we-are/planned-parenthood-at-a-glance.

Stevens, A. B. (2017). What is reproductive justice? *Against the Current*, 32(188), 8–8.

What is Planned Parenthood's mission statement? (2017). Retrieved from https://www.plannedparenthood.org/about-us/who-we-are/mission.

POLIO

Polio is among one of the most well-known vaccine-preventable infectious diseases in the world. Also known as poliomyelitis, the polio disease is caused by an enterovirus called poliovirus. Like other enteroviruses, the poliovirus enters the gastrointestinal tract through the mouth and then spreads into the lymph nodes and the bloodstream. From the bloodstream, poliovirus can enter the central nervous system and cause permanent damage that leads to paralysis. In some cases, where paralysis occurs in muscles necessary for vital functions such as breathing, death will also occur.

The transmission of poliovirus between individuals typically occurs through a fecal-oral route. Usually, the poliovirus from infected patients' stools can contaminate the hands of the carrier, which then touch a variety of surfaces such as cooking or eating utensils. These then carry the poliovirus to the mouth of others who subsequently become infected themselves. This route of transmission is highly contagious. Research studies have found that nearly 100 percent of the household contacts of infected children showed antibodies that indicate the transmission of poliovirus (Centers for Disease Control and Prevention, 2000).

Regardless of the contagious nature of poliovirus, most affected children are asymptomatic and do not show any signs of being infected. The polioviruses are shed from their body through the stool with no central nervous system damage. It is important to note that the stool of these children is still contagious and could spread poliovirus to others. In a smaller subset of infected children, there are some minor symptoms such as low-grade fever, sore throat, or abnormal nerve sensations. Less than 1 percent of children infected with polio show "flaccid paralysis," which involves diminution of muscular reflexes and the aching or spasm of the muscles. In some of these children with "flaccid paralysis," muscle function never recovers to the same degree and therefore causes permanent mild to severe paralysis or even death (Centers for Disease Control and Prevention, 2015). Therefore, much emphasis has been placed on eradicating polio throughout the world with the use of vaccinations that build immunity to the poliovirus in both children and adults.

Although ancient artwork and descriptions have supported the claim that poliomyelitis has afflicted humanity for thousands of years, it was first definitively characterized by an English physician named Michael Underwood in the late 18th century, who described polio as a progressive debilitation of the lower extremities in children. Poliomyelitis outbreaks throughout Europe and the United States continued to be reported in the following century with worsening effect. Even one of the U.S. presidents in the mid-20th century, Franklin Delano Roosevelt, was thought to have suffered from poliomyelitis and was dependent on iron braces when walking. The peak polio outbreak in the United States was reached in 1952, when over 21,000 cases of paralytic poliomyelitis were reported in that year alone.

With the advent and spread of the poliovirus vaccine a few years after 1952, the incidence of poliomyelitis began to decline sharply until it was completely eradicated in the Western Hemisphere by 1991. Although poliomyelitis still occurs not uncommonly in Afghanistan, Pakistan, and Nigeria, the world as a whole has made remarkable progress through systematic vaccinations and polio education. Its incidence has diminished far below historic levels with generations of children throughout the world who have not experienced or even seen poliomyelitis paralysis. Private nongovernmental organizations such as the Bill and Melinda Gates Foundation and Rotary have been instrumental in providing the funding needed to eliminate poliomyelitis through the Global Polio Eradication Initiative alongside national and international governmental agencies such as the Centers for Disease Control, the United Nations Children's Fund, and the World Health Organization. Over $15 billion has been spent for polio eradication around the world since 1988, with another $7 billion anticipated to be spent between 2013 and 2019 (Global Polio Eradication Initiative, 2017).

Oral polio vaccine is administered to a young patient during Afghanistan's national immunization days in 2015. During immunization campaigns, polio teams go door-to-door immunizing all children under the age of five. (Shah Maria/AFP/Getty Images)

The poliovirus vaccine that has been responsible for this great advancement in polio eradication has itself undergone an evolution throughout its existence. Jonas Salk, an American medical virologist, discovered and developed the first poliovirus vaccine. He chose to leave it unpatented under the belief that public health should be a moral commitment. This inactivated poliovirus vaccine (IPV) was first licensed in 1955 and was hailed as a great accomplishment.

The IPV was used for approximately six years before being replaced with oral vaccines, which were themselves replaced by an enhanced-potency IPV by 1988. The enhanced IPV has become more commonly used since then, particularly in the United States. The enhanced IPV is very effective, with greater than 99 percent of vaccine recipients developing antibodies against all three major serotypes of poliovirus after three doses; this immunity is likewise suspected to be lifelong (Centers for Disease Control and Prevention, 2015).

Although the oral vaccine is still used in many parts of the world because of its efficacy and low cost, physicians in the United States use the enhanced IPV because it minimizes the risk of very rare negative side effects such as vaccine-associated paralytic polio. The future of polio eradication involves the building of capacity in developing countries to shift from oral vaccinations to IPV. Advancements in IPV manufacturing and logistical capacity are needed to lower costs, build supply stores, and allow for safe transportation to make IPV a feasible alternative to oral vaccines in developing countries.

Whatever form of the poliovirus vaccine is used, however, it has undoubtedly been credited with saving millions of lives from crippling paralysis and/or death in the United States and throughout the world since its inception. The advent of vaccinations has served to transform poliomyelitis from an epidemic threat into an eradicated disease in the course of several decades.

Shayan Waseh

See also: Cutter Incident, The; Epidemic; Infant Mortality; Infectious Diseases; Influenza; Roosevelt, Franklin Delano; Salk, Jonas; Vaccines; *Controversies in Public Health:* Controversy 3

Further Reading

Centers for Disease Control and Prevention. (2000). Updated recommendations of the Advisory Committee on Immunization Practices. *Morbidity and Mortality Weekly Report*, 49(RR-5), 1–22.

Centers for Disease Control and Prevention. (2015). *Epidemiology and prevention of vaccine-preventable diseases*. Washington, DC: Public Health Foundation.

Chan, M. (2014). The contribution of immunization: Saving millions of lives, and more. *Public Health Reports*, 129(S3), 7–8.

Global Polio Eradication Initiative. (2017). *History of polio*. Retrieved from http://polioeradication.org/polio-today/history-of-polio.

POPULATION HEALTH

The term "population health" appears increasingly in today's public health, health services, and administration arena, yet without a precise meaning. Although the general public tends to view "population health" as exchangeable with "public health," there is no general agreement on the use of the term among contemporary medical scientists and health administrators. To explain its origin, the term was first introduced to the public, arguably, by a group of Canadian medical researchers, Evans, Barer, and Marmor (1994), in their book *Why Are Some People Healthy and Others Not? The Determinants of Health of Populations*. Since then the meaning has undergone some changes and contexts. Two major meanings are used today. One meaning defines population health from the perspective of those who investigate causes of health disparity in a given population and thus defines the term as the "health outcomes of a population." Therefore, improving population health means *reducing the health disparities of at-risk populations*. The other meaning is "population health" from the standpoint of the general public's demand that the current health care system should be improved and promoting ways to a healthier lifestyle, thereby giving meaning the "general population's health status in reference to the existing health care systems and lifestyle." This definition sees "improving population health" as referring to *developing and enhancing the overall quality of the present health care system and promoting health-conscious culture among the general population.* The former sense of the term originates in *Why Are Some People Healthy and Others Not?* So it is the original or traditional meaning of the word. However, when Marmor and his colleagues first introduced it to the public, they never formally defined it in their essays. Rather, their work was focused on the understanding of the determinants of health of populations without giving a clear meaning to the term. It is later that the medical scientists David Kindig and Greg Stoddart undertook efforts to give a definitive meaning to the term, drawing on Marmor's work. In Kindig and Stoddart's 2003 article, "What Is Population Health?," they state that population health should be defined as "the health outcomes of a group of individuals, including the distribution of such outcomes within the group" (2003). And they add: "These populations often are geographic regions like nations or communities but also can be other groups, like employees, specific ethnic groups, disabled persons, or prisoners" (2007).

Those who understand population health in the traditional meaning see "population health" associated with the two fundamental inquiries: first, why some people live healthier and longer lives than others; second, how to ensure that every person has equal opportunity for quality life free of disease and disability. To answer the first, the researchers examine multiple varying determinants, such as the population's general income level, genetic traits, environmental exposures, communicable diseases, general work environment, work-life balance, availability of health care resources (and services), and others. The researchers' overall focus tends to be on economic factors, which are many times associated with geographic area. In other words, they believe that the causes of the health disparity should be investigated within or in reference to the economic framework. Their argument follows that the reason why life expectancy of residents in Appalachia is shorter and lifestyle is unhealthier than those living in the other parts of the eastern United States is primarily due to economic factors creating low incomes. This form of investigative inquiry has great common sense. It is a common truth that in a capitalist society an individual's income level determines length and quality of life. The wealthier one is, the better nutrition, recreational facilities, and health care one can access, and poverty creates a cycle. Physicians graduating from U.S. medical schools are reluctant to practice in poor communities. As a result, low income families have less access to quality health services.

How to improve the health of the underprivileged population is a serious challenge, which leads to the second concern of the population health inquiry, how to eliminate health disparities. The primary task involved here is to find relatively cost-effective ways of allocating health care resources and services to disadvantaged populations while also tackling the sources of health inequity. The financial-administrative concern is significant because, whether the population in question is seen in a global, domestic, or local level, the available resources are not unlimited. In most cases, policy makers are under tight budget constraints. Thus, achieving maximum return from the invested resources is a crucial part of population health thinking. Mechanisms to achieve the best cost benefit are expanding insurance coverage, increasing health education, promoting community health promotion programs, and using evidence-based programs.

The other prevalent meaning of "population health" used today is found in a group of researchers' effort to respond to the public's alleged demand or outcry that the current society can and should do better about providing health care. As a methodological solution, the researchers put their focus on improving the overall quality of the existing health care system and propagating health-conscious culture. In this scheme of thought, the population health is defined as the "general population's health status in reference to the existing health care system and the population's health lifestyle." The most organized type of this population health thinking may be found in Berwick, Nolan, and Whittington's 2008 article, "The Triple Aim: Care, Health, and Cost." Berwick and his colleagues, a team of medical researchers-administrators from the Institute for Health Improvement (IHI), argue that the U.S. health care system should pursue, simultaneously, three aims to improve its overall quality: patients' experience of health care, which includes quality and satisfaction; the health of populations; and reducing per capita costs of health care (2008). With respect to quality of care and patient satisfaction, 4 out of 10 Medicare patients treated for congestive heart failure are readmitted to the hospital within 90 days. Studies show that the rate can be reduced to less than 1 out of 10 readmissions. According to the 2006 WHO statistics, "the United States ranks thirty-first among nations on life expectancy, thirty-sixth on infant mortality, twenty-eighth on male healthy life expectancy, and twenty-ninth on female healthy life expectancy" (2008). Based on these data, Triple Aim scholars call for greater investment to improve the health care system, as well as to encourage healthier lifestyles in the entire population, including increased physical activity, healthy eating, and avoidance of smoking, alcohol, and other substances. Efforts to achieve this goal are clearly focused on improving the system for all populations typically in a national scale, instead of addressing the health inequality of specific populations, the fact of which has invited criticisms particularly from the users of the former meaning of population health. The main criticism is that this approach to population health draws attention away from the economic factor of the health care system. The critics also recommend that this approach to population health should use the terms "population health management," "population medicine," or "population health movement," instead of "population health." The two definitions of population health are neither logically contradictory to each other in their linguistic contents, nor practically opposed to each other when the policy implementations are carried out with good plans. Given that the former group of researchers' concern as a way of improving population health is primarily closing the gap of the health disparity of populations, they do not mean closing the gap by downgrading the quality of health for the wealthy but by uplifting the standard of care for the poor. The latter researchers can say that improving the general standard of health care system and educating the public in healthy lifestyle is an effective way to provide better health care for all, including the poor, though the disparity between the rich and the poor may be unavoidable. One important component measuring the success of any type of health care system is whether it makes the most vulnerable classes suffer less. The proposed program (e.g., Triple Aim) attempts to provide the most suffering population with a better health care *than now* by improving the system's general quality and thereby seeks medical justice, as much as the former group does. It is true that uplifting the general standard of health care will improve the quality of care for the poor. However, it remains also true that, as mentioned above, the group's emphasis and focus take attention away from the particular problems that the geographically isolated impoverished groups are facing. Thus, it is best to conceive both definitions of population health as complementary to each other. Accordingly, the health policy makers and administrators should be sensitive to the claims from both groups.

There are other interpretations of population health worthy of mention. Dunn and Hayes (1999) and Jacobson and Teutsch (n.d.) engage in a similar research on the health of population and health disparity as Kindig and Greg, but with slightly different foci. Dunn and Hayes pay particular attention to measurement and identify population health as the health of a population *measured by* health status indicators and influenced by social, economic, and physical determinants. The latter group proposes to clarify the ambiguity of the term by abandoning it and replacing population health with "total population health." Another prominent researcher, T. Kue Young, defines population health as "a conceptual framework for thinking about why some populations are healthier than others, as well as the policy development, research agenda, and resource allocation that flow from it." This definition sets the investigative perimeter to include health determinants affecting not just ill but the entire populations.

The many and various definitions of population health, backed by respectable scholarly positions, roughly fall into or revolve around two major meanings. Population health refers to health of the population, systems used to ensure and promote health, and seeking equality of health between various populations. More important than any particular scholarly definition is how to draft and implement effective health care policies and regulations based on science derived from the many definitions.

Marvin J. H. Lee

See also: Epidemiology; Ethics in Public Health and Population Health; Health Disparities; Social Determinants of Health

Further Reading

Berwick, D., Nolan, T., & Whittington, J. (2008). The triple aim: Care, health, and cost. *Health Affairs*, 27(3), 759–769.

Dunn, J. R., & Hayes, M. V. (1999). Toward a lexicon of population health. *Canadian Journal of Public Health, 90*(Suppl. 1), S7.

Evans, R. G., Barer, M. L., & Marmor, T. R. (1994). *Why are some people healthy and others not? The determinants of health of populations*. New York: Aldine de Gruyter.

Hartley, D. (2004). Rural health disparities, population health, and rural culture. *American Journal of Public Health*, *94*(10), 1675–1678.

Jacobson, D. M., & Teutsch, S. (n.d.). *An environmental scan of integrated approaches for defining and measuring total population health by the clinical care system, the government public health system, and stakeholder organizations.* Washington, DC: National Quality Forum. Retrieved from http://www.improvingpopulationhealth.org/PopHealthPhaseIICommissionedPaper.pdf.

Kindig, D., & Stoddart, G. (2003). What is population health? *American Journal of Public Health*, *93*(3), 380–383.

Kindig, D. A. (2007). Understanding population health terminology. *Milbank Quarterly*, *85*(1), 139.

Young, T. K. (2004). *Population health: Concepts and methods*. New York: Oxford University Press. doi:10.1093/acprof:oso/9780195158540.001.0001

PRECAUTION ADOPTION PROCESS MODEL (PAPM)

The precaution adoption process model (PAPM) presents the sequence of cognitive and behavior stages that individuals go through when confronted with a health hazard. The model proposes that when individuals first encounter a health issue, they are in a state of ignorance. As they gain more information on the topic, they move to a state of awareness and subsequently decide whether to address the problem. The stages or constructs are:

- Unaware of the issue
- Aware of the hazard, not concerned
- Concerned with the hazard and deciding on possible actions
- Deciding not to act

OR

- Deciding to act
- Acting
- Maintaining

Each PAPM stage has different characteristics of decision making and action as well as factors or determinants that influence the process. Public health professionals use the PAPM to study, plan, and understand individual motivation and behavior in health promotion and disease prevention.

There are several well-known stage models in the field of behavioral health. Stage models propose that people do not stop, start, or change health behaviors suddenly. Individuals go through stages. First, the individual must recognize the issue as a potential threat or desired change. After acknowledgment, the individual weighs the benefits and costs of change, develops a plan of action, implements the plan (act), and works to sustain the behavioral change. Stage theories are useful in that they define very clear steps and what an individual thinks and needs at a particular stage. The earliest and most well-recognized stage model, the transtheoretical model (TTM) or stages of change model was developed from observations of people who were trying to quit smoking (Prochaska & DiClemente, 1983). Initially, the smoker is unaware of the health consequences of smoking (unaware of the hazard). Small signs, such as a morning cough, smelly clothes, bad breath, stained teeth, the cost of cigarettes, or loss of free will may force the smoker to acknowledge health, social, and financial cost of smoking (aware of the hazard but not concerned). As the signs become unavoidable, the smoker will start to recognize the problem and investigate options (concerned with the hazard and deciding what to do). If the smoker decides to act, he or she will develop a plan of action. Action involves seeking professional help, destroying any remaining cigarettes, or purchasing nicotine replacement therapy. While the person is in action and maintenance stages, he needs to avoid places and people that might exacerbate cravings. Whether the individual is stopping a harmful behavior or adopting a positive behavior, there is a clear and logical sequence to changing behavior. The PAPM varies from the TTM in three ways. The PAPM adds an earlier stage of *completely unaware*; separates the first TTM stage, precontemplation, into *aware/not concerned* and *aware/deciding*; and separates the second TTM stage, contemplation, into *decided to act* and *decided not to act*. The PAPM categories provide further distinction of the different cognitive stages. A practical limitation of these refinements is that each stage requires a clear definition. In order to follow the PAPM with integrity, researchers and program planners must recruit and retain participants that represent each stage. This means many more program and study participants and greater costs to run the study or program.

In comparison to models that present behavioral change as a continuum, stage theories can be complex and challenging to use. The advantage of these models is that they apply to just about every intentional behavioral change from developing a daily routine of dental flossing to practicing regular breast self-exam or testicular self-exam. The PAPM has been used in disaster preparedness, mature driver safety, premenstrual syndrome, oral hygiene, falls in the elderly, and home radon testing. Further testing and refinement of the PAPM may help public health professionals to personalize disease prevention and health promotion programs to individual participants and have greater impact of health behaviors.

Sally Kuykendall

See also: Behavioral Health; Environmental Health; Evidence-Based Programs and Practices; Transtheoretical Model

Further Reading

Elliott, J. O., Seals, B. F., & Jacobson, M. P. (2007). Use of the Precaution Adoption Process Model to examine predictors of osteoprotective behavior in epilepsy. *Seizure: European Journal of Epilepsy*, *16*, 424–437. doi:10.1016/j.seizure.2007.02.016

Hassan, H., King, M., & Watt, K. (2017). Examination of the precaution adoption process model in understanding older drivers' behaviour: An explanatory study. *Transportation Research: Part F, 46,* 111–123. doi:10.1016/j.trf.2017.01.007

Prochaska, J. O., & DiClemente, C. C. (1983). Stages and processes of self-change of smoking: Toward an integrative model of change. *Journal of Consulting and Clinical Psychology, 51,* 390–395.

Weinstein, N. D. (1988). The precaution adoption process. *Health Psychology*, *7*(4), 355–386. doi:10.1037/0278-6133.7.4.355

Weinstein, N. D., & Sandman, P. M. (1992). A model of the precaution adoption process: Evidence from home radon testing. *Health Psychology*, *11*(3), 170–180. doi:10.1037/0278-6133.11.3.170

Weinstein, N. D., Sandman, P. M., & Blalock, S. J. (2008). The precaution adoption process model. In K. Glanz, B. K. Rimer, K. Viswanath, K. Glanz, B. K. Rimer, & K. Viswanath (Eds.), *Health behavior and health education: Theory, research, and practice* (4th ed., pp. 123–147). San Francisco: Jossey-Bass.

PRECEDE-PROCEED PLANNING MODEL

The *p*redisposing, *r*einforcing, and *e*nabling *c*onstructs in *e*ducational *d*iagnosis and *e*valuation—*p*olicy, *r*egulatory, and *o*rganizational *c*onstructs in *e*ducational and *e*nvironmental *d*evelopment (PRECEDE-PROCEED) planning model is a framework for public health program planning and evaluation (Green, Kreuter, Deeds, & Partridge, 1980). The model consists of nine phases: (1) social diagnosis, (2) epidemiological diagnosis, (3) behavioral and environmental diagnosis, (4) educational and organizational diagnosis, (5) administrative and policy diagnosis, (6) implementation, (7) process evaluation, (8) impact evaluation, and (9) outcome evaluation. The phases are represented as a diagram that starts with the desired goal of the project. Phase 1 identifies the health problem of interest, and Phases 2 to 5 examine factors that inhibit or promote the health issue. These moderating factors lead into Phase 6, public health actions, policies, or interventions. Phases 7 to 9 represent process and impact evaluations of the planned action, leading back to the health problem identified in Phase 1. The main advantage of the model is that it outlines the many, many factors the program planner or policy maker must consider when addressing complex health issues. Use of the model promotes efficiency and effectiveness of efforts. A disadvantage of the model is that it is very complex and requires a diverse set of knowledge and skills. It is easy to become lost in all of the possible options the model presents. The PRECEDE-PROCEED model is different from other public health models because it is typically used in conjunction with other public health models or theories, such as the health belief model or the transtheoretical model.

Phase 1 of the PRECEDE-PROCEED model is *social diagnosis*. In social diagnosis, the public health planner works with key stakeholders in the community to identify health concerns that interfere with *quality of life*. Consulting with members of the community, a concept known as *public participation,* ensures that the project identifies issues that community members believe are important, not the program planner. The process of gathering community consensus is time consuming, but it supports community empowerment, and community members will be more likely to support and sustain the effort. Defining the problem or quality of life issue may be difficult. For example, community members may express concern with increasing rates of Type 2 diabetes among area youth. Because Type 2 diabetes is a consequence of obesity or overweight, the true underlying issue is actually childhood obesity. Identifying the underlying problem rather than a consequence or symptom of the larger problem ensures that efforts are focused in the right direction and expands the possibility for grant funding, community collaborations, or other support.

Phase 2, *epidemiological diagnosis,* examines the health problems related to the quality of life issue. In addition to Type 2 diabetes, children who are overweight or obese are at risk for arthritis, asthma, impaired self-esteem, cardiovascular disease, and social discrimination. Through a needs assessment, public health program planners might gather data on children's weight from local schools, health clinics, or other sources. The needs assessment would enumerate and validate the community's concerns. The planning group would use the data to develop a measurable objective. For example, if the needs assessment showed that 16 percent of local youth were obese, the planning group may select a target goal of reducing obesity to 14.5 percent of area youth. The objective should be specific, measurable, accurate, realistic, and timely (SMART). The epidemiological diagnosis considers behavior, lifestyle, and environment that impact the quality of life issue. Phase 3, the *behavioral diagnosis,* may reveal lifestyle choices such as sedentary activities whereas the *environmental diagnosis* may reveal a lack of safe places to play. Phase 4 is *educational and organizational diagnosis*. This phase identifies enabling, predisposing, and reinforcing factors that initiate or maintain the desired behavioral change. Enabling factors are resources such as sports programs, access to recreational areas, or access to nutritious fresh fruits and vegetables. Predisposing factors are influences related to the individual, such as knowledge, attitudes, or beliefs that promote healthy weight. Predisposing factors that affect weight management include social attitudes, knowledge of nutrition information, or food preferences. Reinforcing factors are influences that occur subsequent to health actions, which strengthen the behavior. Reinforcing factors might be emotional incentives such as compliments or praise from peer or family in reaction to weight loss. Phase 5, *administrative and policy diagnosis,* identifies policies, assets, or conditions that promote or interfere with implementation. Policies limiting park usage could interfere with organized athletic groups. The program group would focus on organizing resources that promote physical activity and minimize barriers. The program, policy, or activity is implemented during Phase 6.

The final phases consist of evaluating the program activities. *Process evaluation* (Phase 7) measures short-term changes in the predisposing, reinforcing, and enabling factors. *Impact evaluation* (Phase 8) measures changes in behavioral and environmental factors. *Outcome evaluation* (Phase 9) measures how well the project affected quality of life. Did the project reach the goal of reducing childhood obesity to 14.5 percent? One limitation of this last phase is that it may take several years to realize changes. To implement the entire model, from start to finish, may not be possible within the two- to three-year time frame of many public health grants.

The PRECEDE-PROCEED planning model is used by public health planners to understand, investigate, and plan public health interventions. The model applies to complex health issues that are influenced by lifestyle, personal behaviors, the environment, public policy, and knowledge of health. It allows practitioners to think on a broad scale considering all of the factors, while still keeping focus on the primary quality of life issue.

Sally Kuykendall

See also: Community Organizing; Evaluation; Health Belief Model; Health Education; Health Policy; *Healthy People 2020*; Needs Assessment; Transtheoretical Model

Further Reading

Glanz, K., Lewis, F. M., & Rimer, B. K. (Eds.). (1997). *Health behavior and health education: Theory, research, and practice* (2nd ed.). San Francisco: Jossey-Bass.

Green, L. W., Kreuter, M. W., Deeds, S. G., & Partridge, K. B. (1980). *Health education planning: A diagnostic approach.* Mountain View, CA: Mayfield.

National Cancer Institute. (2005). *Theory at a glance: A guide for health promotion practice* (2nd ed.). NIH Publication Number 05-3896.

PRESCRIPTION DRUGS

Prescription drugs, or medications, continue to be prescribed at an increasing rate as disease states become more and more complex. Many individuals now seek to self-treat certain ailments with over-the-counter medications, but based on the severity of the ailment a prescribed medication may be necessary. Prescription medications are broken up into multiple categories, or classes, to include treatments to help fight infectious diseases, diabetes, chronic pain, high blood pressure, depression, mental illness, cancer, and gastrointestinal disorders, to name a few.

Prescription medication spending grew at the highest rate in 2014 with the last growth of this magnitude seen in 2011. Accounting for $373.9 billion in costs in 2014, which was up by 13.1 percent since 2001 (growth of 17 percent in spending), prescription medication sales increased due to medicines innovative in nature, patents that were not up for expiration, and prices that were listed as a higher dollar amount than previous years. Implementation of the Affordable Care Act (ACA) in 2014 expanded the ability for some patients to fill prescription medication requests than were able in previous years. Forty-two new ingredients, active in nature, were brought to the market in 2014, up from 36 introduced in 2013. Specialty medications continue to rise as illnesses become more and more complex with the majority of today's research focused on cancer (oncology), diabetes (antidiabetics), pain (analgesics), high blood pressure (antihypertensives), infectious diseases (antibacterials), and mental health (IMS Institute, 2015).

Medications to treat pain continue to be dispensed at a high rate by pharmacists. Continued focus is being placed on identifying safe practices behind prescribing and dispensing medications for pain relief as increased deaths are on a rise with the inappropriate use of pain medications by patients. Drug poisoning and misuse of pain medication called "opioids" has been on a rise since 1990 and is being called an epidemic of national magnitude (Paulozzi, Budnitz, & Xi, 2006). Prescription medication must be prescribed by health care professionals who are licensed to prescribe medication. Prescription medications are then filled and dispensed through a licensed pharmacy with final approval from a state licensed and boarded pharmacist. New research is being conducted to identify advanced roles of pharmacy technicians related to filling and checking of prescription medications providing pharmacists greater time to counsel patients on the proper use of such medications. Additional one-on-one time with pharmacists and patients has become increasingly necessary due to complex prescription medication dosing, decreased time spent with physicians, nurses and prescribers, and multiple prescription medications for many patients (Adams, Martin, & Stolpe, 2011).

Prescription medications must be approved by the Federal Drug Administration (FDA) and must follow a stringent approval process. This approval is called the "drug review process" and includes stages that must thoroughly be met in order for approval review. The drug review process is best described in 12 stages with the first stage being preclinical testing or animal testing. Once preclinical testing is complete, manufacturers submit an Investigational New Drug (IND) application, which describes proposed human testing. Human testing is then conducted in three phases: (1) healthy volunteers to identify any medication side effects, drug metabolism in the body, and excretion of the medication; (2) those affected by the disease or illness to show if the medication is effective; and (3) studies the safety and additional effectiveness of the medication (U.S. Food and Drug Administration, 2015a). Once all of these phases are met and safety and efficacy are ensured, the manufacturer can submit a New Drug Application (NDA) asking the FDA to consider approval. Drugs may enter into the animal testing stage and never make it to an NDA or review of approval by the FDA. All clinical testing must follow strict approvals starting with a protocol to explain the manufacturer's intent to study the drug, how they plan to perform these studies, and approval of a local institutional review board (IRB).

There are a number of medications that are on the market that treat the same illnesses and the same symptoms; however, medications may work very differently on different individuals. Brand medications are those that are patented by the founding manufacturing company. Once the medication goes off patent, the medication is available for generic companies to manufacture and sell. Generic medications are sometimes sought out by individuals as they can be less expensive, and insurance companies now seek to identify generic alternatives with the rising costs of prescription medications. Patients with and without prescription medication coverage many times struggle to pay for necessary medications. This can inadvertently result in the lack of medication adherence, where individuals may take less medication than prescribed to stretch the medication over longer periods of time. Illegal purchase of prescription medications can also occur where individuals purchase prescribed medications outside of the country to avoid the high U.S. medication costs. This can be dangerous to patients if the medication is of a different chemical formula, dosage, or quantity than prescribed by their health care professional (Kesselheim et al., 2015).

In 2000, researchers reported approximately 44,000 to 98,000 deaths annually in hospitals from medical errors with a high rate of these deaths occurring because of medication errors. In 1993, medication errors attributed to 7,391 deaths compared to 2,876 in 1983 (Institute of Medicine [U.S.] Committee on Quality of Health Care in America, 2000). The FDA currently reports one death per day from medication errors and approximately 1.3 million annual patient injuries in the United States due to "prescribing, repackaging, dispensing, administering, or monitoring" with causes resulting from communication gaps, confusion in names, directions, and abbreviations of prescription medications, and the lack of understanding of medication use by patients (U.S. Food and Drug Administration, 2015b). Enhanced systems must continually be put into place to help reduce the risk of errors faced with prescription medications (Adams, Martin, & Stolpe, 2011).

The terms "on label" and "off label" arise quite frequently when discussing prescription medications. "On label" is when the medication is prescribed for an FDA-approved use and listed in the FDA-approved package insert, or otherwise called "labeling" for that medication. "Off label" is when a medication is prescribed for a use, which has been discussed in the medical literature, but such a use has not been approved by the FDA and is therefore not listed in the FDA-approved package insert for that medication. Prescription medications used in an off label manner can offer great insight to the medical community and to drug manufacturers. However, since there is no FDA approval for these off label uses, risk versus benefit needs to fully be assessed by prescribing health care professionals. Important uses of prescription medications may be found accidentally through their use off label. It is, however, critical to keep in mind that the FDA approval process should be sought for all prescription medication uses to ensure the appropriate drug trials have been performed, safety and efficacy are properly shown, and the medication is reviewed in a multidisciplinary fashion (U.S. Food and Drug Administration, 2015a).

Continued education is necessary regarding prescription medications. Both health care professionals and patients require additional knowledge regarding the safety, efficacy, and proper use of such medications. As chronic illnesses rise and continue to become more complex, misuse potential rises with prescription medications. This misuse potential can be a result of increased illness-related symptoms, increased communication gaps between health care professionals and patients, increased dosing complexity of specialty medications, and changes in health care coverage regarding prescription medications. As one can attest, health care is in a state of significant change, and more and more focus must be placed on the safety, efficacy, and appropriate use of prescription medications.

Eileen L. Sullivan

See also: Affordable Care Act; Care, Access to; Elder Maltreatment; Food and Drug Administration; *Controversies in Public Health:* Controversy 1

Further Reading

Adams, A. J., Martin, S. J., & Stolpe, S. F. (2011, October 1). Tech-check-tech: A review of the evidence on its safety and benefits. *American Journal of Health-System Pharmacy, 68*(19), 1824–1833.

IMS Institute. (2015). *Medicine use and spending shifts: A review of the use of medicines in the U.S. in 2014.* Retrieved from http://www.fdanews.com/ext/resources/files/04-15/IIHI_Use_of_Medicines_Report_2015.pdf?1429048559.

Institute of Medicine (U.S.) Committee on Quality of Health Care in America. (2000). *To err is human: Building a safer health system.* In L. T. Kohn, J. M. Corrigan, & M. S. Donaldson (Eds.). Washington, DC: National Academies Press. Retrieved from http://www.ncbi.nlm.nih.gov/books/NBK225182/.

Kesselheim, A. S., Huybrechts, K. F., Choudhry, N. K., Fulchino, L. A., Isaman, D. L., Kowal, M. K., & Brennan, T. A. (2015, February). Prescription drug insurance coverage and patient health outcomes: A systematic review. *American Journal of Public Health, 105*(2), e17–e30.

Paulozzi, L. J., Budnitz, D. S., & Xi, Y. (2006, September). Increasing deaths from opioid analgesics in the United States. *Pharmacoepidemiology and Drug Safety, 15*(9), 618–627.

U.S. Food and Drug Administration. (2015a). *The FDA's drug review process: Ensuring drugs are safe and effective.* Retrieved from http://www.fda.gov.

U.S. Food and Drug Administration. (2015b). *U.S. Food and Drug Administration medication error report.* Retrieved from http://www.fda.gov/Drugs/DrugSafety/MedicationErrors/ucm080629.htm.

PREVENTION

Each year in the United States, approximately 600,000 people die of heart disease, 590,000 people die of cancer, 145,000 people die of lower respiratory illnesses, 136,000 people die of unintentional injuries, 128,000 people die of stroke and cerebrovascular diseases, 76,000 people die of diabetes, and 43,000 people die of suicide (National Center for Injury Prevention and Control, 2015). The majority of these deaths are linked to four lifestyle behaviors: high fat, high concentrated carbohydrate diet, lack of physical activity, tobacco use, and alcohol abuse (National Center for Chronic Disease Prevention and Health Promotion, 2009). The financial cost of lifestyle-related illnesses is enormous. Americans pay an average of $9,403 per year for health care (World Bank Group, 2017). Prevention is a medical strategy that aims to stop health problems before they start or before they progress to more serious problems. Prevention activities work by enhancing knowledge, attitudes, and behaviors or through policy or environmental actions. Over time, public health practitioners learned to tailor programs to the target population's level of risk. Despite a critical need for prevention programs, such programs frequently encounter cultural and political obstacles. American society is an impatient culture, a society that values instant results. Prevention programs offer delayed benefits. Thus, the hard work of prevention is often overlooked in favor of programs that promise instant results, even if the promises are false. Furthermore, cost versus benefit calculations can be difficult. When prevention is effective, health problems do not occur. It is difficult to measure a problem that does not occur, which means it is difficult to justify program costs.

The idea of preventive medicine emerged from several sources. As advancements in sanitation, microbiology, and immunizations reduced deaths due to infectious illness, medical professionals turned their attention to chronic illnesses. In 1949, the American Hospital Association, the American Medical Association, the American Public Health Association, and the American Public Welfare Association founded the Commission on Chronic Illness. The first objective of the commission was to:

> modify the attitude of society that chronic illness is hopeless; to substitute for the prevailing over-concentration on the provision of institutional care, a dynamic program designed as far as possible to prevent chronic illness, to minimize its disabling effects, and to restore its victims to a socially useful and economically productive place in the community. (Commission on Chronic Illness, 1949, p. 1344)

In the first of four volumes, the commission identified the importance and role of prevention. Primary prevention was defined as "averting the occurrence of disease," and secondary prevention was defined as "halting the progression of disease from its early unrecognized stage to a more severe one and preventing complications" (Commission on Chronic Illness, 1957, pp. 1–68). In 1953, Drs. Leavell and Clark published a handbook on preventive medicine for community practitioners. They presented a theoretical framework with five levels of prevention: (1) health promotion, (2) targeted protection, (3) early diagnosis and treatment, (4) disability limitation, and (5) rehabilitation. In later editions, Leavell and Clark reduced the framework to three levels, primary prevention (health promotion), secondary prevention (combining targeted protection and early diagnosis and treatment), and tertiary prevention (combining disability limitation and rehabilitation).

The emerging field of psychology formally entered the prevention arena in 1964. Several decades earlier, on November 28, 1942, 492 people died and hundreds were injured when Boston's popular Cocoanut Grove nightclub caught fire. Although the nightclub had a maximum occupancy rate of 460 people, more than 1,000 people crowded into the club that evening. A member of the staff lit a match so that he could see to change a lightbulb. The match ignited the fronds of fake palm trees and highly flammable wall coverings and decorations. The fire spread throughout the building. Fire exits were either hidden or nonfunctional. Patrons pushed and stampeded toward the main entrance. Piles of bodies jammed the revolving exit doors. The disaster shocked the nation. Because of the Cocoanut Grove fire, the nation initiated new fire safety regulations. Two psychiatrists at Massachusetts General Hospital—Eric Lindemann and Gerald Caplan—treated Cocoanut Grove survivors and family members of victims. Their clinical observations helped to develop crisis theory, how people respond to and recover from traumatic experiences. Using the framework of primary, secondary, and tertiary prevention, Caplan expanded the field of prevention into counseling, mental health, and public health (Caplan, 1964).

The idea of primary, secondary, and tertiary prevention applies to a vast array of public health problems. Primary prevention aims to stop the problem before it occurs. Secondary prevention aims to detect the problem early in order to halt progression. Tertiary prevention aims to stop adverse consequences after a problem has already begun. In the case of fires, primary prevention consists of eliminating fire hazards in the home and workplace, regulations against open flames, and fire safety education. Secondary prevention consists of smoke detectors, fire sprinkler systems, and functional fire escapes. Tertiary prevention includes specialized burn units, pain management, physical therapy, and mental health treatment.

In 1987, Dr. Robert S. Gordon Jr., special assistant to the director of the National Institutes of Health, suggested using a risk perspective for prevention activities. Gordon noted that the terms "primary," "secondary," and "tertiary" could be confusing to nonpractitioners. On the surface, primary sounds preferable to secondary, when, in fact, all three types of prevention are equal and necessary. Gordon also noted that the current terminology focused on biomedical chronology (before or after diagnosis). Public health and epidemiology consider level of risk. Gordon proposed the terms "universal prevention," "selective prevention," and "indicated prevention." Universal prevention focuses on preventing illness among the broad population regardless of level of risk. Selective prevention aims at people with heightened risk. Indicated prevention aims at people who currently manifest the behavior or condition. Gordon also differentiated between intervention and treatment, noting that treatment relieves symptoms while interventions are used for asymptomatic clients. Experts continue to refine the definitions with some advocating that indicated prevention should apply to both symptomatic and asymptomatic populations. Weisz, Sandler, Durlak, and Anton (2005) added two new categories of prevention to create the scale: health promotion/positive development strategies, universal, selective, indicated, and treatment interventions. Whereas universal prevention aims to reduce risk factors, health promotion/positive development strategies aim to enhance protective factors in order to promote health and well-being. And where indicated prevention focuses on those with symptoms of a disorder who do not meet diagnostic criteria, treatment interventions focus on those with diagnosable disorders.

Many doctors, nurses, physical therapists, and health care providers enter public health after decades of caring for patients with devastating injuries or disease. For many experienced health professionals, preventing disease is preferable to treating disease. Prevention saves lives, resources, and promotes quality of life, free from disability. Prevention is key in public health. Sanitation, mass immunizations, mammography screenings, heart health programs, and substance abuse prevention programs are all designed to reduce potential for disease. With the rising cost of health care and increasing aging population, prevention programs will continue to play an important role in helping to enhance quality of life.

Sally Kuykendall

See also: Centers for Disease Control and Prevention; Chronic Illness; Intervention; National Center for Injury Prevention and Control; Social Determinants of Health; Truth Campaign, The; Upstream Public Health Practices

Further Reading

Caplan, G. (1964). *Principles of preventive psychiatry.* New York: Basic Books.

Commission on Chronic Illness. (1949). Announces its program. *American Journal of Public Health, 39*(10), 1343–1344.

Commission on Chronic Illness. (1957). *Chronic illness in the United States* (Vol. 1). Cambridge, MA: Harvard University Press.

Gordon, R. (1987). An operational classification of disease prevention. In J. A. Steinberg & M. M. Silverman (Eds.), *Preventing mental disorders* (pp. 20–26). Rockville, MD: Department of Health and Human Services.

Leavell, H.R., & Clark, E.G. (1953). *Preventive medicine for the doctor in his community: An epidemiologic approach.* New York: McGraw-Hill.

National Center for Chronic Disease Prevention and Health Promotion. (2009). *The power of prevention: Chronic disease . . . the public health challenge of the 21st century.* Centers for Disease Control and Prevention. Retrieved from https://www.cdc.gov/chronicdisease/pdf/2009-Power-of-Prevention.pdf.

National Center for Injury Prevention and Control. (2015). *10 Leading causes of death by age group, United States—2014.* National Vital Statistics System, National Center for Health Statistics, CDC. Retrieved from https://www.cdc.gov/injury/wisqars/leadingcauses.html.

Weimar, R. H. (1973). Toward a model of primary prevention of drug abuse in elementary schools. *British Journal of Addiction to Alcohol & Other Drugs, 68*(1), 57.

Weisz, J., Sandler, I., Durlak, J., & Anton, B. (2005). Promoting and protecting youth mental health through evidence-based prevention and treatment. *American Psychologist, 60*(6), 628–648.

World Bank Group. (2017). *Health expenditures per capita (current US$).* Retrieved from http://data.worldbank.org/indicator/SH.XPD.PCAP?end=2014&start=1995&view=chart&year_high_desc=true.

PUBLIC HEALTH DEPARTMENT ACCREDITATION

Public health department accreditation is a voluntary review to determine whether a state, tribal, local, or territorial health department's processes, services, and outcomes meet nationally recognized, evidence-based standards in public health practice. Many government and health care service institutions, such as schools, hospitals, and nursing homes, undergo an accreditation process. Accreditation ensures that the organization is providing quality services and achieving intended outcomes. The standards by which public health departments are judged are based on the Ten Essential Public Health Services (Essential Services Work Group, n.d.). Accreditors assess the health department's ability to identify community health needs, investigate health hazards, communicate health matters to the general public, engage with the community in health promotion activities, develop public health policies and strategic plans, enforce public health laws, promote access to quality health care, maintain a competent public health workforce, ensure quality improvement, employ evidence-based practices, maintain an effective system of management, and collaborate with the governing entity. The goal of accreditation is to "protect and improve the health of the public by advancing the quality and performance of all public health departments in the country—local, state, territorial and tribal" (Centers for Disease Control and Prevention [CDC], 2017).

In 2003, the Institute of Medicine report *The Future of the Public's Health in the 21st Century* recommended action items to improve public health. One recommendation was to create a formal system of accreditation for health departments. With leadership and support from the Centers for Disease Control and Prevention (CDC) and the Robert Wood Johnson Foundation (RWJF), approximately 400 public health leaders and experts developed accreditation standards and measures. It was important that the standards would work for any health department regardless of size, governance, internal structure, and community health needs (De Milto, 2015). In 2007, the Public Health Accreditation Board (PHAB) was incorporated as the independent accrediting body. From 2009 to 2010, the standards and accreditation process were pilot tested in 30 different health departments. The standards and measures were finalized to 12 domains, and formal accreditation assessment was launched in 2011. The first 11 health departments were awarded accreditation on February 27, 2013.

The accreditation process requires a serious commitment of time, resources, and expertise. To become accredited, the health department undergoes rigorous self-review, reporting, and external evaluation. PHAB lists seven steps to accreditation: pre-application, application, document selection and submission, site visit, accreditation decision, reports, and reaccreditation. During the pre-application stage, the health department learns about the accreditation process, standards, and measures and appoints their accreditation coordinator. The accreditation coordinator leads the accreditation review. Both the accreditation coordinator and the health department director must complete PHAB's online orientation. To proceed to the next stage, the health department registers an intention to apply for public health accreditation. In the application stage, the health department submits the formal application with the accreditation fee. PHAB is a 501(c)3 nonprofit organization. Accreditation fees are used to support PHAB services and staff. In 2014–2015, fees varied from $12,720 to $95,400 based on size of the population that the health department served. In comparison, the Joint Commission International (n.d.), the organization which accredits hospitals, reports an average fee of $46,000 in 2010. Accreditation fees are consistent with similar agencies. After application, the accreditation coordinator attends a two-day, in person training to review PHAB standards, measures, and the documentation needed to support accreditation.

For the health department, the document selection and submission stage is the most intensive part of accreditation. PHAB sets up an electronic database whereby members of the health department's accreditation team can upload documents. The documents provide evidence of the department's ability to meet the required standards. For example, Domain 10 assesses the health department's use of evidence-based practices. The health department staff would identify a few strong, evidence-based programs and practices and upload grants, advertisements, technical reports, or published research that showed the successful use of evidence-based programs or practices. All documents must be submitted within 12 months of database access. During the site visit, PHAB volunteers go to the health department and check to ensure that the documents match what is actually happening at the site. The visitors also clarify any ambiguity or questions regarding the documents, highlight areas of excellence, and discuss areas for improvement. The site visitors report to the Accreditation Committee who reviews the evidence and makes a final determination on accreditation. Health departments that fail to meet accreditation standards may submit an action plan. The Accreditation Committee and site visitors review the action plan to determine whether the plan is realistic and adequately addresses any deficiencies. If the plan is sufficient, the Accreditation Committee can grant accreditation at that time. To maintain accreditation, the health department must submit annual reports showing evidence of ongoing commitment to high-quality, evidence-based practice and progress in any areas identified for improvement. Accreditation is granted for five years at which time the health department must submit a new application and documents and undergo a new site visit.

Public health department accreditation is a comprehensive review of current resources and public health practices. PHAB examines a department's performance, use of evidence-based practices, ability to engage community partners, and plans for ongoing quality improvement. Reviewers look for a system of shared decision making, strong community partnerships, quality services and programs, and a program for ongoing evaluation and improvement. Whether the department achieves accreditation or not, the process requires that the applicant consider current services, community needs, best practices, strengths and weaknesses, areas for improvement, and future directions. Going through the accreditation process encourages accountability and transparency and improves communication within the department and with external partners (Kronstadt, Meit, Siegfried, Nicolaus, Bender, & Corso, 2016). Accreditation enhances the credibility and reputation of the department and expands opportunities for grant funding. Clients of accredited public health departments are assured that the department uses resources appropriately, delivers quality services, and is accountable to the populations that it serves. The goal for public health is to have the majority of Americans covered by an accredited public health department.

Sally Kuykendall

See also: Community Health Centers; Core Competencies in Public Health; National Association of County and City Health Officials

Further Reading

Centers for Disease Control and Prevention. (2017). *National voluntary accreditation for public health departments.* Retrieved from https://www.cdc.gov/stltpublichealth/accreditation.

De Milto, L. (2015). *Establishing a national public health accreditation organization.* Robert Wood Johnson Foundation. Retrieved from http://www.rwjf.org/en/library/research/2015/05/establishing-a-national-public-health-accreditation-organization.html.

Essential Services Work Group. (n.d.) *Ten essential services: Purpose and practices of public health.* Atlanta: Centers for Disease Control and Prevention. Retrieved from http://www.cdc.gov/stltpublichealth/hop/pdfs/Ten_Essential_Public_Health_Services_2011-09_508.pdf.

Institute of Medicine. (2003). *The future of the public's health in the 21st Century.* Washington, DC: The National Academies Press.

Joint Commission International. (n.d.). *Costs of accreditation.* Retrieved from https://web.archive.org/web/20111016171113/http://www.jointcommissioninternational.org/Cost-of-Accreditation.

Kronstadt, J., Meit, M., Siegfried, A., Nicolaus, T., Bender, K., & Corso, L. (2016). Evaluating the impact of National Public Health Department accreditation—United States, 2016. *Morbidity and Mortality Weekly Report, 65*(31), 803–806. doi:10.15585/mmwr.mm6531a3

Public Health Accreditation Board. Retrieved from http://www.phaboard.org.

Riley, W. J., Bender, K., & Lownik, E. (2012). Public health department accreditation implementation: Transforming public health department performance. *American Journal of Public Health, 102*(2), 237–242. doi:10.2105/AJPH.2011.300375

PUBLIC HEALTH DEPARTMENTS

See State, Local, and Territorial Health Departments

PUBLIC HEALTH IN THE UNITED STATES, HISTORY OF

The annals of public health in the United States are rich with great accomplishments, daunting challenges, and even cautionary events. Public health in the United States is as old as the country itself and has always responded to the conditions of the country particular to each unique stage of its history.

At the end of the 18th century, Congress passed one of its first great public health laws, the Act for the Relief of Sick and Disabled Seamen. Since seamen were a transient population, they faced difficulty in securing health care in local towns. Congress used the act to authorize the formation of a U.S. Marine Hospital Service. The Marine Hospital Service provided health care for all merchant sailors. This universal health care service was originally paid for by a twenty-cents-per-month tax on seamen before eventually becoming allocated for by congressional funds over a century later. This act marked the first time that the U.S. federal government worked to coordinate a public health service for a specific population of citizens. Albeit, the primary motivation was a concern for national security rather than a desire to promote public and general welfare.

The 19th century was filled with public health actions and achievements in the United States, even more so than in the preceding century. The development of systematic record-keeping and the implementation of vital public health legislation were instrumental in setting the stage for a vibrant and effective public health system in the United States. At the initial turn of the century, in the year 1800, Dr. Benjamin Waterhouse (1754–1846) introduced the smallpox vaccine into the United States for the first time, indicating the initial step in a journey that would lead to the eradication of smallpox. In 1842, Massachusetts began to keep records of births and deaths; this record-keeping was then emulated by the other states in the country, allowing public health professionals to study the causes of mortality in the population and craft public health interventions more effectively for the first time. In the later part of the 19th century, Massachusetts again took the lead in establishing laws that implemented a precursor to mandated reporting, which requires all dangerous communicable diseases to be reported to a central public health authority. This requirement forms the foundation of the contemporary Centers for Disease Control and Prevention's ability to track epidemics and disease outbreaks throughout the nation and to respond swiftly and effectively to curtail their spread. The end of the 19th century was also responsible for the creation of the precursor of the National Institutes of Health (NIH), which provides immense public health and biomedical research funding and direction for the country in modern times (Boston University of Public Health, 2015). A modest laboratory was established in New York to study and diagnose infectious diseases in sea travelers. This laboratory would later move to Washington, DC, and evolve into the NIH.

Although many of the laws and accomplishments of the 19th century were monumental in establishing the framework behind many of the great public health systems in the United States in the Modern Era, the 20th century was responsible for the birth of some of the great and most famous public health laws in the United States. Upton Sinclair, an American journalist and novelist, wrote the famous expository novel *The Jungle* in 1906, which brought national attention to the gruesome health violations and poor conditions in the meatpacking industry. In response to the national outcry related to the reality depicted in *The Jungle*, Congress passed the Federal Meat Inspection Act and the Pure Food and Drug Act. This gave the federal government a tremendous amount of regulatory power and control to assure that different foods and drugs were prepared and distributed in a manner that was conducive to the public's health and well-being. For the first time, the federal government of the United States was able to mandate that foods be appropriately labeled and chemicals remain unadulterated and pure. Likewise, the Pure Food and Drug Act of 1906 mandated that chemicals such as alcohol, caffeine, and morphine be accurately labeled and appropriately dosed so that overdose and harmful side effects be mitigated. In fact, these laws at the beginning of the 20th century were instrumental in establishing the federal government as a powerful regulatory agent in matters related to the public health and well-being of the country.

Inspectors at the Swift & Company meatpacking plant in Chicago, ca. 1906. Upton Sinclair's description of filthy conditions in the meatpacking industry sparked public outcry, forcing Congress to create the Federal Meat Inspection and Pure Food and Drug Acts of 1906. (Library of Congress)

Throughout the 20th century, landmark public health studies and epidemiological investigations began to find important results with far-reaching implications. In the middle of the century, the Framingham Heart Study began to show findings that linked behavior, diet, and exercise with physiological issues such as heart disease. This was influential in highlighting the need for public health interventions that targeted the determinants of health before health problems develop. Around the same time, the first large-scale clinical trial of the Salk polio vaccine was beginning, eventually leading to the eradication of crippling polio before 1980.

While public health organizations and regulatory laws were being established, environmental protection was likewise slowly developing. In the second half of the 1900s, laws such as the Clean Water Act, the Clean Air Act, the Safe Drinking Water Act, and the Comprehensive Environmental Response, Compensation, and Liability Act were passed by Congress. These laws were instrumental in public health even though they were concerned with regulating the levels of chemicals in the environment. By regulating the amount of chemicals such as lead in the water, particulate matter in the air, and other hazardous materials at sites such as landfills, the public was increasingly becoming shielded from the harms of environmental exposure to harmful chemicals that cause cancer, respiratory issues, and other diseases.

It is important to note, however, that the history of public health in the United States, no matter how filled with great accomplishments and achievements, was also marred by some deeply troubling ethical violations. The United States Public Health Service, which evolved from the marine health service system established in the Act for the Relief of Sick and Disabled Seamen, was responsible for one of the greatest public health misconducts in human history during the syphilis-related Tuskegee Study. In 1932, the Public Health Service began to study the effects of syphilis in black males (Centers for Disease Control and Prevention, 2016). The population that was studied was in Tuskegee, Alabama, and did not give appropriately informed consent for the study. The public health and health care professionals involved in the study examined the course of disease in nearly 400 individuals while withholding the appropriate treatment that could have protected them from the terrible and harmful effects of untreated syphilis infection. This study went on for nearly 40 years while the patients did not receive the readily available treatment for syphilis infection. The ethical issues and inhumanity of the actions of the government and public health professionals responsible for the Tuskegee Study are of great importance in public health throughout the world. Now, public health professionals learn about the Tuskegee Study, and institutions such as institutional review boards are required at every facility in the United States that carries out research; the aim of such requirements is to avoid unethical studies such as the one in Tuskegee from ever happening again. Any members of the public participating in research must receive ample information regarding risks and procedures so that they can give informed consent for their participation, and unethical studies that cause undue harm to patients are forbidden.

The history of public health in the United States is one that is filled with many profound events, both good and bad. The public health domain in the United States grew by dealing with the specific events and challenges faced by the American population at each point in time throughout its history. The accomplishments and growing powers of public health agencies in the United States, such as the Centers for Disease Control and U.S. Food and Drug Administration, were incremental and attributable to the needs of each era that the United States went through. Importantly, the accomplishments of the United States in many public health arenas, such as vaccination and the eradication of multiple infectious diseases, were not only vital for the domestic public health but were also responsible for saving many millions of lives throughout the world. The polio vaccine, for example, has helped eradicate polio from nearly every country in the world. By understanding the history of such public health accomplishments in the United States, the role that public health has played in shaping the country's history as a whole is more readily discernable.

Shayan Waseh

See also: Affordable Care Act; Centers for Disease Control and Prevention; Food and Drug Administration; Medicaid; Medicare; Modern Era, Public Health in the; National Cancer Institute; National Center for Injury Prevention and Control; National Heart, Lung, and Blood Institute; National Institute on Drug Abuse; National Institutes of Health; Planned Parenthood; Social Security Act

Further Reading

Boston University of Public Health. (2015). *Public health in the United States.* Retrieved from http://sphweb.bumc.bu.edu/otlt/mph-modules/ph/publichealthhistory/publichealthhistory8.html.

Centers for Disease Control and Prevention. (2016). *Tuskegee Study—Timeline.* Retrieved from https://www.cdc.gov/tuskegee/timeline.htm.

Duffy, J. (1974). *A history of public health in New York City, 1866–1966.* New York: Russell Sage Foundation.

Rosen, G. (1993). *A history of public health* (Expanded ed.). Baltimore: The Johns Hopkins University Press.

Sinclair, U. (1906). *The jungle.* New York: Doubleday, Jabber & Company.

Tulchinsky, T. H., & Varavikova, E. (2000). *The new public health: An introduction for the 21st Century.* San Diego: Academic Press.

Turnock, B. J., & Atchison, C. (2002). Governmental public health in the United States: The implications of federalism. *Health Affairs, 21*(6), 68–78.

PUBLIC HEALTH LAW

Laws are the rules that society uses to resolve disagreements between members. Some of the greatest public health achievements were accomplished through public health law. The 100 percent reductions in deaths due to smallpox, diphtheria, poliomyelitis, and measles were achieved through mandatory vaccinations (CDC, 1999a). The Highway Safety Act and National Traffic and Motor Vehicle Safety Act decreased motor vehicle fatalities from 18 deaths per million vehicle miles traveled to 1.7 deaths per million miles traveled (CDC, 1999b). The Occupational Safety and Health Administration (OSHA) and Fair Labor Standards Act (FLSA) were critical in reducing unintentional work-related injuries from 37 injuries per 100,000 workers to 4 injuries per 100,000 workers (CDC, 1999c). Laws are highly effective tools used by federal, state, tribal, local, and territorial authorities. Because laws are so effective, we see many, many different laws, regulations, statutes, and ordinances designed to prevent disease and promote health. There are laws restricting the sale of pet turtles to prevent salmonella transmission, laws on tobacco advertising to reduce lung cancer, and laws on preparing for emergencies to prevent death and injury due to natural and man-made disasters. Although states and local health authorities carry substantial responsibility for protecting health, they must do so within the constraints of the individual freedoms guaranteed by the U.S. Constitution. Throughout history, efforts in disease prevention come in conflict with personal liberties. The Clean Indoor Air Act, regulating smoking in the workplace, was initially criticized as violating the rights of smokers. As society develops legislation on pressing issues such as opioid addictions, environmental health, food safety, emergency preparedness, and childhood obesity, public health administrators are challenged to balance the health of the community with personal freedom.

Public health law is a vast database of constitutional, legislative, administrative, and judicial laws. Legal authority comes from five sources: (1) federal, state, tribal, and territorial constitutions; (2) international agreements; (3) legislative or administrative; (4) regulations; and (5) common law. Federal law, primarily the Constitution, defines how legal powers are divided between individual states and federal authorities. Although the majority of power is directed to individual states, territories, and tribal nations, the federal government has ultimate authority in matters related to national defense, foreign diplomacy, and the economy. This is why, despite mass shootings in many places throughout the United States, state and local authorities are unable to pass legislation controlling gun ownership. Constitutional law supersedes local laws. International agreements include historical agreements, such as the Declaration of Helsinki (1964), which provides ethical guidelines for medical research involving human participants. More recent agreements include the International Health Regulations (2005), which build capacity and coordinate services in response to global health alerts. In addition to developing a worldwide response, the International Health Regulations also provide guidelines to control transmission of disease at international airports, ports, and ground crossings. Legislative or statutory laws and regulations reflect state and local government choices and priorities. These laws determine funding allocations, program support, and prohibitions of certain activities. Oftentimes, laws are established in reaction to events or experiences. After residents converted a rental dumpster into a swimming pool for a block party, the City of Philadelphia's Department of Licenses and Inspections issued the statement: "In view of the City's commitment to public health, safety, and basic common sense, we will not issue permits for block party dumpster pools. And while you would think this decision would not require an explanation, three days of press requests have proven otherwise. So, Philly, here's why you shouldn't swim in a receptacle most often used for waste . . ." (Peralta, 2016). From international agreements to local ordinances, public health laws and regulations are intended to protect health. The final form of legal authority is common law or judicial law, which is based on previous court cases. To ensure consistency and fairness, legal precedents are used whenever possible.

All laws, even laws regarding health behaviors, are enforced by police powers. Punishments for violation can range from warnings to misdemeanor fines to felony charges with imprisonment. Under police power, public health officials have the authority to investigate outbreaks of infectious diseases, mandate vaccinations, seize property, destroy toxic substances, and involuntarily detain individuals who are a threat to the public health. The case of Kaci Hickox demonstrates the use and hazards of such power. On October 24, 2014, Kaci Hickox arrived in Newark Airport returning from a month in Sierra Leone where she worked as a nurse with the international aid organization Médecins Sans Frontières (Doctors Without Borders). In Africa, Hickox cared for patients with Ebola, a rare, frightening, and fatal viral disease transmitted through direct contact. While providing patient care, Médecins Sans Frontières workers adhered to strict infection control protocols, washing hands in chlorinated water, using protective gear, and not touching infected people. In response to Ebola, the state of New Jersey implemented a 21-day mandatory quarantine for anyone arriving from Sierra Leone, Liberia, or Guinea with possible Ebola contact. Despite following infection control procedures and being asymptomatic, the nurse was held involuntarily for 80 hours including quarantine in a tent. Hickox believed that her well-publicized custody and comments that she was infectious were based on political aspirations by the New Jersey governor, rather than public health science. She later sued Governor Chris Christie alleging false imprisonment, invasion of privacy, and violation of due process. Although public health authorities have powers equal to police officers, enforcement must be used judiciously. In neighboring New York City (NYC), officials developed different strategies, an algorithm of education, identification, and monitoring. Working with many diverse groups and focusing efforts on at-risk West African communities in the Bronx, Harlem, and Staten Island, the NYC Department of Public Health asked people to report potential exposure to their Active Monitoring Call Center. At-risk individuals took their own temperature and communicated regularly with the Department of Public Health through the call center. By the end of the global outbreak, NYC personnel had worked with more than 5,000 individuals (NYC Health, 2016). The NYC algorithm became a model for other cities throughout the nation. Although public health officials have the authority to enforce laws, educating and empowering the affected community is often the preferred course of action.

The field of public health law encompasses many different jobs. Lawyers provide legal advice to public health administrators, try cases, write contracts for services, draft and interpret statutes, conduct research, advocate for marginalized groups, and develop policies. Lawyers interpret existing laws, such as HITECH, EMTALA, and the Stark law, and provide advice on Medicare, Medicaid, the Affordable Care Act or private health insurance coverage. Not typically viewed as public health, medical examiners who investigate deaths are part of the larger public health system of a city or county. In general, public health law professionals must have the ability to balance legal practices, policies, social justice, and ethics.

Public health law is made up of a complex patchwork of statutes, regulations, and litigation. Laws ranging from state laws mandating immunizations at school entry to local ordinances forbidding unleashed dogs in public parks are highly effective in promoting health. However, the complexity of the legal system and varying authority can result in conflict. Public health has the responsibility to promote public good yet must do so within constitutional rights to personal freedom and property ownership. Other problems occur when laws are overly zealous or poorly contrived in response to health alerts. Thoughtful regulations, based on science and trust, can impact challenging health problems.

Sally Kuykendall and Leapolda Figueroa

See also: Affordable Care Act; Emergency Medical Treatment and Labor Act; False Claims Act; Health Information Management; Health Insurance Portability and Accountability Act; Health Policy; Stark Law

Further Reading

Association of State and Territorial Health Officials. (2016). *Public health law.* Retrieved from http://www.astho.org/Public-Policy/Public-Health-Law/?terms=public+health+law.

Centers for Disease Control and Prevention (CDC). (1999a). Achievements in public health, 1990–1999 impact of vaccines universally recommended for children—United States, 1990–1998. *Morbidity and Mortality Weekly Reports, 48*(12), 243–248. Retrieved from https://www.cdc.gov/mmwr/preview/mmwrhtml/00056803.htm.

Centers for Disease Control and Prevention (CDC). (1999b). Achievements in public health, 1990–1999 motor vehicle safety: A 20th century public health achievement. *Morbidity and Mortality Weekly Reports, 48*(18), 369–374. Retrieved from https://www.cdc.gov/mmwr/preview/mmwrhtml/mm4818a1.htm.

Centers for Disease Control and Prevention (CDC). (1999c). Achievements in public health, 1990–1999: Improvements in workplace safety—United States, 1990–1999. *Morbidity and Mortality Weekly Reports, 48*(22), 461–469. Retrieved from https://www.cdc.gov/mmwr/preview/mmwrhtml/mm4822a1.htm.

Centers for Disease Control and Prevention (CDC). (2016). *Public health law program.* Retrieved from https://www.cdc.gov/phlp/.

Health Care (HHS). (2014). *The role of public programs.* Retrieved from http://www.hhs.gov/healthcare/about-the-law/read-the-law/.

Hickox, K. (2014). Her story: UTA grad isolated at New Jersey hospital in Ebola quarantine. *The Dallas Morning News.* Retrieved from http://www.dallasnews.com/ebola/headlines/20141025-uta-grad-isolated-at-new-jersey-hospital-as-part-of-ebola-quarantine.ece and http://www.dallasnews.com/ebola/headlines/20141025-uta-grad-isolated-at-new-jersey-hospital-as-part-of-ebola-quarantine.ece.

The Network for Public Health Law. (2016). *Public health law.* Retrieved from https://www.networkforphl.org/.

NYC Health. (2016). *With Guinea declared Ebola-free, health department concludes its response and closes monitoring program for incoming travelers.* Press Release # 002-16. Retrieved from https://www1.nyc.gov/site/doh/about/press/pr2016/pr002-16.page.

Peralta, E. (2016, August 4). *Philadelphia to its residents: Don't swim in dumpsters.* NPR. Retrieved from http://www.npr.org/sections/thetwo-way/2016/08/04/488695414/philadelphia-to-its-residents-dont-swim-in-dumpsters.

Q

QUARANTINE

Quarantine is a public health measure dating back to early civilization where people or animals arriving from foreign areas are isolated from others to prevent the spread of communicable disease. The practice of isolation is routinely used in health care. Isolation separates people with infectious diseases from healthy people. The practice stops transmission from the infected carrier to a new host. Quarantine separates and restricts movement for a period of time. During this time, the isolated person is monitored to determine if he or she has a communicable disease. The term "quarantine" originates from Italian, *quaranta giorni,* meaning 40 days, the length of time used to monitor for illness. Before antibiotics and routine childhood immunizations, quarantine was a common (and frequently ineffective) way to prevent an epidemic. The control or eradication of cholera, yellow fever, smallpox, and typhus has reduced the need for quarantine stations. In 2017, 20 quarantine stations were located at strategic entry points throughout the United States in cities such as Anchorage, Seattle, San Francisco, Honolulu, El Paso, Miami, New York City, Boston, Chicago, and Minneapolis. Quarantine personnel are federal government employees empowered to apprehend, detain, examine, or conditionally release individuals suspected of carrying the quarantinable diseases of cholera, diphtheria, infectious tuberculosis, plague, smallpox, yellow fever, viral hemorrhagic fevers (e.g., Ebola), or severe acute respiratory syndrome (SARS).

Early records of quarantine practices date to 549 CE (Tyson, 2004). In a world besieged by the bubonic plague, Eastern Roman Emperor Justinian enacted a law to isolate people arriving from plague-infested regions. In 583 CE, the Council of the Roman Catholic Church in Lyon, France, isolated people with leprosy from society. In the 600s CE, China detained sailors and passengers who appeared to be suffering from the plague. In the 1300s, European and Asian countries created areas of forced quarantine. Surrounded by guards, victims who attempted to escape were either captured and returned to the area or executed. In 1348, Venice appointed a committee to detain ships in the harbor for up to 40 days. Quarantine was intended to prevent the Black Death from entering the city. Efforts were unsuccessful. In 1403, Venice established one of the first quarantine stations, located on an island in the Venice lagoon. In colonial America, early efforts of quarantine were sporadic, regulated by state or local governments. In 1647, Boston passed an ordinance requiring all arriving ships to stop at the harbor entrance for inspection. In 1663, New York City passed a law requiring people arriving from areas with smallpox to be reviewed by sanitary officials before entering the city. Seventy-five years later, New York City established a quarantine station at Bedloe's Island. The station isolated immigrants, travelers, and sailors who may be carrying smallpox or yellow fever. New York's quarantine act passed in 1863, giving quarantine officials the power to detain a ship or to order fumigation before permission to dock. In 1878, Congress passed the National Quarantine Act, a law that focused primarily on yellow fever prevention. In 1892, a cholera epidemic forced President Benjamin Harrison to expand the National Quarantine Act, allowing officials to order detention of 20 days or longer. Local quarantine stations were gradually turned over to the federal government with the last station passing to federal control in 1921.

Although the idea of confining individuals in order to protect a greater number of people seems like a logical action, there is, unfortunately, the potential for abuse. In 1900, Chick Gin, a Chinese businessman died of bubonic plague in a San Francisco basement. Officials allowed whites to leave the area and cordoned off a 15-block neighborhood, closing many Chinese American businesses. The court later ruled that the quarantine was unjust and based on racism and lifted the restriction. From 1907 to 1910 and from 1915 until her death in 1938, Irish immigrant, Mary Mallon (Typhoid Mary) was held on North Brother Island. The intention was to prevent Mary from spreading typhoid fever. However, she was held without trial, raising the question of public health's right to detain people. From 1917 to 1919, the federal government was concerned with the high number of young men ineligible for the draft due to sexually transmitted infections. Authorities incarcerated more than 30,000 women suspected of having syphilis or gonorrhea. Many of the women were poor and unable to afford treatment, and some of the women were married, having been infected and reported to authorities by vindictive spouses (University of Kansas, 2015). On October 24, 2012, Doctors Without Borders nurse Kaci Hickox returned from treating patients with Ebola in West Africa and was involuntarily held for three days by New Jersey officials. Hickox was never infected with the virus and later sued for false imprisonment, violation of due process, and invasion of privacy. Hickox asserted that her detention was based on fear and politics rather than on the science of disease transmission. Any law that allows officials the right to limit the individual freedom of other people has the potential for abuse. It is critical that such policies have a system of checks and balances in place to prevent abuse and to protect vulnerable populations of immigrants, minorities, women, children, and poor people.

Today, quarantine is regulated under the Division of Global Migration and Quarantine, part of the Centers for Disease Control and Prevention's (CDC) National Center for Emerging and Zoonotic Infectious Diseases. Quarantine personnel review the origin of each traveler to assess health risk and determine the appropriate public health response. To minimize the need for quarantine, the CDC monitors global epidemics and works with countries to intervene at the source of the contamination.

Sally Kuykendall

See also: Ancient World, Public Health in the; Cholera; Epidemic; Infectious Diseases; Middle Ages, Public Health in the; Renaissance, Public Health in the; Smallpox; Surgeon General; U.S. Public Health Service; World Health Organization; *Controversies in Public Health:* Controversy 3

Further Reading

Centers for Disease Control and Prevention (CDC). (2017). *Quarantine and isolation.* Retrieved from https://www.cdc.gov/quarantine/index.html.

Tyson, P. (2004). *A short history of quarantine.* NOVA. Retrieved from http://www.pbs.org/wgbh/nova/body/short-history-of-quarantine.html.

The University of Kansas. (2015). *Researcher documents gender, class bias in quarantine law measures.* Retrieved from https://news.ku.edu/2015/07/29/researcher-documents-gender-class-bias-quarantine-law-measures.

R

RE-AIM (REACH, EFFECTIVENESS, ADOPTION, IMPLEMENTATION, AND MAINTENANCE)

RE-AIM (reach, effectiveness, adoption, implementation, and maintenance) is a model to plan and evaluate community health programs. Before RE-AIM was developed, public health program evaluations mirrored clinical studies. This means that programs were primarily assessed on whether they worked or not. The problem is that clinical studies are carried out under highly controlled conditions with participants who meet certain criteria. Community-based programs are carried out in the real world and must navigate day-to-day problems. For example, clinical or pilot studies in smoking prevention attract and recruit highly motivated individuals. Selected participants are more likely to stay in the program, take the necessary steps to stop smoking, and will yield high rates of program success. Unfortunately, hand-selected study participants may not represent smokers in the community, people that a program hopes to help. Under real-world conditions, such as with larger groups of people or with people at the earlier stages of change, programs may not demonstrate the same effectiveness. Selective recruitment, limited resources, conflicting priorities, and day-to-day demands create gaps between clinical research findings and findings in the real world. To correct the issue, researchers from the AMC Cancer Research Center in Denver, Colorado, the Kaiser Permanente Center for Health Research, and the Oregon Research Institute developed a model that included program outreach and participants (Glasgow, Vogt, & Boles, 1999). RE-AIM considers the broader effects of a program, such as how many people are impacted, how participants are impacted, and who is impacted.

The RE-AIM model consists of five major constructs, presented in chronological order: *reach, effectiveness, adoption, implementation*, and *maintenance*. *Reach* describes how well the project attracts and retains people who need the program the most. *Effectiveness* refers to the program's ability to achieve the intended changes in participant knowledge, attitude, or behavior. This construct also notes any adverse consequences experienced by participants as a result of participating in the program. *Adoption* assesses how well other sites or settings are able to use the program. Another term for adoption is replicability, which means how well a program can be reproduced at another site. *Implementation* reflects how well the content and materials presented during the program match the program developer's original program. Also known as fidelity of implementation, this construct shows whether the program required major modifications in order to meet the audience's needs and whether the changes altered the program to such a degree that it was no longer consistent with the original program. *Maintenance* refers to whether the individual participants are able to sustain the changes and whether the organization is able to integrate the program into day-to-day operations after initial support ends. The model outlines all of the various factors that program managers need to consider in planning and evaluating a program.

The GLAMA! (Girls! Lead! Achieve! Mentor! Activate!) program is an example of how public health professionals use the RE-AIM framework to plan and assess programs (Jenkinson, Naughton, & Benson, 2012). GLAMA! is a school-based program designed to develop leadership skills, social connectedness, and physical activity among adolescent females. School-based interventions are a popular forum for community-based interventions. Schools have sustained access to a wide audience of youth throughout critical periods of emotional, social, and physical development. School buildings offer suitable program sites without having to worry about transportation, outside activities, or personal schedules. The GLAMA! program was piloted in Melbourne, Australia. Researchers used the RE-AIM framework to assess:

1. *Reach:* Who participated in the program and why? Who did not participate in the program and why?
2. *Effectiveness:* How did the program impact participants?
3. *Adoption:* What factors attracted the schools to accept the program?
4. *Implementation:* Which program components did the schools use?
5. *Maintenance:* Did participants and schools continue the intervention and if so, which parts of the intervention did they use?

Based on the pilot program, the researchers concluded that teacher professional development, integration of the program into the school schedule, and more practical opportunities to apply leadership skills could enhance future GLAMA! interventions (Jenkinson, Naughton, & Benson, 2012). The RE-AIM model was a valuable framework to identify and analyze specific parts of the program, obstacles, and opportunities for improvement.

The RE-AIM model has been used to develop programs in residential dementia care, chronic kidney disease, children's nutrition and physical activity, Type 2 diabetes, workplace wellness programs, and many other public health topics. The framework helps program planners to consider the multiple factors that influence program success in order to maximize program effectiveness.

Sally Kuykendall

See also: Community Health; Evidence-Based Programs and Practices; Logic Model; Prevention

Further Reading

Glasgow, R. E., Vogt, T. M., & Boles, S. M. (1999). Evaluating the public health impact of health promotion interventions: The RE-AIM framework. *American Journal of Public Health*, 89(9), 1322–1327.

Jenkinson, K. A., Naughton, G., & Benson, A. C. (2012). The GLAMA (Girls! Lead! Achieve! Mentor! Activate!) physical activity and peer leadership intervention pilot project: A process evaluation using the RE-AIM framework. *BMC Public Health, 12,* 55. doi:10.1186/1471-2458-12-55

RE-AIM. Retrieved from http://re-aim.org.

RECIPROCAL DETERMINISM

Reciprocal determinism describes mutuality between the individual and the environment where the environment influences the individual and the individual influences the environment. The concept of reciprocal determinism developed from social cognitive theory (SCT) by Dr. Albert Bandura. SCT describes how individuals learn new skills or behavior by watching others (Bandura, 1986). Public health professionals use the concept of reciprocal determinism to understand, investigate, and change negative behaviors or to promote positive behaviors. The concept applies to numerous public health topics such as job stress, pediatric obesity, nutrition, prenatal health, workplace safety, and social activism. For example, when someone starts a new job at a restaurant, he or she learns skills and practices by watching the experienced workers. If mentoring workers use good handwashing techniques, the individual will also learn to use and practice good handwashing techniques. Likewise, if senior workers neglect food safety practices, the new employee is also likely to neglect such practices. Over time, the employee becomes a model for other trainees. Thus, the environment of good food safety practices influences the individual, and the individual eventually becomes part of an environment to influence others. Once food safety practices are established, good handwashing becomes endemic, engrained in the environment of this particular restaurant. Social cognitive theory describes additional factors that impact the individual's ability to learn and practice a task. Overall, reciprocal determinism is useful in helping public health practitioners to identify ways to disrupt negative behaviors and introduce positive behaviors.

Sally Kuykendall

See also: Handwashing; Social Cognitive Theory

Further Reading

Bandura, A. (1962). Social learning through imitation. In M. R. Jones (Eds.), *Nebraska Symposium on Motivation, 1962* (pp. 211–274). Lincoln: University of Nebraska Press.

Bandura, A. (1986). *Social foundations of thought and action: A social cognitive theory*. Englewood Cliffs, NJ: Prentice Hall.

Glanz, K., Lewis, F. M., & Rimer, B. K. (Eds). (1997). *Health behavior and health education: Theory, research, and practice* (2nd ed.). San Francisco: Jossey-Bass.

RENAISSANCE, PUBLIC HEALTH IN THE

The social and civilizational forces operating during the Renaissance were responsible for birthing some of the most foundational components of public health, particularly in the fields of epidemiology, infectious disease, and medical science. As the structure of society was transformed during the Renaissance, especially throughout Europe between the 14th and 17th centuries, public health began to become of greater importance. Public health approaches became empowered with a greater understanding of how wellness and disease operate. Additionally, the scientific and intellectual advancements of the Renaissance were essential in laying the framework for contemporary public health and medical practice. In this way, the evolution of public health during the Renaissance is still of tremendous import today, and the accomplishments and discoveries of the Renaissance Era have produced profound reverberations in the history of both public health and medicine.

Interestingly, one of the most infamous public health problems in humanity's history was at least partly responsible for contributing to the start of the Renaissance itself. In the era immediately preceding the Renaissance, the feudal structure of society was incrementally dissolving, and populations of people became increasingly connected. As medieval trade and commerce began to spread and evolve to include trade with far off lands and peoples, outbreaks of communicable diseases such as syphilis became more common, and outbreaks of these infectious diseases were frequent and harmful. The most influential of these communicable diseases was *Yersinia pestis*—commonly known as the Black Death—which devastated European and worldwide populations. This population depletion was partly responsible for creating the conditions of ample land, high workforce demand, and concentrated wealth that contributed greatly to the start of the Renaissance (Woodville, 2013). Although much of the understanding of disease at that time was related to spirituality and divinity, the devastation of the Black Death was enough to motivate the initial attempts at raising the level of public sanitation and developing greater governmental regulation in public life (University of Virginia, 1994). It was the epidemiological challenge of the Black Death and other profound infectious disease outbreaks that motivated much of the public health advances in sanitation and hygiene at a population level.

Although the Black Death devastated much of the trade and commercial networks within the world and Europe, the post–Black Death Renaissance period was marked by an increase of trade beyond the original baseline level, and the management of communicable diseases became of even greater importance. Therefore, communicable disease management techniques and regulations were implemented throughout the world. For example, in order to combat the spread of syphilis in Europe—an illness that was attributed at that time to travelers returning from the New World as well as prostitution—public health regulations were implemented that mandated the registration of prostitutes, the reporting of disease cases, and the quarantining of sick patients.

Additionally, throughout the Renaissance, the European monarchs and governments invested greater amounts of capital and resources to establishing a stronger public health care framework to foster the growth and health of their populations. Utilizing his available resources, the Russian czar Ivan IV developed a network of major health care pharmacies in large urban centers and began to open the first series of secular hospitals to meet the health care needs of the population (Tulchinsky & Varavikova, 2009). This represents one of the first large coordinated efforts in Russia to establish a coherent and comprehensive health network to meet the civilian and military health needs of the country. In England, the increasing urbanization of the population provided the needed impetus to encourage the development of hospitals. In addition, the urban sprawl and pollution on city streets drove the British government to clarify that responsibility for sanitation, and public health fell on local British government at the level of the parish; this responsibility at the time was then placed on individual citizens who were then responsible for ensuring that their strip of the street was clean and well kept. Although this governmental regulation did not effectively prevent streets from becoming overcrowded with fecal matter and disease in Renaissance England, the clarification of the public health responsibility of local government was important in establishing public health as a responsibility of local authorities.

In addition to the fact that the societal advancements in the way that European countries conceived of and dealt with public health challenges were highly influential and laid the foundation of future public health practice, the scientific advancements of the Renaissance were of even greater importance. These scientific discoveries, in the fields of medicine, chemistry, and public health, were of immense importance in the path to humanity's contemporary understanding of health and disease. The natural science-based disciplines of anatomy and physiology contributed to the systematization of the clinical practice of medicine. For one of the first times in Western medicine, the internal anatomy of the body began to be extensively and systematically studied, and new theories about cardiovascular structure, hemodynamics, and neuromuscular function were born.

The contagion theory of disease was also developed in this era, profoundly influencing the way that public health professionals conceived of hygiene and health. This model of infectious diseases is still prevalent today and is the foundation of society's approach to managing disease outbreaks. Rather than consider diseases as exclusively divine punishment, or as resulting from bad air, public health professionals began to understand the microbial basis of infectious diseases for the first time. This scientific understanding was made possible in no small part by the invention of the microscope by van Leeuwenhoek in 1676, allowing scientists and physicians to see the microorganisms behind disease for the first time. The development of a microbial (or contagion) understanding of disease allowed public health professionals and physicians to understand the importance of tracking the spread of diseases through regulations that established and mandated record-keeping of deaths and causes of death.

One example of how government regulation aided public health was the implementation of the "Bills of Mortality" in English society. These bills kept records of deaths by cause, allowing public health professionals to analyze trends and notice epidemics and outbreaks. Much like the Centers for Disease Control and Prevention's

MEMENTO MORI

LONDON'S Dreadful Visitation:
Or, A COLLECTION of All the
Bills of Mortality
For this Present Year:
Beginning the 27th of December 1664. and
ending the 19th. of December following:
As also, The GENERAL or whole years BILL:
According to the Report made to the
KING'S Most Excellent Majesty,
By the Company of Parish-Clerks of London. &c

LONDON:
Printed and are to be sold by E. Cotes living in Aldersgate-street.
Printer to the said Company 1665.

During the Great Plague of London (1665–1666), parish clerks recorded local deaths in Bills of Mortality. Records indicate that bubonic plague killed almost one out of four Londoners. (Jupiterimages)

reportable disease system in the modern-day United States, the Bills of Mortality in England allowed the public health authorities to better understand how diseases were spread and impacted on society. This was important in informing attempts to curtail and diminish the spread of disease.

Building on this, another large development for public health during the Renaissance came in the middle of the 17th century in England, where John Graunt analyzed these Bills of Mortality and was therefore able to articulate how mortality was deeply connected to the living conditions in which people lived. John Graunt is now considered one of the first demographers in the world due to his work with the Bills of Mortality. His observations represented one of the first times that statistical analysis was used with governmental mortality data to generate public health insights. This practice is now essential to contemporary public health practice and is one of the most common ways that public health organizations and governmental agencies shape and guide their initiatives and projects. Additionally, the record-keeping and systematization of health information of the Renaissance Era is responsible for the development of the disciplines of demography and vital statistics, and it is even responsible for the practice of collecting basic population health measurements such as height, age, weight, and race.

The period of the Renaissance, which was born from one of the greatest public health catastrophes of all time—the Black Death—became one rich with an evolving understanding of the fundamental disciplines of medical science, infectious disease, sanitation and hygiene, and population health. With the emergence of great thinkers and revolutionary scientists that shed new insights on anatomy, physiology, microbiology, clinical science, and epidemiology, the foundational understanding of the human body and population health was transformed and was started on the path to society's contemporary understanding. The Renaissance, in this way, was a great transitional era where medicine and public health moved from the religious and spiritual domain into the natural sciences. This transition set the foundation for the following Enlightenment Era and the next few centuries of rapid medical advancements. Another important aspect of the Renaissance was that as the structure of civilization changed throughout Europe and the rest of the world to become more urbanized, the need for public health approaches to urban sprawl, pollution, and contamination became more urgent and clearly discernible. This phenomenon set the stage for public health to evolve to the level of importance and influence that it has today in the modern world. The Renaissance, in this way, served as the launching pad for modern public health practice.

Shayan Waseh

See also: Ancient World, Public Health in the; Infectious Diseases; Middle Ages, Public Health in the; Quarantine; Smallpox

Further Reading

Cipolla, C. M. (1976). *Public health and the medical profession in the Renaissance.* Cambridge, UK: Cambridge University Press.

MacNalty, A. S. (1945). The Renaissance and its influence on English medicine, surgery, and public health. *The British Medical Journal*, 2(4430), 755–759.

Tulchinsky, T. H., & Varavikova, E. (2009). *The new public health.* Cambridge, MA: Academic Press.

University of Virginia. (1994). *Plague and public health in Renaissance Europe.* Retrieved from http://www2.iath.virginia.edu/osheim/plaguein.html.

Woodville, L. (2013). *The Black Death.* Retrieved from https://www.khanacademy.org/humanities/renaissance-reformation/late-gothic-italy/beginners-guide-late-gothic/a/the-black-death.

RESEARCH

Public health research is a systematic process that explores problems and provides insights so that public health professionals can develop the knowledge and skills needed to prevent and treat diseases and to improve quality of life for individuals and communities. People do informal research every day. From identifying the best type of pet for a family to adopt, exploring new career options, or improving an old family recipe, people collect information, develop new ideas, and pilot test their ideas. Formal research uses a methodical, planned approach. To perform research, the investigator learns as much as possible about the subject of interest, designs a study, collects data, analyzes the results, and reports the results to other people. A research study can be simple or elaborate, inexpensive or expensive. Regardless of effort and cost, there is no guarantee of success. Sometimes research studies produce usable results, sometimes they do not. Research guides practice by informing professionals of the best treatment options, the most effective prevention mechanisms, or how to streamline systems. Conversely, practice guides research. Researchers develop research studies based on current and emerging health problems reported by public health professionals.

The research process starts with reading and reviewing what experts have written and what is known about the topic of interest. The literature review is an essential first step in planning a research study. The Nuremberg Code—a set of guidelines developed as a result of the atrocities committed by Nazi scientists during World War II—requires the investigator to justify the research. No research study should be undertaken without first determining what is known about the problem and what needs to be studied next. To do this, the researcher reads as many books, articles, and publications as possible. Reading materials are carefully selected. Only good quality resources are read, not popular articles, advertisements, or other sources that might have a vested interest in the information presented. By excluding lower quality resources, the researcher ensures that the justification is based on scientific evidence, not personal or political beliefs. Through reading what others have written and published on the topic, the researcher learns how other experts defined and limited the problem, how the problem affects humans and societies, how many people are impacted by the problem, high-risk groups, and recommendations for other researchers. The literature review helps the researcher to develop research questions or a research hypothesis of what needs to be studied next.

The research question is a general question that describes what the researcher would like to explore. Here are some examples: "What factors increase risk of autism?" "Which program is more effective in reducing substance abuse?" "How does social support influence diabetes management?" The research hypothesis is a testable statement, phrased as a statement. An example of a research hypothesis is: "Diabetic patients with positive social support will report more stable blood sugars than diabetic patients without positive social support." The research hypothesis names the variables (social support and stability of blood sugar) and the relationship between the variables (the higher the social support, the more stable the blood sugar). The research question or research hypothesis provides structure to the research study. Compare the research hypothesis provided above with the research hypothesis: "After receiving positive social support, diabetic patients will report greater stability of blood sugars." The first hypothesis compares two groups of diabetic patients, an experimental and control group. The experimental group has positive social support, and the control group does not have positive social support. The second hypothesis compares blood sugars of one group of diabetic patients, pre-intervention and post-intervention. The research hypothesis states the study group, the variables that the researcher is studying, and the expected outcome of the study. Research hypotheses provide clues as to who the researcher will study (sample population), what data are collected (variables), and how data are analyzed.

After designing the study, the researcher collects information or data directly or indirectly from the study sample. In public health, the study sample is often people. However, the study sample could also be patient charts, water samples, or advertisements in magazines that influence people's health behaviors. The researcher obtains or recruits the study sample and collects data from the sample. Public health researchers perform research studies in many different locations, such as hospitals, clinics, communities, schools, businesses, and homes. The data collected may be qualitative or quantitative. Qualitative data are descriptions using words and ideas. Quantitative data are descriptions using numbers. In the study of blood sugar management and social support, the qualitative researcher might investigate how social support influences diabetic management. The qualitative researcher may learn that positive social networks provide a sense of belonging that reduces stress and makes it easier to manage the challenges of diabetes; increases self-esteem, encouraging the person with diabetes to take good care of his or her body; and increases access to information providing guidance that helps the diabetic patient to manage potential problems and concerns more quickly and easily. The qualitative researcher looks at how social support works and develops major themes or ideas that are common across the study sample of diabetic patients. The quantitative researcher looks at how social support works by counting the concepts of interest. The quantitative researcher would measure social support and blood sugar and calculate any differences. The quantitative researcher may conclude that the blood sugars of diabetic patients with positive social support are not significantly different from diabetic patients without positive social support. However, diabetic patients with positive social support are 70 percent more likely to check their blood sugars regularly, which could prevent complications due to too high or too low of a blood sugar. Neither form of data, qualitative or quantitative, is superior to the other. Both forms of data work together to help public health professionals to understand and address health problems.

After collecting the data, the researcher presents the results. This process, known as data conversion, requires the researcher to take large masses of data and convert them into understandable concepts while still maintaining accuracy of the results. To convert the data, the researcher may need to read more than 100 pages of interview transcripts or enter and calculate answers from thousands of surveys. Fortunately, computer software packages are available for some types of data conversion. Analyzing the data and presenting the data in a format that is easy to understand requires critical thinking and mathematical skills. The researcher attempts to focus the data so that readers can pull out the most important and relevant results without getting lost in details. The ultimate purpose of presenting the data is to share the information with others so that health professionals can improve the current ways that they work and take care of people. Researchers are responsible for sharing results with interested communities through books and popular social media and reporting results to other scientists through professional conferences and journal articles. Presenting results allows the researcher to share information with others, encourages the exchange of ideas, and provides a check that results are accurately reported. Results are discussed, questioned, or confirmed. These discussions are critical to ensuring that changes in practice and further research are based on good science.

Throughout history, there have been times when researchers were too eager to make new discoveries and ignored the health, safety, and free will of study participants. Experiments, such as the Tuskegee Syphilis Study, Willowbrook Hepatitis Studies, or cancer studies at New York City's Jewish Chronic Disease Hospital, reveal an embarrassing history of unethical human experimentation. To ensure that researchers focus on the rights and welfare of study participants, the National Commission for the Protection of Human Subjects of Biomedical and Behavioral Research was formed and developed *The Belmont Report* (1979). *The Belmont Report* is a document that outlines and describes the three basic bioethical principles of respect for persons, beneficence, and justice. Respect for persons requires researchers to treat participants as autonomous individuals who are able to make their own decisions regarding study participation. According to this principle, selected populations may be more vulnerable to coercion or manipulation. Vulnerable populations require more stringent safeguards. The second principle, beneficence, obligates researchers to maximize the benefits to study participants and minimize the harms. The final principle, justice, mandates that each person is treated fairly and provided the same benefits and opportunities as others. All research studies involving human participants are reviewed for human participant protections by an independent group of scientists and nonscientists known as an institutional review board (IRB). The IRB members review studies to ensure that the study is founded in good science and follows the bioethical principles of human participant protections.

Research is an ongoing cycle of learning and investigation designed to discover new information and make connections between what we know and what we need to know. Research seeks to improve how public health practitioners identify, treat, and prevent illnesses. Researchers are bound by a code of ethics and professional practices that ensure protection of human participants and honesty in collecting and reporting results.

Sally Kuykendall

See also: Belmont Report, The; Causality; Code of Ethics; Ethics in Public Health and Population Health; National Cancer Institute; Tuskegee Syphilis Study

Further Reading

Babbie, E. R. (2015). *The practice of social research*. Independence, KY: Cengage.

National Institute of Health, Office of Extramural Research. (2015, July 1). *Protecting human research participants.* Retrieved from https://phrp.nihtraining.com/users/login.php.

U.S. Department of Health and Human Services, Office of Human Research Protections. (2015, July 1). *The Belmont Report.* Retrieved from http://www.hhs.gov/ohrp/humansubjects/guidance/belmont.html.

RISK-BENEFIT ANALYSIS

Risk-benefit analysis, also referred to as cost-benefit analysis or benefit-cost analysis, is a principle of public health that compares the risk or cost of an action to financial and human gains. The concept is used in many disciplines and is particularly relevant to public health where interventions and programs are often financed through public funds or private foundations. Risk-benefit analysis tells whether the expected or actual outcomes of a policy or program justify the risk or cost. The concept has been used to quantify the value of syringe exchange programs, newborn phenylketonuria (PKU) testing, early childhood education programs, the Clean Air Act, mental health services, vaccinations, and stroke prevention efforts.

Risk-benefit comparison requires a careful consideration of all relevant factors. In public health, such considerations encompass financial costs, likelihood of the disease or injury, likelihood of serious complications or adverse consequences due to disease or injury, life expectancy, current quality of life, and currently available alternatives. In terms of life expectancy, a public health action that prevents 10 premature deaths of newborns has greater value than 10 premature deaths of octogenarians (O'Brien, 2002). The challenge is in quantifying the value of human life.

To ensure accurate and honest comparisons, statisticians must identify a logical common denominator or adjust for risk. For example, when comparing the number of deaths due to automobiles in 1997 to 1925, statisticians must account for the fact that there were fewer vehicles on the roads in 1925. Instead of comparing the actual number of deaths, safety experts calculate deaths per 100 million vehicle miles traveled (VMT). Standardizing to 100 million VMT yields better comparable data and more accurate conclusions. In 1925, there were 18 deaths per 100 million VMT. In 1997, there were 1.7 deaths per 100 million VMT (Achievements in public health motor-vehicle safety: A 20th century public health achievement, 1999). A 90 percent reduction in deaths due to motor vehicle crashes demonstrates significant advancements in driver, passenger, and pedestrian safety. A risk-benefit analysis would also consider the cost of those advancements, that is, the cost of the National Highway Safety Act, the cost of raising the minimum drinking age, and the cost of driver education programs, sidewalks, restricted traffic flow, seat belts, air bags, and child safety seats. To keep it simple, let's examine one intervention, graduated driver licensing programs. Between 1995 (before graduated driver licensing programs) and 2008 (after graduated driver licensing programs), fatal crashes of 16-year-old drivers decreased from 13.4 per 100 million VMT to 9.1 per 100 million VMT (National Safety Council, 2015). Allstate Foundation estimates that implementing comprehensive graduated driver licensing programs in all states could save 2,000 lives and $13.6 billion per year. Oregon, reported to have the strictest graduated driver licensing program, estimates annual administrative costs of $150,000 and annual estimated savings of $11 million (Insurance Institute for Highway Safety, n.d.). Thus, for every $1 that Oregon invests in graduated driver licensing program, $73 is saved.

With limited funding for public health programs, risk-benefit analysis is a useful tool to assess the value of a program. On the other hand, cost-benefit analyses raise ethical questions, such as what is the dollar value of a life or of quality of life, and whether all lives have equal value or are some more valuable than others. Focusing exclusively on cost-benefit analyses could eliminate public investment in valuable research and treatment of rare diseases or emerging health problems. There are dangers in trying to reduce the value of a program or policy to a quantitative number.

Sally Kuykendall

See also: Anderson, Elizabeth Milbank; Syringe Service Programs; Truth Campaign, The; Veterans' Health

Further Reading

Achievements in public health motor-vehicle safety: A 20th century public health achievement. (1999). *Morbidity and Mortality Weekly Report*, *48*(18), 369–374. Retrieved from https://www.cdc.gov/mmwr/preview/mmwrhtml/mm4818a1.htm.

Allstate Foundation. (2016). *Teen safe driving*. Retrieved from https://www.allstatefoundation.org/teen_safe_driving_driver_license.html.

Boden, L. I. (1979). Cost-benefit analysis: Caveat emptor. *American Journal of Public Health*, *69*(12), 1210.

Insurance Institute for Highway Safety. (n.d.). *Graduated driver licensing*. Retrieved from http://adtsea.org/Resources%20PDF%27s/NHTSA%20Graduated%20Driver%20Licensing.pdf.

National Safety Council. (2015). *Injury Facts®, 2015 edition.* Itasca, IL: Author. Retrieved from http://www.nsc.org/Membership%20Site%20Document%20Library/2015%20Injury%20Facts/NSC_InjuryFacts2015Ed.pdf.

Neenan, W. B. (1971). Distribution and efficiency in benefit-cost analysis. *Canadian Journal of Economics*, *4*(2), 216.

O'Brien, B. J. (2002). Book review: Risk-benefit analysis. *New England Journal of Medicine, 346,* 1099–1100.

Reid, R. J. (2000). A benefit-cost analysis of syringe exchange programs. *Journal of Health & Social Policy*, *11*(4), 41–39.

Wilson, R., & Crouch, E. A. C. (2001). *Risk-benefit analysis.* Cambridge, MA: Harvard University Press.

ROOSEVELT, ELEANOR (1884–1962)

Eleanor Roosevelt was the first wife of a president to use her position to fight for the rights of disadvantaged populations. Eschewing a life of privilege and ease, Roosevelt worked diligently to improve living and working conditions of minorities, women, and the destitute. Her efforts in public advocacy and legislature created a safety net for many Americans. After her husband died, she expanded her responsibilities, playing an important role in human rights through the fledgling United Nations.

Anna Eleanor Roosevelt was born on October 11, 1884, to Anna Rebecca (Hall) and Elliott Bulloch Roosevelt. Her parents were members of New York City's wealthy elite related to Philip Livingston (signer of the Declaration of Independence), William Livingston (signer of the U.S. Constitution), and President Theodore Roosevelt.

Although her wealthy background assured her social position and her attendance at the best private schools provided her with ample training, she had a difficult childhood with an unsympathetic mother and an alcoholic father. Her parents died when she was very young, leaving her to be raised by a strict grandmother. Roosevelt attended finishing school at Allenswood Academy, Wimbledon, England. Under the progressive leadership of the headmistress Marie Souvestre, Roosevelt flourished. However, in 1902, her grandmother summoned her home for her formal social debut. As a young, social debutante, Roosevelt volunteered at the Rivington Street Settlement House and the Consumers League where she was confronted by the low wages and working conditions of New York City's poor. The young Roosevelt considered herself unattractive and never acquired a superior upper-class demeanor. Shy instead of coy, clumsy instead of poised, she was just as surprised as everyone else when her dashing, handsome, distant cousin Franklin D. Roosevelt proposed marriage.

For 14 years after their marriage, until 1919, Roosevelt dutifully suffered domination by Franklin's mother, Sara; bore six children; and fulfilled the traditional social obligations of a wealthy politician's wife. The discovery at the end of World War I that her husband loved another woman prompted Roosevelt to establish an identity of her own. Instead of devoting an afternoon a week to aid the less fortunate, she made it a full-time career. She also became active in women's affairs and the Democratic Party. When Franklin was stricken later that year with polio, she helped him to continue his political career by taking over some of his tasks. Franklin returned to active political life in 1928 and won election as governor of New York, and Roosevelt resumed her own growing public life.

After her husband's election as president in 1932, Roosevelt refused to live only in Franklin's shadow. After the inauguration, her first official act was touring poor neighborhoods in Washington, DC. The unsanitary living conditions prompted her to start a campaign to provide decent affordable housing with indoor plumbing and toilets to every home in America. In her capacity as first lady, Roosevelt visited workers in mines and factories, held press conferences, and wrote a newspaper column. Strongly committed to civil equality for African Americans, she was often the only person close to the White House who was willing to speak up on race issues. FBI director J. Edgar Hoover compiled a report of over 3,000 pages documenting Roosevelt's activities against segregation, fascism, racial injustice, and later, the Cold War and nuclear weapons. When Eleanor's sometimes controversial statements and behavior on behalf of the less fortunate worried his aides, Franklin smiled and replied, "I can always say, I can't do a thing with my wife." Although despised by some for her outspokenness, Roosevelt was admired and loved by many more for her tireless efforts to encourage social reform for African Americans, women, youth, and the poor. In a half-hearted apology to her friend, Roosevelt wrote, "I am sorry that all these attacks against me are causing so much grief to my friends. But in these troubled times I intend to go right on saying and doing what must be said and done. And I intend to provide lots of ammunition for attack in the future" (Cook, 1993, p. 26).

In 1939, when the Daughters of the American Revolution refused to let Marian Anderson, an African American singer, perform in Washington's Constitution Hall, Roosevelt resigned from the organization. Then she helped arrange for Anderson to give a triumphant outdoor concert on federal property at the Lincoln Memorial.

Roosevelt's frequent trips across the country enabled her to learn the mood of the public. She became a major domestic policy adviser in her husband's administration. As one New Deal aide recalled, "No one who ever saw Eleanor Roosevelt sit down facing her husband, and holding his eye firmly, say to him, 'Franklin, I think you should . . .' ever forgot the experience." Eleanor Roosevelt was instrumental in the development of the National Labor Relations Act, the Fair Labor Standards Act, and the Social Security Act. She served briefly as codirector of the Office of Civilian Defense in 1941 and played a major role in Franklin's selection of Frances Perkins as secretary of labor, the first woman to hold a Cabinet-level position.

During World War II, Roosevelt visited troops in the United States, England, the Caribbean, and the South Pacific. After Franklin's death in 1945, she continued her public life, writing her newspaper column, serving as a delegate until 1952 to the United Nations (where she was instrumental in drafting the Declaration of Human Rights), and working with emotionally disturbed children. She supported reform Democrats in New York and worked for Adlai Stevenson in his campaigns for president in 1952 and 1956. President John F. Kennedy reappointed her to the United Nations in 1961, the year before she died on November 7, 1962.

Steven G. O'Brien and Sally Kuykendall

See also: Centers for Medicare and Medicaid Services; Medicaid; Medicare; Roosevelt, Franklin Delano; Social Security Act; Wald, Lillian

Further Reading

Cook, B. W. (1992). *Eleanor Roosevelt.* New York: Viking.

Cook, B. W. (1993). Eleanor: Loves of a First Lady [Cover story]. *Nation, 257*(1), 24–26.

Hareven, T. K. (1968). *Eleanor Roosevelt: An American conscience.* Chicago: Quadrangle Books.

Lash, J. P. (1972). *Eleanor: The years alone.* New York: Norton.

O'Farrell, B. (2009). Restoring workplace democracy: Eleanor Roosevelt and labor law reform. *Journal of Workplace Rights, 14*(3), 329–350. doi:10.2190/WR.14.3.e

Roosevelt, E. (1937). *This is my story.* New York: Harper.

Roosevelt, E. (1949). *This I remember.* New York: Harper.

Roosevelt, E. (1958). On my own, Part Three: I learn about communists. *Saturday Evening Post, 230*(34), 30–62.

Roosevelt, E. M. (1958). *On my own.* New York: Harper.

ROOSEVELT, FRANKLIN DELANO (1882–1945)

Franklin Delano Roosevelt was the 32nd president of the United States and the only president to serve more than two terms. His presidency marked numerous advancements in public health. Stricken with polio at the age of 39, Roosevelt was the first president with a noticeable disability. His experience with chronic illness provided insight and empathy for the suffering of disadvantaged people in the United States. Roosevelt led the fight against polio, introduced the New Deal, enhanced the U.S. Public Health Service, implemented Social Security, and initiated a national housing program. His major contributions to public health were providing economic security and supporting mental health, proper nutrition, and access to medical care for millions of Americans.

Franklin Delano Roosevelt was born on January 30, 1882. He enjoyed a privileged youth, spending his early years at the family estate in Hyde Park, New York, and attending the exclusive Groton School before going on to Harvard University and Columbia University Law School. In 1905, he married Eleanor Roosevelt, his distant cousin and the niece of former president Theodore Roosevelt. He was elected to the New York Senate in 1910 and quickly made a name for himself by challenging the Tammany Hall political machine's control over the Democratic Party. In 1920, Roosevelt ran as the vice presidential candidate with James M. Cox. Although the Democratic Party lost the election, Roosevelt used the opportunity to establish a national reputation. His political future seemed assured until he was stricken with polio and paralyzed in the lower extremities. Because polio tended to strike infants and children, Roosevelt was initially misdiagnosed. The first consulting doctor believed that Roosevelt suffered a blood clot in his spinal cord or a spinal lesion and prescribed regular back massages. The doctor who made the diagnosis of polio stopped the massages believing that the massages may have spread the infection.

Knowing that his paralysis would be perceived as infirmity or defect, Roosevelt and his aides carefully orchestrated public appearances. This picture is one of three known photographs of Roosevelt in his wheelchair. (Franklin D. Roosevelt Library)

For two years, Roosevelt struggled to teach himself how to cope with the loss of physical function. On the recommendation of a friend, he sought treatment at a resort in Warm Springs, Georgia. The warm mineral waters were said to cure infantile polio. Roosevelt was not cured but enjoyed the resort so much that he continued to make regular visits. In 1926, the resort experienced financial difficulties. The Roosevelts bought the resort and converted it to a hydrotherapeutic center for polio survivors. The treatment center struggled to survive until 1934 when, in lieu of birthday gifts, Roosevelt encouraged friends and colleagues to donate money to the Georgia Warm Springs Foundation. The first annual Birthday Ball raised one million dollars. Subsequent Birthday Balls were also highly successful.

In 1937, Roosevelt decided that a more comprehensive approach to polio control was needed. In notes, Roosevelt explains the purpose and mission of a National Foundation for Infantile Polio:

> The general purpose of the new foundation will be to lead, direct, and unify the fight on every phase of this sickness. It will make every effort to ensure that every responsible research agency in this country is adequately financed to carry on investigations into the cause of infantile paralysis and the methods by which it may be prevented. It will endeavor to eliminate much of the needless after-effect of this disease—wreckage caused by the failure to make early and accurate diagnosis of its presence. We all know that improper care during the acute stage of the disease, and the use of antiquated treatment or downright neglect of any treatment, are the cause of thousands of crippled, twisted, powerless bodies now. Much can be done along these lines right now. The new foundation will carry on a broad-gauged educational campaign, prepared under expert medical supervision, and this will be placed within the reach of the doctors and hospitals of the country. (Roosevelt, 1937)

The National Foundation for Infantile Polio funded massive research toward the discovery of a vaccine against polio, the most notable of which were Drs. Jonas Salk and Albert Sabin. After the discovery of the polio vaccine, the foundation evolved into the March of Dimes with the mission of reducing infant mortality and preventing birth defects.

Many people thought Roosevelt's paralysis would end his political career. The image of a "cripple" might prevent many Americans from voting for him. With Eleanor's help, Roosevelt developed a bold personal style. The press was complicit in covering up his disability. Very few pictures exist of Roosevelt in a wheelchair. He posed for pictures in a standing position, leaning on his cane, a podium, or personal aide for balance. His leg braces were painted black so as not to be seen in photographs. His charming, persuasive persona outshone his disability. In 1928, Roosevelt won the race for governor of New York.

The roaring twenties brought enormous growth and prosperity to the inner cities. Consumer confidence was high, and easy credit enticed people to take out large loans. The Federal Reserve and economists warned that the boom could not last forever. The warning triggered investors to sell stocks, causing the stock market to drop. Hoping to stabilize the market, big banks purchased large blocks of blue chip stocks, stocks in corporations that had a solid reputation for making a profit. The strategy worked temporarily and the market rallied. However, the events were reported in the weekend newspapers and by Monday, many investors tried to sell stocks in order to get out of the market. By Tuesday October 29, 1929, widespread panic and chaos ensured. The Dow lost 30 points. "Black Tuesday" triggered the start of the Great Depression. Consumer confidence in the market dropped, people stopped making large purchases, businesses closed, unemployment rates reached 25 percent, full-time workers were relegated to part-time work, banks foreclosed, and people lost homes and properties. Roosevelt established a reputation as a compassionate, reform-oriented governor.

In 1932, Roosevelt became the presidential nominee for the Democratic Party. During the campaign, he promised to balance the federal budget and to provide aid to the needy. Confident that he would win the election, Roosevelt began preparing for the presidency. He enlisted the aid of a number of experts and college professors to assist him so that he could move quickly to deal with the national crisis. This group of professors—Rexford Tugwell, Adolph Berle Jr., and Raymond Moley—were nicknamed the *brain trust*. In his inaugural address, Roosevelt announced that he would call Congress into an immediate special session to pass the New Deal legislation necessary to deal with the banking crisis and the collapse of the economy. The special session of Congress lasted from March 9, 1933, to June 16. During that period of 100 days, more important legislation was passed than at any other comparable period in U.S. history.

The three aims of the New Deal were recovery, relief, and reform. To stop the rush on bank withdrawals, banks closed temporarily. The Agricultural Adjustment Administration (AAA) was established to limit production and increase farm prices. The Civil Works Administration, the Civilian Conservation Corps, the Public Works Administration, and later the Works Progress Administration were created to relieve unemployment by providing temporary jobs. The Federal Emergency Relief Administration was created to provide funds to local relief agencies. Other innovative programs were:

- The Home Owners' Loan Corporation, which worked to protect people from mortgage foreclosures.
- The National Recovery Administration (NRA), which was designed to regulate business competition.
- The National Labor Relations Board, which was established to guarantee the right of labor to organize.
- The Tennessee Valley Authority project, which brought low-cost power and jobs to millions of people in the Tennessee River Valley area.

Among the many relief efforts was the Social Security Act, a landmark policy to provide social insurance for the elderly. The idea of social insurance for the elderly was first proposed by Isaac Max Rubinow. Rubinow was a Russian immigrant, economist, and medical doctor caring for poor immigrants in New York City's Lower East Side. The elderly were at high risk for suffering the effects of inflation and unemployment. Using data from the U.S. Department of Commerce and Labor, Rubinow estimated that 500,000 men and 1,400,000 women over the age of 65 were unable to earn a living wage. The burden of care often shifted to families or charities. In the summer of 1934, Roosevelt named the Committee on Economic Security with Rubinow serving as consultant. On August 14, 1935, Roosevelt signed the Social Security Act, providing social insurance for the nation's elderly into law.

Although these efforts failed to end the Great Depression, they provided a sense of the government's commitment to relieving people's suffering and led to Roosevelt's landslide reelection in 1936. They also marked the first extensive use of the government's fiscal powers to stimulate mass purchasing and thereby promote economic recovery. Although New Deal legislation provided substantial relief for the American people, it was World War II that returned the United States to prosperity.

By the time Roosevelt won reelection in 1936, he had realized that the dictatorial regimes in Japan, Germany, and Italy were hoping to solve their economic problems through military expansion. Although Roosevelt wanted to keep the United States out of war, he provided aid to Great Britain. In 1940, Roosevelt decided to run for an unprecedented third term. Roosevelt promised to keep Americans out of any foreign wars and easily defeated his Republican rival, Wendell Willkie. Japan's surprise attack on Pearl Harbor on December 7, 1941, forced a declaration of war against Japan. Germany and Italy then declared war on the United States, and the United States found itself fighting in both Asia and Europe. On the home front, Roosevelt issued Executive Order 9066, authorizing the "relocation" of more than 100,000 Japanese Americans in the United States. The Japanese American internment has since been recognized as a gross violation of civil liberties.

Roosevelt was severely criticized for some of the ways he directed the war effort, but he behaved in his characteristically pragmatic fashion. His goal was to win the war with as few American casualties as possible. To do this, he needed to keep the wartime alliance of Great Britain, the Soviet Union, and the United States together until after Germany and Japan were defeated, and he did. Meanwhile, war created prosperity, and Americans widely believed that they were fighting "the Good War." These factors sustained national unity and enough popularity for Roosevelt for him to win reelection to a fourth term in 1944.

In 1945, the Allies (the United States, Great Britain, and the Soviet Union) met in Yalta to discuss the composition of postwar Europe. After Roosevelt returned from Yalta, his doctors ordered him to rest. He traveled to his retreat at Warm Springs, Georgia, where he suffered a massive cerebral hemorrhage and died on April 12, 1945. Roosevelt's vice president, Harry Truman, succeeded him as president.

No other president in the 20th century was as adored by the masses as Roosevelt. Through his speeches and famous "fireside chats," Roosevelt spoke to millions of Americans. Hundreds of thousands sent him letters detailing their hardships, asking for assistance, and thanking him for his help. Reporting on Roosevelt's death, the *American Journal of Public Health* noted:

> [Roosevelt] was a great humanist in the sense defined by Archibald MacLeish when he said, 'It is necessary to believe in man, not only as the Christians believe in man,

> out of pity, or as the democrats believe in man out of loyalty, but also as the Greeks believed in man, out of pride.' Humanism in this connotation was perhaps the keynote of President Roosevelt's personality. He understood human needs and he had faith in human power. To justify that faith by carrying forward the age-long struggle for a better world is our obligation and our opportunity. (Roosevelt, 1945)

Roosevelt inspired both intense loyalty and opposition. His critics and supporters agree, however, that he did more to establish the U.S. welfare state and government responsibility for individual social welfare than any other president has. Roosevelt's impact on the United States through his social and economic legislation was huge and lasting.

Sally Kuykendall

See also: Centers for Medicare and Medicaid Services; Cutter Incident, The; Infectious Diseases; Medicaid; Medicare; Polio; Roosevelt, Eleanor; Salk, Jonas; Social Security Act; Vaccines

Further Reading

Berish, A. (2016). *FDR and polio.* FDR Presidential Museum and Library. Retrieved from https://fdrlibrary.org/polio.

Brown, T. M., & Fee, E. (2002). Isaac Max Rubinow. *American Journal of Public Health, 92*(8), 1224–1225.

Burns, J. M. (1956). *Roosevelt: The lion and the fox.* New York: Harcourt Brace.

Burns, J. M. (1970). *Roosevelt: The soldier of freedom.* New York: Harcourt Brace Jovanovich.

Fraser, S., & Gerstle, G. (Eds.). (1989). *The rise and fall of the New Deal order, 1930–1980.* Princeton, NJ: Princeton University Press.

Helfand, W. H., Lazarus, J., & Theerman, P. (2001). ". . . So that others may walk": The March of Dimes. *American Journal of Public Health, 91*(8), 1190.

Lash, J. P. (1971). *Eleanor and Franklin: The story of their relationship, based on Eleanor Roosevelt's private papers.* New York: Norton.

Parran, T. J. (1936). Health security. *American Journal of Public Health, 26,* 329–335.

Richardson, S. (2015). FDR on global disease threats, 1940. (2015). *American History,* 49(6), 14.

Roosevelt, F. D. (1937). *Personal notes.* FDR Library. Retrieved from https://fdrlibrary.org/documents/356632/390886/polio_nfipcreation.pdf/e0c36fdc-5a79-4d7c-a57c-c8b43637e019.

Roosevelt, F. D. (1945). *American Journal of Public Health, 35*(5), 509.

Schlesinger, A. M., Jr. (1957–1960). *The age of Roosevelt* (Vols. 1–3).

Troy, T. (2017). Presidents and public-health crises. *National Affairs, 31,* 54–66.

ROSEN, GEORGE (1910–1977)

George Rosen was a prolific writer, medical historian, public health physician, and social scientist. Rosen's drive, determination, energy, and vision created two unique fields within public health: history and social medicine. Repeatedly denied entrance into the hallowed halls of academia, Rosen stood firmly between the worlds of public health practice and academic scholarship. From his research on miners' diseases to factory conditions, he was an advocate for the working people. He carefully detailed the conflicting interests of industry, public policy, and occupational health. The resulting observations and insights brought social medicine to the forefront of public health practice. Throughout his lifetime, Rosen authored more than 200 articles and nine books and translated numerous medical-historical texts into English. His greatest contribution was in researching and documenting the history of public health through which he highlighted the relationship between social circumstances and health. Although he was never a political activist, Rosen worked steadily to educate others on the living and working conditions of the poor and disadvantaged.

The son of working-class Jewish immigrants, Rosen was born in Brooklyn and grew up in a world where social status determined health. His father, Morris Rosen, was a shirt presser and union activist. As a child, George tagged along to union functions, although he was uninterested in union politics. His mother, Rose Handelman Rosen, was homemaker for the family of four. George did not learn English until he started elementary school and quickly became an avid reader of any and every subject. In 1930, he completed his undergraduate degree at the College of the City of New York and applied to medical school. Denied admission due to *numerus clausus*, an anti-Semitic practice, which limited the number of Jewish students attending an institution, a friend suggested going to medical school in Germany. In the fall, Rosen joined other American medical students in attending Berliner Universität.

The Berlin University was not the traditional backup or safety school. Also known as Friedrich Wilhelms Universität and Humboldt Universität, the university boasts 40 Noble Prize winners along with notable alumni and lecturers, W. E. B. Du Bois, Albert Einstein, James Franck, Robert Koch, Max Planck, and Erwin Schrödinger, to name a few. In Germany, Rosen was introduced to a lifestyle far different from that of his working-class roots. He was impressed by the national health system, European culture, and most of all by his medical school classmate and future wife, Beate Caspari. The Caspari family, also Jewish, had survived the turmoil of World War I and hyperinflation of the Weimar Republic. Believing that the worst was behind them, the Caspari family enjoyed a comfortable life. Beate intended to follow her father's example as a family physician. However, their time at school coincided with the Nazi rise to power. Rosen's American citizenship protected him. Beate's family was not as fortunate. The American students walked a fine line of wanting to help the Jewish families, yet enjoying immunity from a growing anti-Semitic movement. Beate Caspari recalled one incident where the family feared that their house would be searched by the Schutzstaffel (SS). Her father carried a pistol to protect himself from robbery during house calls. If the SS found the pistol, her father could be jailed. To protect the family, George wrapped the pistol in paper and threw it in a nearby river. Beate and George intended to be married but moved their wedding earlier so that Beate would also have the protection of American citizenship and thus be able to finish medical school. The partnership proved to be long, successful, and productive.

Rosen's medical program included a dissertation requirement. He was determined to write on the little known topic of the history of American medicine. His adviser referred him to Dr. Henry Ernest Sigerist, director of the Institute of the History of Medicine at Johns Hopkins and the world's leading expert on the history of medicine. Sigerist and Rosen worked well together. The final dissertation was on American physician and physiologist William Beaumont. Rosen would have liked to work full-time with Sigerist after graduation. However, Hopkins did not have funding for another medical historian. The Rosens moved to New York City where George began an internship at Beth-El Hospital in Brooklyn and regularly contributed articles to Sigerist's journal *Bulletin of the History of Medicine.* The responsibility of regular articles with monthly deadlines forced George to investigate numerous different topics. He decided to write a book, and Sigerist suggested the topic of the history of miners' diseases. Mining was and is one of the most dangerous jobs in the world. Miners risk injury and death from collapsed mine shafts, explosions, and collisions with locomotives or mine cars. In 1930, the Bureau of Mines reported 103,821 injuries and 2,063 fatalities (Adams, Geyer, & Chenoweth, 1932). Rosen's book, *The History of Miners' Diseases: A Medical and Social Interpretation,* carefully studied mining practices and diseases, advancing from ancient Greece and Rome through the 1900s. The work presented social reforms in Belgium, Britain, Germany, and France, which led to improvements in the industry. Rosen's ability to simultaneously dissect and weave together history, economy, occupational health and safety, social conditions, and acute and chronic diseases appealed to a wide audience of physicians, engineers, historians, chemists, and social scientists.

In 1937, Rosen started his own medical practice and took a part-time job at New York City Department of Public Health to help pay the bills. He would have preferred working as a university scholar. He enjoyed reading and writing and lacked or did not care to invest in developing the interpersonal skills of a bedside doctor. The public health experience created the desire to get a master of public health (MPH) degree. In the fall of 1939, Rosen started sociology courses at Columbia University. Continuing to juggle his clinical practice and scholarship, Rosen earned his PhD in sociology while working full-time as a health officer with the NYC Department of Health (1942) and for the United States Army (1943). The army sent him to England to interview German doctors about Nazi experimentation on humans. In Great Britain, Rosen connected with Henry Schulman who invited him to edit the *Journal of the History of Medicine and Allied Sciences.*

Discharged from the army in 1946, Rosen returned to the NYC Department of Health and enrolled in the MPH program at Columbia University. By this time, Sigerist was retiring from Johns Hopkins. Rosen, having established himself as a medical historian in his own right, was hoping to take Sigerist's positon. Race and politics once again stood in the way. Johns Hopkins would not consider a Jewish chairholder. Sigerist, a vocal advocate for social medicine, created enemies within the institution. Rosen was guilty of communism by association. Therefore, he continued his day job in public health, writing on the side. In 1949, Rosen became the director of health education for NYC and founded the Department of Health Education and Preventive Services at the Health Insurance Plan of Greater New York (HIP). Through HIP, Rosen was able to apply his ideas of social medicine. He became active in the American Public Health Association and eventually became editor for the *American Journal of Public Health (AJPH)*. Through the *AJPH*, Rosen focused efforts on bringing public health together as a profession. This was a challenging task since public health professionals encompass a wide array of professions. As a natural extension of his interests, Rosen started the *AJPH* feature *Public Health: Then and Now*. The feature continues today, reflecting on the history of public health and lessons for the future. In 1951, Rosen finally earned an appointment as part-time faculty at Columbia University School of Public Health. The position later became full-time, and in 1969 he moved to Yale University to become professor of history of medicine and public health. Rosen continued to lecture and write about social medicine from a global/historical perspective until his sudden death by heart attack (July 27, 1977) while on lecture tour in England.

The legacy of George Rosen is a reflection of his life experiences. The son of poor Jewish immigrants, repeatedly denied entry into elite institutions, and witness to the overexaggerated nationalism of Nazi Germany, George Rosen worked tirelessly to envision a public health system that focused on the needs of the people, effectively sidestepping ethnocentric, class-centric politics. Although he was never a vocal political activist, Rosen used his pen to create activism. He presented unavoidable facts, forced enlightened knowledge, and drove logical reasoning. His pen was his political activism. And through his writing, he advocated for those who could not advocate for themselves. Rosen died at the relatively young age of 67, which begs the question, if Rosen or others like him had the voice, power, and support of formal institutions earlier in life, what would our public health system look like today?

Sally Kuykendall

See also: American Journal of Public Health; Modern Era, Public Health in the; Social Determinants of Health

Further Reading

Adams, W. W., Geyer, L. E., & Chenoweth, L. (1932). *Coal-mine accidents in the United States.* U.S. Department of Commerce. Washington, DC: U.S. Government Printing Office. Retrieved from http://digital.library.unt.edu/ark:/67531/metadc12525/m2/1/high_res_d/Bulletin0355.pdf.

Caspari-Rosen, B. B. (n.d.). *Autobiographical essays, posted by Susan Koslow (née Susan Joan Rosen).* Retrieved from http://profkoslow.com/beatecasparirosen/index.html.

Hamilton, A. (1944). The history of miners' diseases: A medical and societal interpretation [Book]. *New Republic, 111*(10), 283.

Mormon, E.T. (2015). George Rosen: Public health and history. In G. Rosen, *A history of public health* (Rev. expanded ed.). Baltimore, MD: Johns Hopkins University Press.

Rosenkrantz, B. G. (1979). George Rosen: Historian of the field. *American Journal of Public Health*, *69*(2), 165.

Schmacke, N. (1998). Health promotion through Neighborhood Health Centers: A tribute to George Rosen on the 20th anniversary of his death. *Health Promotion International*, *13*(2), 151.

Terris, M. (1979). George Rosen and the American public health tradition. *American Journal of Public Health*, *69*(2), 173–176.

RURAL HEALTH

The first important issue in discussing rural health is the definition of "rural." The federal government uses two different major definitions of "rural." The Census Bureau defines as rural all population, housing, and territory that does not fit within the urban definitions of either urbanized areas of 50,000 or more people or urban clusters of at least 2,500 and less than 50,000 people. The Office of Management and Budget (OMB) classifies counties as metropolitan, micropolitan, or neither. A metro area will have a core urban area of 50,000 people or more, while a micro area has an urban core of at least 10,000 people but less than 50,000 people. All counties that are not part of a metropolitan statistical area are considered rural. Using this definition, about 15 percent of the population of the United States is rural, covering roughly 72 percent of the land area of the United States. The general consensus is that each definition has limitations, with the Census Bureau standard providing an overcount of the rural population whereas the OMB standard represents an undercount. The Federal Office of Rural Health Policy (FORHP) classifies all nonmetro counties as rural and uses an additional adjustment, coming up with about 18 percent of the population and 84 percent of the land area of the United States as rural (FORHP, 2017).

Most experts in public health agree that there are obstacles faced by both rural health care providers and patients that are different from those in urban areas. Important differences include workforce shortage problems, socioeconomic factors, and health inequalities. Considering first the issue of workforce shortages, access to physicians and other health care services is much more difficult in rural areas. The patient to primary care physician ratio in rural areas is only 39.8 physicians per 100,000 people, as compared with a figure of 53.3 physicians per 100,000 people in urban areas. The same is true for other types of health providers, such as dentists, where there are only 22 per 100,000 in rural areas versus 30 per 100,000 in urban areas (National Rural Health Association, 2017). Given the lower numbers of providers, access to care is a problem even if people have good health insurance and transportation (National Rural Health Association, 2017).

The next issue, socioeconomic factors, helps to illustrate why issues of access to care become even more complicated and problematic in rural areas than the simple figures on workforce shortages might indicate. People living in rural areas tend to be poorer than those in urban areas. Per capita income in rural areas is over nine thousand dollars lower than the average per capita income in the United States. As part of this, rural Americans are more likely to live below the poverty level. This is even truer for minorities and a major problem for children (about 25 percent of rural children live in poverty). Rural residents are more likely to depend on the Supplemental Nutrition Assistance Program (SNAP), with almost 15 percent of rural households using the benefits versus less than 11 percent of metropolitan households (National Rural Health Association, 2017). Adding to the issues of greater poverty are more transportation problems, both because of the greater distances that must be traveled and the less reliable transportation sources of the rural poor. In addition, rural communities have more uninsured people, along with higher rates of unemployment. In this era of the importance of the Internet as a source of health information, rural residents also have problems with access to high-speed Internet connections, with over half of rural residents not having Internet connections of the basic bandwidth recommended by the Federal Communications Commission.

Given these problems, it is perhaps not surprising that rural residents report a range of more serious and concerning health issues. Some of these apply to all rural populations, and some are of special concern to the young or to older age groups. For the young, one example is tobacco use. Over a quarter of rural youth over the age of 12 smoke cigarettes versus 19 percent in large metro areas. The rates of smokeless tobacco usage are three times higher for rural youth (National Rural Health Association, 2017). Another example is that rural youth are twice as likely to commit suicide. For middle-aged and older rural populations, diabetes and coronary heart disease are more common. A recent Centers for Disease Control and Prevention (CDC) study found that rural Americans are more likely to die from five leading causes of death than those living in urban areas. Many of these deaths were considered potentially preventable by the CDC, such as 25,000 from heart disease, 19,000 from cancer, 11,000 from chronic lower respiratory disease, and 4,000 from stroke (CDC, 2017). In general, rural residents are poorer, older, and sicker than urban counterparts. Rural residents have higher rates of cigarette smoking, high blood pressure, and obesity. They have less leisure-time physical activity and lower seat belt use than their urban counterparts.

For all rural residents, injuries are more common, with a 22 percent greater risk of injury-related death. Some of this relates to vehicle crashes, as more than 50 percent of vehicle crash-related fatalities occur in rural areas, even though the miles traveled are less (only one-third of miles traveled in vehicles occur in rural areas) (National Rural Health Association, 2017). In the CDC study, they found 12,000 potentially preventable deaths in rural areas from unintentional injuries (CDC, 2017). Also in the CDC study, they reported that unintentional injury deaths were approximately 50 percent higher in rural areas than in urban areas, partly due to greater risk of death from motor vehicle crashes and opioid overdoses. Additionally, the greater distances between health care facilities and trauma centers create more issues of gaining access to specialized care for people injured in rural areas.

A last area of greater problems for rural residents is mental health. Issues of availability of mental health professionals are one problem, as is the issue of accessibility due to travel times and lack of insurance. Another issue is that rural residents have more negative views about mental health services, leading to reluctance to use such services, in addition to the barriers of cost, travel time, and lack of enough professionals providing these services. A recent issue that crosses boundaries between physical and mental health but is a serious problem in rural areas is opioid addiction.

Jennie Jacobs Kronenfeld

See also: Food Insecurity; Health Disparities; Health Resources and Services Administration; Nutrition; U.S. Department of Agriculture

Further Reading

Centers for Disease Control and Prevention (CDC). *Rural health.* Retrieved from https://www.cdc.gov/ruralhealth.

Centers for Disease Control and Prevention (CDC). (2017). *Rural Americans at higher risk of death from five leading causes.* Retrieved from https://www.cdc.gov/media/releases/2017/p0112-rural-death-risk.html.

Eberhardt, M. S., & Pamuk, E. R. (2004). The importance of place of residence: Examining health in rural and nonrural areas. *American Journal of Public Health, 94*(10), 1682–1686.

Federal Office of Rural Health Policy (FORHP). *Basic website information.* Retrieved from https://www.hrsa.gov/ruralhealth/index.html.

Hale, N. L., Smith, M., Hardin, J., & Brock-Martin, A. (2015). Rural populations and early periodic screening, diagnosis, and treatment services: Challenges and opportunities for local public health departments. *American Journal of Public Health, 105*(S2), S330–S336. doi:10.2105/AJPH.2014.302449

National Rural Health Association. (2017). *About rural health.* Retrieved from https://www.ruralhealthweb.org/about-nrha/about-rural-health-care.

S

SABIN, FLORENCE RENA (1871–1953)

Florence Sabin, born in 1871, is regarded as one of the outstanding woman scientists in the medical field in the first half of the 20th century. Sabin was the first female professor at Johns Hopkins School of Medicine, the first female elected to the National Academy of Sciences, and the first female to direct a department at the Rockefeller Institute for Medical Research. After ground-breaking discoveries in the lymphatic system and tuberculosis, Sabin focused on reorganizing public health in Colorado. In 1951, she was awarded the prestigious Lasker Award for public service.

Florence Rena Sabin was born on November 9, 1871, in Central City, Colorado. Her mother, Rena (Miner), was a schoolteacher from Vermont who taught in the South until the Civil War (1861–1865), before moving west. Florence's father, George Kimball Sabin, was from a prestigious New England family. He abandoned his plans to study medicine following the gold rush and becoming a mining engineer. Florence attended school at the Vermont Academy at Saxton's Rover, Vermont. In 1893, she graduated from Smith College with a bachelor of science degree. She hoped to study medicine. However, many medical schools did not accept females, and George Sabin did not have the funds to send his daughter to medical school. Dr. Grace Preston, the resident physician at Smith College, told Sabin that Johns Hopkins was trying to start a medical school with the aid of a group of prominent women. The founders gave two conditions. The medical school must have high standards for admission and must accept women who met the entrance criteria. With the plan to save money for medical school, Sabin returned to Colorado and taught mathematics at Wolf Hall in Denver. In Denver, Sabin also worked as a private tutor, teaching the children of Ella Strong Denison. A wealthy philanthropist, Denison partially supported Sabin through medical school. Sabin returned to Smith College where she worked during the school year as a substitute teacher and during the summer as a researcher at the Biological Laboratory in Woods Hole, Massachusetts.

When Sabin attended Johns Hopkins Medical School, she found gender stereotypes were not completely eliminated. All of the professors were male, and many refused to mentor female students on the assumption that the women would only drop out of medicine and have babies. Female students were easily overlooked for valuable clinical and research opportunities. Dr. Franklin Mall, chair of the Anatomy Department, noticed that Sabin showed great interest in research. He encouraged her to study the controversial topic of the origin of the lymphatic system. Injecting lymphatic channels with India ink, Sabin showed that the vessels derived

After retiring from her prestigious career at the Rockefeller Institute for Medical Research in New York, Dr. Florence Rena Sabin returned to her native Colorado where she completely reorganized the State Board of Health. (National Library of Medicine)

from the venous system. Sabin published her first paper and continued research into the brain anatomy of newborns, leading to several publications before graduation.

Sabin received her medical degree in 1900 and chose to continue in research and teaching. Her major areas of research were lymphatic vessels, red and white blood cells, development of supravital staining techniques for living cells, and the identification of the monocyte as a definitive type of white blood cell. In 1902, Johns Hopkins Medical School appointed her as the first female instructor, and by 1917 she had advanced to full professor. A few months after her promotion, her mentor, Dr. Mall, died. Sabin seemed a natural choice for the chair's position. However, Johns Hopkins administration passed her over and awarded the position to Sabin's student Lewis Weed. Other current and former students were furious. Many assumed she would leave Johns Hopkins. However, she stayed with the explanation that she had research projects in progress. In 1925, Simon Flexner convinced Sabin to leave Johns Hopkins to direct the new Department of Cellular Studies at the Rockefeller Institute.

The Rockefeller Institute was modeled after the Pasteur Institute in France and the Koch Institute in Germany. Offering a well-equipped research laboratory, decent salary, and freedom from teaching responsibilities and university politics, the Rockefeller Institute attracted the best U.S. scientists. Sabin studied the role of white blood cells in fighting infections. Her research led to a major interagency project studying the body's response to tuberculosis. Although the scientists were unable to find a cure for tuberculosis, they did gain benchmark discoveries into the anatomy and physiology of the immune system. Living in New York, Sabin enjoyed an active social life of concerts, museums, and dinner parties.

Sabin retired from the Rockefeller Institute in 1938 and returned to her native Colorado where she wrote up her research, traveled, and served on several foundations, including the Henry Strong Denison Foundation. In 1944, the governor of Colorado was establishing a postwar committee on health. He wanted a woman who would not challenge the status quo to lead the group. A journalist from the *Denver Post* recommended the little old lady, except, Sabin was not unfamiliar with public health. She had volunteered at a woman's health clinic in Baltimore and worked closely with public health departments on the tuberculosis project. On appointment, Sabin immediately applied her research skills and infectious disease training to Colorado's public health system. Her first project was to conduct health surveys of Colorado residents and to consult with public health experts. The surveys showed high morbidity and mortality rates. Yet, state funding for public health allocated less than ten cents per person per year. Sabin wrote and introduced several pieces of public health legislation to address the poor health care systems in the state. The "Sabin Bills" reorganized Colorado's State Board of Health so that administrative positions in the board could not be used as political patronage appointments; provided district health services using federal, state, and local funds; increased the stipends for indigent hospitalized tuberculosis patients; and gave provisions so that the Department of Public Health could obtain funding for the construction of new hospitals under the Hill-Burton Act. In December 1947, Sabin was appointed manager of Denver's Department of Health and Charities. In the most populated city of Colorado, Sabin worked on improving sanitation in restaurants and hospitals, regulating the milk industry to ensure safe, uncontaminated milk, and reducing industrial contamination of waterways. She finally retired in 1951 and died on October 3, 1953, after a prolonged case of pneumonia.

Sabin was recognized for many scientific and public health accomplishments. She was the first woman elected to the National Academy of Sciences (1925) and the first female president of the American Association of Anatomists (1924–1926). She received honorary degrees from a dozen universities. Among her other honors and awards were the National Achievement Award (1932), the M. Carey Thomas Prize (1935), the Trudeau Medal of the National Tuberculosis Association (1945), and the Albert Lasker Public Service Award (1951). A bronze statue was placed in her honor in Statuary Hall in Washington, DC. In addition to her numerous scientific papers, she was the author of *An Atlas of the Medulla and Mid-Brain* (1901) and *Biography of Franklin Paine Mall* (1934). She was a member of the American Association for the Advancement of Science, the American Physiological Society, the Society for Experimental Biology and Medicine, the Harvey Society, and the National Tuberculosis Association, and an honorary member of the New York Academy of Sciences. In public health, Sabin is credited with reorganizing Colorado's public health system to ensure that positions in a state public health department are not used as a reward for political contributions or support.

Tiffany K. Wayne and Sally Kuykendall

See also: Health Policy; Infectious Diseases

Further Reading

Andriole, V. T. (1959). Florence Rena Sabin—Teacher, scientist, citizen. *Journal of the History of Medicine & Allied Sciences, 14*(3), 320–350.

Dunn, E. C. (2011). The pasteurized state: Milk, health and the government of risk. *Endeavour, 35*(2/3), 107–115. doi:10.1016/j.endeavour.2011.06.004

National Institutes of Health. *The Florence R. Sabin Papers.* Profiles in Science, National Library of Medicine. Retrieved from http://profiles.nlm.nih.gov/RR.

Sabin, F. R. (1947). People win for public health in Colorado. *American Journal of Public Health, 37,* 1311–1316.

Sabin, F. R. (1948). Ailments of health departments. *American Journal of Public Health, 38,* 1508–1511.

Sabin, F. R. (1952). Trends in public health. *American Journal of Public Health, 42,* 1267–1271.

Wayne, Tiffany K. (Ed.). (2010). *American women of science.* Santa Barbara, CA: ABC-CLIO.

SALK, JONAS (1914–1995)

Jonas Salk developed the first safe and effective vaccine against poliomyelitis (polio). Polio is a devastating illness that primarily affects children. The deadly virus moves rapidly, attacking the nervous system. Five to ten percent of polio victims died due to respiratory muscle paralysis (World Health Organization, 2016). The introduction of the inactivated polio vaccine in 1955 was one of the most important public health advances of the 20th century.

Salk was born on October 28, 1914, in New York City to Russian immigrant parents. He was a young child during the beginnings of epidemic polio. He attended New York University School of Medicine and became a physician, but he was drawn to research rather than to direct patient care. Salk's interest in virology (the study of viruses) was piqued by a lecture in medical school. The lecturer stated that the only way for a person to become immune to a viral disease was to suffer the disease, because a killed vaccine would not work on viruses. The lecturer also said that it was possible to make a person immune to the bacterial disease diphtheria by inoculation with a vaccine made from killed bacteria. Salk felt that the statements were contradictory. Both statements could not be true.

After completing his medical training, Salk entered the University of Michigan's School of Public Health working as assistant professor of epidemiology and researching influenza virus. In 1947, biochemist and virus researcher Max Lauffer recruited Salk to move to the University of Pittsburgh. In a note of reference, Salk's former laboratory supervisor at Columbia Medical School described his former student, "[Salk] showed a high aptitude for experimental work . . . Casual encounters since that time have left me with the impression that he has continued to be very fond of himself" (Pitz, 2014). Salk became director of the virus research laboratory and professor in bacteriology (1949–1954) and preventive medicine (1954).

Salk obtained a research grant to participate in a poliovirus-typing project commissioned by the National Foundation for Infantile Paralysis (NFIP). Scientists across the country were in a race to find a safe and effective polio vaccine. Albert Sabin's vaccine used attenuated (weakened) forms of all three polio serotypes while Jonas Salk used the most deadly Type 1 (Mahoney) poliovirus. Salk's lab adopted a new technique that allowed the growth of the virus on monkey kidney tissue. Poliovirus could suddenly be grown in large amounts with less time, money, and monkey specimens. Salk deactivated (killed) the virus with formalin so that the body still produced antibodies, but there was no possibility of transmitting disease. After successfully testing the vaccine in rhesus monkeys, a small trial was conducted with previously infected children.

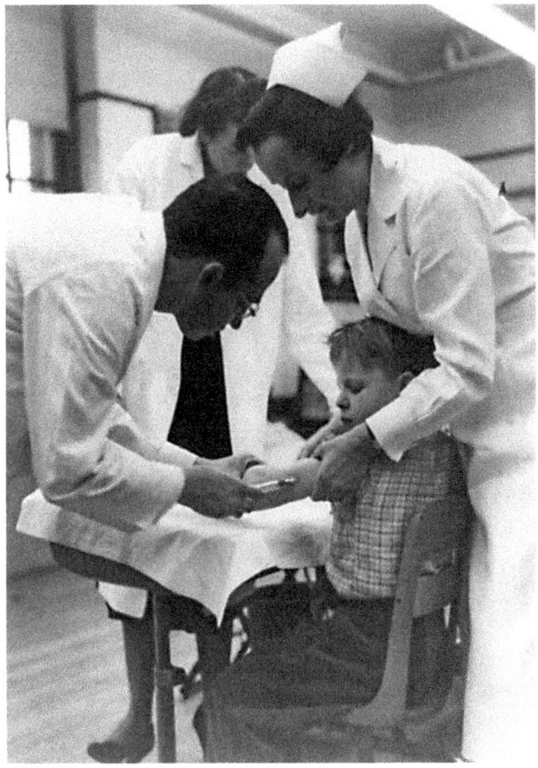

Dr. Jonas Salk tests his polio vaccine in a large-scale placebo-controlled trial of 1.8 million children. When Salk's vaccine was pronounced "safe, effective, and potent," church bells rang and air-raid sirens shrieked. (Library of Congress)

In 1953, 35,592 Americans were infected with polio, resulting in 1,450 deaths and 15,648 cases of permanent paralysis (Freyche & Payne, 1956). The following year, Salk commenced a placebo-controlled trial of the vaccine with 1.8 million children. When Salk's vaccine was pronounced "safe, effective, and potent," church bells rang and air raid sirens shrieked. However, the joy was short-lived. Within a few weeks of the start of the nation's mass immunization campaign, six children immunized with vaccine from Cutter Laboratories became paralyzed. Although the Cutter vaccine had passed government safety standards, some of the potent Mahoney virus had survived the manufacturing process, causing an estimated 40,000 cases of polio, including 200 cases of paralysis and 10 deaths (Fitzpatrick, 2006). The Cutter cases revealed serious flaws in manufacturing, bottling, and quality assurance testing. The government revised safety standards and resumed the polio vaccination program in the fall of 1955. Five years after introduction of the Salk vaccine, the incidence of poliomyelitis cases dropped 90 percent, and the vaccine proved to be safe, potent, and effective. In September 2015, world health experts announced the worldwide eradication of Type 2 polio, and the last cases of Type 3 wild poliovirus were seen in November 2012. The Global Polio Eradication Initiative is working to eradicate polio throughout the world.

In 1960, Salk established the Salk Institute in California, a nonprofit research institution devoted to biological research related to health. After his work on the polio virus, Salk began research on the AIDS virus and contributed his remaining career in search of a cure. Salk died in La Jolla, California, on June 23, 1995.

Lara J. Kunschner and Sally Kuykendall

See also: Cutter Incident, The; Infectious Diseases; Polio; Roosevelt, Franklin Delano; Vaccines; World Health Organization; *Controversies in Public Health:* Controversy 3

Further Reading

Blum, N., Katz, E., & Fee, E. (2010). Professor Natan Goldblum: The pioneer producer of the inactivated poliomyelitis vaccine in Israel. *American Journal of Public Health, 100*(11), 2074–2075. doi:10.2105/AJPH.2010.192922

Bredeson, C. (1993). *People to Know. Jonas Salk: Discoverer of the polio vaccine.* Berkeley Heights, NJ: Enslow.

Byrne, J.P. (Ed.). (2008). *Encyclopedia of pestilence, pandemics, and plagues.* Westport, CT: Greenwood.

Fitzpatrick, M. (2006). The Cutter incident: How America's first polio vaccine led to a growing vaccine crisis. *Journal of the Royal Society of Medicine, 99*(3), 156.

Freyche, M. J., & Payne, A. M. (1956). Poliomyelitis in 1954. *Bulletin of the World Health Organization, 15*(1–2), 43–121.

Global Polio Eradication Initiative. (2017). *History of polio.* Retrieved from http://polioeradication.org/polio-today/history-of-polio.

Kluger, J. (2004). *Splendid solution: Jonas Salk and the conquest of polio.* New York: G. P. Putnam's Sons.

Martin, W. (1977). *Medical heroes and heretics.* Old Greenwich, CT: Devin-Adair.

Offit, P. A. (2005). *The Cutter incident: How America's first polio vaccine led to the growing vaccine crisis.* New Haven, CT: Yale University Press.

Oshinsky, D. (2006). *Polio: An American story.* New York: Oxford University Press.

Pitz, M. (2014, May 21). Letters reveal how Pitt recruited Dr. Jonas Salk. *Pittsburgh Post-Gazette* (PA).

Salk, J. E. (1951). Direction of research on vaccination against influenza. *American Journal of Public Health, 41,* 669–677.

World Health Organization. (2016). *Poliomyelitis.* Retrieved from http://www.who.int/topics/poliomyelitis/en.

SANGER, MARGARET LOUISE HIGGINS (1879–1966)

Margaret Sanger was a social reformer who advocated for the right of poor men and women to control the number and spacing of their children. As a visiting nurse, Sanger witnessed hemorrhage, sepsis, and deaths that resulted from self-induced and backstreet abortions. Determined to stop the unnecessary fatalities, Sanger provided sex education through news columns and pamphlets. Through multiple arrests and prosecutions, Sanger persevered and started the nation's first birth control clinic. In the end, public opinion and the demand for birth control overruled regulations. Today, family planning and women's reproductive health are one of the greatest health achievements of the 20th century.

Margaret was born on September 14, 1879, in Corning, New York, to Anne Purcell and Michael Hennessey Higgins. Mr. Higgins was a stone carver, sculpting angels for tombstones. When he declared himself an atheist, local churches ostracized him. In her autobiography, Margaret recalled life as the sixth of 11 children of Irish immigrants: "Very early in my childhood, I associated poverty, toil, unemployment, drunkenness, cruelty, quarreling, fighting, debts, and jails with large families" (Sanger, 1931, p. 5). Despite family dysfunction, Michael taught his children to stand up for what they believed in and to accept the consequences of those beliefs. Margaret's mother, Anne, died at the age of 48 from tuberculosis, a bacterial infection of the lungs that causes severe muscle wasting. Margaret blamed her father for her mother's death. Pregnant 18 times, including seven miscarriages, Anne was very frail and weak when she died. Margaret decided to become a nurse, caring for pregnant women. She started her studies at Claverock College and Hudson River Institute before transferring to the nursing program at White Plains Hospital.

Before graduating from nursing school, Margaret married architect William Sanger. She contracted tuberculosis the following year and, like her mother, struggled with the wasting disease for the rest of her life. The couple moved to Hastings-on-Hudson where they had three children—Stuart, Peggy, and Grant. William was happy in the suburbs, but Margaret yearned for the intellectual stimulation of the city. In 1910, the family moved to New York City (NYC). Margaret worked as a visiting nurse on the Lower East Side, and William struggled as a painter. The couple immersed themselves in the life, activities, and culture of Greenwich Village. Margaret joined the Liberal Club and the Women's Committee of the New York Socialist Party, taking part in many pickets and worker strikes.

Margaret's patients were a continual reminder of her own childhood of poverty, immigrant health, food insecurity, and competition for food and resources within the family. In July 1912, truck driver Jack Sachs called Sanger to attend to his wife, Sadie Sachs. Mrs. Sachs was 28 years old, pregnant, and the mother of three children. Jack barely earned enough to support the family. Mrs. Sachs had attempted a self-abortion and almost died. Sanger provided around the clock care for three weeks. As the young woman recovered from severe sepsis, she asked the doctor how she could avoid another pregnancy. The doctor responded that Jack should sleep on the roof. Three months later, Jack Sachs called Sanger again. Sanger recalled:

> His wife was sick again and from the same cause . . . Mrs. Sachs was in a coma and died within ten minutes. I folded her still hands across her breast, remembering how they pleaded with me, begging so humbly for the knowledge which was her right . . . Jake was sobbing, running his hands through his hair and pulling it out like an insane person. Over and over again he wailed, "My God! My God! My God!" (Sanger, 1931, p. 900)

Sadie Sachs was one of more than 2 million women who attained illegal abortions each year in the United States. Another 25,000 women died in childbirth while others committed suicide (Coigney, 1969). Sanger decided to shift her attention from treating abortions to preventing abortions, a public health principle known as *upstream*.

Sanger wrote a series of seven news articles on female reproduction and sex education. The articles, entitled "What Every Girl Should Know," were published in the socialist newspaper, the *New York Call*. However, when Sanger attempted to publish an article on syphilis and gonorrhea, the *New York Call* rejected it. Under federal Comstock Law (1873), information on sex education, prevention of conception, and abortion was illegal and banned from distribution by the U.S. Post Office. The chief proponent of the law, Anthony Comstock, served as special agent to the post office. Rather than drawing a salary, he kept a portion of the fines gathered from violations. Comstock was relentless in seeking offenders. Storekeepers who left mannequins unclothed in store windows were liable to prosecution. Medical schools could not send books through the mail. Doctors, such as the Sachs's doctor, were banned from discussing birth control with one exception. They could counsel men on the use of condoms as a way to prevent sexually transmitted infections.

On October 27, 1916, women with baby carriages queue for birth control outside Margaret Sanger's clinic at 46 Amboy Street in Brooklyn, New York. Police raided the clinic multiple times, arresting Sanger, confiscating medical records, and holding patients until they gave names and addresses. (Library of Congress)

Sanger viewed birth control as a human rights issue and a women's rights issue. She tried collaborating with the suffragettes and with labor groups. However, the groups were focused on their own causes, and birth control seemed too radical. In 1914, the Sanger family traveled to France. William studied art while Margaret investigated birth control in Europe. Within a month, Margaret returned to the United States and began publishing a monthly newspaper, *The Woman Rebel*. The publication was the first to introduce the term "birth control." She was immediately convicted and indicted on three counts of violating Comstock Law. Facing 45 years in prison, Sanger fled to England. However, as she left the United States, she signaled a printer to distribute 100,000 booklets. *Family Limitation* detailed the various birth control methods she had learned about in France and England. Back in Europe, Sanger met with birth control experts, toured health clinics, and prepared birth control brochures in multiple languages. She once again joined with groups of artists and authors, a lifestyle that resulted in multiple extramarital affairs and raised questions of whether her efforts were for her own benefit. Margaret eventually sent a letter to William asking for a divorce. Ironically, Comstock was setting a trap for William. He tricked William into giving away his last copy of *Family Limitation*. William was jailed for 30 days but refused to reveal his wife's location.

When Peggy—the Sanger's six-year-old daughter—contracted pneumonia, Margaret returned earlier than planned. Despite intensive nursing care by Margaret, Peggy died. Margaret became despondent. Her crusade for birth control was partially driven by a desire to make a better life for Peggy. With Sanger back in the states, Comstock was seeking aggressive prosecution. He wanted Sanger to serve five years of hard labor for each copy of *Family Limitation*. However, he underestimated the power of public opinion. By now, the majority of Americans favored birth control. And the news images of a pale, tiny woman suffering from a lifetime of tuberculosis and despondent over the death of her daughter attracted public sympathy. The government dropped all charges against Sanger.

In 1916, Sanger opened the first birth control clinic in the United States. The location was carefully selected based on invitations from the community and maternal health data from the NYC Board of Health. A patron living in California donated $50 for rent. A sympathetic landlord gave discounted rent of 46 Amboy Street in Brooklyn and even helped paint the clinic rooms. The Brownsville clinic staff consisted of Margaret Sanger, Ethel Byrne (Sanger's sister who was also a nurse), and Fania Mindell (a translator). The opening was well advertised with 5,000 flyers printed in English, Italian, and Yiddish. Sanger contacted Brooklyn's district attorney to let him know she intended to distribute birth control information. Clients traveled from New Jersey, Pennsylvania, Massachusetts, and Connecticut. Women who were unable to come sent their husbands in their place. On the first day, the staff saw 100 women and 80 men (Jacobs, n.d.). Women with baby carriages lined the street waiting for care. Sanger was prepared for any legal consequences. The police raided the clinic multiple times, arresting Sanger and the others, holding patients in the waiting rooms until they gave their names and addresses, and confiscating medical records. Each time, Sanger paid her bail and reopened the clinic. After nine days, the clinic closed. Once again, the case attracted public attention. Sanger was convicted and served 30 days in jail. Byrne was sentenced to 30 days and immediately went on a hunger strike. The hunger strike attracted even more attention. When Byrne became seriously ill, the governor pardoned her. Mindell was convicted and fined. The case resulted in a landmark ruling that allowed physicians to provide medically indicated birth control information. This meant that doctors could legally run birth control clinics. Unfortunately, the Comstock Law had stymied medical training. Doctors did not know how to counsel patients on birth control. Margaret hired a physician to travel around the country to educate doctors. They collected a list of 20,000 doctors willing to provide counseling on birth control. Women wrote to Sanger from across the nation, seeking advice on where and how to find information on birth control. In 1921, Sanger founded the American Birth Control League, the organization that eventually became Planned Parenthood.

In 1922, Sanger married J. Noah Slee. The millionaire president of Three-in-One Oil Company and a conservative church leader, Slee was an unlikely match for the headstrong, adventurous younger woman. The relationship did not deter Margaret's activities. In 1923, she opened a birth control clinic with Dr. Hannah Stone. Stone worked without pay and used the opportunity to collect data. Stone discovered that out of 1,655 clinic patients, 1,434 (87 percent) had self-aborted, and one woman reported self-aborting 40 times (Gray, 1979). The finding that nearly 9 out of 10 women reported self-aborting was eye-opening to the medical establishment. As information on birth control became accessible, demand for birth control methods increased. Yet, there were no suppliers in the United States. Sanger arranged for diaphragms to be shipped from Germany to Canada and smuggled them across the U.S. border in Three-in-One Oil boxes. In 1929, the police raided Sanger's clinic, collected the names and addresses of patients, and confiscated medical records. This time, the medical establishment stepped in, criticizing the police for violating doctor-patient confidentiality.

After World War II, the major opponent of birth control was the Catholic Church. The public generally accepted birth control. However, the cost of a diaphragm was prohibitive, and the device was awkward for some women. Sanger envisioned an inexpensive pill. The major pharmaceutical companies did not believe that women would take a pill every day of their lives for something that was not related to disease. With the financial support of Katharine Dexter McCormick (1875 II, the major opponent of birist capable of developing an oral contraceptive. Dr. Gregory Pincus was a struggling chemist who was denied tenure at Harvard for his controversial experiments with in vitro fertilization. Using a formula by G. D. Searle Pharmaceutical Company, Pincus developed and tested the pill. The U.S. Federal Drug Administration approved the pill for use in 1960.

Margaret Sanger was a pioneer in women's reproductive health. Contrary to federal laws that viewed sex education as crude and vulgar, Sanger embraced human sexuality and worked to empower both men and women to control reproduction. Sanger's investment in health education, contraception, and women's rights created a system of care that prevents 1.9 million pregnancies per year and reduces the demand for elective abortions (Guttmacher Institute, 2016). The ability to control reproduction improves women's health, frees women to pursue career and volunteer opportunities, and interrupts the poverty and stress of disadvantaged families.

Sally Kuykendall

See also: Dunham, Ethel Collins; Family Planning; *Healthy People 2020*; Infant Mortality; Maternal Health; Planned Parenthood; Prevention; Social Determinants of Health; Upstream Public Health Practices; Women's Health; *Controversies in Public Health:* Controversy 5

Further Reading

Centers for Disease Control and Prevention (CDC). (1999). Achievements in public health, 1900–1999: Family planning. *Morbidity and Mortality Weekly Report, 48*(47), 1073.

Centers for Disease Control and Prevention (CDC). (2017). Maternal and infant health. Retrieved from https://www.cdc.gov/reproductivehealth/maternalinfanthealth/.

Coigney, V. (1969). *Margaret Sanger: Rebel with a cause.* Garden City, NY: Doubleday.

Gray, M. (1979). *Margaret Sanger: A biography of the champion of birth control.* New York: Richard Marek.

Guttmacher Institute. (2016). *Publicly funded family planning services in the United States.* Retrieved from https://www.guttmacher.org/fact-sheet/publicly-funded-family-planning-services-united-states.

Jacobs, E. (n.d.). *Places that matter: Margaret Sanger Clinic (former).* Retrieved from http://www.placematters.net/node/1329.

New York University. (n.d.). *The Margaret Sanger Papers Project.* Retrieved from http://www.nyu.edu/projects/sanger/.

Office of Disease Prevention and Health Promotion. (2017). *Healthy People 2020.* Retrieved from https://www.healthypeople.gov/.

Sanger, M. (1931). *My fight for birth control.* New York: Farrar & Rinehart.

Wardell, D. (1980). Margaret Sanger: Birth control's successful revolutionary. *American Journal of Public Health, 70*(7), 736.

SCHOOL HEALTH

School health is an important topic in the United States and has been a special part of public health for over the past 100 years. More recently, there has been much discussion of the establishment of comprehensive school health programs (CSHPs). A push for CSHPs has emphasized both the public health and the educational advantages of such programs. From an educational standpoint, CSHPs improve students' academic performance and thus the employability and productivity of future citizens. From the public health perspective, CSHPs are an important way to decrease morbidity and mortality in school age populations and also to impact health care expenditures. One important aspect of school health programs is that one-third of the objectives in public health approaches such as the *Healthy People* projects are either directly attained or significantly influenced through schools (Institute of Medicine, 1997). There are often three different aspects of school health programs: traditional provision of limited health care services to children during the school day often through the services of a school nurse, health education provided to children through the school setting (sometimes with the help of a school nurse or through the efforts of classroom teachers), and, more recently, school-based comprehensive clinics.

Some of the same arguments in support of the importance of general child health programs also relate to school health. If children are healthy, they are more likely to be ready and able to learn and, as adults, to be healthy and able to contribute to the workforce and the overall vitality of society. In earlier eras, disease and death in children were due largely to infections. During this time period, childhood deaths were common, and there was concern over the spread of infectious disease within a school setting. Over the past century, both childhood mortality and infectious disease rates in the United States have been drastically lowered, so it is now uncommon for a child to die in childhood, whereas 150 years ago many families experienced the death of at least one child. In addition, in the United States, at least from age five on, children spend a large proportion of their waking hours in a school setting. Participation in public schools is one of the most commonly shared experiences in society.

One of the founders of modern nursing in the United States, Lillian Wald (1867–1940), was also recognized as the first school nurse in the United States. She worked in New York City in the poorer sections of the city. New York City was one of the first cities with mandatory school attendance laws and also had a large number of immigrant children with health care problems. From their efforts, the idea of general physical evaluations of children became more common, and New Jersey was the first state to require this by law in 1910. The poor health of some Americans had become evident during World War II (1939–1940) with high rejection rates of recruits into the military service due to health problems. In 1946, partially as a response to this, the National School Lunch Act was passed to promote better childhood nutrition and thus improve child health.

As immunizations became a more important part of the health of children, laws for mandatory immunization for school entrance became important, and often the school nurse had to help enforce these requirements. By the 1950s, often school nurses were very busy with school health examinations, including screening for vision and hearing deficits, and keeping immunization records. Another major role of school nurses is first aid and the evaluation of sick children. As concern about child abuse has grown, identification of violence-related injuries treated in the school setting has become another important task for school nurses (Igoe, 1994).

Another part of school health is a comprehensive health education program. Such programs are an important part of the curriculum in most school districts. Classroom teachers in lower grades have always included some health content in their teaching throughout the year. Programs generally start in kindergarten and continue through high school, and focus on providing an introduction to the human body and to factors that prevent illness and promote or damage health. National standards for such programs were established in the 1990s and have helped school districts create better curriculum content in the area of health. There has been a growth in evidence-based programs and evaluation of the content of educational programs in school health. In recent decades, more of the focus has been on elementary and middle schools, as the emphasis on more advanced courses has become one focus of changes in high school education in the United States.

Beginning in the 1980s and increasing in the 1990s, there was a move to provide more comprehensive school-based clinics in some schools. Groups such as the American Public Health Association created a Center for School, Health and Education in 2010 to advocate for and help organize school-based health care as a comprehensive strategy for preventing school dropouts and improving graduation rates for K–12 students. School-based health clinics grew from 31 in 1984 to 327 in 1991 to over 500 in 1992 (Kronenfeld, 2000). In 2004, the W. K. Kellogg Foundation launched a six-year initiative to expand school-based health care. Such clinics were included as a safety net provider in the 2009 Child Health Insurance Reauthorization Program, formerly SCHIP. The expansion of health care insurance coverage for children with the passage of the Affordable Care Act (ACA) under President Barack Obama made school-based clinics less important, especially in states that adopted the Medicaid expansions. The future of the ACA is currently uncertain, as are issues related to comprehensive school-based clinics.

Another area of uncertainty and problems in school health is the decline in school nurses, especially those with training at the registered nurse (RN) level. Since the early 2000s, and even more so since the Great Recession (roughly 2007–2012), the number of school nurses has been declining. Less than half of the country's public schools employ a full-time nurse, and in some of the worst cases—largely in poor, urban school systems—there's only one school nurse for every 4,000 students (Camera, 2016). This is another area of concern for the future in the school health area.

Jennie Jacobs Kronenfeld

See also: Children's Health; Community Health; Evidence-Based Programs and Practices; Health Education; Wald, Lillian; *Controversies in Public Health:* Controversy 5

Further Reading

Camera, L. (2016, March 23). Many schools don't have enough school nurses. *U.S. News & World Report* online. Retrieved June 30, 2017, from https://www.usnews.com/news/articles/2016-03-23/the-school-nurse-scourge.

Centers for Disease Control and Prevention. *Healthy Schools.* Retrieved from https://www.cdc.gov/healthyschools.

Centers for Disease Control and Prevention. (2011). School health guidelines to promote healthy eating and physical activity. *Morbidity and Mortality Weekly Report, 60*(5), 1–78.

Igoe, J. B. (1994). School nursing. *Nursing Clinics of North America, 29,* 443–458.
Institute of Medicine. (1997). 6 Challenges in school health research and evaluation. *Schools and health: Our nation's investment.* Washington, DC: The National Academies Press. doi:10.17226/5153
Kronenfeld, J. J. (2000). *Schools and the health of children: Protecting our future.* Thousand Oaks, CA: Sage.

SELF-EFFICACY

Self-efficacy is the personal belief that one is capable of performing the tasks necessary to attain a desired goal (Bandura, 1977, pp. 191–215). Self-efficacy is an important principle in public health because public health practitioners are constantly striving toward teaching people new skills and behaviors that will promote and maintain health. The concept of self-efficacy focuses less on the actual behavioral objective and centers on the individual's beliefs regarding his or her own ability to both meet and accomplish the challenges associated with attaining that objective. In the case of teaching individuals who are newly diagnosed with diabetes to measure and inject their own dose of the drug insulin, the patients must believe that they have the ability to perform the skill. High self-efficacy is related to a range of positive outcomes, including overall well-being and approaching tasks with interest and commitment. In contrast, individuals with low self-efficacy are more likely to avoid difficult challenges because they do not believe that they are capable of successfully accomplishing the necessary task. In order to encourage healthy behaviors and treatment compliance, public health professionals must understand, gauge, and promote self-efficacy among the patients who they serve.

Self-efficacy is developed in three primary ways: through mastery experiences, observing others who model the behavior, and persuasion (Bandura, 1986, pp. 359–373). Mastery experiences are challenges that take moderate to high levels of perseverance to accomplish a task. As a diabetic person is being taught to self-inject insulin, it is common to practice inserting the syringe into an orange or other model. In these situations, maintaining effort, even in the face of adversity, acts as evidence and allows the person to realize that he or she can effectively accomplish the task. A second pathway to develop self-efficacy is through observing others—social models who maintain effort. The most effective model is someone who is similar to the observers. Physical similarities suggest that they can also be successful in completing the task. This means that a child learning to self-inject insulin may be more successful when the behavior is modeled by another child rather than an adult. A third method to develop self-efficacy is through social persuasion. Social persuasion occurs when the communicator attempts to change another person's thoughts or behaviors. In this instance, the public health professional attempts to convince someone that he or she is capable of performing the behavior. Persuasive messages are most effective when they are realistic. Improbable messages are quickly discounted, especially if the person attempts and fails in the task. Persuasive messages can come from public health practitioners, medical professionals, and family members and ultimately increase the person's self-efficacy.

Perceived self-efficacy is appraised in three areas: magnitude and strength (van der Bijl & Shortridge-Baggett, 2001, pp. 189–207) and generality (Lunenburg, 2011, pp. 1–6). Magnitude is an external appraisal in which a person judges the level of difficulty of the task. For example, a student might evaluate his or her psychology exam to be moderately challenging. This assumed level of difficulty will accordingly influence his or her perception of self-efficacy regarding studying for the test. Strength is an internal appraisal referring to the level of confidence a person has about his or her ability to successfully complete a task. For example, a student is likely to judge his or her ability to effectively accomplish a goal-related task, such as putting in the long hours to study for an exam. Generality is a global perception of self-efficacy in which a person generalizes his or her expectations of self-efficacy across situations. In this instance, generality refers to the expectation of a level of self-efficacy in a range of tasks, not just one task. Together and individually, these characteristics influence how one perceives one's level of self-efficacy.

An important aspect of public health is empowering people to care for their own bodies, minds, and spirits. This may include engaging in regular physical activity, following a healthy diet, stopping smoking, or controlling anger and frustration. Public health professionals can use the concepts of self-efficacy to ensure that the patient realizes and appreciates the advantages of learning and practicing a specific health behavior, that the behavior is appropriately modeled, and by encouraging healthy behaviors through a variety of sources. Self-efficacy is an important principle in determining and guiding self-care and healthy lifestyles.

Stephen K. Trapp

See also: Children's Health; Diabetes Mellitus; Health Education; Locus of Control; Social Cognitive Theory

Further Reading

Bandura, A. (1977). Self-efficacy: Toward a unifying theory of behavioral change. *Psychological Review*, *84*(2), 191–215.

Bandura, A. (1986). The explanatory and predictive scope of self-efficacy theory. *Journal of Social and Clinical Psychology*, *4*(3), 359–373.

Bandura, A. (1994). *Self-efficacy*. Hoboken, NJ: Wiley.

Bandura, A. (2012). On the functional properties of perceived self-efficacy revisited. *Journal of Management*, *38*(1), 9–44.

Lunenburg, F. C. (2011). Self-efficacy in the workplace: Implications for motivation and performance. *International Journal of Management, Business, and Administration*, *14*(1), 1–6.

van der Bijl, J. J., & Shortridge-Baggett, L. M. (2001). The theory and measurement of the self-efficacy construct. *Research and Theory for Nursing Practice*, *15*(3), 189–207.

SHATTUCK, LEMUEL (1793–1859)

By today's standards, Lemuel Shattuck was a brilliant public health epidemiologist with incredible stamina and vision. At the time that Shattuck lived, however, public health was in its infancy, and official records of births, deaths, and diseases were nonexistent or haphazard. A self-educated man, Shattuck nurtured and developed many talents. He was a teacher, bookseller, publisher, researcher, and statistician. He served as a member of the Massachusetts State Legislature, a member of the Massachusetts Historical Society, and founder of the American Statistical Society. In public health, he is recognized as the main researcher and author of the *Report of the Sanitary Commission of Massachusetts* of 1850. Also known as *The Shattuck Report*, the document collected statistics on the living conditions of Massachusetts state residents and proposed ways to improve health through sanitation, regulations on the quality of food and drugs, and community planning. Shattuck is considered the architect of the public health system in the United States. He designed a framework for public health that was later adopted by many states and towns. C. E. A. Winslow described *The Shattuck Report* as "perhaps the most significant single document in the history of public health."

Lemuel Shattuck was born on October 15, 1793, in Ashby, Massachusetts. He was the fifth of six children of Betsey (Miles) and John Shattuck. In 1794, the Shattuck family relocated to southern New Hampshire where they purchased a farm. The land was rocky and poor. The family labored to survive. The children worked on the farm, attending school only five or six weeks per year. John Shattuck worked the farm during the day and as a shoemaker in the evening. Betsey Shattuck died of consumption (tuberculosis) in 1798, and John remarried the following year. The Shattuck children were self-taught, studying together as a group. Lemuel attended Appleton Academy for only two quarters, enough for him to qualify as a teacher and supplement the family income.

The summer of 1816 was particularly bad for farmers. Unseasonably cold weather wrecked crops and forced many to migrate westward, including Shattuck. On his travels, Shattuck worked as teacher, first in New York and then in Detroit. In Michigan, he founded the first Sunday school. Direct interactions with students and their families plus an insatiable curiosity gave him insights into the living and working conditions of residents in the various places he lived. By 1823, Shattuck returned to Massachusetts to help his brother manage a general store in Concord. Two years later, he married Clarissa Baxter, and the couple eventually had five children. Managing the store in Concord allowed Shattuck to pursue his passion of reading, studying, and learning. He researched and wrote his first book, *A History of Concord, Middlesex County Massachusetts, from the Earliest Settlement to 1832; and the Adjoining Towns, Bedford, Acton, Lincoln and Carlisle; Containing Various Notices of County and State History Not before Published*, which was published in 1835. At the time, a book on the history of Concord was not novel. There were several existing books on the history of Concord. These works primarily reported church or town records. What was novel about Shattuck's book was the extent that he went to in order to gather information. Shattuck visited the towns and people of the area, gathered stories, and documented interesting bits of information, which brought the tedious records to life. He did what is now known as field research or an oral history project. In addition to compiling personal stories, Shattuck gave recommendations to improve the living conditions of local residents. His research was concurrent with serving on Concord's school committee and gave him insights into improving the school system. He is credited with organizing school finances and developing policies, including a plan for teachers to record and report academic lessons to the town committee each year.

In 1834, the Shattuck family moved to Cambridge, Massachusetts, where he managed a store. The following year, they moved to Boston where Shattuck worked as a bookseller and publisher. He served on the City Council and the Massachusetts General Court. Colleagues recalled that Shattuck was extremely conscientious in his public duties. Whenever he was assigned to a committee or a project, he gave it all of his effort. He firmly believed that data could be used to identify social problems and to appropriately guide wise government policy. His pursuit of data led to the creation of the American Statistical Association in 1839. Shattuck's reputation as a hard worker came at a price. Other members on a committee with Shattuck would sit back and not work as hard. Shattuck often carried the weight of public responsibilities.

Although the study of genealogy was frowned upon at the time, Shattuck enjoyed researching his heritage. He traced his ancestors back to the original emigration to America. This research was an enormous task because of the lack of official records and high degree of population movement. And yet, Shattuck took the genealogical research one step further by presenting stories of each of the six to eight generations. He created a system of genealogical research that became a model for others. In 1841, he published *A Complete System of Family Registration*. In 1855, he published *Memorials of the Descendants of William Shattuck, the Progenitor of the Families in America That Have Borne His Name; Including an Introduction and an Appendix Containing Collateral Information*. The following year, Shattuck published *Blank Book Forms for Family Registers, Devised and Constructed upon a New, Simple, and Comprehensive Plan; Containing Suggestions and Directions for an Improved System of Family Registration, Designed for General Use in Every Family*. Shattuck's genealogical research was not simply focused on recording family births and deaths. He cared deeply about people. He believed that in presenting births, marriages, deaths, residences, illnesses, social conditions, income, and anecdotes, he was giving evidence of human connectedness and brotherly affection. His *Memorial of the Descendants of William Shattuck* (1855) became a model for the preservation of family histories. His genealogical research also impressed on him the need for a formal census.

In Boston, Shattuck successfully advocated for and organized a town census. In 1849, the Massachusetts governor and council requested that Shattuck, N. P. Banks, and Jehiel Abbott prepare a census report on the sanitary conditions of the state. Shattuck did most of the research and writing. The *Report of the Sanitary Commission of Massachusetts* of 1850 is considered one of the greatest documents in the history of public health. In introducing the purpose of the report, Shattuck wrote:

> We believe that the conditions of perfect health, either public or personal, are seldom or never attained, though attainable; that the average length of human life may be greatly extended, and its physical power greatly augmented; that in every year within this Commonwealth, thousands of lives are lost which might have been prevented; that a vast amount of unnecessarily impaired health, and physical debility exists among those not actually confined by sickness; that these preventable evils require an enormous expenditure and loss of money, and impose upon the people unnumbered and immeasurable calamities pecuniary, social, physical, mental, and moral, which might be avoided; that means exist, within reach, for their mitigation or removal; and that measures for prevention will effect infinitely more than remedies for the cure of disease.

The report was divided into four parts. The first two sections presented the history of the sanitary movement in France, Germany, England, and colonial America, with a review of major epidemics. The third section presented statistical analyses of mortality data by place, season, occupation, and cause followed by 50 recommendations for public health. The recommendations reflected a combination of thoughtful long-range planning and common sense. The final section gave support for the recommendations and offered suggestions for state policies to support public health.

Prior to *The Shattuck Report*, boards of health were small organizations that dealt with acute epidemics and public nuisances. *The Shattuck Report* recommended:

- Establishing formal state and local boards of health.
- Sanitary surveys of other cities and towns.
- Uniform nomenclature for causes of death.
- Collection of data on diseases including research of malaria and tuberculosis.
- Control of nuisances that affect health.
- Supervision of the construction of new buildings for safety.
- Sanitary requirements for schools and lodging houses.
- Periodic vaccinations for smallpox.
- Control of the sale of spoiled food, drink, and medicine.
- Quarantine measures.

The report recommended using civil engineering to promote health. Communities should be planned with trees and green spaces for recreation, public walkways, and access to clean air and water. Shattuck expressed concerns for the use of the criminal justice system in controlling mentally ill people. He argued that people suffering from mental illness should be turned over to the boards of health for care rather than be put in jail. He also called for the education of nurses and specialty training in sanitary science. To put this in perspective, Shattuck's report was published in 1850. Florence Nightingale did not establish the first nursing school until 1860. Finally, the report advocated for public health education. He envisioned that clergy should speak to their congregations on public health issues at least once a year. Shattuck estimated the annual cost of reducing preventable diseases in Massachusetts was $7,512,000 and requested $3,000 for the state board of health. Despite the effort, foresight, and economic benefits, the recommendations were initially disregarded. Dr. Henry Ingersoll Bowditch described Shattuck's report as falling "stillborn from the hands of the State printer."

In 1869, Massachusetts established the first state board of health. Other states quickly followed suit, and *The Shattuck Report* served as a valuable guide in defining roles and responsibilities of the new agencies.

Shattuck was a self-educated man, a teacher, an enthusiastic and focused visionary, and man of high faith and morals. He believed in the value of data in defining and charting social progress. His hard work helped to design a plan for arranging and preserving public documents and family records. More importantly, he had the wisdom and courage to call attention to social problems, filthy living conditions, and disease, and the stamina to work toward a vision of prosperity for all. The sanitary report increased awareness and helped to implement measures to provide clean water and adequate ventilation, to safely dispose of sewage, and to restrict the sale of unsafe food and drink. *The Shattuck Report* not only describes life in 1850 but also provides the infrastructure for public health today.

Sally Kuykendall

See also: American Journal of Public Health; Bowditch, Henry Ingersoll; Food Safety; Social Determinants of Health; State, Local, and Territorial Health Departments; Winslow, Charles-Edward Amory

Further Reading

Shattuck, L. (1850). *Report of the Sanitary Commission of Massachusetts.* Cambridge, MA: Harvard University Press. Retrieved from https://archive.org/details/b21359131.

Smillie, W. G. (1949). Lemuel Shattuck, still a prophet. *American Journal of Public Health, 39,* 135–144.

Winklestein, W. (2008). Lemuel Shattuck: Architect of American public health. *Epidemiology, 19*(4), 634.

SKIN CANCER

Prolonged exposure to the sun damages the skin and can result in tumors, disfigurement, and death. Over the past 50 years, skin cancer has steadily increased, especially in Australia, North America, and Northern Europe. An estimated one in five Americans will develop some form of skin cancer in their lifetime. There are more skin cancers in the U.S. population than all other cancers combined. Annual treatment costs are estimated at $8.1 billion. In many areas of the country, there is limited access to dermatologists for treatment. To prevent skin cancer, the surgeon general of the U.S. Public Health Service appealed to businesses, schools, communities, and federal, state, tribal, local, and territorial governments to increase public awareness of skin cancer and to promote skin cancer prevention.

Skin cancer is classified into two main categories: nonmelanoma skin cancer (NMSC), which includes basal cell carcinoma (BCC) and squamous cell carcinoma (SCC), and melanoma, which is less common than NMSC representing less than 2 percent of all skin cancers, but is responsible for the majority of skin cancer–related deaths. Of the NMSCs, 75 percent are BCC and the remaining 25 percent are SCC.

There are several well identified risk factors for skin cancer. The most important risk factor is the average annual ultraviolet (UV) radiation exposure received from the sun or tanning beds. Most UV exposure occurs during childhood, before the age of eight. Other known risk factors include occupational hazards and genetics. Pilots, sailors, and farmworkers are just a few of the at-risk occupations due to prolonged exposure outdoors. Certain genetic phenotypes are at greater risk. People with light complexion, blue eyes, and blonde or red hair have higher risk. Both SCC and BCC are found more often in males than females. SCC and BCC are commonly found on the head, neck, and upper extremities.

Skin cancer is detected by a dermatologist performing a full body skin examination (FBSE). For every 400 patients screened, approximately one melanoma is detected. Diagnosis is made by biopsy and pathological examination. The "ABCDEs" guide is used to identify which lesions require biopsy. Asymmetry, irregular Borders, Color changes, Diameter greater than 6 mm, and Evolving or changing in appearance suggests the need for biopsy. Several biopsy types are possible including excisional, incisional, and shave. Excisional biopsies remove the entire lesion in one section with margins. It results in a larger specimen for examination, but also results in a larger scar. Incisional biopsies include punch biopsies that only remove a piece of the lesion. Although this limits the scar, it also limits the amount of material for exam. Shave biopsies are done for superficial lesions where the entire lesion is removed by slicing under the lesion. It does not require suturing.

Skin cancer is treated by surgical excision, electrodessication, topical chemotherapy, laser, radiation, or chemotherapy. NMSC are easily treated with local treatments. Melanoma treatment requires precise diagnosis, staging, and excision. An excisional biopsy is used to measure the depth of invasion, known as Breslow thickness. A wide excision with 2-cm margins ensures the entire tumor is removed with a border of adjoining healthy tissue. The five-year survival rate for early localized disease is 91 percent whereas advanced, metastatic disease has a poor prognosis. Advanced melanoma is relatively resistant to chemotherapy, radiation, and immunotherapy. Diagnosis and treatment should be performed by a board certified dermatologist, surgeon, or primary care physician. In areas with poor access to medical care, doctors use telemedicine, communicating through electronic means, including video, to help diagnose and treat a suspected lesion.

Skin cancer is easily preventable. Unfortunately, in a large study of teenagers, less than 40 percent regularly used sunscreen, 83 percent experienced sunburn in the last year, and 33 percent experienced more than three sunburns. Only a minority of the survey respondents knew the correct amount of sunscreen to apply, the need for reapplication, or the need to apply 30 minutes before going outdoors

(Federman, Kirsner, & Viola, 2013). Regular daily sunscreen use is better at reducing skin cancer than discretionary application—only using sunscreen when the individual feels it is needed (Green, Williams, Logan, & Strutton, 2011). Furthermore, although sunscreen helps prevent SCC, it has little effect on BCC. *The Surgeon General's Call to Action to Prevent Skin Cancer* recommends:

- Educating people about skin cancer so that they may take action to protect their skin.
- Providing more opportunities for shade or sun protection in outdoor settings.
- Reducing the dangers of indoor tanning.
- Developing policies to advance skin cancer prevention.
- Advancing the science of skin cancer prevention through research, surveillance, and evidence-based programs. (U.S. Department of Health and Human Services, 2014)

A number of nonprofit, government, and professional organizations support public service announcements (PSAs) to educate the public about the dangers of skin cancer. Impact Melanoma, formerly the Melanoma Foundation of New England, created PSAs, *Tanning Is Out, Your Skin Is In,* to highlight the dangers of tanning beds. *Practice Safe Skin: Skin Cancer Prevention Project* provides brightly colored sunscreen dispensers in convenient, high-traffic outdoor spaces, such as at beaches, parks, day care centers, zoos, and golf courses. Skin cancer prevention is also integrated into schools, workplaces, parks, and recreational facilities through policies that discourage tanning and by providing adequate shaded areas.

Skin cancers are increasing in the United States and worldwide. Regular screening with early diagnosis and treatment can effectively take care of many of these cases. However, not all cases are easily treated, and treatment can be expensive and time consuming. To prevent skin cancer, physicians, dermatologists, and public health professionals recommend regular application of sunscreen before going outside, reapplication every half an hour and after swimming or sweating, and minimizing overall exposure to UV radiation.

Erin Mathews and Neil Mathews

See also: Cancer; Intervention; Logic Model; National Cancer Institute

Further Reading

American Academy of Dermatology. Retrieved from https://www.aad.org.

Centers for Disease Control and Prevention. *Skin cancer.* Retrieved from https://www.cdc.gov/cancer/skin/index.htm.

Federman, D. G., Kirsner, R. S., & Viola, K. V. (2013). Skin cancer screening and primary prevention: Facts and controversies. *Clinics in Dermatology, 31,* 666–670. doi:10.1016/j.clindermatol.2013.05.002

Geller, A. C., Oliveria, S. A., Bishop, M., Buckminster, M., Brooks, K. R., & Halpern, A. C. (2007). Study of health outcomes in school children: Key challenges and lessons learned from the Framingham Schools' Natural History of Nevi Study. *Journal of School Health*, 77(6), 312–318.

Green, A.C., Williams, G. M., Logan, V., & Strutton, G.M. (2011). Reduced melanoma after regular sunscreen use: Randomized trial follow-up. *Journal of Clinical Oncology, 29*(3), 257–263.

Impact Melanoma. Retrieved from http://mfne.org.

Kimbrough, C. W., et al. (2017). Melanoma and cutaneous malignant neoplasms. In C. M. Townsend, Jr., R. D. Beauchamp, B. M. Evers, & K. L. Mattox (Eds.), *Sabiston textbook of surgery: The biological basis of modern surgical practice* (20th ed., pp. 724–753). Philadelphia: Elsevier.

Kimbrough, C. W., McMasters, K. M., & Davis, E. G. (2014). Principles of surgical treatment of malignant melanoma. *Surgical Clinics of North America, 94*(5), 973–988. doi:10.1016/j.suc.2014.07.002

Soyer, H. P., Rigel, D. S., & Wurm, E. M. (2012). Actinic keratosis, basal cell carcinoma, and squamous cell carcinoma. In J. L. Bolognia, J. J. Jorizzo, & J. V. Schaffer (Eds.), *Dermatology* (pp. 1773–1793). Philadelphia: Elsevier.

U.S. Department of Health and Human Services. (2014). *The Surgeon General's call to action to prevent skin cancer*. Retrieved from https://www.surgeongeneral.gov/library/calls/prevent-skin-cancer.

SMALLPOX

Smallpox is a viral infection caused by one of two varieties of a virus subdivided as *Variola major* and *Variola minor*. This microorganism takes a horrific toll on the human body, first manifesting as a high fever followed by a distinctive, bumpy rash with blistering of the skin, mouth, and throat. Mortality can range from 1 percent in cases of *Variola minor* to more than 33 percent with *Variola major*. Death occurs roughly a week and a half to two weeks after initial infection from a combination of viremia (overabundance of virulent matter in the bloodstream), immune system collapse, and heart failure. Historically, smallpox caused millions of deaths around the world and decimated entire populations. Those who survived were often left with permanent facial scars, blindness, or limb deformity. The discovery of smallpox inoculation in the 18th century and later innovations in vaccination science significantly decreased the number of cases, with a few notable exceptions. In 1950, the Pan American Health Organization developed the goal of eradicating smallpox in North, South, and Central America. Initial efforts were promising, and effective public health strategies were extended throughout the world. By 1979, the World Health Organization (WHO) officially declared smallpox eradication. The eradication of smallpox is one of the leading public health accomplishments of all time. This incredible feat was accomplished by all countries working together and using thoughtful public health measures.

The variola virus is part of a family of orthopox viruses that characteristically replicate in the cell's cytoplasm instead of the nucleus. The family includes variola, vaccinia, cowpox, and monkeypox. Although variola only infects humans, vaccinia, cowpox, and monkeypox are animal diseases that can also attack humans. The majority of cases of smallpox are classified as *ordinary*, where the entire body beginning with the forehead and face is covered by distinctive pustules that harden, burst, and leave pockmarks on the skin. Less than 10 percent of cases are *malignant* with softened, flat lesions that produce a high fever and toxemia, a profusion of toxins in the bloodstream. Malignant cases nearly all result in fatality. Less than 3 percent of cases are *hemorrhagic* and characterized by lesions that bleed beneath the skin, giving the body a black appearance, hence its common name *black pox*. Hemorrhagic cases, like malignant ones, are nearly always fatal.

Smallpox is contracted in the same manner one catches other highly contagious human-contact diseases. The virus is primarily transmitted through airborne inhalation or face-to-face contact with an infected person. Exposure to infected bodily fluids or contaminated objects, such as clothing or blankets, can also act as a means of transmission. Infected persons are highly contagious from the first appearance of rash and blisters until the last one disappears, a period lasting many weeks. In order to eradicate smallpox, public health professionals had to break the chain of transmission from the carrier or reservoir to other susceptible hosts. This interruption was achieved through *disease surveillance*. Public health epidemiologists studied the patterns of past smallpox epidemics and predicted where future outbreaks were most likely to occur. Health professionals around the world and specifically in high-risk areas were vigilant for patients with symptoms of smallpox. In 90 to 100 percent of cases, early, preeruptive (before the rash appears) symptoms are high fever, headache, and backache. The classic smallpox rash starts as macules, small red spots on the tongue and mouth. These spots turn into lesions that break open, releasing viral particles into the mouth. The challenge for health professionals was to quickly and accurately differentiate the macules from other childhood rashes, such as chickenpox. Once potential cases were identified, the case was immediately reported for epidemiological tracking, the patient was isolated, and everyone who came in contact with the infected individual was vaccinated, a strategy known as ring vaccination. Normally, public health practices herd immunity where immunizing a certain threshold of individuals effectively prevents the spread of that disease. With smallpox, 83 to 85 percent of individuals would have to be immunized for effective herd immunity. With ring vaccination, 100 percent of individuals surrounding the infected person are immunized. Ring vaccination provides a complete blockade. The virus can no longer move from one host to the next. All bed linens or other materials that came in contact with the patient's open wounds are destroyed.

Smallpox could be either epidemic, striking in a particular area with a burst of fatalities, or endemic, in which the disease reoccurs each year as part of everyday life. The earliest historical cases of smallpox can be traced to the Indian subcontinent in 1500 BCE, China in 1122 BCE, and Egypt in 1145 BCE, where the disease was endemic to these populations. It is less clear when smallpox arrived in Europe. Some speculate about outbreaks in ancient Greece or Rome. The first direct references date from the early Middle Ages. By the 16th century, smallpox was endemic in Western civilization. European explorers and settlers carried smallpox to the New

World and Australia, causing great loss of life in native communities. The Native Americans were especially hard hit, decimating many tribes until widespread government immunizations in 1833. By the 18th century, smallpox was wreaking havoc in Europe. In the later part of the century, an estimated 400,000 Europeans died each year from the disease. Children were the hardest hit.

The ancient Chinese were the first to practice and perfect methods to prevent the spread of smallpox. Methods of inhaling the dried powder of smallpox pustules or in-grafting, rubbing a strain of the virus into a scratch on the skin, successfully controlled the spread and reduced mortality. As people migrated or traded between countries, in-grafting practices spread across India, Persia, Turkey, and Africa, eventually gaining the attention of physicians at the Royal Society of London. European doctors were initially reluctant. There was the potential of spreading smallpox even more or rejection by peers and society. Lady Mary Wortley Montagu (1689–1762), the wife of the British ambassador to the Ottoman Empire (modern-day Turkey), is credited with changing attitudes toward in-grafting or variolation. Lady Montagu had contracted smallpox as a young adult and was left with permanent scarring. Her brother died from smallpox. While living in Turkey, she noticed a distinct absence of the disease and curiously investigated variolation practice. She arranged for her six-year-old son to be variolated but not her infant daughter. After returning to England and facing another smallpox epidemic, she arranged for variolation of her three-year-old daughter, the first recorded in London. Very learned and persuasive, Lady Montagu encouraged her friends in the royal court to get variolated. Now that the practice was commonplace among the influential aristocracy, British physicians felt more comfortable with the technique.

Although variolation helped lower smallpox mortality, there were still considerable risks to introducing children to viral strains. Inoculation remained a great controversy and was not universally accepted. In 1796, a British physician named Edward Jenner noticed that milkmaids caught the benign cowpox disease but rarely contracted the deadly smallpox. He hypothesized that inoculating material from the pustules of cowpox could provide immunity against smallpox. He named the cowpox material "vaccina" from the Latin word for cow, *vacca*. Later, during the 19th century, *vaccinia*, a relative of variola, was substituted as a means for vaccination, and the riskier method of smallpox inoculation was banned in many countries.

A number of nations, including the United States and Russia, continue to maintain specimens of the smallpox virus for current and future laboratory experiments. The general population is no longer routinely vaccinated against smallpox. The only people who are vaccinated are military personnel who could be exposed to smallpox through bioterrorism or scientists who work with the virus. Should an outbreak occur, smallpox can be diagnosed in a laboratory environment through electron microscope replication and observation. Upon diagnosis, the physician would gauge the time elapsed from initial infection to determine whether vaccination will be helpful. Vaccination accomplished within three days of the infection greatly alleviates symptoms in the majority of cases. Administered between the fourth and seventh days carries less effectiveness. There are no drugs approved within the last 50 years for the treatment of smallpox, meaning medical facilities can only provide supportive care such as hydration and dressing of wounds.

Smallpox was once one of the greatest scourges to mankind. Millions of people infected by the variola virus suffered permanent disability or early death. The first public health measures to stop the transmission of smallpox started in ancient China as in-grafting. Chinese medical practitioners purposely introduced small amounts of dried viral particles through breaks in the skin. This strange, but effective practice was passed along trade routes through India and Turkey. In Europe, the practice was met with controversy, interest, rejection, and fear. In an act of informed desperation, members of the British aristocracy started opting for variolation. Early results were mixed, and British physicians and scientists eventually improved the technique to develop safe and effective vaccinations. Armed with effective vaccines and new techniques in disease surveillance, global health organizations realized the potential to completely eliminate smallpox, and in 1979 smallpox was officially eradicated. The techniques used to control smallpox may be effective in eradicating other infectious diseases plaguing mankind.

Sean P. Phillips

See also: Bioterrorism; Epidemic; Immigrant Health; Indian Health Service; Infectious Diseases; Jenner, Edward; Modern Era, Public Health in the; Public Health in the United States, History of; Quarantine; Renaissance, Public Health in the; Vaccines; World Health Organization; *Controversies in Public Health:* Controversy 3

Further Reading

Behbehani, A. M. (1983). The smallpox story: Life and death of an old disease. *Microbiological Reviews*, 47(4), 455–509.

Fenn, E. A. (2002). *Pox americana: The great smallpox epidemic of 1775–82.* New York: Hill and Wang.

Hopkins, D. (2002). *The greatest killer: Smallpox in history.* Chicago: University of Chicago Press.

Williams, G. (2011). *Angel of death: The story of smallpox.* London: Palgrave Macmillan.

SMITH, JAMES MCCUNE (1813–1865)

Physician, pharmacist, and abolitionist James McCune Smith was the first African American to obtain a medical degree and to publish in an American medical journal. His staunch opposition to the recolonization of blacks back to Africa and his advocacy for abolitionism are indicative of the issues that concerned free black activists in the North in the mid-18th century. Smith advanced public health by deconstructing ideas of the day and harmful stereotypes against blacks. A prolific and eloquent writer, Smith countered Thomas Jefferson's *Notes on Virginia,* which presented and validated slave-owner fears of violent retaliation by former slaves.

Smith was born on April 18, 1813, in New York City to parents who had successfully obtained their freedom. As a young boy, he was educated in the African Free Schools, where he established lifelong relationships with others who would also become significant activists, including Henry Highland Garnet and George Downing. Even as a child, Smith's intelligence singled him out for special recognition. At the age of 11, he was selected by the African Free School teachers to prepare a speech in honor of a visit from Revolutionary War hero general Marquis de Lafayette.

When he was 14, Smith witnessed one of the most historic occasions in New York City's free black community, the Emancipation Day celebration. Despite his young age, Smith later wrote one of the most revealing accounts of the commemorative activities, which included a parade complete with drums, dancing, and music. Smith was denied admission to American medical schools on the basis of race. Sorely disappointed, he sought assistance from activist Peter Williams Jr., who arranged for Smith to enroll at the University of Glasgow in Scotland. Thus, in 1832, Smith sailed for Scotland, where he spent the next five years earning three degrees: a bachelor's degree (1835), a master's degree (1836), and a medical degree (1837).

In 1837, Smith returned to his home in New York City and opened a successful medical practice and two pharmacies. His political activism began almost immediately; he fought openly against slavery and helped to create the Young Men's Anti-Slavery Society shortly after his return home. Yet he soon found that most of his associates were obsessed with another political issue: the emergence of the American Colonization Society, an organization that they feared would forcibly remove free blacks from the United States. Smith responded to the call by joining the anti-colonization struggle.

On January 8, 1839, African American New Yorkers convened the "Great Anti-Colonization Meeting" in order to protest against the "scheme" of African colonization. Smith was among the strongest leaders who addressed the crowd, offering an unequivocal manifesto on colonization. Describing the notion as antirepublican and un-Christian, they asserted the United States as the only logical home for free blacks. Smith's reputation as an orator also led him to deliver two additional addresses in the 1840s: "A Lecture on the Haitian Revolution" in 1841 and "The Destiny of the People of Color" in 1843.

Smith's determination to eradicate racism and claim U.S. citizenship for African Americans often caused him to assume rather controversial positions. During the 1840s, for example, he was extremely outspoken in his opposition to separate African American organizations. He believed that, given racial conflict in the United States, it was necessary to form successful biracial coalitions. As a result, he opposed the call for a statewide colored convention in New York on the grounds that independent African American action was a form of racial exclusivity that threatened the cause of racial advancement. After considerable debate and conflict, Smith was finally convinced to attend the New York State colored conventions, but he never relinquished his concerns about potential racial divisiveness. Instead, he increased his public activities on a wide range of political issues locally and nationally.

On the local level, Smith demonstrated his growing concern with the plight of working-class African Americans. In 1843, he became the physician for the Colored Orphan Asylum and diligently worked for more than a decade on behalf of these children. In 1850, Smith also assisted in the establishment of a new organization to address the needs of African American workers, the American League of Colored Laborers, which advocated for education and training in mechanical skills as a method to improve conditions.

In the following year, he convened a gathering of African American New Yorkers to assess the state of their community. Smith prepared a rather elaborate statement on the socioeconomic status of the African American community, outlining the vice plaguing their people and the economic problems that drove people to desperation. He revealed that African Americans had been denied equal access to education and skilled training and had therefore been reduced to the lowest occupations. In response, Smith developed a solution. Although similar plans had not been successful, Smith suggested that African Americans should abandon the city en masse and relocate back to the country. Through this project, Smith developed a friendship with white abolitionist Gerrit Smith, and the two men collaborated for many years thereafter. The plan never fully took shape, but Smith's plan for a return to an agricultural lifestyle demonstrated both his desperation and his dedication to improving conditions for the African American community.

Smith's national activism manifested itself in a wide range of issues during the 1850s. At the opening of the decade, he became particularly active following the passage of the Fugitive Slave Act. Outraged by this legislation, Smith joined the Committee of Thirteen, an organization designed to protect and defend fugitives. He became particularly famous for a public confrontation with his white pastor at St. Phillip's Church, during which Smith chastised him for not opposing the Fugitive Slave Act. After the minister declared that they must uphold the laws of the United States, Smith confronted him and reportedly "raised the Devil" with his anger.

His activism with the Committee of Thirteen eventually caused Smith to refocus his energies on the cause of anticolonization. In January 1852, the Committee of Thirteen convened the African American community in Abyssinian Baptist Church to declare their opposition to colonization and assert their rights as American citizens. They were particularly concerned because New York governor Hunt had endorsed colonization and was apparently considering a plan to provide funds to finance forced removal of the African American population. Smith was elected as a delegate to a meeting with the governor and ultimately convinced Hunt to reverse his position.

During this period, Smith also gained a reputation within the national African American leadership. He was a regular contributor to Frederick Douglass's newspapers under the pseudonym Communipaw. He also represented New York City at the 1853 Colored Convention and played a critical role in attempting to create a national African American organization, the National Council of the Colored People (NCCP). The idea for the NCCP was to implement the success of local associations on the national level and create a power base of African American leaders across the North. However, the NCCP was plagued by disorganization from its inception, and the organization never fully developed. Unable to reproduce their local effectiveness on the national level, activists abandoned the NCCP in 1855, only two years after it commenced.

Despite the failure of the NCCP, however, Smith remained nationally active. In particular, in 1855, he became the first African American to chair a national political convention. The Radical Abolition Party, formerly the Liberty Party, held its inaugural convention in Syracuse, New York, in June 1855 and hoped to gain the endorsement of African American voters by selecting Smith as its chair. However, Smith had opposed the Liberty Party in the 1840s because he believed the organization had not sufficiently advocated on behalf of the free black population. However, the reorganized political party made a concerted effort to incorporate African American men, and Smith had been convinced to provide his support to the struggling organization. Smith was rewarded for his loyalty, for they selected him as the nominee for secretary of state in 1857. Yet despite their best efforts, the Radical Abolition Party did not make major inroads with either the African American community or the American political system. As a result, by 1858, most African American leaders, including Smith, had abandoned the organization.

Even with all of Smith's political activism, perhaps his most well known activity was his very public conflict with Garnet beginning in 1858. Garnet had recently founded the African Civilization Society, an organization designed to spread religion and establish business relationships in Africa. In particular, the society was interested in exploring the possibility of cotton production in West Africa, an endeavor it hoped would provide competition for southern cotton and destroy the system of slavery. However, the controversial portion of the plans lay in the idea that free blacks should migrate from the United States and assist in the development of Liberia. Although Garnet insisted that emigration should be entirely voluntary, both Smith and fellow activists Downing and Douglass denounced Garnet and his society. There was, in particular, a very public confrontation between Smith and Garnet that played out in the pages of the *Anglo-African Magazine*. Smith challenged Garnet to focus his energy on the condition of African Americans in the United States, instead of other countries throughout the world. According to Smith, he and Garnet had made a pledge 25 years earlier that they would devote their lives to uplift the black race, fight for abolition, and gain the suffrage. Smith maintained that because they had not yet achieved their goals, Garnet was obligated to honor his agreement. For months, the two men exchanged ugly words about each other and the colonization issue. Smith and Garnet remained at odds until 1862 when they reunited over the cause of slaves during the Civil War.

Up until his death, Smith remained active in the African American community. In 1861, he helped finance the creation of the African American newspaper the *Anglo-African Magazine* and, in 1863, was appointed as a professor of anthropology at Wilberforce College. However, a continuing heart problem prevented Smith from actually joining the faculty, a condition that eventually took his life in November 1865. His final major contribution was authoring an introduction to Garnet's address before Congress in February 1865. His ideas on social indicators of health provide a critical foundation to today's public health practice. Smith died on November 17, 1865, just weeks after the passage of the Thirteenth Amendment.

Leslie M. Alexander

See also: Bousfield, Midian Othello; Bowditch, Henry Ingersoll; Health Disparities; Kelley, Florence; Social Determinants of Health; Tubman, Harriet

Further Reading

Alexander, L. M. (2008). *African or American? Black identity and political activism in New York City, 1784–1861.* Champaign: University of Illinois Press.

Blight, D. W. (1985). In search of learning, liberty, and self-definition: James McCune Smith and the ordeal of the antebellum black intellectual. *Afro-Americans in New York Life & History*, 9(2), 7–25.

Harris, L. (2003). *In the shadow of slavery: African Americans in New York City, 1626–1863.* Chicago: University of Chicago Press.

Houston, H. R. (2009). Smith, James McCune (1813–1865). In J. C. Smith & L. T. Wynn (Eds.), *Freedom facts and firsts: 400 Years of the African American civil rights experience.* Canton, MI: Visible Ink Press. Retrieved from https://ezproxy.sju.edu/login?url=http://search.credoreference.com/content/entry/vipfff/smith_james_mccune_1813_1865/0?institutionId=473.

Stauffer, J. (2000). *The black hearts of men: Radical abolitionists and the transformation of race.* Cambridge, MA: Harvard University Press.

SNOW, JOHN (1813–1858)

Dr. John Snow was a British physician who worked to improve the unsanitary living conditions existing in industrialized cities during the 19th century. Snow pioneered the early use of anesthesia and advocated for public hygiene reforms. He is best remembered for his ingenuity and tenacity in tracing the source of contamination of a virulent outbreak of cholera in London in 1854. To accomplish this feat, Snow developed a theory of how cholera was spread, tested his theory by mapping the outbreak of the disease, and traced the problem to one specific source. Snow's ideas and vision spurred the development of public works and city planning, creating sanitary reform within urban areas.

Snow was born as the oldest of nine children of a working-class family living in York, England. At the age of 14, he apprenticed with a surgeon and went on to assist other medical practitioners in the Durham and Yorkshire region from 1833 to 1836. In 1836, Snow enrolled in London's Hunterian School of Medicine. He later earned his doctorate from the University of London (1844) and joined the Academy of Physicians (1850). Snow was one of the first physicians in Great Britain to study the administration of anesthetic agents. He believed that chloroform and ether might be used as a way to alleviate pain during surgery. This was a dangerous endeavor because anesthesia slows the body systems, and incorrect or reckless administration can cause death. To support patients under anesthesia, Snow invented a rudimentary artificial respirator and identified five characteristic stages of anesthesia. The equipment and knowledge allowed physicians to administer anesthesia with greater accuracy and safety. Snow published a number of articles advocating the use of anesthetics during medical procedures and childbirth. His ideas on the use of chloroform gained public attention and acceptance in 1853 and 1857 when Queen Victoria and her husband employed Snow to administer anesthesia during the childbirth of her youngest two children.

Snow was a founding member of the Epidemiological Society of London, and his greatest legacy remains in epidemiology. Throughout the early 1800s, the world had experienced several major outbreaks of cholera. More than 1 million people died during these epidemics and pandemics. A new outbreak occurred in London in 1854. Snow, who was working as a doctor in the area of the outbreak, performed a geographical analysis of deaths. He drew a map of London, noting where the infected people lived. Through this map, he was able to pinpoint the place of origin, tracing it to a single water pump at Broad Street in London's Soho District. Snow's report provided sufficient evidence to convince civil officials to act. The pump handle was removed, causing the pump to be nonfunctional and stemming further transmission of the disease. Snow conducted a further analysis comparing the water supplies of the Lambeth and the Southwark and Vauxhall companies. This investigation revealed that deaths by cholera may be related to the water source of the household. Southwark and Vauxhall water had eight to nine times greater instances of disease compared to the Lambeth company. The difference appeared to be that the Lambeth company had

Memorial pump honors Dr. John Snow's contribution to public health. Snow traced London's 1854 cholera cases to the water pump on Broad Street. Removing the pump handle stopped the epidemic. (Betsy Weber)

recently moved its water supply to a cleaner source outside of London. Although Snow's advances in epidemiology were groundbreaking, many of his findings on the transmission of disease were not fully appreciated until the 20th century.

Snow suffered from poor health throughout his life. An early teetotaler and vegetarian, declining health prompted him to abandon these practices. In June 1858, while writing a new work on anesthetics, Snow suffered a stroke and died from complications. Snow's discovery of water as a means for the transmission of cholera had a profound impact on the development of public health medicine and urban planning. Geographic mapping is a valuable tool used by epidemiologists today to track patterns in disease transmission and to identify sources of an infection and at-risk populations. Snow was also instrumental in demonstrating the intersect between public health and social responsibility. By identifying a health problem among a disadvantaged population and working to alleviate that problem, Snow developed strategies to prevent further spread of the disease.

Sean P. Phillips

See also: Cholera; Epidemic; Epidemiology; Infectious Diseases; Intervention; Pandemic; Waterborne Diseases

Further Reading

Friis, R. H., & Sellers, T. (2015). *Epidemiology for public health practice* (5th ed.). Burlington, MA: Jones & Bartlett.

Hamlin, C. (2007). *Cholera: The biography.* Biographies of diseases 2. Oxford, UK; New York: Oxford University Press.

Hempel, S. (2007). *The strange case of the broad street pump: John Snow and the mystery of cholera.* Berkeley: University of California Press.

Kudlick, C. J. (1996). *Cholera in post-revolutionary Paris: A cultural history.* Studies on the history of society and culture 25. Berkeley: University of California Press.

Rosenberg, C. E. (1987). *The cholera years: The United States in 1832, 1849, and 1866.* Chicago: University of Chicago Press.

Vinten-Johansen, P., et al. (2003). *Cholera, chloroform, and the science of medicine: A life of John Snow.* New York: Oxford University Press.

SOCIAL COGNITIVE THEORY (SCT)

Social cognitive theory (SCT) is a theory that describes how individuals watch and assess other people in order to learn new skills or behavior (Bandura, 1986). Public health professionals use the theory to understand, investigate, and change negative health behaviors and to promote health-enhancing behaviors. SCT applies to numerous health topics such as violence, medication compliance, parents' intention to vaccinate children, maternal nutrition, weight loss, and adolescent pregnancy. Although SCT developed from social research, recent discoveries suggest that biology may also play a role in observational learning. The theory presents multiple constructs that are highly relevant to public health practice.

In early 1962, Canadian American psychologist Dr. Albert Bandura conducted a series of experiments investigating aggressive behavior. Bandura believed that children learn aggression by watching others act aggressively. To test his hypothesis, he created eight different scenarios or skits. All of the scenes featured an adult in a room with toys. Some of the scenes featured the adult attacking an inflatable clown while other scenes showed nonaggressive play. Young study participants were divided by gender. Half of the male children observed a male actor while the other half observed a female actor. Female children were similarly assigned to either same gender or different gender role models. Bandura found that the children who observed the aggressive play were 16 to 17 times more likely to act aggressively, and the children who observed an adult of the same gender displayed aggression more than children who observed aggression by someone of the different gender. A higher number of males exhibited violent behavior in comparison to females. Bandura was alarmed to see that the children's aggression was not limited to imitation. The children created their own novel forms of violence, substituting toys as weapons to attack the clown. Bandura's studies provided overwhelming evidence that children learn violence by watching others.

Constructs are the building blocks or concepts that combine to create a theory or model. The constructs of SCT are observational learning, behavioral capability, self-efficacy, expectations, expectancies, reinforcements, emotional coping, environment, situation, and reciprocal determinism. *Observational learning* is the idea that people learn by watching other people. If someone wants to learn how to snowboard, she starts by watching other people snowboard. *Self-efficacy* is the degree of confidence that the observer has in her ability to perform the observed behavior. *Behavioral capability* is the physical or cognitive aptitude to perform the desired action. Snowboarding requires leg strength, power, agility, flexibility, core strength, and the ability to navigate geographic situations. *Expectations* are the consequences or outcomes that observers believe may occur because of the behavior. If the observer is unsure of what might happen after performing the behavior or fears injury or punishment, she may be less likely to try the behavior. If the expected outcome is positive, a concept known as *expectancies*, the observer will be more willing to try the behavior. *Reinforcements* are material or psychosocial rewards that affirm the behavior. The beginner snowboarder will feel some sense of pride in successfully navigating a difficult slope. *Emotional coping* refers to how the individual deals with any psychological or physical arousal that results from the action. If the snowboarder falls, how does she cope with the fall? Does she get up and try again, or is she embarrassed and wanting to leave the slope? *Environment* is the physical or social surroundings that promote or inhibit the specific behavior. How do experienced snowboarders respond to the novice snowboarder? Are they friendly and supportive, or do they dismiss or belittle efforts? *Situations* refer to how the individual interprets the environmental conditions. Are environmental obstacles simply challenges to be overcome, or do they block learning? *Reciprocal determinism* describes mutuality between the individual and the environment. The novice snowboarder learns by watching others, and within a few months other novice snowboarders will be watching her. She will create the environment for others. The SCT constructs outline the underlying factors that influence learning and explain how people acquire new behaviors.

Although SCT was envisioned over half a century ago, the theory continues to evolve. Scientists have identified specialized nerve cells in primates and birds. These cells, known as mirror neurons, become active when the animal observes another animal performing an interesting behavior (Dipellegrino, Fadiga, Fogassi, Gallese, & Rizzolatti, 1992). Mirror neurons may play a significant role in helping people to learn social rules and to accurately interpret the emotions of others. Such skills are important when people move to a new region, join a social group, or start a new job. Some experts speculate that defects in the mirror neurons may be associated with social-emotional disturbances such as autistic spectrum disorders or schizophrenia.

Social cognitive theory is used extensively to study a wide range of health issues. For example, Hasking and Rose (2016) used social cognitive theory to study nonsuicidal self-injury (NSSI). The researchers found that individuals who were aware of peers who self-injured were more likely to self-injure. The findings suggest that health educators focus on negative expectancies, such as infection, nerve damage, hair loss, shame, and depression, to reduce NSSIs and also raise questions about how media portrays harmful behaviors. In describing the psychosocial factors that influence learning, SCT is a valuable tool for public health researchers and practitioners.

Sally Kuykendall

See also: Diffusion of Innovations Theory; Health Communication; Health Education; Locus of Control; Reciprocal Determinism; Self-Efficacy

Further Reading

Bandura, A. (1962). Social learning through imitation. In M. R. Jones (Eds.), *Nebraska symposium on motivation, 1962* (pp. 211–274). Lincoln: University of Nebraska Press.

Bandura, A. (1986). *Social foundations of thought and action: A social cognitive theory*. Englewood Cliffs, NJ: Prentice Hall.

Dipellegrino, G., Fadiga, L., Fogassi, L., Gallese, V., & Rizzolatti, G. (1992). Understanding motor events—A neurophysiological study. *Experimental Brain Research*, *91*(1), 176–180.

Glanz, K., Lewis, F. M., & Rimer, B. K. (Eds.). (1997). *Health behavior and health education: Theory, research, and practice* (2nd ed.). San Francisco: Jossey-Bass.

Hasking, P., & Rose, A. (2016). A preliminary application of social cognitive theory to nonsuicidal self-injury. *Journal of Youth and Adolescence*, *45*(8), 1560–1574. doi:10.1007/s10964-016-0449-7

Kuykendall, S. (2012). *Bullying: Health and medical issues today*. Santa Barbara, CA: Greenwood.

SOCIAL DETERMINANTS OF HEALTH (SDOH)

The social determinants of health (SDOH) are the causes underlying the major health problems and diseases in the United States and around the world. SDOH are referred to as the *causes of the causes* or the *actual causes* of death. Currently, deaths are classified by biological cause, the disease or problem that resulted in fatality. In the United States, the leading biological causes of death are heart disease, cancer, respiratory diseases, injuries, cerebrovascular disease, Alzheimer's disease, and diabetes mellitus. These diseases are all related to common risk factors of poor nutrition, lack of physical activity, smoking, substance abuse, and poor mental health. Digging deeper, major health risk factors are created by social, environmental, and material resources. For example, the person who lives alone in an impoverished neighborhood, lacks the means for fresh fruits and vegetables, and lacks access to safe places for exercise is at greater risk for heart disease, diabetes mellitus, violence, and cancer than the person who lives in a comfortable home, in an area with walking paths, farmers' markets and grocery stores, and a wide selection of fresh fruits and vegetables. Thus, the cultural, social, economic, wellness opportunities, and environmental conditions that surround us—individually and collectively—impact health. Public health epidemiologists decided to calculate deaths by social determinants, rather than biological causes. An estimated 245,000 people die every year in the United States as a result of lack of education, 176,000 people die from racial segregation, 162,000 people die from limited social support, 133,000 people die due to individual-level poverty, 119,000 people die due to income inequality, and 39,000 people die due to area-level poverty (Galea, Tracy, Hoggatt, Dimaggio, & Karpati, 2011). This means that more people die every year as a result of racial segregation than from Alzheimer's disease (93,541 deaths/year) and diabetes mellitus (76,488 deaths/year), combined. Analyzing deaths and health from the social determinants standpoint offers a deeper understanding of the leading causes of death, revealing the existence of unnatural causes and providing opportunity to improve health beyond disease-based approaches.

Social determinants of health result from social structures. Economic and political systems determine how power and resources are distributed, creating unnatural systems that impact health. Socially disadvantaged and marginalized groups are often segregated to noxious environments and hazardous, low-paying jobs with limited access to resources, further education, and other opportunities to improve living conditions. Social conditions, particularly race and socioeconomic status, are among the fundamental causes of health disparities. The landmark Whitehall studies tracked the health status of thousands of civil servants in the United Kingdom. These cohort studies consistently found that the mortality rate was three times higher among low paid workers in comparison to workers in the highest pay grades (Marmot & Brunner, 2005). The Healthcare Cost and Utilization Project studied earning and preventable hospitalizations in the United States. To compensate for regional cost of living differences, participants were divided into four groups based on pay. Quartile 1 was people earning in the lowest 25 percent. Quartile 2 was people earning in the middle to lower percentiles (25–50 percent). Quartile 3 was people earning in the middle to higher percentiles of 50–75 percent, and Quartile 4 was people earning in the highest percentiles of 75 percent and above. In comparison to people in Quartile 4, people in Quartile 1 reported an additional 500,000 hospitalizations, people in Quartile 2 reported an additional 220,000 hospitalizations, and people in Quartile 3 reported an additional 90,000 hospitalizations. Income disparity accounted for an additional $6 billion in preventable hospitalizations (Centers for Disease Control and Prevention [CDC], 2014). Statistic after statistic demonstrates substantial differences in health status based on the color of a person's skin. Infant mortality rate is 5.5 deaths per 1,000 live births among infants of white mothers and 12.7 deaths per 1,000 live births among infants of black and African American mothers (CDC, 2014). The five-year breast cancer survival rate is 91.4 percent for white women and 77.4 percent for black women (National Center for Health Statistics, 2012). The homicide rate of men, aged 15–29 years, is 4.3 per 100,000 for white males and 75.3 per 100,000 for black males (CDC, 2014). Community resources dictate quality of life, and quality of life influences health. Depriving people of community resources condemns that group to poorer health status. Although the impact of social conditions may be greatest in early life, health effects often last and accumulate over time and across generations.

Absolute and relative measures of social conditions are important in understanding health disparities between and within countries. Among less developed nations, higher country-level income (i.e., GDP) is associated with health gains. The life expectancy of the Polynesian Island of Tuvalu, the country with lowest GDP of approximately $37 million, is 65 years old, while the life expectancy of the United States with a GDP of approximately $18 trillion is 79 years old. After a country attains a certain standard of living, the extent of social inequality within the country is more important in explaining between-country variations in health and well-being. Among rich, developed countries, health and well-being are better in countries with low inequality as measured by comparing the gap between the top 20 percent and lowest 20 percent of society or using the Gini coefficient. Denmark has a low income inequality (Gini coefficient = 0.25), an infant mortality rate of 3.8 deaths per 1,000 live births and 1.01 homicides/100,000 people. The United States, with a high income inequality (Gini coefficient = 0.40) has an infant mortality rate of 6.9 deaths per 1,000 live births and 5 homicides/100,000 people. In countries with greater inequality, the health outcomes for all groups—even for the best-off—are worse compared to countries with lower inequality. Social inequality also explains some within-country health disparities. In the United States, states with lower inequality have better health indicators on average compared to states with greater inequality.

A large body of research evidences a strong and consistent link between the environment and health and well-being indicators, including disability, chronic conditions, mental health, birth outcomes, and domestic violence. Although behaviors are proximate determinants of these health outcomes, a key understanding in the social determinants of health perspective is that health behaviors and other downstream health determinants are substantially impacted by upstream factors. The environment, both physical and social, influences health by shaping the choices available to individuals as well as the choices they are likely to make regarding health behaviors and other life experiences that impact health, such as whether they attend college—one of the factors most strongly associated with morbidity and mortality in developed countries. Cigarette smoking, the leading cause of preventable death worldwide, is a useful example of how the environment impacts health. Who smokes, and why smoking is more common among certain population groups, may be linked to multiple factors—the availability of cigarette retailers, social norms surrounding smoking in one's social networks, stress, and occupation and work environment. There is some evidence that a greater availability of cigarettes in proximity to one's home (measured through the density of cigarette retailers) and greater exposure to tobacco advertising, which may be regulated by governments, are associated with a greater likelihood of smoking. However, cigarette retailers and tobacco marketing are often concentrated in low income and predominantly minority neighborhoods in the United States; it is therefore not surprising that smoking is more common among low income and minority groups in the United States. These conditions do not occur by chance, but are shaped by the political economy.

The physical environment encompasses both the natural and built environments. Aspects of the natural environment that influence health include air quality, which affects respiratory health. Features of the built environment, including sewage and sanitation infrastructure, parks, buildings, streets and other man-made features, may also promote or hinder healthy behaviors. For instance, access to usable parks and supermarkets (which provide fresh produce) near one's home is associated with lower obesity, whereas a lack of parks and greater access to convenience stores are associated with greater obesity. Researchers have questioned whether the association between neighborhoods and health is causal—that is, whether neighborhood environment impacts health or whether individuals with characteristics that predispose them to illness elect to live in the same neighborhoods. The Moving to Opportunity program, initiated in the United States in 1994, was a randomized experiment in which very low income families were given vouchers to move to more advantaged neighborhoods. This permitted the examination of the effects of the conditions in which people live on their quality of life and outcomes. Although earlier studies found null results, recent longitudinal research finds that moving to a better-off neighborhood in childhood is associated with several improved outcomes later in life compared to those who continue living in poor areas (Chetty et al., 2016). This Moving to Opportunity program provides evidence of the causal impact of neighborhood on health and suggests that changing the environment may change health. Future research should leverage longitudinal data to better understand the mechanisms by which the environment influences health.

In terms of the social environment, a large body of literature finds that positive social ties are crucial to health. Since Emile Durkheim's studies of social integration, social scientists have documented the salubrious effects of positive social relationships, which can buffer against the harmful health effects of stressors. Conversely, strained relationships and interactions are deleterious to health. Racial discrimination, for example, has been linked with poor mental health and greater risk of obesity and cardiovascular disease. Moreover, the physical and social aspects of the environment are interrelated, often having cascading effects. For example, deteriorations in the physical environment (e.g., more abandoned buildings) can change the social environment (e.g., increased crime), and vice versa.

Recognizing the critical importance of physical and social environments on health, many organizations have adopted formal strategies that incorporate the social determinants of health into their approaches to improving population health. The Commission on Social Determinants of Health, initiated by the World Health Organization (WHO), proposed three overarching principles of action: (1) improving daily living conditions; (2) tackling inequitable distribution of power, money, and resources; and (3) measuring the problem and evaluating the impact of action. To achieve this, an increasing number of public health organizations are promoting a "health in all policies" strategy that addresses how all social policies can affect individual and community health. This approach advocates for the use of health impact assessments to understand how policies in diverse areas—ranging from community planning, education, transportation, and agriculture, to housing and law—impact health. Through cross-sector collaboration, organizations can strategically target neighborhood conditions that contribute to poor health to efficiently and effectively ameliorate various social determinants simultaneously. For instance, planners and developers can work together to create safe, affordable housing that maximizes health by enhancing access to recreational space and facilitating neighborhood cohesion through innovative design.

Social determinants of health range from basic physiological requirements for food and safety to psychosocial needs for living wages, supportive relationships, quality education, and justice. Economics, housing, community, policy, environment, social support, and material resources influence people psychologically and behaviorally. Social determinants explain many public health disparities and offer ways to improve the health of disadvantaged groups. Ultimately, the social determinants of health are pivotal to improving population health because they address the root causes of morbidity, mortality, and health disparities.

Georgiana Bostean and Sally Kuykendall

See also: Adverse Childhood Experiences; Anderson, Elizabeth Milbank; Care, Access to; Chadwick, Edwin; Children's Health; Cornely, Paul B.; Cultural Competence; Disability; Disability Movement; Health; Health Disparities; Healthy Places; Infant Mortality; Leading Health Indicators; Lesbian, Gay, Bisexual, and Transgender Health; Population Health; Shattuck, Lemuel; Smith, James McCune; Social Ecological Model; Spiritual Health

Further Reading

Braveman, P., Egerter, S., & Williams, D. R. (2011). The social determinants of health: Coming of age. *Annual Review of Public Health, 32,* 381–398. doi:10.1146/annurev-publhealth-031210-101218

Chetty, R., Hendren, N., & Katz, L. F. (2016). The effects of exposure to better neighborhoods on children: New evidence from the Moving to Opportunity experiment. *American Economic Review, 106*(4), 855–902. doi:http://dx.doi.org.ezproxy.sju.edu/10.1257/aer.106.4.855

Centers for Disease Control and Prevention. (2014). Centers for Disease Control and Prevention Health Disparities and Inequalities Report—United States, 2013. *Morbidity and Mortality Weekly Report,* 62(Suppl. 3). Retrieved from http://www.cdc.gov/mmwr/pdf/other/su6203.pdf.

Durkheim, E. (1951). *Suicide: A study in sociology.* New York: The Free Press.

Galea, S., Tracy, M., Hoggatt, K. J., Dimaggio, C., & Karpati, A. (2011). Estimated deaths attributable to social factors in the United States. *American Journal of Public Health, 101*(8), 1456–1465. doi:10.2105/AJPH.2010.300086

Link, B. G., & Phelan, J. (1995). Social conditions as fundamental causes of disease. *Journal of Health and Social Behavior,* 80–94.

Marmot, M., & Brunner, E. (2005). Cohort profile: The Whitehall II study. *International Journal of Epidemiology, 34*(2), 251–256.

Marmot, M., Friel, S., Bell, R., Houweling, T. A., & Taylor, S. (2008). Public health: Closing the gap in a generation: Health equity through action on the social determinants of health. *The Lancet, 372,* 1661–1669. doi:10.1016/S0140-6736(08)61690-6

National Center for Health Statistics. (2012). *Health, United States, 2011: With special feature on socioeconomic status and health.* Hyattsville, MD. Retrieved from http://www.cdc.gov/nchs/data/hus/hus11.pdf.

Wilkinson, R. G., & Pickett, K. (2009). *The spirit level: Why greater equality makes societies stronger.* New York: Bloomsbury Press.

Williams, D. R., & Sternthal, M. (2010). Understanding racial-ethnic disparities in health: Sociological contributions. *Journal of Health and Social Behavior, 51*(Suppl.), S15–S27.

World Health Organization. (2008). *Closing the gap in a generation: Health equity through action on the social determinants of health.* Commission on Social Determinants of Health final report.

SOCIAL ECOLOGICAL MODEL

Ecological models consider the many psychosocial, environmental, political, and regulatory factors that influence individual and community well-being. The idea that the social and political environment influences health applies to numerous public health concerns. Community violence, obesity, oral health, suicides, substance abuse, and occupational health and safety are influenced by family, peers, community, and the regulatory environment. The ecological perspective is used to plan multilevel public health research, programs, interventions, and media campaigns. The models differentiate levels of influence, suggesting opportune points for interventions. Key principles to understanding the ecological perspective are (1) an individual's health behaviors are influenced by intrapersonal, interpersonal, organizational, community and, public policy circumstances; (2) in addition to influencing the individual, ecological factors also interact across systems to accentuate or inhibit behavior; (3) effective interventions work on multiple levels; and (4) programs that focus on behavioral change (as opposed to systems-level change) offer greater impact (Glanz, Lewis, & Rimer, 1997).

Charles Darwin was the first to suggest that the environment influences living beings. The theory of evolution states that some species adapt novel physical or behavioral traits as a way to enhance survival, and this process results in natural selection. Dr. Sigmund Freud applied Darwin's theory to human beings. Freud proposed that the ego develops to mediate between the instinctual id and the moralistic superego. Thus, the human psyche develops because of interactions with parents, family, peers, and society. Sociologist George Herbert Meade expanded the idea of human-environmental influence to sociology. Meade noted that people observe the world around them, interpret the world, and interact with others based on their interpretation. He used the term *symbolic interactionism* to describe how individuals communicate, interpret, and adjust to social groups and the term *social behaviorism* to describe how social interactions influence the mind and behaviors. Meade's work was advanced by his mentee Herbert Blumer. Blumer noted that interactions are *dynamic*, occurring as ongoing processes. Although a person interprets the social world based on previous experiences, that interpretation can change through continued experiences and interactions. Dr. Kurt Lewin (1935) furthered Blumer's work by introducing the idea of *group dynamics*. Group dynamics describe how individuals and groups interact, react, and adapt to changing circumstances.

The expert most often associated with ecological systems theories is developmental psychologist Dr. Urie Bronfenbrenner. In 1973, Bronfenbrenner noted that children's emotional and social development is dependent on interactions with other people. Bronfenbrenner proposed four subsystems, presented as concentric circles with the individual at the center. The individual is encircled by the *microsystem* of family, peers, close neighbors, school, and other close social network. The microsystem is encircled by the *mesosystem*, which represents connections between parts of the microsystems, such as relationships between parent and teacher. The mesosystem is encircled by the *exosystem*, social institutions that indirectly impact the child, such as the parent's workplace, social services, adult neighbors, the media, or political systems. The exosystem is encircled by the *macrosystem*. The macrosystem is the predominant culture to which the child is exposed, that is, socioeconomic status, ethnic identity, or social norms and values. Each system influences the individual and other systems, *and* the effects occur over time, an idea referred to as *chronosystem*. Bronfenbrenner's model has many different applications. Researchers in Australia used the model to understand community resilience during natural disasters (Boon et al., 2012). Individual characteristics include past experiences with disaster (bushfire, flood, or cyclone), personal health, gender, or indigenous vulnerability or resilience. The microsystem consists of concerns for and by family and friends. The mesosystem reflects warnings, by word of mouth, phone, or Internet.

The exosystem consists of relief centers, insurance, emergency management agencies, charities, and other disaster relief agencies. The chronosystem covers initial response and capacity as well as recovery after the event. Each level influences one another, and effective disaster management must address all levels. The advantage of Bronfenbrenner's model, as well as other ecological models, is that they point out the many factors outside of individual control that influence behaviors. They do not blame the victim for the problem. One limitation is that the models explain behavior; they do not advise how to alter the behavior.

Using Bronfenbrenner's model, public health experts developed the social ecological model (McLeroy, Bibeau, Steckler, & Glanz, 1988). Under the social ecological model, influencing factors are presented as individual, interpersonal, institutions and organizations, community, and structures and systems. The model is used to examine and suggest multilevel interventions for complex health issues, such as obesity. For example, the individual factors for obesity include gender, ability or disability, genetics, epigenetics, and knowledge or attitudes toward physical activity and diet. Interpersonal factors include food traditions, preferences, and choices, which are heavily influenced by family, friends, and culture. Institutions and organizations include school, workplaces, or faith-based institutions, which also influence dietary choices and food access. Community factors include neighborhood walkability and safety, access to physical activity facilities or programs, and access to fresh fruits and vegetables. Policy level factors are zoning for recreational areas, access to bike paths or trails, public transportation, housing, and other health or social policies. Local programs to reduce obesity must consider multiple levels for intervention activities. Experts suggest that future directions for the use of ecological models are to place greater emphasis on the relationships between systems. In the interrelationship design, influencing factors are presented as a series of overlapping, roulette curves rather than in the traditional nested arrangement.

The social ecological model tailors well known ecological theories to public health practice. The model presents the individual as a center point, influenced by multiple social, community, institutional, and government factors. Ecological models are widely used and critical to public health practice. They are listed within the public health core competencies and as curricular frameworks in schools of public health. Advantages of the models are that they highlight the many factors that initiate and maintain health behaviors and suggest points of intervention. Ecological models also demonstrate the complexity of health behaviors and the need for sophisticated, multifactorial approaches in health promotion.

Sally Kuykendall

See also: Care, Access to; Cultural Competence; Disability; Disability Movement; Environmental Health; Healthy Places; Infant Mortality; Leading Health Indicators; Reciprocal Determinism; Social Determinants of Health; Spiritual Health

Further Reading

Boon, H., Cottrell, A., King, D., Stevenson, R., & Millar, J. (2012). Bronfenbrenner's bioecological theory for modelling community resilience to natural disasters. *Natural Hazards*, *60*(2), 381–408. doi:10.1007/s11069-011-0021-4

Bronfenbrenner, U. (1973, February 26–March 1). *An emerging theoretical perspective for research in human development.* Paper presented at the annual meeting of the American Educational Research Association, New Orleans, LA.

Bronfenbrenner, U., Alvarez, W. F., & Henderson, C. R. (1984). Working and watching: Maternal employment status and parents' perceptions of their three-year-old children. *Child Development*, *55*(4), 1362–1378. doi:10.2307/1130006

Centers for Disease Control and Prevention. (2013). *Addressing obesity disparities.* Retrieved from https://www.cdc.gov/nccdphp/dnpao/state-local-programs/health-equity/framing-the-issue.html.

Glanz, K., Lewis, F. M., & Rimer, B. K. (Eds.). (1997). *Health behavior and health education: Theory, research, and practice* (2nd ed.). San Francisco: Jossey-Bass.

Lewin, K. (1935). *A dynamic theory of personality*. New York: McGraw-Hill.

McLeroy, K. R., Bibeau, D., Steckler, A., & Glanz, K. (1988). An ecological perspective on health promotion programs. *Health Education & Behavior*, *15*(4), 351. doi:10.1177/109019818801500401

Trickett, E., Beehler, S., Deutsch, C., Green, L., Hawe, P., McLeroy, K., & . . . Trimble, J. (n.d.). Advancing the science of community-level interventions. *American Journal of Public Health*, *101*(8), 1410–1419.

SOCIAL SECURITY ACT (SSA)

During the Great Depression of the 1930s, people in the United States grew their own vegetables for food, walked rather than rode, and avoided the unnecessary expense of cigarettes or alcohol. As a result, life expectancy increased. However, the state-run pension plans did not take into account America's increasing elderly population or inflation. Pension payments fell short on providing a reasonable income to the aging population. Many elderly who had worked their entire lives were starving or unable to pay for basic health care. The Social Security Act (SSA) of 1935 is a federal program enacted in response to the vast number of the aging workforce who could not support themselves. With the intention of providing social insurance, Franklin D. Roosevelt signed the SSA into law on August 14, 1935. The concept of social insurance was built on the philosophy of a government-sponsored subsidy to benefit senior citizens. The program and system have been expanded to provide assistance to children, elderly, or the disabled who cannot or do not earn enough to support themselves. Every feature of the SSA is related directly or indirectly to public health. Providing economic security supports mental health, proper nutrition, and means to medical care.

The original intent of the SSA was to provide guaranteed income for retired persons aged 65 or older. According to SSA.gov, "benefits were to be based on payroll tax contributions that the worker made during their working life" (SSA.gov, 2017).

President Franklin D. Roosevelt signs the Social Security Act into law on August 14, 1935. The program supports children, elderly, and disabled people who cannot earn enough to support themselves. (Social Security Administration)

These contributions would be placed into a joint fund where workers actively saved for their retirement. The fund would be overseen by the government. The Social Security Board (SSB) was established to oversee the system. Initially, the board compensated for the lack of bank funding by borrowing money from other federal agencies. The SSB acted as an independent entity until it was eliminated in 1946 and replaced by the present Social Security Administration (SSA) under the direction of a single administrator.

In order to allocate benefits, the United States Postal Service was given the task of assigning and distributing Social Security numbers. The USPS then forwarded the applications to satellite Social Security offices where the Social Security cards were issued. Federal Insurance Contributions Act (FICA) taxes were withdrawn from an employee's earnings and the monies forwarded to the Social Security Trust Fund. The fund dispersed payments as a one-time payout to individuals who were not able to fully contribute to the program. The monthly payments that are known today were not implemented until 1940.

In 1939 several amendments were made to the original act. Two additional sections were added to provide benefits for spouses and children of qualified workers as well as "survivors' benefits paid to the family in the event of the premature death of a covered worker" (SSA.gov, 2017). The inclusion ultimately changed the act from one of individual retirement plan to that of a family income protection plan. The amendment also allowed an increased payment amount. No further changes were made to the program until 1950.

In response to the inefficiencies of act, the Social Security Administration announced major changes. The first change was to increase the monetary payments for those enrolled in the plan as well as providing additional incentives for the current workforce that would utilize the system at a later time. The increases were named cost-of-living allowances (COLAs) and would be completed in two phases, in 1950 and 1952. These increases accounted for inflation.

In 1954 the Social Security Administration began the disability insurance program for disabled workers aged 50–64 as well disabled minor children (SSA.gov, 2017). This program provides those with documented disabilities income to prevent economic uncertainty. In 1960 this was changed to include disabled workers of any age and their dependents.

In 1960 there were substantial changes to the Social Security program. The first modification was to adjust the age that men could apply for benefits to age 62. By decreasing the age at which benefits were granted, it decreased the allowance paid out. This resulted in substantially more beneficiaries being enrolled at the time. By far the most powerful change was launching the health insurer, Medicare, in 1966. The implementation of Medicare meant that recipients were now eligible to receive health insurance funded by the Social Security Administration. The Medicare program provided two forms of coverage, Part A covering hospital service and Part B covering physicians' services.

The 1970s brought about additional changes for the Social Security Administration. Although the initial act of 1935 provided benefits for the elderly, the poor, and the blind, and in 1950 the disabled were added, these groups were considered "adult categories" (SSA.gov, 2017). These categories were not managed by the SSA but instead by the state and local administrations that were given monetary funding from the federal government. Due to the state and local government inability to properly manage and distribute benefits, the Secretary of Health, Education and Welfare determined that the benefits should be managed by the Supplemental Security Income (SSI), which is supervised by the SSA.

Medicare benefits were extended to individuals that received disability payments for a minimum of two years and those ill with chronic renal disease. The provisions also "liberalized the retirement earnings test" as well as allowed for deferred retirement credits and increased allowances for individuals that chose to postpone their benefits after the age of 65 (SSA.gov, 2017). Automatic COLAs' increases were also implemented. This resulted in increases of the Social Security tax additionally modifying the wage-base assessment that is used to determine allowance amounts. COLA specifically regulates prices whereas wage-based assessment regulates wages. These modifications were done to preserve the future of the Social Security system, but the ramifications of the current system meant that benefit payments would exceed the salary contributions made. Due to the problematic impact of future benefits, these modifications were not successful and thereby had to be changed, which resulted in modification in the 1980s that included an increase in the retirement age and the collection of taxes on benefits.

In the years since there have been changes but none greater than that as previously discussed. The SSI program has been modified to eliminate previous health conditions that were believed to be considered a disability, such as alcoholism and drug addiction. Legislation has been established to combat fraud, determine immigrant eligibility, establish employment incentives for disabled workers, eliminate the retirement earnings test, add health insurance coverage for prescription drugs, and eliminate potential benefits for incarcerated individuals. Overall, the program functions to support members of the community who are unable to support themselves due to age or disability.

Leapolda Figueroa and Sally Kuykendall

See also: Centers for Medicare and Medicaid Services; Medicaid; Medicare; Public Health Law; Roosevelt, Eleanor; Roosevelt, Franklin Delano

Further Reading

Coffey, E. R. (1941). Public health expands its facilities under Title VI, federal Social Security Act. *American Journal of Public Health, 31,* 297–304.

Eliot, M. M. (1936). Progress in maternal and child welfare under the Social Security Act. *American Journal of Public Health, 26,* 1155–1162.

Hood, R. C. (1940). Services for crippled children under the Social Security Act. *American Journal of Public Health, 30,* 935–937.

Social Security Administration. (2017). *Social Security history: Historical background and development of Social Security.* Retrieved from https://www.ssa.gov/history/briefhistory3.html.

Waller, C. E. (1935). Social Security Act in its relation to public health. *American Journal of Public Health, 25,* 1186–1194.

SOCIETY OF PUBLIC HEALTH EDUCATION (SOPHE)

The Society of Public Health Education (SOPHE) is the primary professional association of public health educators. The organization's main purpose is to improve public health education practice by identifying and addressing the challenges and needs of community-based and clinical health professionals. Founded in 1950, this international organization brings together practitioners, academics, researchers, administrators, grant funders, nonprofit agencies, policy makers, and students to share best practices, innovations, and tools. Membership benefits include access to SOPHE publications and newsletters, continuing education opportunities, discounts on conferences and SOPHE health education and career resources. In addition to offering professional education, SOPHE also offers awards, scholarships, and fellowships to members. SOPHE is a good way to build a professional network and to stay current in the field of health education. Students are eligible for discounted memberships.

Knowledge of the human body and diseases advances quickly, and professional health educators are responsible for keeping up to date with scientific progress and refuting false information while planning, managing, and advancing the health of those whom they serve. Professional organizations such as SOPHE help health educators to stay current in the field by offering annual conferences, newsletters, and quality, peer-reviewed journals. Attendees of SOPHE's annual meeting learn new techniques in health education, current information, best practices, and can earn continuing education to maintain professional certifications. Electronic newsletters provide information on upcoming events of interest to health educators, workshops, advocacy information, brief research reports, and news on the achievements and efforts of current members.

SOPHE publishes three quality, peer-reviewed professional journals, *Health Promotion Practice, Health Education & Behavior,* and *Pedagogy in Health Promotion: The Scholarship of Teaching and Learning.* The journals are published by Sage journals and adhere to the Committee on Publication Ethics (COPE) guidelines. This means that the journal articles are checked by experts to ensure that the information presented is accurate, honest, and original. *Health Promotion Practice* examines practical strategies and applications in health education and health promotion programs. Articles on community interventions, worksite wellness, school health, and international settings share best practices, suggestions for improvement, and problem-solving strategies. This journal is for readers interested in the practical application of health promotion programs. *Health Education & Behavior* examines the theory and process of planning, implementing, and evaluating health behavior and health education programs. The journal publishes empirical research studies, case reports, evaluation research, literature reviews, and articles on health behavior models and theories. This journal is appropriate for the reader who is interested in theoretical concepts of how people learn or how people change or adapt health behaviors. *Pedagogy in Health Promotion* focuses on best practices in training future generations of health care practitioners and educators. The primary audience is faculty members and instructors of continuing education courses or those who are interested in teaching health educators. All three journals offer self-study articles providing continuing education contact hours for Certified Health Education Specialists (CHES).

SOPHE advances health of the general public by partnering efforts with community-based organizations, federal government agencies, decision makers, and members. For example, the ACHIEVE program (Action Communities for Health, Innovation & EnVironmental ChangE) is a national network of organizations working together to create healthy places to live, work, and play. ACHIEVE organizations offer a number of resources and tools to help community members develop health programs within their own communities. SOPHE also advocates for effective health policies by educating local and national decision makers on current health issues and by keeping members informed on current policies under consideration.

SOPHE supports health educators in communities, workplaces, and health centers by keeping them informed of best practices, by ensuring access to accurate health information, and by promoting health policies and systems that support individual efforts of members.

Sally Kuykendall

See also: American Public Health Association; Core Competencies in Public Health; Health Education; Health Policy; School Health

Further Reading

ACHIEVE Healthy Communities. (2017). Retrieved from http://www.achievecommunities.org/.

Committee on Publication Ethics. (2017). Retrieved from http://publicationethics.org/.

Society of Public Health Education. (2017). Retrieved from http://www.sophe.org/.

SPIRITUAL HEALTH

In earlier views of health, especially in the ancient world, there was a recognized and even unquestioned connection between physical well-being and religious practices and beliefs. Beginning with Hippocrates (ca. 460–370 BCE), health and medicine began to focus on natural, biological determinants and causes, gradually developing into a science that eventually led to better treatment, research, and outcomes. However, as modern medical science became more prominent and mainstream, the medicalization of health care became dominant, and the connection between health and spiritual aspects of a person's life and makeup was lost or diminished. It has been a relatively recent phenomenon for health to be viewed again as something broader than the physical or biological well-being. Such a shift has impacted both medical and public health treatments and interventions.

Health care today is typically seen in the context of holistic health, which takes into account the physical, emotional, social, psychological, and spiritual needs of the person. Public health research and practice also follows this comprehensive view. For example, in studies regarding population health and health-related quality of life, the Centers for Disease Control and Prevention (CDC) defines and measures health broadly. Quality of life surveys take into account factors of culture, employment, availability of schools, nature of community or neighborhood, values, and spirituality (Taylor, 2000). Spirituality and considering spiritual needs, then, are key components to understanding a person's overall health and important to consider in the prevention and treatment of disease or injury.

There are no standard definitions for spirituality or spiritual well-being, although there are common characteristics among the various definitions. One of the better definitions of spirituality comes from the Consensus Conference, a group of over

40 health care providers that included chaplains, physicians, nurses, social workers, psychologists, and pastors: "Spirituality is the aspect of humanity that refers to the way individuals seek and express meaning and purpose and the way they experience their connectedness to the moment, to self, to others, to nature, and to the significant or sacred" (Puchalski et al., 2009, p. 887). The "significant" referred to in this definition could be God or other supreme being, or it could also be family, a particular social cause, organization, or vocation. Spiritual health, then, can be described as integrating, or finding a balance, regarding purpose and meaning in light of one's connections to self, others, and to the significant or sacred.

When assessing spiritual health, it is essential to consider a number of related matters and concerns. Besides purpose and meaning, it is helpful to address other areas of life, such as love and belonging, guilt and forgiveness, acceptance, gratitude, and a sense of hope or hopelessness. It is also critical to understand that spiritual health is less about a cure than it is about healing. For instance, individuals who are dealing with a life-limiting illness like cancer can experience spiritual health and healing even though there may be no cure for their illness.

Another aspect of spiritual health is knowing and recognizing the difference between spirituality and religion or being religious. Religion can be viewed as "a group's enculturation of an organized system of beliefs, texts, roles and practices related to spirituality" (Robinson, Thiel, Backus, & Meyer, 2006, p. 720). The religious focuses on the corporate and communal nature of spirituality, while spirituality concerns the individual and personal search for meaning. Religion has to do with codifying rituals and beliefs, whereas spirituality involves what meaning the person gives to a particular ritual, how they internally experience a practice like prayer or Eucharist. The religious is more external, while spirituality deals with one's inner beliefs. Everyone can be considered spiritual, but not everyone is religious. This difference is critical to public health practice and research, especially regarding outcomes or the way information is analyzed. For example, a researcher may want to study the direct link between a religious ritual, like prayer, and positive medical outcomes. However, such a study may fail to recognize that personal spirituality and faith experience help a patient to know that God is with them whatever the medical outcome. If the investigation examines only the connection between the ritual and positive medical outcomes, and not the meaning behind the ritual, critical information and connection may be missed.

Spirituality or attending to spiritual well-being can be seen as one of a cluster of needs when addressing overall health. Attending to the spiritual health of a patient may involve singing a hymn or saying a prayer at the bedside, a conversation about life's meaning, or addressing a deep hurt. Dealing well with a person's spiritual health may or may not affect their physical health or outcomes. However, discovering the effect of spirituality on physical or overall health is also important to consider. In spite of the differences between science and religion, or biology and spirituality, many have insisted that there is a definite relationship between spirituality, or religious practices, and overall health (especially mental and medical health). For example, one might think it is plausible that the more at peace people feel, the better their health, or the more able they will be to cope with a serious illness.

The first known study investigating spirituality and health was performed in 1872 (Harrington, 2010). Further research has only gained momentum over the past 30 years. Numerous studies have been conducted investigating relationships between prayer and health, attending religious services and mortality, spirituality and end of life issues, spiritual practices and stress reduction, the impact of faith and belief on recovery from serious illness, forgiveness and health, as well as the role of the physician and other health care workers regarding spiritual care. Many have attempted to discover a deeper, definitive relationship between spirituality or being religious and positive health outcomes, especially physical ones. Although a number of investigations have indicated a positive relationship between religious practices or rituals and positive health outcomes, there are others that have shown the opposite.

Although there have been nearly 1,600 studies regarding religion or spirituality and health, more research needs to be done to discover what relationship there is and how to make the most of these connections to improve health (Koenig, King, & Carson, 2012). Even though more study needs to be accomplished, it is important to understand that spiritual issues and spirituality impact how a patient approaches health-related behaviors, treatment, end of life decisions, or how they cope with the disease. Such insights can be integrated into public health ensuring optimal health.

Louis Kuykendall Jr.

See also: Behavioral Health; Disease; Health; Healthy Places; Indian Health Service; Mental Health; Social Determinants of Health

Further Reading

Harrington, A. (2010). *God and health: What more is there to say?* [e-book]. Templeton Foundation Press. Available from Digital Access to Scholarship at Harvard (DASH), Ipswich, MA.

Idler, E. (2014). *Religion as a social determinant of public health.* New York: Oxford University Press.

Koenig, H. G., King, D. E., & Carson, V. B. (2012). *Handbook of religion and health* (2nd ed.). New York: Oxford University Press.

Meanley, S., Pingel, E. S., & Bauermeister, J. A. (2016). Psychological well-being among religious and spiritual-identified young gay and bisexual men. *Sexuality Research & Social Policy: A Journal of the NSRC, 13*(1), 35–45. doi:10.1007/s13178-015-0199-4

Musgrave, C. F., Allen, C. E., & Allen, G. J. (2002). Spirituality and health for women of color. *American Journal of Public Health, 92*(4), 557.

Puchalski, C., Ferrell, B., Virani, R., Otis-Green, S., Baird, P., Bull, J., & . . . Sulmasy, D. (2009). Improving the quality of spiritual care as a dimension of palliative care: The report of the Consensus Conference. *Journal of Palliative Medicine, 12*(10), 885–904. doi:10.1089/jpm.2009.0142

Robinson, M. R., Thiel, M. M., Backus, M. M., & Meyer, E. C. (2006). Matters of spirituality at the end of life in the pediatric intensive care unit. *Pediatrics, 118*(3), 719–729.
Stone, R. T., Whitbeck, L. B., Chen, X., Johnson, K., & Olson, D. M. (2006). Traditional practices, traditional spirituality, and alcohol cessation among American Indians. *Journal of Studies on Alcohol*, 67(2), 236–244. doi:10.15288/jsa.2006.67.236
Taylor, V. R. (2000). *Measuring healthy days: Population assessment of health-related quality of life* [Electronic resource]. Atlanta: U.S. Department of Health and Human Services, Centers for Disease Control and Prevention, National Center for Chronic Disease Prevention and Health Promotion, Division of Adult and Community Health.

SPORTS-RELATED CONCUSSIONS (SRCs)

Sports-related concussions (SRCs) are defined as a traumatic brain injury induced by biomechanical forces. They are a common public health problem in the United States with estimates ranging between 1.6 and 3.8 million cases per year. Due to underreporting, these figures might underestimate the actual incidence. Football has the highest incidence, and females have a greater incidence than males. SRCs account for approximately 9 percent of all high school sports injuries. There has been an increase in the number of concussions over the past decades, likely due to several factors, including greater involvement in team sports and an increased awareness of concussions along with better diagnostic techniques (Sprouse, Harris, Sprouse, Humerick, & Miller, 2016). Public health efforts to prevent SRCs focus on educating parents, youth, coaches, health care providers, and the general public.

SRCs share some common features. They are caused by either a direct blow to the head, neck, face, or elsewhere on the body with the impulse force being transmitted to the head. Suffering an SRC does not need an impact directly to the head to occur. Typically, this force results in rapid onset of short-lived impairment of neurological function that resolves spontaneously, but some symptoms may develop over minutes to hours. An SRC may result in neuropathologic changes, but signs and symptoms are of functional disturbances, not structural injury, which would be shown on standard neuroimaging like computed tomography (CT) or magnetic resonance imaging (MRI). Finally, the diagnosis may or may not include loss of consciousness.

Athletes suspected of having an SRC may exhibit signs and symptoms across many domains. Symptoms may include somatic (headache, dizziness, blurred vision, photophobia, phonophobia), cognitive (decreased attention, feeling in a fog, distractibility), or emotional (lability, depression, personality changes). Physical signs encompass loss of consciousness, blank or vacant look, seizure, amnesia, or neurologic deficits. Other helpful aspects for diagnosis include balance impairment (gait unsteadiness, ataxia), behavioral changes (anger, irritability), cognitive impairments (slow reaction times, attention deficit), and sleep disturbances (somnolence, drowsiness, hypersomnia).

The hallmark of diagnosis of an SRC is a thorough history and physical exam. The history should include the mechanism of injury, history of prior concussions,

Athletic trainer Brandon Nolt and Director of Sports Medicine Rennie Sacco check Kutztown University defensive back Corey Harris for neurological deficits after injury. (Shutterstock.com)

and symptom inventory. A graded symptom checklist, such as the Standardized Assessment of Concussion (SCAT), can aid in reviewing pertinent symptoms and be followed over several visits. Physical exam should include a detailed neurologic exam covering mental status, cognitive function, ocular function, vestibular function, gait, and balance. Brain imaging is reserved for those patients suspected of having more severe injuries, such as skull fractures or intracranial bleeding. Worsening symptoms over time would also be an indication for advanced imaging.

Most SRCs resolve in 7–10 days; children and adolescents usually recover more slowly due to the developing, immature brain. Numerous studies have demonstrated longer recovery times for younger athletes compared to college and professional athletes. Most consensus statements agree that the initial treatment should be rest until the patient is symptom free. This includes both physical and cognitive rest to allow the brain to heal. Activities such as video games, cell phone use, reading, schoolwork, and exercise need to be limited until symptoms have abated. Once symptoms at rest have resolved, a graded, stepwise rehabilitation strategy is employed to return the athlete to sports and academics. Athletes are started on very low exertion exercise and observed for reemergence of symptoms, then progressed every day to the next level if symptoms do not reappear. Typically, this progression takes a minimum of five days to complete. These programs and exercises should be supervised by a certified athletic trainer or other professional. Certain strategies may have to be employed to support academic success, such as shortened school days, extra time for tests, help with note taking, and restrictions on classes that induce symptoms (e.g., computer science or music).

A serious but rare event is the second impact syndrome. This occurs in a young athlete who suffers a second concussion when he or she has not recovered from the first. The proposed hypothesis is uncontrolled brain swelling from the second insult and carries a 50 percent mortality rate. This situation has only been described in athletes under 20 years old.

Unfortunately, 10–15 percent of SRCs do not improve in the first couple weeks and may develop post-concussive syndrome (PCS). It is not a prolonged concussion, but a separate clinical entity characterized by headache, dizziness, nausea, memory disturbance, confusion, fatigue, sleep disturbance, concentration problems, and fogginess. Although data are limited, treatments are directed at symptoms and include medications and various forms of physical and occupational therapy such as cognitive, visual, and vestibular therapy. Medications are aimed at specific symptoms such as analgesics for headaches, stimulants for fatigue, or antidepressants for anxiety and depression.

A recent concern has been the possible connection between repeated SRCs and the development of chronic traumatic encephalopathy (CTE) first described by Nigerian American physician Bennet Omalu in 2004. CTE is clinically associated with mood disorders, neuropsychiatric disturbances, and cognitive impairments. To date, there are no epidemiological, prospective, or cross-sectional studies that demonstrate a cause and effect relationship between SRC and CTE.

Public health efforts directed toward decreasing the incidence and severity of SRCs focus on education of athletes, coaches, parents, and health care providers in the signs and symptoms of SRC; instruction of proper fit and use of equipment; teaching proper athletic technique (tackling in football, heading in soccer, etc.); encouraging athletes to report concussive symptoms; and developing better methods to diagnose SRC such as biomarkers and advanced imaging. Equipment modifications have demonstrated mixed results. Football helmets, for example, have greatly reduced some injuries, like skull fractures, but have not impacted concussions to the same degree. However, headgear in rugby has had a protective effect. Use of mouth guards has not shown any reductions in SRCs. Rules changes in some sports have had a more dramatic effect. In junior ice hockey, the rule change to prohibit body-checking before age 13 has markedly reduced concussion rates in this sport. Heads Up is a resource center provided by the Centers for Disease Control and Prevention that provides information on best practices in preventing SRCs. Future efforts seek to change the culture of sports to one which emphasizes the safety and wellness of the athlete over the outcome of the game.

Neil Mathews

See also: Injuries; National Center for Injury Prevention and Control; School Health

Further Reading

Almeida, A. A., & Kutcher, J. S. (2016). Sports and performance concussion. In R. B. Daroff, J. J. Jankovic, J. C. Mazziotta, & S. L. Pomeroy (Eds.), *Bradley's neurology in clinical practice* (7th ed.). Maryland Heights, MO: Elsevier Saunders.

Centers for Disease Control and Prevention. (2017). *HeadsUp*. Retrieved from https://www.cdc.gov/headsup/index.html.

Dashnaw, M. L. (2017). Mild traumatic brain injury in adults and concussion in sports. In H. R. Winn (Ed.), *Youmans and Winn neurological surgery.* London, UK: Elsevier.

Giza, C. C., Kutcher, J. S., Ashwal, S., Barth, J., Getchius, T. D., Gioia, G. A., & . . . Zafonte, R. (2013). Summary of evidence-based guideline update: Evaluation and management of concussion in sports: Report of the Guideline Development Subcommittee of the American Academy of Neurology. *Neurology*, *80*(24), 2250–2257. doi:10.1212/WNL.0b013e31828d57dd

Halstead, M. E., & Walter, K. D. (2010). Sport-related concussion in children and adolescents. *Pediatrics*, *126*(3), 597–615. doi:10.1542/peds.2010-2005

McCrory, P., Meeuwisse, W., Dvořák, J., Aubry, M., Bailes, J., Broglio, S., & . . . Johnston, K. M. (2017). Consensus statement on concussion in sport: The 5th international conference on concussion in sport held in Berlin, October 2016. *British Journal of Sports Medicine*, *51*(11), 838. doi:10.1136/bjsports-2017-097699

Omalu B. (2004). Chronic traumatic encephalopathy and the National Football League. *Journal of Neuropathology & Experimental Neurology*, *63*(5), 535.

Sprouse, R. A., Harris, G. D., Sprouse, G. E., Humerick, M., & Miller, R. T. (2016). Sport-related concussion: How best to help young athletes. *Journal of Family Practice*, *65*(8), 538–546.

STARK LAW

The Stark law prohibits physician self-referral—a practice in which doctors refer patients to health services where the physician or a physician's family member has a financial interest. Doctors have a lot of power in prescribing medical tests or treatments and where patients go for such services. Ethical conflicts arise when doctors are directly or indirectly compensated by a business related to their practice. The physician may prescribe unnecessary services or favor certain organizations, blocking competition and increasing regional health care costs. In Sumter, South Carolina, Tuomey Healthcare System administrators engaged in such practices. Hospital administrators were concerned with a new freestanding surgicenter, which was being built nearby. The administrators feared that Tuomey would lose revenue if doctors performed minor surgeries in the doctor's office or the ambulatory service center rather than in the hospital's facility. To counter losses, the health care system contracted 19 area specialists to exclusively use Tuomey's outpatient surgicenter. The contracts were unusual in that they allowed the physicians to continue as independent practitioners and focused on number of surgeries rather than number of hours worked at Tuomey's facility. The 10-year contracts prohibited the physicians from performing surgeries within a 30-mile radius of the hospital for another two years after the end of the contract. In the case against Tuomey, the U.S. Department of Justice alleged the contract payments were higher than market rate for specialist services, and the hospital was padding the Medicare bills to compensate the physicians (U.S. Department of Justice, 2015). Tuomey was found guilty and fined $237 million for improper financial relationships. The case eventually settled for $72.4 million, and Tuomey was taken over by Palmetta Health.

Named after the bill's sponsor, U.S. Congressman Pete Stark, the Stark law became effective in 1992 and has gone through several modifications. Stark I was originally a provision of the Omnibus Budget Reconciliation Act (OBRA) of 1989. The regulation applied to self-referrals to clinical laboratory services. OBRA 1993 created Stark II, expanding the law to cover *designated health services* such as inpatient and outpatient treatment or rehabilitation services, radiology, medical equipment, and prescription drugs. The law has been criticized. In communities with limited access to health resources, the Stark law could conceivably block physicians from creating needed treatment centers. Oftentimes, physician-created services are less expensive because they do not carry the overhead expenses of hospitals. The Stark law could also block physicians from participating in managed care networks where the physicians might act as advocates for their patients. The Stark law does allow some exceptions. Hospitals and physicians may enter into contracts if the proposed payment amounts are reasonable in comparison to market value, the payment amount is identified in advance and not based on volume, and the physician services are clearly named. Contracts should last longer than one year to avoid predatory agreements that take advantage of a natural disaster or regional epidemic. Examples of acceptable contracts are bona fide employment, incidental benefits (such as free parking or meals while on call), and renting medical office space.

Penalties for violation of the Stark law start with denial of Medicare or Medicaid payment for the services in question, fines of up to $15,000 per incident, and possible expulsion from federally financed health programs. This is why we see a hospital such as Tuomey, bought out by a neighboring institution. If a hospital cannot bill for Medicare services, the organization is essentially out of business. The loss not only affects the hospital but also hurts the community who needs those medical services. A violation must meet four main criteria: (1) physician; (2) referral for designated health services; (3) entity that bills Medicare; and (4) financial relationship between the organization and the physician or the physician's immediate family member (Fredricksen & Egan, 2015). For the purposes of the law, "physician" refers to any medical or osteopathic doctor, podiatrist, dentist, optometrist, or chiropractor. "Designated health services" include clinical laboratory services, physical therapy, occupational therapy of speech therapy, radiological services, home health services, medical equipment, and outpatient prescription drugs or hospital services, both inpatient and outpatient. "Financial relationship" is defined as direct or indirect ownership or investment interest or direct or indirect compensation arrangement. Although Stark was designed primarily to avoid Medicare fraud, the law has been used to settle fraudulent Medicaid claims. The final amendment from the Patient Protection and Affordable Care Act (PPACA) states that the Centers for Medicare and Medicaid Services will allow providers to initiate a process of self-reporting for possible or actual breaches of the act. Physicians, who try to circumvent the Stark law by putting ownership in another person's name or through other contrivance, can be fined up to $100,000 per scheme.

The Stark law is related but not the same as the False Claims Act and the federal Anti-Kickback law. The Stark law is intended to protect patients and prevent corruption and abuse of the Medicare program by physicians and health care–related businesses. The law safeguards medical care by ensuring that the doctor is acting in the patient's best interests and that prescribed treatments and tests are not financially motivated.

Leapolda Figueroa and Sally Kuykendall

See also: Administration, Health; Affordable Care Act; False Claims Act; Medicare; Public Health Law

Further Reading

Frederiksen, M., & Egan Weaver, E. (2015). Understanding the federal physician self-referral statute: "Stark law." *Journal of Health Care Compliance, 17*(2), 47–65.

U.S. Department of Justice. (2015, October 16). *United States resolves $237 million false claims act judgment against South Carolina hospital that made illegal payments to referring physicians.* Washington, DC. Retrieved from https://www.justice.gov/opa/pr/united-states-resolves-237-million-false-claims-act-judgment-against-south-carolina-hospital.

STATE, LOCAL, AND TERRITORIAL HEALTH DEPARTMENTS

State, local, and territorial health departments are government agencies responsible for preventing diseases and promoting the health of people living within the respective jurisdiction. The agencies were originally organized as a way to prevent and control epidemic diseases. Over time, functions, scope, and regulatory authority extended to other areas of health. Organizational structures varied based on the area, state governance, or population served. Generally, health departments are responsible for (1) developing policies to protect, promote, and improve public health; (2) ensuring adequate resources for essential public health services; (3) ensuring compliance with federal, state, and local laws and regulations related to public health; (4) organizing and leading public health efforts; (5) collaborating with community partners to promote health; and (6) ensuring continuous quality improvement (Public Health Law Center and William Mitchell College of Law). Services tend to cover certifying agencies for federal reimbursement for health services, mental health care, tuberculosis control, medical examiner services, health planning, minority health services, and rural health services. These services may be performed directly by the health department or indirectly through contracts with for-profit or nonprofit agencies. Public health departments are also responsible for responding to emerging health issues. In the past few decades, public health departments have assumed leading roles in bioterrorism preparedness, emergency response, toxicology prevention, chronic disease epidemiology, cancer screenings, state health insurance programs, and human participant protections review boards.

The first state board of health was founded in 1869 by Massachusetts physician and social reformer Henry Ingersoll Bowditch. Bowditch envisioned an organization, supported by the government, which used science to provide medical and social care to disadvantaged people. Within a few years, other states and large cities created their own departments of health. These early public health departments focused on sanitation and hygiene, maintaining disease registries, immunizations, and treatment. During World War I (1914–1918), many draftees were rejected due to poor physical or mental health. It became apparent that success as a nation depended on healthy citizens. Health departments expanded efforts to provide health education, visiting nurses to support new mothers, infants, and children, and community health clinics. Through the mid-20th century federal activities in disease research, prevention, and control grew with the establishment of the National Institutes of Health, the Public Health Service, and the Centers for Disease Control and Prevention. The roles of state and local boards of health changed to keep relevant with federal activities and funding opportunities. For example, maternal and child health services, family planning services, sexually transmitted disease control, and tuberculosis control became standard services within state and local health departments when the federal government offered financial and technical assistance for such services.

Today, there are approximately 2,600 local health departments in the United States (Yeager, Ferdinand, Beitsch, & Menachemi, 2015). Primary health department functions are to identify community health needs, investigate health hazards, communicate health matters to the general public, engage with the community in health promotion activities, develop public health policies and strategic plans, enforce public health laws, promote access to quality health care, maintain a competent workforce, employ evidence-based programs and practices, collaborate with the governing entity, and ensure ongoing quality improvement. The Public Health Accreditation Board (PHAB) offers a voluntary review of health departments to ensure quality services. A growing challenge for all health departments is the skyrocketing cost of medical services. Despite scientific advances in the prevention of infectious diseases, improved nutrition, and evidence-based practices in behavioral health, the nation still struggles with political, economic, and social values that contradict public health, and this leaves public health departments in the difficult position of justifying the need for care and services to disadvantaged populations.

Sally Kuykendall

See also: Association of State and Territorial Health Officials; Bowditch, Henry Ingersoll; Community Health Centers; National Association of County and City Health Officials; U.S. Public Health Service; *Controversies in Public Health:* Controversy 4

Further Reading

Association of State and Territorial Health Officials. (2016). Retrieved from http://www.astho.org.

Essential Services Work Group. (n.d.). *Ten essential services: Purpose and practices of public health.* Atlanta: Centers for Disease Control and Prevention. Retrieved from http://www.cdc.gov/stltpublichealth/hop/pdfs/Ten_Essential_Public_Health_Services_2011-09_508.pdf/.

Hyde, J. K., & Shortell, S. M. (2012). The structure and organization of local and state public health agencies in the U.S.: A systematic review. *American Journal of Preventive Medicine*, 42(5, Suppl. 1), S29–S41. doi:10.1016/j.amepre.2012.01.021

Institute of Medicine. (2003). *The future of the public's health in the 21st century.* Washington, DC: The National Academies Press.

Miller, C. A. (1977). Statutory authorizations for the work of local health departments. *American Journal of Public Health, 67,* 940–945.

Miller, C. A. (1977). Survey of local public health departments and their directors. *American Journal of Public Health, 67,* 931–939.

Public Health Accreditation Board. Retrieved from http://www.phaboard.org.

Public Health Law Center and William Mitchell College of Law. Retrieved from http://www.publichealthlawcenter.org/sites/default/files/resources/phlc-fs-state-local-reg-authority-publichealth-2015_0.pdf.

Shipley, A. E. (1917). Health administration on the district plan. *American Journal of Public Health, 7,* 248–259.

The state health department—Services and responsibilities. (1954). *American Journal of Public Health, 44,* 235–252.

Yeager, V. A., Ferdinand, A. O., Beitsch, L. M., & Menachemi, N. (2015). Local public health department characteristics associated with likelihood to participate in national accreditation. *American Journal of Public Health, 105*(8), 1653–1659. doi:10.2105/AJPH.2014.302503

SUBSTANCE ABUSE AND MENTAL HEALTH SERVICES ADMINISTRATION (SAMHSA)

An estimated 22.7 million Americans need treatment for substance abuse, yet only 2.5 million people actually receive treatment from qualified facilities (National Institute on Drug Abuse [NIDA], 2015). The Substance Abuse and Mental Health Services Administration (SAMHSA) is the federal agency responsible for leading national efforts in prevention, treatment, and recovery of substance abuse, mental illness, and behavioral health problems. SAMHSA's mission is to "reduce the impact of substance abuse and mental illness on America's communities" (SAMHSA). To carry out this mission, SAMHSA creates and disseminates information through public awareness campaigns, offers research and community grants, analyzes and develops national policies, advocates for evidence-based programs, and works to improve access to quality services for people suffering from substance abuse and mental illness. The agency is one of the eight operating divisions of the Department of Health and Human Services (DHHS). Current initiatives address substance abuse, suicide, trauma and violence, workforce wellness, veterans' health, homelessness, mental illness, prescription drug misuse, disaster preparedness and response, HIV/AIDS, and criminal and juvenile justice. SAMHSA serves members of the general population and populations vulnerable to socioemotional trauma, such as lesbian, gay, bisexual, transgender, and queer (LGBTQ) individuals, ethnic minorities, veterans and their families, and college students and youth in transitional stages. SAMHSA studies and encourages best programs and practices in substance abuse prevention and promotion of mental health.

Federal organizing against the problem of substance abuse prevention traces back to 1935 when a research facility was established for addiction research within the Public Health Service hospital in Lexington, Kentucky. The facility eventually became the Addiction Research Center (ARC) and later the National Institute on Drug Abuse (NIDA). Before the science of addictions or mental illness was realized, people with neurological disorders, addictions, or mental illness were housed in mental institutions and isolated from the rest of society. Mental asylums struggled with overcrowding, underfunding, seriously ill patients, and unqualified staff. The popular opinion was that people with mental illness were morally defective and did not deserve humanity or compassion. The field of medicine was complicit in the problem. Few doctors chose to go into psychiatry, and little was known (or even cared to be known) about effective treatments. As veterans returned from World War II, the nation was confronted by an epidemic of post-traumatic stress disorder, anxiety, depression, and paranoia. Witnessing the trauma of war, death, torture, destruction, and fear took a toll on the sons, brothers, uncles, and fathers who served the nation. Over one million service men and women were admitted to military hospitals for neuropsychiatric problems (Appel, Beebe, & Hilger, 1946). The nation could no longer depersonalize, blame, or stereotype the mentally ill as morally defective. There was a moral obligation to care for the nation's veterans. In 1946, President Harry S. Truman signed the National Mental Health Act. The law called for research into mental health disorders, prevention and treatment programs, training in care of the mentally ill for medical professionals, and the creation of the National Advisory Mental Health Council. The obligation to care for the nation's veterans helped to stimulate research, training, and programs in mental health.

In 1970, President Richard M. Nixon signed the Comprehensive Alcohol Abuse and Alcoholism Prevention, Treatment, and Rehabilitation Act, also known as the Hughes Act after recovering alcoholic senator Harold Hughes. The act supported research, prevention, and treatment of alcohol abuse and led to the creation of the National Institute on Alcohol Abuse and Alcoholism (NIAA). The NIAA was responsible for many new discoveries in treatment of alcohol addiction, fetal alcohol syndrome, and underage drinking as well as advocating for effective policies, programs, and treatments. The public started to recognize alcoholism as a disease in need of medical treatment, rather than a moral deficit. The Alcohol, Drug Abuse, and Mental Health Administration (ADAMHA) was established to take NIAA's discoveries and apply the information to addiction treatment. ADAMHA was quickly replaced by SAMHSA. Whereas ADAMHA focused on the treatment of addictions, SAMHSA focused on promoting mental health among all people. Thus, SAMHSA's focus is holistic, geared toward disease prevention and health promotion.

SAMHSA serves as the nation's leading authority on behavioral health. The organization provides accurate resources and information to states, territories, tribes, communities, local organizations, health professionals, and individuals. SAMHSA is a clearinghouse for quality information on alcohol, tobacco and other drugs, behavioral health treatment, mental disorders, school and campus health, suicide prevention, trauma and violence, and vulnerable populations. Mentalhealth.gov is a resource for individuals experiencing mental health problems, concerned friends looking to help a loved one, parents and caregivers, teachers, and faith and community leaders. The site describes attributes of mental health, warning signs of mental health problems, ways to promote positive mental health, and recovery from mental illness. The website links directly to the National Suicide Prevention Lifeline, 1-800-273-TALK (8255), for those who need someone to connect with. *SAMHSA News* is a national newsletter providing the latest information in substance use and mental disorder prevention, treatment, and recovery. Article topics include building trauma-informed resilient communities, self-care for health care professionals, and partnering with faith-based organizations. Stopbullying.gov is where experts in bullying turn for the latest information, news, and updates in bullying prevention research. Written for all audiences, the site defines bullying, risk factors, effective strategies for prevention, and constructive responses. Stopbullying.gov deconstructs many of the myths and misperceptions regarding bullying in order to bring accurate information into homes, schools, and communities. SAMHSA provides a wealth of current and accurate information to support mental health.

The nation has come a long way in recognizing mental illness and addictions as chronic diseases in need of medical treatment. Much of the progress can be attributed to federal partners working with communities to study and understand behavioral health problems. SAMHSA focuses specifically on increasing public awareness and understanding of mental disorders and substance use, promoting mental health among all people in the nation, preventing substance abuse and mental illness, supporting recovery, and increasing access to evidence-based programs and treatments. Over the next several years, the organization will focus on building a competent, qualified behavioral health workforce, integrating behavioral health services into existing health systems, exposing the connections between trauma and antisocial behaviors, preventing substance abuse and mental illness, and strengthening the systems that support people in recovery by partnering with education and employment services. A major challenge will be confronting and controlling the opioid epidemic, as this may divert resources from current needs.

Sally Kuykendall

See also: Addictions; Alcohol; Beers, Clifford Whittingham; Centers for Disease Control and Prevention; Dix, Dorothea Lynde; Emergency Preparedness and Response; Evidence-Based Programs and Practices; Food and Drug Administration; Mental Health; Mental Illness; Prescription Drugs; U.S. Department of Agriculture; U.S. Department of Health and Human Services; Veterans' Health; Violence; *Controversies in Public Health:* Controversy 2

Further Reading

Appel, J. W., Beebe, G. W., & Hilger, D. W. (1946). Comparative incidence of neuropsychiatric casualties in World War I and World War II. *The American Journal of Psychiatry*, *103*, 196–199. doi:10.1176/ajp.103.2.196

National Institute on Drug Abuse. (2015). *Drug facts, nationwide trends.* Retrieved from https://www.drugabuse.gov/publications/drugfacts/nationwide-trends.

Pols, H., & Oak, S. (2007). War & military mental health: The US psychiatric response in the 20th century. *American Journal of Public Health, 97*(12), 2132–2142.
Substance Abuse and Mental Health Services Administration. Retrieved from https://www.samhsa.gov.

SURGEON GENERAL

The surgeon general is the country's senior medical officer responsible for communicating important health information to the nation and managing the U.S. Public Health Service. Only one surgeon general serves at a time. To qualify for the position, the candidate must have experience in public health, and be a member of the U.S. Public Health Service, nominated by the president of the United States, and confirmed by the Senate. The position of surgeon general was founded in 1870 when President Ulysses S. Grant appointed Dr. John Maynard Woodworth as supervising surgeon of the Marine Hospital Service, a national health system for sick, injured, and disabled seamen. Over the years, the role of the surgeon general evolved from treating and preventing communicable diseases to treating and preventing acute and chronic health issues. Today, the Office of the Surgeon General reviews the latest scientific advances in health and makes recommendations for the nation's health. As a public health professional, the surgeon general is bound by ethical principles of honesty, integrity, respect for persons, beneficence, and justice. This means that the surgeon general must act in the best interests of the nation and the people in the nation and cannot selectively review scientific information in order to support or oppose political ideology.

The Office of the Surgeon General traces back to 1798 when President John Adams signed the Act for the Relief of Sick and Disabled Seamen. The act was designed to hold shipping merchants and crews accountable for compensating local hospitals caring for sick or injured sailors. As shipping trade developed and the system grew, the Marine Hospital Service (MHS) was created to supervise and coordinate services. In 1871, Dr. John M. Woodworth was appointed as the first supervising surgeon. Woodworth created a uniformed federal workforce responsible for examining sailors and immigrants, investigating outbreaks of infectious diseases, and regulating local sanitation. The Commissioned Corps of the U.S. Public Health Service is a nonmilitary organization composed of public health professionals responsible for protecting, promoting, and advancing the health and safety of the United States. In 1873, the position of supervising surgeon became supervising surgeon general and was later changed to surgeon general.

The surgeon general holds the rank of a two-star rear admiral (RADM) or three-star vice admiral (VADM). The surgeon generals and acting surgeon generals who have served the nation are:

- John M. Woodworth (1871–1879)
- RADM John B. Hamilton (1879–1891)
- RADM Walter Wyman (1891–1911)

- RADM Rupert Blue (1912–1920)
- RADM Hugh S. Cumming (1920–1936)
- RADM Thomas Parran Jr. (1936–1948)
- RADM Leonard Scheele (1948–1956)
- RADM Leroy E. Burney (1956–1961)
- RADM Luther L. Terry (1961–1965)
- VADM William H. Stewart (1965–1969)
- RADM Richard A. Prindle (acting surgeon general, 1969)
- RADM Jesse L. Steinfeld (1969–1973)
- RADM S. Paul Ehrlich (acting surgeon general, 1973–1977)
- VADM Julius B. Richmond (1977–1981)
- Edward Brandt, Jr. (acting surgeon general, 1981–1982)
- VADM C. Everett Koop (1982–1989)
- ADM James O. Mason (acting surgeon general, 1989–1990)
- VADM Antonia C. Novella (1990–1993)
- RADM Robert A. Whitney (acting surgeon general, 1993)
- VADM M. Joycelyn Elders (1993–1994)
- RADM Audrey F. Manley (acting surgeon general, 1995–1997)
- ADM/ VADM David Satcher (1998–2002)
- RADM Kenneth P. Moritsugu (acting surgeon general, 2002)
- VADM Richard H. Carmona (2002–2006)
- RADM Kenneth P. Moritsugu (acting surgeon general, 2006–2007)
- RADM Steven K. Galson (acting surgeon general, 2007–2009)
- RADM Donald L. Weaver (acting surgeon general, 2009)
- VADM Regina M. Benjamin (2009–2013)
- RADM Boris D. Lushniak (acting surgeon general, 2013–2014)
- VADM Vivek H. Murthy (2014–2017)
- RADM Sylvia Trent-Adams (acting surgeon general, 2017)

The surgeon general is the chief authority for public health issues in the nation. For example, under President John F. Kennedy, Surgeon General Luther L. Terry led a committee of experts to investigate the health effects of smoking. Mounting evidence contradicted the popular belief that cigarettes cleared the lungs and aided breathing. The committee reviewed more than 7,000 research articles and Surgeon General Terry concluded that cigarette smoking is a health hazard. From the surgeon general's report, Congress passed the Federal Cigarette Labeling and Advertising Act of 1965 requiring the surgeon general's warning label on all cigarette packages and banning cigarette advertising on television.

Although the surgeon general is responsible for ensuring and promoting the health of people in the nation, political pressures often strain the person and the role. In 1968, the position of Assistant Secretary of Health (ASH) was created to oversee the surgeon general's office. Whereas the Office of the Surgeon General is a service position, legally and ethically forbidden from engaging in political activities, the Assistant

Secretary of Health is a political position. This means that the surgeon general has a responsibility to promote public health while the surgeon general's boss has a responsibility to promote the current administration's political agenda. This creates problems. Such as when the Reagan administration attempted to pressure Surgeon General C. Everett Koop, MD, into saying that abortion was psychologically harmful to women. Fortunately, members of Congress accepted and supported the conclusions from Terry's smoking and health advisory committee. If members had acted in the best interest of tobacco companies, cigarette advertising companies, or small shopkeepers, more people would have died from cancer and smoking-related diseases.

The surgeon general is the nation's top doctor or nurse, responsible for identifying pressing health concerns, investigating the latest science, and developing recommendations. Overall, the system works. The surgeon general's office is cautious knowing that announcements could make or break a business. Unfortunately, the current system of oversight is based on politics, and this can become a problem if the current political regimen has an agenda that conflicts with public health.

Sally Kuykendall

See also: Association of State and Territorial Health Officials; Cancer; Centers for Disease Control and Prevention (CDC); Cutter Incident, The; Elders, Joycelyn; Health Policy; *Healthy People 2020*; National Heart, Lung, and Blood Institute (NHLBI); Obesity; Research; Tuskegee Syphilis Study; U.S. Department of Health and Human Services; U.S. Public Health Service; Skin Cancer; Violence; Wynder, Ernst Ludwig; *Controversies in Public Health:* Controversy 2; Controversy 4

Further Reading

Carmona, R. (2017). Instant admirals and the plague of politics in the United States Public Health Service: Back to the future. *Military Medicine, 182*(5), 1582–1583. doi:10.7205/MILMED-D-17-00039

Furman, B. (1973). *A profile of the United States Public Health Service, 1798–1948*. Washington, DC: U.S. Department of Health, Education, and Welfare.

Mullan, F. (1989). *Plagues and politics: The story of the United States Public Health Service.* New York: Basic Books.

Surgeon General. Retrieved from https://www.surgeongeneral.gov.

SYRINGE SERVICE PROGRAMS

When injection drug users (IDUs) inject heroin, cocaine, methamphetamine, or other substance, they draw a tiny amount of blood from the vein into the syringe to check that the needle is properly positioned. If the blood is infected with HIV, hepatitis B, hepatitis C, or other blood borne disease, the pathogen can be transmitted to other people who use the syringe. As the AIDS epidemic advanced, one-quarter to one-third of all new cases were due to needle sharing (HIV/AIDS surveillance report, 1993). Half of all heterosexually acquired AIDS cases traced to unprotected sex with an IDU, carrying the infection to newborns and nursing infants. Improperly discarded syringes risk injury and infection to children, sanitation workers, and members of a community. Needle exchange programs (NEPs) reduce blood borne infections by offering injection drug users (IDUs) free sterile syringes in exchange for used, potentially contaminated needles. Syringe service programs (SSPs) are comprehensive public health programs offering needle exchange, alcohol swabs, bleach, safe needle disposal bins, condoms, health education on safe injection practices and wound care, overdose prevention, counseling, testing for HIV and hepatitis, and referral to drug treatment programs or other mental health services. NEPs, SSPs, and syringe exchange programs (SEPs) are also called *harm reduction* programs because the programs focus on reducing the harm of injection drug use, rather than treating the addiction. Multiple evaluation studies show that SSPs effectively reduce the transmission of HIV, hepatitis, and other blood borne diseases among at-risk populations (Des Jarlais, Sloboda, Friedman, Tempalski, McKnight, & Braine, 2006; Kaplan & O'Keefe, 1993; Wodak & Cooney, 2006). However, since inception NEPs have been highly controversial, criticized as promoting illegal and self-destructive behavior. The Consolidated Appropriations Act of 2016 limits the use of federal funds to support NEPs. The federal government provides partial support to state, local, tribal, and territorial health departments that demonstrate the need for SSPs. To qualify, the organization must present strong epidemiological evidence of increased cases or risk of HIV and hepatitis due to injection drug use. Taxpayer dollars may not be used to support illegal drug activities. From a public health perspective, SSPs are effective in reducing HIV and hepatitis among IDUs and sexual partners of IDUs. An added benefit is that they provide access to closed, hard to reach communities. This access will become increasingly important as the United States grapples with the emerging opioid and heroin epidemics.

Needle exchange programs started in Edinburgh, Scotland, when a pharmacist distributed sterile syringes to IDUs in order to stop an epidemic of hepatitis B and hepatitis C. In 1983, a large, centrally located pharmacy in Amsterdam stopped selling syringes to IDUs after an outbreak of hepatitis B. Junkiebond, a community of IDUs, partnered with the local health department to establish a program of needle exchange. The onset of AIDS prompted other NEPs in major cities of the Netherlands, the United Kingdom, and Australia. In the United States, NEPs started as underground movements. Yale student and former heroin addict Jon Stuen-Parker created the Boston AIDS Brigade and the Yale AIDS Brigade, which evolved into the National AIDS Brigade. Working out of his home or car along the northeastern corridor of the United States, Stuen-Parker was arrested 27 times in seven states for the possession and delivery of drug paraphernalia (McLean, 2011). Despite evidence supporting the effectiveness of SSPs, the United States lagged well behind other nations (Wodak & Cooney, 2006). America's War on Drugs and other national drug policies focused on crime and punishment at the expense of public health. Without effective prevention or intervention mechanisms, the United States developed the highest HIV/AIDS incidence rates of any non–third world country (Wodak & Cooney, 2006).

The first legal NEP in the United States was established in Tacoma, Washington, in 1988. In 1994, 55 SEPs exchanged approximately 8 million syringes (Syringe Exchange Programs—United States, 1995). By 2002, 119 SEPs exchanged almost 25 million syringes as well as offering referrals for substance abuse treatment, on-site HIV and hepatitis counseling, tuberculosis and sexually transmitted disease (STD) screening, and on-site medical care (Update: Syringe Exchange Programs—United States, 2005). Early evaluation of SSPs showed limited efficacy in reducing HIV transmission. Critics argued that SSPs encouraged drug use and increased blood borne diseases. Experts responded that study results may have been confounded by the fact that SSPs attract chronic IDUs. SSP participants have higher risk of HIV than nonparticipants. Researchers concluded that programs may be most effective during early drug use and suggested expanding services to include STD prevention and addiction treatment services.

Multiple studies refute the arguments used to oppose SSPs and SSP funding. From 1991 to 2001, the U.S. government sponsored seven evaluation studies (Wodak & Cooney, 2006). All seven studies showed that SSPs reduced HIV transmission among IDUs, their partners, and children. Researchers in New Haven, Connecticut, estimated a 33 percent reduction in HIV infection rate among program users (Kaplan & O'Keefe, 1993). The World Health Organization (2004) analyzed over 200 reports from around the world and concluded that SSPs:

1. Substantially reduce HIV.
2. Are more effective than bleach or other forms of disinfection.
3. Do not increase illicit drug use.
4. Are cost effective.
5. Provide opportunity for referral to drug treatment programs and other health services.

International experts noted that NEPs combined with other HIV prevention programs are an appropriate public health response to HIV transmission. They also cautioned that U.S. laws against drug paraphernalia impeded public health efforts. Despite overwhelming evidence in support of SSPs, it is illegal to buy or own syringes without a prescription, and federal regulations heavily restrict the use of federal funds for NEPs.

SSPs are public health programs that protect against HIV transmission and seroconversion. Studies show that the programs work in at least 10 countries and are cost effective (Wodak & Cooney, 2006). However, simply exchanging needles is not enough to control HIV or hepatitis among IDUs. Programs that target transmission of pathogens to sexual partners and children or assist with treatment and recovery provide an umbrella of services that can have greater public health impact.

Sally Kuykendall

See also: Addictions; Evidence-Based Programs and Practices; Hepatitis; Infectious Diseases; Mental Illness; Risk-Benefit Analysis; *Controversies in Public Health:* Controversy 2

Further Reading

Burris, S., Finucane, D., Gallagher, H., & Grace, J. (1996). The legal strategies used in operating syringe exchange programs in the United States. *American Journal of Public Health*, *86*(8), 1161–1166.

Centers for Disease Control and Prevention. (2016). *Syringe service programs.* Retrieved from https://www.cdc.gov/hiv/risk/ssps.html.

Des Jarlais, D., Sloboda, Z., Friedman, S. R., Tempalski, B., McKnight, C., & Braine, N. (2006). Diffusion of the D.A.R.E and syringe exchange programs. *American Journal of Public Health*, *96*(8), 1354–1358.

Harm Reduction Coalition. Retrieved from http://harmreduction.org.

HIV/AIDS surveillance report. (1993). Atlanta, GA: U.S. Department of Health and Human Services, Public Health Service, Centers for Disease Control and Prevention, National Center for Infectious Diseases, Division of HIV/AIDS; Rockville, MD: CDC National AIDS Clearinghouse [distributor].

Kaplan, E. H., & O'Keefe, E. (1993). Let the needles do the talking! Evaluating the New Haven needle exchange. *Interfaces*, *23*(1), 7–26.

McLean, K. (2011). The biopolitics of needle exchange in the United States. *Critical Public Health*, *21*(1), 71–79. doi:10.1080/09581591003653124

North American Syringe Exchange Network. Retrieved from https://nasen.org.

Syringe Exchange Programs—United States, 1994–1995. (1995). *Morbidity and Mortality Weekly Report*, *44*(37), 684.

Update: Syringe Exchange Programs—United States, 2002. (2005). *Morbidity and Mortality Weekly Report*, *54*(27), 673–676.

van Ameijden, E., van den Hoek, J., van Haastrecht, H., & Coutinho, R. (1992). The harm reduction approach and risk factors for human immunodeficiency virus (HIV) seroconversion in injecting drug users, Amsterdam. *American Journal of Epidemiology, 136*(2), 236. Retrieved from https://doi.org/10.1093/oxfordjournals.aje.a116489.

Wodak, A., & Cooney, A. (2006). Do needle syringe programs reduce HIV infection among injecting drug users: A comprehensive review of the international evidence. *Substance Use & Misuse*, *41*(6–7), 777–813. doi:10.1080/10826080600669579

World Health Organization. (2004). *Effectiveness of sterile needle and syringe programming in reducing HIV/AIDS among injecting drug users.* Geneva, Switzerland: Author. Retrieved from http://www.who.int/hiv/pub/idu/pubidu/en.

T

TRANSTHEORETICAL MODEL (TTM)

The transtheoretical model (TTM) was developed in 1983 by two researchers, Dr. James O. Prochaska and Dr. Carlo C. DiClemente, while investigating how people successfully stopped cigarette smoking. The model presents the cognitive stages that people go through when they are intentionally changing health behaviors. Also known as "stages of change," TTM describes both adopting a positive health behavior, such as increasing exercise, and stopping a negative behavior, such as substance abuse. Originally applied to addictive disorders, the model has been found to relate to many other behaviors such as intimate partner violence, bullying, physical activity, mammography screening, safe sexual practices, diet, and sunscreen use. TTM depicts multiple concepts that play a role in intentional behavioral change. The main constructs or building blocks of the model are the stages of change, cognitive and emotional factors that influence the ability and decision to change, and activities that help people to progress through the specific stages. It is an important tool for public health professionals to use for dealing with issues that can affect health,

The core constructs of TTM are the actual stages of behavioral change: *precontemplation, contemplation, preparation, action, maintenance,* and *termination.* The precontemplation stage describes the phase when the person engages in the negative health behavior or, if moving toward a healthy behavior, has yet to adopt the positive behavior. For example, when a person is in an unhealthy relationship, one that includes intimate partner violence (IPV), the victim in precontemplation is fully immersed in relationship with the aggressor and has no intention or need to escape the abusive relationship. The victim either denies or avoids discussing the abuse and may even make excuses for the perpetrator. In the contemplation stage, the individual recognizes the problems of continuing the behavior. Normally, contemplation lasts approximately six months. People can easily get stuck in this stage, a problem that the model's authors refer to as chronic contemplation or behavioral procrastination. In the contemplation stage, the victim of an abusive relationship might start to question the perpetrator's actions and motives. The victim might compare the current relationship to positive interpersonal relationships of friends and family members. In identifying and recognizing acts of disrespect, intimidation, or abuse, the victim becomes more aware of the problem. During preparation, the individual weighs available support systems or options and thinks about using these systems within the next month. The victim of IPV may gather information on different types of counseling services or local domestic violence resources. The action phase is the most obvious and observable of the stages. The action phase is the stage when the individual is actively engaged in stopping the negative behavior or adopting the positive behavior. The person in a violent relationship may break off the relationship, move, change telephone numbers, or terminate social networking sites. The action stage is the most dangerous for victims of IPV because the perpetrator will become more aggressive in order to maintain control. Violence may escalate to physical assault. The maintenance phase occurs when the person has successfully stopped the unhealthy behavior and has few temptations to relapse to the former lifestyle. Although stages are presented in temporal order, TTM is not linear. Individuals can easily become stuck in a stage or relapse to former behaviors. Most importantly, TTM tells us that behaviors rarely stop or start without thought, planning, and awareness. People go through stages to change behavior. This is an important concept because public health programs are often measured by the number of people who take action. The number of people who change behavior is not always an accurate representation of program success. It is just as valuable to move a program participant from precontemplation to contemplation as it is to move someone from preparation to action.

TTM includes ideas from prior research on decision making by Janis and Mann (1977). Decisional balance depicts how people think about and weigh the pros and cons of an intended action. Women in abusive relationships often stay because they do not believe that they have the economic power to support themselves and their children, or the victim may believe that the perpetrator will recognize the hurt and pain and self-correct ways of relating. Physicians and health professionals can help people in the early stages of decisional balance by providing health information and lists of available resources. In many cases, victims of domestic violence, often mothers, will not seek help for themselves but will seek help when they realize the impact of exposure to abuse on their children. Knowing what information will enable healthy decision making can help public health professionals to empower people to make decisions and change behavior. As individuals move through the stages, the advantages of changing the behavior outweigh the concerns or disadvantages.

TTM also provides individuals undergoing behavioral change and the public health educators supporting those individuals with a toolbox of educational and support strategies, known as the "processes of change." The processes of change are techniques that support people through the specific stages. The person in the *precontemplation-contemplation* stage needs accurate and specific information. During this time, the public health educator might use consciousness raising, dramatic relief, environmental reevaluation, or self-reevaluation to support the individual in decision making. The person in the *preparation* stage needs help in making a plan or commitment to stop smoking. This is the stage where pledges, contracts, or resolutions are most useful. The person in the *action and early maintenance* stages needs active and strong support. Controlling situations and events that might cause a relapse, using a reward system, supportive relationships, and substituting the negative behaviors with positive behaviors are ways that people in the action phase succeed in changing the behavior.

TTM is a highly relevant and useful model for today's health issues. Understanding how people consider and change behaviors helps public health professionals to work with communities and individuals to prevent and reduce many chronic diseases.

Sally Kuykendall

See also: Addictions; Behavioral Health; Health Communication; Health Education; Intervention; Self-Efficacy; Substance Abuse and Mental Health Services Administration; *Controversies in Public Health:* Controversy 4

Further Reading

Glanz, K., Rimer, B. K., & Viswanath, K. (Eds.). (2008). *Health behavior and health education: Theory, research, and practice.* San Franscisco: Jossey-Bass.

Janis, I. L., & Mann, L. (1977). *Decision making: A psychological analysis of conflict, choice, and commitment.* New York: Free Press.

Prochaska, J. O., & DiClemente, C. C. (1983). Stages and processes of self-change of smoking: Toward an integrative model of change. *Journal of Consulting and Clinical Psychology, 51,* 390–395.

Transtheoretical Model. (2015, July 9). Cancer Prevention Research Center, University of Rhode Island. Retrieved from http://web.uri.edu/cprc/transtheoretical-model/.

TRUTH CAMPAIGN, THE

A national tobacco counter marketing campaign branded as *Truth* was launched by the American Legacy Foundation (ALF) in February 2000. The ALF was founded only a few years earlier as a result of the 1998 Master Settlement Agreement between the tobacco industry, 46 states, and five U.S. territories. Among other provisions, this agreement set standards for, and imposed restrictions on, the sale and marketing of cigarettes to youth (Schroeder, 2004). The resulting Truth campaign, the largest national youth smoking prevention campaign, targets an audience that is primarily adolescents aged 12 to 17 years who are susceptible to tobacco use. From the onset, Truth sought to capitalize on the desire of adolescents to be rebellious and independent by exposing them to the tobacco industry's deceptive marketing practices toward teens (Holtgrave, Wunderink, Vallone, & Healton, 2009). The Truth campaign exposed teens to easily digestible truths about the detrimental effects of tobacco use and encouraged them to make their own decisions about smoking.

By marketing an anti-smoking message as a brand, the campaign was able to appeal to adolescents who were at risk for tobacco use. TV and print commercials in line with the latest trends, along with street marketing and a website, allowed Truth to reach a large portion of its target audience (Farrelly et al., 2002). Rather than simply telling youths to "just say no" to smoking, similar to previous anti-smoking campaigns, Truth delivered straightforward facts about the tobacco industry's motives and marketing practices toward teens. The Truth campaign often used direct, and often sobering, quotes from the tobacco companies themselves that revealed their youth-centric marketing and their denial of the negative health effects caused by tobacco (Biener & Siegel, 2000). Truth advertisements showed teens taking on the tobacco industry and tearing down the attractiveness of smoking that tobacco companies tried to establish in their marketing to youths. For example, one Truth commercial known as "The Real Cost" features a young teenage girl trying to buy a pack of cigarettes. The cashier tells her that she will need to give a little more beyond the cash value of the cigarettes, so the girl pulls off a piece of skin from her face and puts it alongside the money. The commercial fades out with a message asking what the real cost of cigarettes is, and then ends by saying that smoking causes wrinkles that age you prematurely. These hard-hitting commercials are meant to catch the attention of adolescents and portray information about the negative effects of smoking in a shocking manner.

The national Truth campaign was modeled after the highly successful Truth program in Florida. Within two years of the 1998 launch, the prevalence of smoking by Florida middle and high school students dropped by 40 percent and 18 percent, respectively (Bauer, Johnson, Hopkins, & Brooks, 2000). The decline was determined to be related to exposure to the Florida counter advertising program (Sly, Hopkins, Trapido, & Ray, 2001). After the nationwide launch, youth smoking decreased 22 percent between 1999 and 2002 (Farrelly, Davis, Haviland, Messeri, & Healton, 2005). The decline was directly attributable to the national Truth campaign. Smoking rates among youth were 1.6 percent lower than they would have been in the absence of the campaign; an estimated 300,000 fewer youth smoked as a result of Truth. Further study found that from 2000 to 2004, Truth prevented 450,000 adolescents from initiating the habit of smoking (Farrelly, Nonnemaker, Davis, & Hussin, 2009). Truth not only reduced the number of youth who were smoking, but the program also changed attitudes toward smoking. Among young people aged 12–17 years, exposure to the Truth campaign was associated with an increase in anti-tobacco attitudes and beliefs, and this effect increased at higher doses of the Truth exposure (Farrelly et al., 2005). More importantly, these effects were sustained over three years, indicating that counter marketing campaigns can successfully sustain young people's attitudes and beliefs in a positive way (Farrelly, Davis, Duke, & Messeri, 2009). The Truth campaign is associated with substantial declines in the youth smoking and has accelerated the recent decline in youth smoking prevalence (Farrelly et al., 2005). There is also evidence that youth-focused anti-smoking campaigns do not just impact youth, but they also promote attitudinal and behavioral changes in young adults not (Richardson, Green, Xiao, Sokol, & Vallone, 2010).

Despite having nationwide reach and markedly improving the public's health with a substantial decrease in youth smoking, this public health campaign did not impose a large economic burden. Expenditures for Truth totaled just over $324 million to develop, deliver, evaluate, and litigate the campaign (Holtgrave et al., 2009). Even when using conservative estimates of the campaign's positive health impacts, Holtgrave and colleagues found that Truth resulted in a savings of approximately $1.9 billion in shared medical costs in just its first two years. An optimistic estimate speculates that this savings was upwards of $5.4 billion. Ultimately, the campaign recouped its expenditures and was extremely cost effective.

The ALF was able to fund the highly successful Truth campaign due to a settlement from litigation between state attorney generals and the tobacco industry. According to the Master Settlement Agreement, ALF funding was dependent on the collective total market share of the four participating tobacco manufacturers, reaching 99.05 or higher (extremely unlikely) (Holtgrave et al., 2009). Due to this stipulation, the ALF has been slowly reducing its expenditures on the Truth campaign in recent years, and it is only being funded by income generated from its reserve fund. In 2014, Truth launched the *Finish It* campaign targeted at the next generation of youth. This campaign encourages upcoming youth to step up to the challenge of becoming the generation that ends smoking for good.

Salini Inaganti

See also: Addictions; Birth Defects; Children's Health; Evaluation; Master Settlement Agreement; RE-AIM (Reach, Effectiveness, Adoption, Implementation, and Maintenance); Risk-Benefit Analysis; Rural Health; Surgeon General; Wynder, Ernst Ludwig

Further Reading

Bauer, U. E., Johnson, T. M., Hopkins, R. S., & Brooks, R. G. (2000). Changes in youth cigarette use and intentions following implementation of a tobacco control program: Findings from the Florida youth tobacco survey, 1998–2000. *Journal of the American Medical Association*, *284*, 723–728. Retrieved from http://doi.org/10.1001/jama.284.6.723.

Biener, L., & Siegel, M. (2000). Tobacco marketing and adolescent smoking: More support for a causal inference. *American Journal of Public Health*, *90*, 407–411. Retrieved from http://doi.org/10.2105/AJPH.90.3.407.

Farrelly, M. C., Davis, K. C., Duke, J., & Messeri, P. (2009). Sustaining "truth": Changes in youth tobacco attitudes and smoking intentions after 3 years of a national antismoking campaign. *Health Education Research*, *24*, 42–48. Retrieved from http://doi.org/10.1093/her/cym087.

Farrelly, M. C., Davis, K. C., Haviland, M. L., Messeri, P., & Healton, C. G. (2005). Evidence of a dose-response relationship between "truth" antismoking ads and youth smoking prevalence. *American Journal of Public Health*. Retrieved from http://doi.org/10.2105/AJPH.2004.049692.

Farrelly, M. C., Healton, C. G., Davis, K. C., Messeri, P., Hersey, J. C., & Haviland, M. L. (2002). Getting to the truth: Evaluating national tobacco countermarketing campaigns. *American Journal of Public Health*, *92*, 901–907. Retrieved from http://doi.org/10.2105/AJPH.92.6.901.

Farrelly, M. C., Nonnemaker, J., Davis, K. C., & Hussin, A. (2009). The influence of the national truth campaign on smoking initiation. *American Journal of Preventive Medicine*, *36*, 379–384.

Holtgrave, D. R., Wunderink, K. A., Vallone, D. M., & Healton, C. G. (2009). Cost-utility analysis of the national Truth® campaign to prevent youth smoking. *American Journal of Preventive Medicine*, *36*, 385–388. Retrieved from http://doi.org/10.1016/j.amepre.2009.01.020.

Richardson, A. K., Green, M., Xiao, H., Sokol, N., & Vallone, D. (2010). Evidence for truth? The young adult response to a youth-focused anti-smoking media campaign. *American Journal of Preventive Medicine*, *39*, 500–506. Retrieved from http://doi.org/10.1016/j.amepre.2010.08.007.

Schroeder, S. A. (2004). Tobacco control in the wake of the 1998 Master Settlement Agreement. *New England Journal of Medicine*, *350*, 293–301. Retrieved from http://doi.org/10.1056/NEJMsr031421.

Sly, D. F., Hopkins, R. S., Trapido, E., & Ray, S. (2001). Influence of a counteradvertising media campaign on initiation of smoking: The Florida "truth" campaign. *American Journal of Public Health*, *91*, 233–238. Retrieved from http://doi.org/10.2105/AJPH.91.2.233.

TUBMAN, HARRIET (1822–1913)

The enslavement of African people is one of the darkest moments of American history. Deprived of the basic human rights of health, liberty, and the pursuit of happiness, millions of people lived in squalid confinement. At risk for violence, injuries, malnutrition, and infection, slaves had an average life expectancy of 21 or 22 years. Harriet Tubman was a fugitive slave who is best known for helping slaves escape to freedom on the Underground Railroad. Historians estimate that Tubman rescued approximately 70 people making 13 trips across the Mason-Dixon Line. She was also one of 20,000 women who worked as nurses, cooks, laundry workers, and cleaners, caring for soldiers during the Civil War (1861–1865). After the war, she continued to work actively for the rights of African Americans, women, the elderly, and the disabled. She opened a nursing home for the elderly and ill in New York. Hailed as "the Moses of her people" because of her courageous leadership on the Underground Railroad, Tubman was a living symbol of human rights activism in the formation of the United States.

Tubman was born as Araminta "Minty" Ross in 1822, one of eight children of Harriet "Rit" (Green) and Ben Ross. Her parents were enslaved on the Anthony Thompson plantation in Dorchester County, Maryland, and Tubman was born into slavery. She began working as a field hand when she was seven years old. She received no schooling and never learned to read or write. Despite the subordination of slavery, Tubman grew up strong-willed and independent. When she was 13, an abusive overseer threw a two-pound dry goods weight at another young slave. Tubman jumped to protect the lad and the weight struck her in the head causing permanent neurological damage. Throughout her life, she suffered seizures, headaches, sleeping spells, and visions. In 1844, she married John Tubman, a free African American, and changed her name to Harriet Tubman.

Five years later, when the plantation where she lived was sold, Tubman escaped to the North. Her husband did not accompany her, so Tubman traveled by herself on the Underground Railroad. She eventually returned for John Tubman, but he had remarried. Not long after her safe arrival in Philadelphia, Tubman began making trips to the Eastern Shore to help free other slaves. In December 1850, she brought out her sister and two children from Maryland, and later she helped her brother and two other slaves. Tubman's most daring exploit occurred in 1857, when she hired a wagon and brought from Maryland her elderly parents. Armed with a small pistol, Tubman brought out not only her family, but other slaves as well. By her own accounts, Tubman rescued approximately 70 African Americans. The number was later inflated by biographer Sara Bradford.

Deeply religious, Tubman thought all her actions were guided by God. Tubman sang two songs during her rescue operations, "Go Down Moses" and "Bound for the Promised Land." She changed the tempo of the song to signal to those in hiding whether it was safe to come out. Fellow abolitionists extolled her virtues, and in the late 1850s, she began speaking at abolitionist meetings. In 1858, Tubman met radical abolitionist John Brown in St. Catherines, Ontario, where she and her parents were then residing. She became a coconspirator in planning his raid on Harpers Ferry, Virginia, in 1859. She had initially planned to participate in the raid herself but was compelled by illness to miss the opportunity; the raid resulted in Brown's capture and death.

During the first year of the Civil War, Tubman continued her rescue work across enemy lines into the South. In early 1862, she joined the Union forces at Beaufort, South Carolina, serving as a scout and spy. She also worked as a nurse and helped slaves who sought refuge with the Union Army. In 1863, Tubman led an army expedition to free over 700 slaves.

After the war, Tubman returned to Auburn, New York, where she had resettled her parents on a farm in the late 1850s. In 1869, she married Nelson Davis, a disabled veteran. She also cared for a number of African American orphans and elderly former slaves. Part of the money that enabled her to do this came from royalties turned over to her from Sarah Bradford, who wrote two biographies: *Scenes in the Life of Harriet Tubman* (1869) and *Harriet, the Moses of Her People* (1886). Although Tubman repeatedly applied to the federal government for compensation for her wartime services, the only money she received was a small pension as the widow of Nelson Davis, who had died in 1888.

In the last years of her life, Tubman raised money for freedmen's schools and helped spur the growth of the African Methodist Episcopal Church in upstate New York. In 1903, she donated 25 acres of land to the church for the establishment of a shelter for poor and homeless African Americans. Tubman died of pneumonia on March 10, 1913. The importance of Tubman's work as an abolitionist was acknowledged in 2013, when President Barack Obama designated a portion of Maryland's Eastern Shore as the Harriet Tubman Underground Railroad National Monument, the first national monument to honor an African American woman. On April 20, 2016, Secretary of the Treasury Jack Lew announced a plan to recognize Tubman by putting her image on the front of the $20 bill, making her the first African American to appear on the front of U.S. paper currency.

Tubman's life demonstrates the struggles and successes of African Americans in securing basic human rights and the most basic level of health.

William McGuire, Leslie Wheeler, and Sally Kuykendall

See also: Bousfield, Midian Othello; Bowditch, Henry Ingersoll; Health Disparities; Kelley, Florence; Smith, James McCune

Further Reading

Bradford, S. H. (2012). *Harriet, the Moses of her people.* Chapel Hill: University of North Carolina Press.

Daniel, S. I. (1932). *Women builders.* Washington, DC: Associated Publishers.

Harriet Tubman Underground Railroad Byway. (2017). *About Harriet Tubman.* Retrieved from http://harriettubmanbyway.org.

Heidish, M. (1976). *A woman called Moses: A novel based on the life of Harriet Tubman.* Ipswich, MA: Houghton.

Quarles, B. (1969). *Black abolitionists.* New York: Oxford University Press.

Schultz, J. E. (2004). *Women at the front: Hospital workers in Civil War America.* Chapel Hill: University of North Carolina Press.

TUSKEGEE SYPHILIS STUDY

The Tuskegee Syphilis Study was a 40-year observational study of the health consequences of untreated syphilis among black men. The U.S. Public Health Service (USPHS) initiated the study in 1932. Six hundred men participated, 399 with syphilis and 201 without the sexually transmitted disease. After the discovery of penicillin, local doctors were instructed not to treat study participants with the antibiotic. Thus, there was a concerted effort to obstruct treatment. The study not only threatened the men's health, but it also exposed sexual partners and unborn children to the deadly pathogen. The study stopped after media reports raised public outcry. The Tuskegee Syphilis Study is of historical significance for several reasons. The study stands as the longest unethical study in the history of the United States. It brought disgrace to public health, medicine, and research. Many African Americans hold a deep distrust of these systems today because of what happened to these vulnerable families at the hands of people who were obligated to provide care. The case is also a reminder of how professional arrogance and social values can adversely affect science and medicine. Scientists must maintain constant vigilance in the protection of human research participants.

To understand the Tuskegee Syphilis Study, one must understand the fascinating and deadly disease of syphilis and the history of racism in medicine. The bacterium *Treponema pallidum* is spread through sexual contact. Without treatment, disease symptoms progress through four unique stages. In the primary stage, painless sores develop at the sight of entry to the body. The sores may go undetected and will disappear in three to six weeks regardless of treatment. During the secondary stage, the victim has signs of infection—fever, sore throat, muscle aches, fatigue, and rashes. Some rashes appear on the mucous membranes—mouth, vagina, or anus. The classic syphilitic rash is red or reddish brown spots on the palms of the hand or the soles of the feet. Again, the rash will go away regardless of treatment. At this point, the infection is internalized. The person shows no outward signs or symptoms. The latent stage can last for 10–30 years. During the tertiary stage, the disease attacks the brain, nervous system, and eyes. The victim suffers from difficulty with muscle movements, paralysis, dementia, or blindness. Syphilis can be transmitted from mother to unborn baby, causing low birth weight, premature birth, or stillbirth. The origin of syphilis is unknown. The disease was first recorded in Europe in 1494, believed to be carried from the new world by Columbus's sailors. Syphilitic symptoms quickly became associated with prostitution and immorality. Curious doctors performed many early experiments in *syphilization* and cures. Mercury emerged as one early treatment. However, mercury had nasty side effects causing neurological damage and death. From 1891 to 1910, Caesar Boeck, professor of dermatology at the University of Oslo, studied 2,000 cases of untreated syphilis. Boeck believed that mercury interfered with the body's natural healing, and he forbid treatment of his hospital patients. When Salvarsan was created in 1910, Boeck's patients were offered treatment even though Salvarsan contained arsenic and also had harmful side effects. In 1925, E. Bruusgaard followed up with patients from the earlier study. The Boeck-Bruusgaard Oslo Study of Untreated Syphilis became a classic study on the natural course of untreated syphilis. The investigators concluded that *all* cases of syphilis, no matter what stage, should be treated. Although the Oslo Study provided detailed information on the clinical course of syphilis, the study participants were all white. European American anthropologists, biologists, doctors, and scientists believed that African Americans were primitive people who were uneducable, oversexed, and subordinate. Physical, mental, and moral differences were due to evolution, not socioeconomic conditions. Black people were considered naturally inferior and inherently at greater risk of death and disease.

In 1929, the Julius Rosenwald Fund provided the U.S. Public Health Service (USPHS) with a grant to identify the prevalence of syphilis and potential for treatment of black people in the rural South. Prevalence data were collected from six counties. Treatment was never given due to the financial collapse of the economic depression. In 1932, Dr. Taliaferro Clark, chief of the USPHS Venereal Disease Division and author of the Rosenwald report, determined that Macon County, Alabama, could provide a "study in nature." With a large, stable black population and syphilis rates of 39.8 percent, Macon County was as an ideal location for longitudinal research (Olansky, Simpson, & Schuman, 1954). Many former plantation slaves settled in the area, working small tracts of degraded agricultural land. The community was geographically, economically, socially, and culturally isolated. Few people moved out of the area. Medical services were limited to one black and nine white physicians, the John A. Andrew Memorial Hospital on the campus of the prestigious Tuskegee Institute, the Veterans Administration Hospital, and the Macon County Health Department. Even these services were limited. The physicians were located in wealthier areas of the county, difficult to access from the poorer regions. Costs at Andrew Memorial Hospital were prohibitive for low income patients. The VA hospital only treated veterans. It was generally concluded that black residents of Macon County with syphilis did not have access to effective, affordable treatment. Surgeon General H. S. Cummings contacted the director of the Tuskegee Institute requesting cooperation with "an unparalleled opportunity" for scientific research that could not "be duplicated anywhere else in the world."

The USPHS partnered with physicians at the Tuskegee Institute, providing funds, resources, and training internships. Six hundred men were enrolled in the USPHS

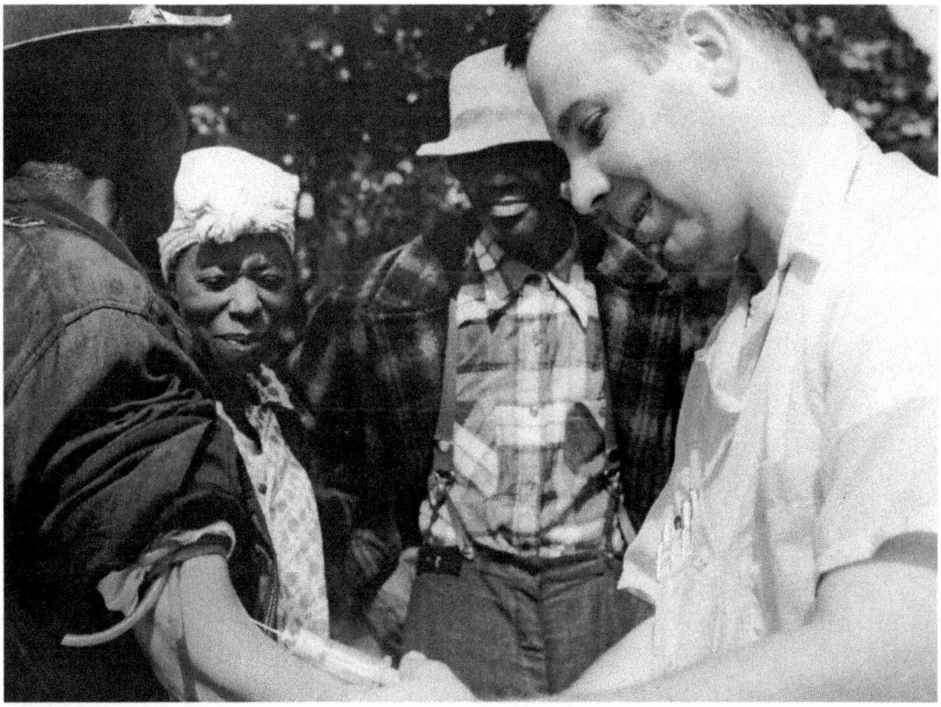

Dr. Walter Edmondson draws blood from an unidentified man enrolled in the Tuskegee Syphilis Study. U.S. Public Health Service doctors exploited black residents of Macon County, Alabama, in a study of syphilis. Study participants were purposefully blocked from getting treatment when penicillin became available. (National Archives)

study. Over 80 percent of the study participants were married. Infected participants had a median age of 60, and uninfected participants had a median age of 61. The researchers hired black staff so that participants would feel more comfortable and less likely to question or resist. A predominant figure was nurse Eunice Rivers. Rivers was a product of her time period. A black woman from the South, Rivers did not question the white doctors. She developed close relationships with the men, ensuring that the men continued in the study despite demands on time and painful procedures. The men were enticed with free medical exams, treatment for disorders not related to syphilis, free meals, certificates of participation, and the promise of burial payment. The men were never given informed consent. They were told that they had "bad blood." The first study report was published in 1936. Interim reports were issued every four to six years. By 1953, Rivers appeared as the principal coauthor on the report, suggesting her growing importance as a member of the study team.

The study was intended to last six months. As funding was renewed, the study continued. By 1947, penicillin became the drug of choice for syphilis. The men were not offered treatment. Their names were sent to local doctors who were asked to refer the patient back to the Tuskegee Institute for care. In 1968, the USPHS social worker and epidemiologist Peter Buxton learned of the study and filed an official protest with the Division of Venereal Diseases. His concerns were dismissed as irrelevant. The following year, the CDC reviewed the study and concluded that it should continue. In 1972, Buxton leaked the story to the *Washington Post*. The next day, it was front page news. Senator Edward Kennedy called for congressional investigation and the study was terminated. By the end of the study, 74 participants were still alive. Over 100 had died from advanced syphilis. The U.S. government settled a class action lawsuit out of court for $10 million and medical care for the surviving men and their wives, widows, and offspring. On May 16, 1997, President Clinton officially apologized to the surviving men and their families on behalf of the nation. The USPHS has taken full responsibility for the civil rights violations.

Reviews of the Tuskegee Syphilis Study determined that the study was unethical. The Oslo study already provided a detailed account of the clinical progression of syphilis. The idea that people with dark skin experience different symptoms or progression was not based in science. The men were never told the purpose of the study or that they had syphilis. Coming from an impoverished minority group, the men were a vulnerable population, easily enticed by minor inducements. The lack of treatment after penicillin was available was maleficent. The risks of study participation did not outweigh the benefits. The Tuskegee Study forced public health and medical scientists to develop a set of guidelines for human participants in research. In 2014, the descendants of the research participants organized to form the *Voices of Our Fathers Legacy Foundation*. The purpose of the foundation is to remember the men who participated in the study, to preserve the history, and to educate others on the human rights violations resulting from the Tuskegee Syphilis Study.

Sally Kuykendall

See also: Belmont Report, The; Centers for Disease Control and Prevention; Ethics in Public Health and Population Health; Hinton, William Augustus; Public Health in the United States, History of; Research; Surgeon General; U.S. Public Health Service

Further Reading

Associated Press (Producer). (1997). USA: President Clinton apologises for syphilis experiment [Streaming video]. Retrieved from Associated Press Video Collection database.

Brandt, A. M. (1978). Racism and research: The case of the Tuskegee Syphilis Study. *The Hastings Center report.* Retrieved from http://nrs.harvard.edu/urn-3:HUL.InstRepos:3372911.

Centers for Disease Control and Prevention. (2016). *U.S. Public Health Service Syphilis Study at Tuskegee.* Retrieved from https://www.cdc.gov/tuskegee/timeline.htm.

Centers for Disease Control and Prevention. (2017). *Syphilis: CDC fact sheet.* Retrieved from https://www.cdc.gov/std/syphilis/stdfact-syphilis.htm.

Final report of the Tuskegee Syphilis Study Ad Hoc Advisory Panel [Microform]. (1973). Washington, DC: U.S. Department of Health, Education, and Welfare, Public Health Service.

Jones, J. H. (1981). *Bad blood: The Tuskegee syphilis experiment.* New York: Free Press; London: Collier Macmillan.

A Matter of Morality. (1972). *Time, 100*(6), 56.

Michigan State University. (n.d.). *Faces of Tuskegee.* Retrieved from https://msu.edu/course/hm/546/tuskegee.htm.

National Center for Bioethics in Research and Health Care. (2017). *Voices of Our Fathers Legacy Foundation.* Retrieved from http://tuskegeebioethics.org/about/voices-for-our-fathers-legacy-foundation.

Olansky, S., Simpson, L., & Schuman, S.H. (1954). Environmental factors in the Tuskegee Study of untreated syphilis: Untreated syphilis in the male Negro. *Public Health Reports (1896–1970), 69*(7), 691. doi:10.2307/4588864

Reverby, S. (2009). *Examining Tuskegee: The infamous syphilis study and its legacy.* Chapel Hill: The University of North Carolina Press.

U

UPSTREAM PUBLIC HEALTH PRACTICES

Upstream public health practices are programs or efforts designed to stop a problem before it starts. Public health offers the story of a fisherman who sees a person drowning in the river. He pulls the person out and resuscitates him. Soon, another person is carried by in the rapids, struggling and gasping for air. The fisherman rescues the second victim. The process continues until the water is filled with drowning people. Villagers arrive to help the drowning victims. Exasperated, one rescuer walks away and the remaining rescuers shout, "Where are you going? We have to help these people!" The frustrated rescuer replies, "I'm going upstream to stop people from falling in the river." While some villagers stay to retrieve victims from the river, others walk upstream, identify the area where people are falling in the water, build a fence, and post warning signs.

The parable demonstrates important principles in public health practice. Stopping a problem before it starts saves valuable resources and lives. Efforts must occur simultaneously upstream and downstream, and neither effort is more important than the other. Success requires multiple people, pooling resources, and working together to address the identified problem.

Paton (1987) credits Dr. Alan Clark, dean and professor of surgery at the University of Otago in Dunedin, New Zealand, with introducing the term *upstream medicine*. Throughout most of his medical career, Dr. Clark found himself performing surgery on tumors that were not diagnosed until late. His training, skill, and efforts were palliative rather than curative. Rather than performing surgery on end-stage cancer, Dr. Clark advocated for screening. He agreed that screening for breast, cervical, and intestinal cancers could be expensive and inconvenient and required personal responsibility. However, he felt prevention was more beneficial and effective. Although many of the screening services have been assumed by technicians, doctors and clinical practitioners use the principle of upstream practices in anticipatory care. Anticipatory care *anticipates* potential health problems and engages the patient as partner in care. An example of anticipatory care is the pediatrician who examines and identifies the physical and emotional development of an infant and counsels the young parent on upcoming developmental milestones. If the health care professional notices that the infant is sitting up and preparing to crawl, she might discuss potential hazards in the home and ways to provide a safe environment for the curious, young explorer. Both upstream and anticipatory care are proactive, foreseeing problems before they occur. Anticipatory care focuses on the patient-provider relationship, envisioning health care as a long-term relationship.

Every effort, every practice, and every program in public health is intended to prevent exposures, experiences, behaviors, and contacts that may result in physical, emotional, mental, social, or spiritual harm. The idea has widespread application to pressing health problems, such as smoking, obesity, opioid abuse, and youth violence. Public health uses the principles of upstream medicine to examine causes and risk factors, effective ways to stop the problem, and methods to prevent future cases.

Sally Kuykendall

See also: Medicine; Precaution Adoption Process Model; Prevention; Risk-Benefit Analysis; Social Determinants of Health; *Controversies in Public Health:* Controversy 4

Further Reading

Bower, E. M. (1978). Pathways upstream: Risks and realities of early screening efforts. *American Journal of Orthopsychiatry*, *48*(1), 131–139. doi:10.1111/j.1939-0025.1978.tb01294.x

Compton, W. M., Boyle, M., & Wargo, E. (2015). Prescription opioid abuse: Problems and responses. *Preventive Medicine: An International Journal Devoted to Practice and Theory*, *80*, 5–9. doi:10.1016/j.ypmed.2015.04.003

Paton, A. (1987). Upstream medicine. *Postgraduate Medical Journal*, *63*(744), 915–916.

U.S. DEPARTMENT OF AGRICULTURE (USDA)

The United States Department of Agriculture (USDA) is a group of 29 federal agencies and offices that provide "leadership on food, agriculture, natural resources, rural development, nutrition, and related issues based on public policy, the best available science, and effective management" (USDA, 2017). The USDA protects and promotes the health of farmworkers, the public, and the environment through food safety, nutrition education, food policies, land management, rural development, research, and education. USDA agencies and offices directly related to public health are the Animal and Plant Health Inspection Service, Center for Nutrition Policy and Promotion, Farm Service Agency (FSA), Food and Nutrition Services, Food Safety and Inspection Service (FSIS), Forest Service (FS), National Agricultural Library (NAL), National Institute of Food and Agriculture (NIFA), Natural Resources Conservation Services (NRCS), Rural Development (RD), Office of Advocacy and Outreach (OAO), Office of the Assistant Secretary for Civil Rights (OASCR), faith-based and neighborhood partnerships (FBNP), and Office of Tribal Relationships (OTR). The roles and responsibilities of each agency are described on the USDA website. The USDA communicates with stakeholders through multiple venues, such as news releases, reports, radio, television, blogs, and live feeds.

In 1906, Upton Sinclair published *The Jungle,* a novel describing the life of a poor Lithuanian immigrant in Chicago. Although the book was intended to expose the harsh and exploitive living and working conditions of recent immigrants, readers were horrified by the descriptions of rats, unsanitary conditions, and health violations in the nation's meatpacking industry. Sinclair later pointed out, "I aimed for the public's heart, and by accident I hit it in the stomach." The book raised public outcry forcing Congress and President Theodore Roosevelt to create the Federal Meat Inspection Act of 1906.

Foodborne illnesses are a serious threat to public health. Approximately 48 million people suffer from foodborne illness each year, resulting in 128,000 hospitalizations and 3,000 deaths (CDC, 2016). Estimated cost of foodborne illnesses is as high as $152 billion per year (Scharff, 2012). The Food Safety and Inspection Service (FSIS) is responsible for ensuring the safety and accurate labeling of meat, poultry, and processed eggs (USDA, 2013). FSIS staff inspects food for bacterial contamination, allergens, mislabeled products, illegal chemical residues, and foreign materials; provides public education and outreach; builds partnerships between public and private sectors to promote food safety; studies foodborne illnesses in order to identify emerging risks; and develops policies to protect the public from foodborne illnesses. The FSIS also ensures that animals are handled humanely at slaughter. Within FSIS is the Office of Public Health Service, an interdisciplinary scientific team of microbiologists, chemists, toxicologists, epidemiologists, and public health professionals who work to identify, manage, and prevent foodborne pathogens and chemical contamination in meat, poultry, and egg products. The Animal and Plant Health Inspection Service (APHIS) ensures the health and care of animals and plants. APHIS's Plant Protection and Quarantine (PPQ) program protects the nation's plants and animals by safeguarding against the entry and spread of nonnative pests.

One in seven U.S. households suffers from food insecurity, not having enough food to nourish all members of the household, or not knowing when safe food can be secured for the next meal (Coleman-Jensen, Rabbitt, Gregory, & Singh, 2016). Food insecurity increases risk for obesity and obesity-related diseases. When people are unsure of how and when they will be able to attain food again, they compensate by overeating or eating unhealthy foods. Food insecurity is particularly harmful to infants and children who need regular nutrition for healthy physical, social, and emotional development. The Food, Nutrition, and Consumer Services (FNS) agency provides children and families in need with access to nutritious foods. FNS programs include Women, Infant and Children (WIC) Program, Supplemental Nutrition Assistance Program, school meals, food distribution programs, disaster assistance, child and adult care food program, summer food service program, farmers' markets nutrition programs, and nutrition education. It is not enough to simply feed people; these programs ensure that families in need are attaining healthy foods that promote health and wellness and prevent disease.

The USDA indirectly combats food insecurity through loans promoting quality of life in rural communities. The agency offers low interest loans for small businesses, home purchases, and rural development. For example, in 2008, the USDA Rural Development partnered with the city of Manistique, Michigan, to upgrade the city's drinking water, sewage, and storm water management systems. In 2012, the USDA

Rural Development invested $28.75 million with Box Butte General Hospital in Alliance, Nebraska. The hospital is using the funds to update services. Local residents no longer need to travel for hours to attain quality health care. Grants and loans are also used to purchase homes, build business spaces for new entrepreneurs, and develop community restaurants. Loans are not limited to rural areas. The USDA also supports microloans for urban farmers and programs, such as Square Roots in New York City, which creates vertical farms using shipping containers.

For 150 years, the U.S. Department of Agriculture has been responsible for ensuring a safe and nutritious food supply for people in the nation and for people importing food products from the United States into other countries. The agency does this through many different mechanisms, such as nutrition education, food safety inspection and monitoring, addressing food insecurity, and investing in human resources by providing loans for home buyers and small businesses in rural communities.

Sally Kuykendall

See also: Agricultural Safety; Environmental Protection Agency; Food and Drug Administration; Food Insecurity; Food Safety; Nutrition; Rural Health; U.S. Department of Health and Human Services

Further Reading

Centers for Disease Control and Prevention. (2016). Foodborne germs and illnesses. Retrieved from https://www.cdc.gov/foodsafety/foodborne-germs.html.

Coleman-Jensen, A., Rabbitt, M., Gregory, C., & Singh, A. (2016). Household food security in the United States in 2015. Economic Research Report No. ERR-215. Retrieved from https://www.ers.usda.gov/publications/pub-details/?pubid=79760.

Scharff, R. (2012). Economic burden from health losses due to foodborne illness in the United States. *Journal of Food Protection*, *75*(1), 123–131.

U.S. Department of Agriculture (USDA). (2013). *One team, one purpose. Food Safety Inspection Service: Protecting public health and preventing foodborne illness.* Retrieved from https://www.fsis.usda.gov/wps/wcm/connect/7a35776b-4717-43b5-b0ce-aeec64489fbd/mission-book.pdf?MOD=AJPERES.

U.S. Department of Agriculture (USDA). (2017). Retrieved from https://www.usda.gov/wps/portal/usda/usdahome.

U.S. DEPARTMENT OF HEALTH AND HUMAN SERVICES (HHS)

The U.S. Department of Health and Human Services (HHS) is the federal agency responsible for managing medical, public health, and social services. The mission of HHS is help Americans achieve healthy and productive lives. The strategic plan to achieve this mission is to strengthen health care; advance scientific knowledge and innovation; advance health, safety, and well-being of Americans; and ensure agency efficiency, transparency, accountability, and effectiveness. Given the wide scope of HHS, the current priorities are to achieve affordable health care, ensure safe food and medical products, provide job assistance, promote access to affordable quality child care, support biomedical research, and address obligations to disadvantaged communities, including tribal communities. Public health falls within the purview of many of HHS agencies.

HHS operations are carried out by 11 divisions, 8 agencies within the U.S. Public Health Service (USPHS) and 3 human service agencies. The operating divisions are Administration for Children and Families (ACF), Administration for Community Living (ACL), Agency for Healthcare Research and Quality (AHRQ), Agency for Toxic Substances and Disease Registry (ATSDR), Centers for Disease Control and Prevention (CDC), Centers for Medicare and Medicaid Services (CMS), Food and Drug Administration (FDA), Health Resources and Services Administration (HRSA), Indian Health Service (IHS), National Institutes of Health (NIH), and Substance Abuse and Mental Health Services Administration (SAMHSA). Much of the day-to-day work is done at the state and local levels or through partnerships with private and nongovernment organizations. Although the divisions may appear to represent separate and distinct responsibilities, in practice, functions are often interdependent. The divisions work with each other to address emerging and reemerging health issues.

A limitation of the agency is that individual and community health are influenced by many economic, demographic, social, and environmental factors outside the scope of the operating divisions. Health issues, such as climate change, community water fluoridation, gun violence, healthy housing, prescription drug overdoses, reproductive and sexual health, and tobacco are influenced by businesses, politics, and personal beliefs. HHS must balance keeping children, adults, families, and communities safe and healthy within the current system of politics and power. Throughout history, ensuring and promoting the health of the nation has come in conflict with politics and economy. Such controversies continue today with gun violence, reproductive health, health disparities, and climate change.

HHS is a complex government agency that oversees and administers programs supporting the health of Americans. Most of the HHS operating divisions address some aspect of public health, whether it is physical, mental, environmental, social, or medical. Challenges emerge when political rights and beliefs conflict with the mission of the agency.

Sally Kuykendall

See also: Affordable Care Act; Centers for Disease Control and Prevention; Centers for Medicare and Medicaid Services; Food and Drug Administration; Indian Health Service; Medicaid; Medicare; National Cancer Institute; National Heart, Lung, and Blood Institute; National Institute on Drug Abuse; National Institutes of Health; Substance Abuse and Mental Health Services Administration; Surgeon General; U.S. Department of Agriculture; U.S. Public Health Service; *Controversies in Public Health:* Controversy 2

Further Reading

U.S. Department of Health and Human Services. (2017). *About HHS*. Retrieved from https://www.hhs.gov/about/index.html.

U.S. PUBLIC HEALTH SERVICE (PHS)

The Commissioned Corps of the United States Public Health Service (PHS) is one of the seven uniformed services under the direction of the executive branch of the federal government. Commissioned by presidential appointment, physicians, dentists, nurses, therapists, pharmacists, environmental health specialists, dietitians, health administrators, veterinarians, scientists, and other public health professionals work to promote health, prevent disease, and advance public health science throughout the nation. Corps members work in biomedical research, novel drug development and approval, safe use of medical devices, design of healthy buildings, and counterterrorism. They also provide needed medical care to underserved, disadvantaged communities. The surgeon general directs the PHS. Corps members wear military uniforms, are assigned to active duty stations, and may be deployed in national and international emergencies. Core values are leadership, service, integrity, and excellence. Commissioned Corps members engage in nonmilitary service. Active duty positions include jobs within the Centers for Disease Control and Prevention, the Food and Drug Administration, Indian Health Service, National Institutes of Health, or other operating divisions of the Department of Health and Human Services (DHHS). Although the Commissioned Corps carries the responsibility to protect and defend the nation's health, this responsibility, many times, has been undermined by politics. Former surgeon general Dr. Richard Carmona (2017) warns that undermining the credibility of the Office of the Surgeon General erodes PHS morale, making it difficult to recruit and retain talented professionals. Given that Commissioned Corps members are highly trained public health professionals who could easily work in more lucrative industry positions, supporting PHS personnel at all ranks is an important step in protecting the health of the nation.

In 1798, President John Adams signed the *Act for the Relief of Sick and Disabled Seamen*. The act authorized port authorities to collect money for the medical care of merchant seamen at local hospitals. The intent was to subsidize local hospitals when ships abandoned sick sailors in port and to halt the transmission of communicable diseases along shipping routes. Each sailor paid the ship's accounting officer twenty cents per month. The funds were given to the port official when the ship docked. Failure to pay resulted in a one hundred dollar fine, and the ship was banned from renewing its shipping license. The nation's first system of national health insurance was highly successful. The fund enabled new hospitals to be built in Boston; Newport, Rhode Island; New Orleans; Charleston; and Washington Point, Virginia. As the system expanded, the need for oversight and coordination of services increased. In 1870, the Marine Hospital Service (MHS) was created, and Dr. John M. Woodworth was appointed as the first supervising surgeon. Woodworth created a workforce that reflected his experiences in the Union Army. Applicants were required to undergo rigorous physical examination. Personnel wore uniforms and could be deployed as needed. When Congress passed the National Quarantine Act in 1878, the PHS gained the responsibility of inspecting and clearing ships as they arrived in port. The PHS Commission Corps was officially created in 1889, and responsibilities expanded to include examining new immigrants, investigating infectious diseases, and regulating local sanitation.

Currently 6,800 USPHS Commissioned Corps members serve in underserved, hard to recruit areas, such as the prison system, Indian Health Services, disaster areas, and military bases. Without these committed professionals, many disadvantaged populations would lack health care services. In 2014–2015, when the deadly Ebola epidemic struck West Africa, PHS personnel were deployed to the area to contain and control the epidemic. With a mortality rate of 51 percent, the virus devastated regional health care workers and disabled local health care systems. The U.S. government mobilized forces. The Army's 101st Airborne Division built Ebola treatment units in West Africa. The U.S. Agency for International Development (USAID) provided logistical support. The Centers for Disease Prevention and Control (CDC) provided training and expertise in infectious diseases. The PHS Commissioned Corps gave direct care. To prepare for treating Ebola-infected health workers in Monrovia, Liberia, PHS doctors, nurses, laboratory staff, and support personnel were specially trained in Ebola, epidemiology, infection control, and current and experimental treatments (Mosquera, Braun, Hulett, & Ryszka, 2015). On October 26, 2014, the first team arrived to staff Monrovia's 25-bed hospital unit. The goal was to treat infected patients and stop transmission. However, typical health care practices encouraging patient-provider interaction had to be set aside for this deadly pathogen. To limit exposure, staff wore heavy personal protective equipment. Patient care was performed by task-specific teams. One team measured vital signs. A second team drew laboratory specimens. A third team provided fluids, nutrition, and hygiene. Over six months, PHS personnel worked 12-hour shifts under hot, stifling conditions. Of the 300 PHS corps members working in Monrovia, none contracted Ebola, the disease was successfully contained, and Liberia was declared Ebola-free in May 2015.

Commissioned Corps members are deployed to many humanitarian crises at home and around the world. PHS members served in New Orleans after Hurricane Katrina (2005), Haiti after the earthquake (2010), Newtown, Connecticut, after the school shooting (2012), Boston after the Marathon bombings (2013), and New Jersey after Hurricane Sandy (2013). Commissioned Corps members risk their lives to work with victims of man-made and natural disasters. In addition to health dangers, PHS efforts are increasingly threatened by political agendas.

In 1968, a new position, the Assistant Secretary of Health, was created to oversee the surgeon general's office. Whereas the Office of the Surgeon General is a service position and forbidden from engaging in political activities, the Assistant Secretary of Health is a political position. This means that the surgeon general has a responsibility to promote public health while the surgeon general's boss has a responsibility to promote the current administration's political agenda. This creates problems. For example, the Reagan administration attempted to pressure Surgeon General Dr. C. Everett Koop into saying that abortion was psychologically harmful to women. There is no evidence to support that abortion is psychologically harmful to women. Former surgeon general Dr. Richard Carmona (2017) notes that politics undermines the integrity, service, and values of the corps and diminishes morale, making it harder to recruit and retain qualified personnel.

The Commissioned Corps of the PHS is responsible for protecting the health and safety of the nation. Members share a greater sense of purpose and camaraderie knowing that they are making a difference and helping underserved communities. Public health professionals say that schools of public health can do much more to prepare and encourage students to commit part of their public health expertise and knowledge to government service (Kolb, 2016). Corps members gain professional training, education, and technical skills that can provide a wonderful springboard to a career in public health.

Sally Kuykendall

See also: Centers for Disease Control and Prevention; Dean, Henry Trendley; National Heart, Lung, and Blood Institute; National Institutes of Health; Quarantine; Roosevelt, Franklin Delano; State, Local, and Territorial Health Departments; Surgeon General; Tuskegee Syphilis Study; U.S. Department of Health and Human Services

Further Reading

Carmona, R. (2017). Instant admirals and the plague of politics in the United States Public Health Service: Back to the future. *Military Medicine*, *182*(5), 1582–1583. doi:10.7205/MILMED-D-17-00039

Commissioned Corps of the U.S. Public Health Service. (2017). Retrieved from https://usphs.gov.

Furman, B. (1973). *A profile of the United States Public Health Service, 1798–1948*. Washington, DC: U.S. Department of Health, Education and Welfare.

Koh, H. K. (2016). Strengthening the U.S. Public Health Service Commissioned Corps: A view from the Assistant Secretary for Health. *Military Medicine*, *181*(1), 12–15. doi:10.7205/MILMED-D-15-00204

Kolb, L. J. (2016). Federal public health service: In retrospect and prospects. *Health Education & Behavior*, *43*(5), 509–517.

Mosquera, A., Braun, M., Hulett, M., & Ryszka, L. (2015). U.S. Public Health Service response to the 2014–2015 Ebola epidemic in West Africa: A nursing perspective. *Public Health Nursing*, *32*(5), 550–554. doi:10.1111/phn.12217

Mullan, F. (1989). *Plagues and politics: The story of the United States Public Health Service*. New York: Basic Books.

Williams, R. C. (1951). *The United States Public Health Service, 1798–1950*. Washington, DC: Commissioned Officers Association of the United States Public Health Service. Retrieved from https://archive.org/details/unitedstatespubl00will.

V

VACCINES

Vaccines are biological agents introduced into a human or animal body with the intention of creating immunity to an infectious agent. Vaccines introduce weakened or dead disease matter that can be easily destroyed and, most importantly, stimulate and aid the body in recognizing and confronting future full-strength instances of the disease. Vaccines can be applied in *preventative* situations to inhibit the development of a disease in an individual or group, or in *therapeutic* situations where vaccines are applied to weaken or ameliorate the conditions of an illness that already exists within the patient. Despite vaccines being originally developed to combat smallpox at the end of the 18th century, vaccines over the last two centuries have proliferated to cure a variety of diseases and conditions. They can also be administered in different ways and in various environments, depending on the particular disease being combatted. The influence of the basic immunological concept behind vaccination on public health policy and globalization ensures that new vaccines will continue to be developed well into the 21st century.

All vaccines stimulate immune system activity and prevent future occurrences of the disease for a period of time. This is achieved by introducing weakened or dead disease matter into the body, whereupon the body recognizes it as foreign and can easily subdue it. This experience allows the immune system to better combat the disease should it enter the body in a strengthened state. Henceforward the person is deemed "immune," meaning his or her body can recognize the protein coating of the pathogen and prevent it from implanting itself into healthy cells. Vaccination (and the immunological concepts that underlie the process) requires an individual and a community commitment. The more people who are vaccinated, the more individuals cease being incubators for particular diseases and fewer people are exposed. This phenomenon is called "herd immunity," and it is a crucial concept in public health, which is the coordination of medical methods and public structures such as hospitals or clinics to improve the health conditions of communities.

There are different types of vaccines available based largely on the biological status of the pathogen used in creating that vaccine. The oldest are heterotypic or "Jennerian" vaccines, which use a related animal disease that only mildly impacts humans. This group includes the smallpox vaccine, the first vaccine. A number of vaccines known as "inactivated" are made from previously virulent material rendered innocuous by heat, chemicals, or radiation. Polio, bubonic plague, influenza, and cholera are vaccinated in this fashion. "Attenuated" vaccines use specially grown versions of the virus whose active, disease-causing attributes are not expressed. This group includes vaccines for measles, mumps, rubella, and typhoid fever. "Subunit" vaccines use fragments of the disease microorganism and are part of vaccinations for hepatitis B. Further experimental vaccines continue to be developed, including ones that make use of DNA material from an infectious agent or the targeting of T-cell receptor peptides, among many elements.

The manner whereby vaccines are introduced into the body has evolved over centuries and has allowed for a variety of methods to be available to medical professionals by the 21st century. Before the widespread introduction of smallpox vaccination at the turn of the 19th century, the West was already familiar with inoculation as a means of disease prevention. Inoculation—later called variolation to differentiate it from vaccination—was an immunological method brought to Europe from Asia during the 18th century that involved the introduction of material from smallpox pustules into the body. This was administered by making a small cut into the skin using a bladed instrument called a lancet and then rubbing the disease material into the wound. A mild case of smallpox would soon develop which, in time, would pass away and leave the patient immune from future instances of the disease. Although helpful in decreasing instances of smallpox, inoculation had great medical and social risks that made its public health application sporadic at best. In using the actual smallpox microorganism, there was a risk the individual might contract the full disease and thus expose himself or herself to disfigurement or even death. It was fears that the medical community was far from introducing a saving method but rather actually exposing people to unnecessary risks that spurred religious and political authorities in Britain and throughout Europe to approach the method with caution and seek out newer, safer methods of disease control.

The development of the smallpox vaccine by the British physician Edward Jenner in 1796 marked the ascendency of vaccination in disease prevention. After observing that milkmaids who contracted cowpox (a nonlethal cousin of smallpox found in cows) were subsequently immune to smallpox, Jenner took material from cowpox pustules on the hand of a milkmaid named Sarah Nelmes and tested his immunological observations on James Phelps, a local boy. Weeks later the boy did not develop smallpox despite being directly exposed to it by Jenner. He named this breakthrough *vaccinia* from the Latin word for cow (*vacca*), which has come to represent both the material (vaccine) and process (vaccination) in many languages. Originally this word applied only to smallpox vaccination; however, by the end of the 19th century the term came to be applied to a succession of immunological advances developed to combat other diseases.

In the 1880s French scientist Louis Pasteur initiated the second generation of vaccines by developing medicines for anthrax and chicken cholera. He advocated the use of "vaccination" to honor these new creations. In 1885 Pasteur also successfully prevented rabies in a patient bitten by a rabid animal in a method called postexposure vaccination. The 20th century witnessed further advances in vaccinations against pressing epidemic diseases. These advances led to treatments for diphtheria, typhoid, whooping cough, and tetanus. The 20th century witnessed a number of landmark vaccines developed in laboratory environments. South African born virologist Max Theiler developed a yellow fever vaccine in 1935 while director of the Rockefeller Institute in New York. In 1955 Jonas Salk developed the first injectable vaccine for poliomyelitis (commonly called polio). Since 1960, vaccines have been developed for measles, mumps, rubella, hepatitis B, and human papillomavirus.

In 1980 the World Health Organization (WHO) declared that increased worldwide access to vaccination and sanitation resulted in the eradication of natural cases of smallpox. Despite great hopes among the medical community for the elimination of other ailments through the development of vaccines, no other human disease has yet been eliminated through vaccination. Vaccines continue to be developed in the hopes of eradicating other diseases, and particular attention has been given to the relationship between vaccines and cells that cause cancer. There remain no vaccines for malaria, herpes simplex, or HIV. The WHO remains confident that polio will be the second human disease to be eradicated, with the disease having disappeared from the Americas in 1994, Europe in 2002, and India in 2014.

The earliest vaccinations were delivered by means of a blade or lancet used to cut or "scarificate" (scrape) the skin and insert the vaccine material into the bloodstream. The first use of a hypodermic needle was by Francis Rynde, an Irish physician, in 1844, and later glass syringes were developed that rapidly replaced the lancet as the primary tool for vaccination even to this day. The development of oral vaccines occurred in the 20th century, including a variety of the polio vaccine in the 1950s. Oral vaccines could be administered by persons with minimal medical training and required less temperature and environment controls than those required to preserve liquid vaccines. Developments in vaccine transmission are allied closely to improvements in creating and distributing vaccines. In the earliest days of vaccination, supply relied on the expertise of individual doctors and the limits of available transportation. Some vaccines were retrieved directly from infected humans and others from animals. By the late 19th century the development of laboratory science streamlined the creation and preservation of vaccine material. The intervention of government oversight of medical materials, such as the 1906 "Wiley Act" that created the Food and Drug Administration in the United States, minimized irresponsible or haphazard medicines. In modern times, vaccines are typically cultivated in laboratory environments from bacteria or virus cultures grown from environments ranging from chicken egg cells to human cells.

The employment of vaccination as a public health tool has remained a matter of contention in the public sphere, particularly after the middle of the 19th century when many governments made certain vaccinations compulsory for entry into schools or occupations. Some dispute the immunological validity of certain vaccines, others contend they pose adverse health effects, and still others claim that not enough clinical study goes into vaccines before they enter the market. Some protest compulsory vaccination on the grounds of religious belief or advocacy of individual liberty. The refusal of part of the population to submit to vaccination could have adverse effects on society as a whole (their "herd immunity"), and public health professionals are dedicated to greater dissemination and education about these issues in the 21st century.

Sean P. Phillips

See also: Cutter Incident, The; Food and Drug Administration; Global Health; Hepatitis; Infectious Diseases; Influenza; Jenner, Edward; Measles; Meningitis; Modern Era, Public Health in the; Pasteur, Louis; Polio; Roosevelt, Franklin Delano; Salk, Jonas; Smallpox; *Controversies in Public Health:* Controversy 3

Further Reading

Bazin, H. (2000). *The eradication of smallpox: Edward Jenner and the first and only eradication of a human infectious disease.* San Diego: Academic Press.
Bliss, M. (2011). *The making of modern medicine.* Chicago: University of Chicago Press.
Largent, M. (2012). *Vaccines: The debate in modern America.* Baltimore: Johns Hopkins University Press.
Oshinsky, D. (2006). *Polio: An American story.* New York: Oxford University Press.

VETERANS' HEALTH

From a public health perspective, there are several reasons why military veterans should be a population of greater interest. First, veterans with a health condition that resulted from their military service are legally entitled to care. The United States has a moral obligation to provide needed medical care to those who have defended its freedom. Additionally, there are more than 20 million veterans (U.S. Census Bureau, 2017). As a demographic group they are similar in size to other populations of public health interest, such as those with smoking-related diseases or vegetarians. Finally, public health endeavors focused on veterans provide insights into the long-term risks and benefits of military service, many components of which are similar to civilian jobs. Such information can inform today's policy makers and health care leaders.

Generally, a veteran is thought of as someone who has fought in a war. The definition is actually much broader: anyone "who served in the active military, naval, or air service, and who was discharged or released therefrom under conditions other than dishonorable" (Pensions, Bonuses, and Veterans' Relief, 38 C.F.R. § 101. 2008, p. 783). So while many people believe all veterans have fought in combat, few actually have. For the purposes of receiving health benefits paid for with federal tax dollars, to be considered a veteran the illness or injury must occur in the line of duty. This means in pursuit of a legitimate, authorized endeavor, such as the person's actual job or training for that job. Health-related consequences of criminal acts or other unauthorized activity are not covered. For example, someone who gets into a motor vehicle crash while under the influence of alcohol likely will not have their medical care paid for by the government.

Many veterans are legally entitled to public health interventions as compensation for service in the military. Upon entry into military service, all veterans take an oath to defend the U.S. Constitution. The implicit agreement is that veterans are willing to risk their life for the sake of their country. In return, Congress—on behalf of the American people—in essence promises vets that if their health is compromised by some aspect of their military service they will get free or affordable health care for the rest of their life. The details of which vets are eligible for what medical care is determined by various legislative acts. For example, the Veterans Health Care Act of 1992 (H.R. 5193) stipulates that psychological counseling is to be provided to all veterans who were sexually assaulted while on active duty.

Actually, Congress has a long history of legislating the medical care of veterans, especially those disabled during wars and conflicts. In 1798 a system of hospitals and domiciliaries was created that served disabled veterans. Eventually known as the Public Health Service, all veterans' medical care was transferred to it in 1919 at the end of World War I. In 1930 Congress established the Veterans Health Administration (VHA), in part, to provide medical care to all eligible veterans. Today the VHA serves nearly 6 million veterans annually through a network of more than 1,000 outpatient clinics and more than 150 hospitals (VHA, 2017).

Based on the most recent census data, there are approximately 18.8 million veterans, of whom 8.5 percent are women, 11.6 percent are African American, and 6.4 percent are Hispanic (U.S. Census Bureau, 2016). Around 20 percent of all veterans have a medical condition that has been officially deemed to be disabling (to some extent), the most common of which are tinnitus/hearing loss, post-traumatic stress disorder (PTSD), back pain, scars, and knee pain (VHA, 2016).

With millions of veterans needing some type of health care, costs are a concern. Congress does not write a blank check to the VHA each year. The total dollars that can be spent on veterans' health is limited. Veterans deemed eligible for VA services are prioritized into several groups. Ideally, the neediest are seen first. In any given year, those lower on the priority list might have to obtain the care they need outside of the VHA system, and pay for it themselves.

Medical care for veterans in the VHA system costs around $65 billion per year, roughly $11,000 per unique patient (VHA, 2016b). As such, any public health efforts to improve veterans' health status or make their care more efficient could likely generate huge savings. For example, studies suggest that it is less expensive in the long run to treat all veterans with any trace of hepatitis C, as opposed to only treating those in advanced stages of the disease. If just 10 percent of all veterans have hepatitis C, the lifetime costs savings for treating all of them would be well over $670 million (Chidi et al., 2016).

Attending to the public health needs of all veterans generates information that is beneficial—not only to the participants themselves—but also to other veterans and civilians who might one day face similar circumstances. However, some in the public health community might argue that investigations of the veteran population are irrelevant to the rest of society. They could say that due to unique exposures

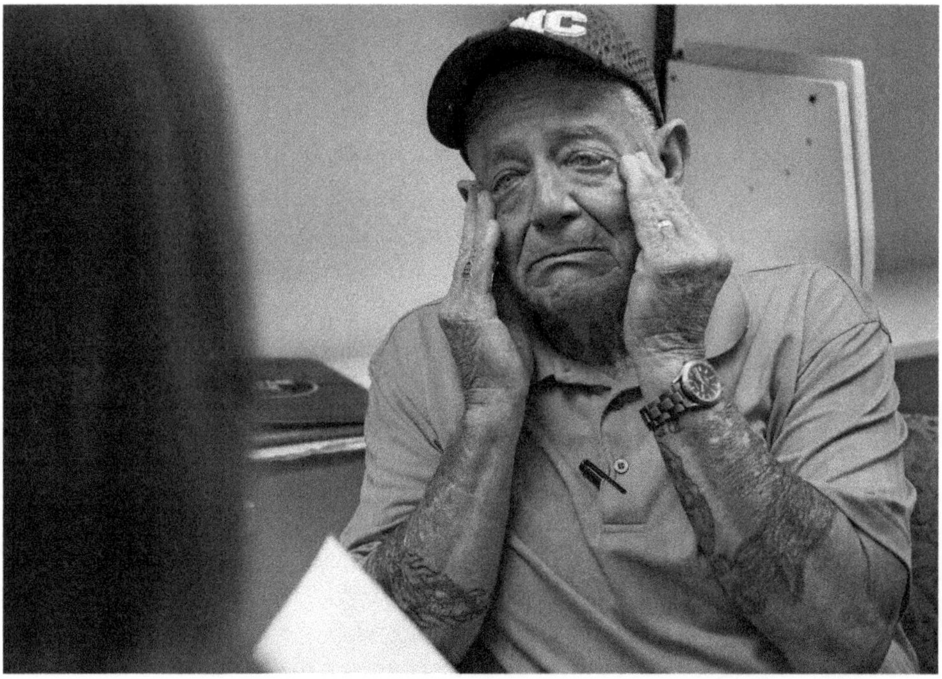

Vietnam veteran Jim Alderman is haunted by the fear, chaos, and odors he experienced as a 19-year-old soldier. Alderman is a patient at Bay Pines Veterans Affairs Medical Center in Bay Pines, Florida, where therapists work with veterans to recognize psychological triggers and to respond with positive coping mechanisms. (E. J. Hersom/Department of Defense)

(combat environments) or various health-related rules and regulations vets had to endure while on active duty, such as having to maintain certain weight standards or mandatory vaccination programs, the findings might not be useful when applied to other populations. It is true that approximately 28 percent of military occupational specialties (i.e., jobs) do not have a civilian equivalent (Sulsky, 2003). These mostly have to do with weapons systems not used by civilians. However, that leaves about three out of every four veterans having been employed in a job with a civilian equivalent. For example, there are military police whose job is very similar to civilian police. And many veterans occupied managerial positions with all of the same stressors and benefits as their civilian counterparts.

One of the most important aspects of public health service that could benefit future generations pertains to the long-term effects of military service. This is true for both health risks and benefits. An example of a health risk is exposure to combat environments. Even though a small minority of veterans has fought in combat, many more have been exposed to combat environments, locations where the threat of attack is possible. This can be very stressful and carries certain health effects such as PTSD. But we don't know how long these effects last. In contrast, a benefit of military service is free and easy access to medical care. What are the long-term effects of this? Perhaps veterans are healthier than their civilian counterparts who did not have health insurance during their early years of employment. These are just some of the questions that could be answered by greater public health interest in the veteran population, something that is owed to them by law, and would likely garner many benefits for a worthy and sizable group many consider heroes.

David J. Reynolds

See also: Bousfield, Midian Othello; Dean, Henry Trendley; Hepatitis; Mental Health; Substance Abuse and Mental Health Services Administration; *Controversies in Public Health:* Controversy 2

Further Reading

Chidi, A. P., Rogal, S., Bryce, C. L., Fine, M. J., Good, C. B., Myaskovsky, L., & . . . Smith, K. J. (2016). Cost-effectiveness of new antiviral regimens for treatment-naïve U.S. veterans with hepatitis C. *Hepatology*, *63*(2), 428–436. doi:10.1002/hep.28327

Gordon, S., & Kizer, K. W. (2017). *The battle for veterans' healthcare: Dispatches from the frontlines of policy making and patient care.* Cornell, NY: Cornell.

Powers, R. (2009). *Veterans benefits for dummies.* Hoboken, NJ: Wiley.

Sulsky, S. I. (2003). On occupational health and safety research in the US Army: Comparability with civilian employee cohorts. *Journal of Occupational and Environmental Medicine*, *45*(3), 220–221.

Title 38—Pensions, bonuses and veterans' relief, 38 C.F.R. § 101. 2008. Washington, DC: U.S. Government Printing Office. Retrieved from https://www.gpo.gov/fdsys/pkg/CFR-2012-title38-vol1/pdf/CFR-2012-title38-vol1-chapI.pdf.

U.S. Census Bureau. (2016). *Facts for features: Veterans' day 2016.* Retrieved from https://www.census.gov/newsroom/facts-for-features/2016/cb16-ff21.html.

U.S. Census Bureau. (2017). *2011–2015 American community survey 5-year profiles.* Retrieved from https://www.census.gov/programs-surveys/acs.

U.S. Department of Veterans Affairs. (2014). *Federal benefits for veterans, dependents, and survivors* (Updated ed.). New York: Skyhorse.

Veterans Healthcare Administration. (2016a). *VBA annual benefits report fiscal year 2015.* Retrieved from http://www.benefits.va.gov/REPORTS/abr.

Veterans Healthcare Administration. (2016b). *Expenditures: 2015.* Retrieved from https://www.va.gov/vetdata/expenditures.asp.

Veterans Healthcare Administration. (2017). *About VHA.* Retrieved from https://www.va.gov/health/aboutvha.asp.

VIOLENCE

Violence presents in many forms with serious public health implications. Homicide cuts short 17,000 deaths per year while suicide claims another 44,000 (Centers for Disease Control and Prevention [CDC], 2017). Over half a million people seek treatment in emergency rooms for injuries due to child maltreatment, elder abuse, intimate partner violence (IPV), youth violence, sexual violence, or suicide attempts. Many more injuries are treated in doctor's offices, emergent care centers, or at home. The estimated cost in medical care and lost productivity for violence-related injuries totaled $70 billion in 2000 (Corso, Mercy, Simon, Finkelstein, & Miller, 2007). Public health aims to reduce and prevent violence through universal, selected, and indicated prevention. Applicable *Healthy People 2020* goals are to reduce homicides from 6.1 per 100,000 people to 5.5 per 100,000 people and to reduce suicides from 11.3 suicides per 100,000 people to 10.2 per 100,000 people. The National Center for Injury Prevention and Control (NCIPC) serves as the nation's leading authority on violence prevention research. The NCIPC monitors the problem, conducts research, and recommends the most effective solutions in violence prevention.

As deaths due to infectious diseases declined, public health officials turned attention to other leading causes of death and disability. Violence was formally acknowledged as a major public health problem in *Healthy People* (1979). This first edition set the goals of reducing suicides, homicides, access to handguns, and child maltreatment. In 1981, CDC staff became formally involved in violence prevention when they assisted Atlanta police investigating the abduction and murder of 28 children and young adults. The CDC used epidemiological tools in the case known as the Atlanta Child Murders (1979–1981). Two years later, the CDC established the Violence Epidemiology Branch to investigate violence-related behaviors and the prevention of violence. Epidemiological data revealed that young black men were dying at significantly higher rates than women and whites. Surgeon General C. Everett Koop (1916–2013; in office 1982–1989) encouraged politicians to invest in youth violence research, which would identify causes, risk and protective factors, and solutions. Guns emerged as one of the leading causes of homicide and suicide in the United States. The National Rifle Association responded by persuading Congress to ban any further CDC-funded research into gun violence. The research ban lasted 17 years and was finally lifted after the Sandy Hook Elementary School shooting in Newtown, Connecticut (2012).

Between 1983 and 1993, politicians realized that they could garner votes by promising to take a hard line on crime. Voters were programmed to fear a new breed of superpredator, represented as a young African American or Latino American male. The costs for housing chronic offenders skyrocketed with estimates totaling $1.7 to $2.3 million per offender in 1997 U.S. dollars (Cohen, 1998). Public health used the tools of epidemiology to investigate the problem and find effective, affordable solutions. In 2001, the Department of Health and Human Services (DHHS) issued *Youth Violence: Report of the Surgeon General*. This comprehensive report described the scope of the problem, presented reliable data, identified risk and protective factors, and reviewed research into existing youth violence prevention programs. Out of hundreds of programs, experts only found a small number of effective programs. Notable programs were home visitation by nurses, multisystemic therapy, Families and Schools Acting Together (FAST), Promoting Alternative Thinking Strategies (PATHS), and Life Skills Training. Even more worrisome was the fact that many of the most popular programs, boot camps, peer mediation, gun buyback programs, and waivers to adult court were found ineffective and, in some cases, exacerbated violence-related behaviors. The surgeon general's report recommended identifying and using evidence-based programs that were proven to work.

Public health addresses a problem by reducing known risk factors. Risk factors for violence-related behavior are categorized as individual level, family level, and community level (DHHS, 2001). Individual-level risk factors are low IQ, antisocial beliefs, exposure to violence, involvement with drugs, alcohol, or tobacco, attention deficit, hyperactivity, and impaired ability to process information. Risk factors at the family level are harsh, negligent, or overbearing parenting practices, poor emotional attachments between parent and child, low income and educational level, dysfunctional communication, and parental substance abuse or criminality. Peer and social factors that promote violence are association with antisocial peers and poor connections to the school. Community-level risk factors are lack of jobs, limited resources, crowded living conditions, lack of community structure, and transient populations with little financial or emotional investment in the neighborhood. In most cases, there is not one specific factor that causes violence. Aggression results from multiple factors working in combination. Thus, solutions require multifaceted approaches.

The CDC, Department of Education (DoE), Office of Justice and Delinquency Prevention (OJJDP), and Substance Abuse and Mental Health Services Administration (SAMHSA) promote evidence-based programs in violence prevention. Programs are categorized as universal, selected, or indicated prevention. Universal prevention programs aim to prevent violence-related behaviors before they emerge. Participants represent varying levels of risk. Examples of universal programs in youth violence prevention are skill building and problem solving, positive youth development, parent training, or bullying prevention programs. Selected prevention programs aim to reduce the risk of violence by working with at-risk populations. Home visitation, academic tutoring, behavioral management, mentoring, and case management work promote protective factors and minimize risk factors. Indicated prevention programs are for populations who have already demonstrated seriously delinquent behavior or violence. Indicated programs focus on skill building, behavioral management, family therapy, or individual therapy. Examples of evidence-based programs in youth violence prevention are Big Brothers Big Sisters Mentoring Program, Chicago Parent Program, cognitive therapy, Early Risers "Skills for Success," Familias Unidas Prevention Intervention, Families and Schools Together (FAST), Life Skills Training, Partners in Parenting, Peacebuilders, and Positive Action Pre–K. The National Registry of Evidence-based Programs and Practices maintains a searchable database of programs that have been reviewed by experts and proven to work.

Violence is one of the leading public health issues in the nation. Although the problem affects all ages, young people, those who offer the most valuable human resource of any society, are at highest risk for injury and death. Using careful epidemiological investigation, public health researchers have been able to identify the risk and protective factors for violence. Program planners developed and tested programs to determine effectiveness. Federal and nonprofit agencies reviewed programs and promote implementation of evidence-based programs. Despite progress, obstacles remain. Too many times, individuals and communities respond to violence with greater violence. Harsh, punitive, and unforgiving policies can aggravate the problem. Long-term solutions are to invest in youth before violence-related behaviors take hold and are transmitted throughout the community.

Sally Kuykendall

See also: Adverse Childhood Experiences; Centers for Disease Control and Prevention; Child Maltreatment; Community Health; Evidence-Based Programs and Practices; Grants; *Healthy People 2020*; Human Trafficking; Immigrant Health; Indian Health Service; Injuries; Intimate Partner Violence; Leading Health Indicators; Mental Health; National Center for Injury Prevention and Control; Prevention; School Health; Substance Abuse and Mental Health Services Administration; U.S. Department of Health and Human Services; *Controversies in Public Health:* Controversy 2

Further Reading

Centers for Disease Control and Prevention. (2017). *Violence prevention at CDC.* Retrieved from https://www.cdc.gov/violenceprevention/overview/index.html.

Cohen, M. A. (1998). The monetary value of saving a high-risk youth. *Journal of Quantitative Criminology, 14*(1), 5–33.

Corso, P. S., Mercy, J. A., Simon, T. R., Finkelstein, E. A., & Miller, T. R. (2007). Medical costs and productivity losses due to interpersonal and self-directed violence in the United States. *American Journal of Preventive Medicine, 32*(6), 474–482. doi:10.1016/j.amepre.2007.02.010

Dahlberg, L. L., & Mercy, J. A. (2009). History of violence as a public health issue. *AMA Virtual Mentor, 11*(2), 167–172. Retrieved from http://virtualmentor.ama-assn.org/2009/02/mhst1-0902.html.

Department of Health and Human Services. (2001). *Youth violence: A report of the Surgeon General.* Rockville, MD: U.S. Department of Health and Human Services, Centers for Disease Control and Prevention, National Center for Injury Prevention and Control; Substance Abuse and Mental Health Services Administration, Center for Mental Health Services; and National Institutes of Health, National Institute of Mental Health. Retrieved from https://www.ncbi.nlm.nih.gov/books/NBK44294.

Kuykendall, S. (2012). *Bullying: Health and medical issues today.* Santa Barbara, CA: ABC-CLIO Greenwood Press.

National Center for Injury Prevention and Control. Retrieved from https://www.cdc.gov/injury/index.html.

National Registry of Evidence-based Programs and Practices. Retrieved from http://nrepp.samhsa.gov/landing.aspx.

W

WALD, LILLIAN (1867–1940)

Lillian Wald was one of the most famous social reformers of the Progressive Era. Wald advanced the welfare of children, developed public health nursing into a profession, and influenced many other social reformers of the era through the Henry Street Settlement in New York City.

Born on March 10, 1867, in Cincinnati, Ohio, into a prosperous family, Lillian D. Wald grew up in Rochester, New York, where she attended Miss Cruttenden's English-French Boarding and Day School. At age 16, she applied to Vassar College but was rejected because she was considered to be too young. After several years spent enjoying an active social life, Wald decided she wanted serious work and entered the New York Hospital training school for nurses. Graduating in 1891, she worked for a year as a nurse at the New York Juvenile Asylum. This experience proving unsatisfactory, Wald enrolled in the Woman's Medical College in New York to obtain additional training. At the same time, she began teaching home-nursing classes for immigrant families.

The turning point in Wald's life occurred in March 1893, when she was called from the classroom to help a sick woman in a run-down tenement building. Horrified by the wretched living conditions, Wald decided to devote herself to public health nursing. Together with Mary Brewster, Wald set up an office first at the College Settlement on the Lower East Side and then on the top floor of a tenement on Jefferson Street. With the financial help of Mrs. Solomon Loeb and her banker/philanthropist son-in-law, Jacob H. Schiff, Wald and Brewster were able to move to a permanent home on Henry Street, where in 1895 they established the Nurses' Settlement.

The Nurses' Settlement was the only social settlement to emphasize nursing, which in Wald's view extended beyond caring for the sick to include education aimed at preventing disease. By 1896, the settlement had 11 residents, 9 of whom were trained nurses, and was known as the Henry Street Visiting Nurses Service. By 1913, there were nine such houses in Manhattan and the Bronx, with a total residential staff of 92 nurses, who made more than 200,000 visits a year. The idea of public health nursing had been born and spread rapidly.

Wald also established the country's first public-school nursing program in New York City. She was instrumental in setting up a department of nursing at Columbia University in 1910, and two years later, she helped the Red Cross establish the Town and Country Nursing Service. Having played a prominent role in the creation of the National Organization for Public Health Nursing, Wald was elected president of the organization in 1912.

A public health nurse climbs across a roof while visiting patients in the tenements of New York's lower east side, 1920. Lillian Wald envisioned specially trained nurses who possessed a fundamental understanding of life in the inner city. (MPI/Getty Images)

The Nurses' Settlement, meanwhile, soon outgrew its nursing focus and became known as the Henry Street Settlement, providing a full complement of community programs. A system of scholarships was started for children from poor families, and career guidance and vocational training were offered. In addition, the Henry Street Settlement was involved in efforts to provide better education for children with intellectual disabilities, to improve housing, to establish more parks and playgrounds, and to eradicate tuberculosis. Henry Street was always dependent on donations, and Wald proved to be a good fund-raiser.

Wald also became active in the child welfare movement. She pushed for legislation prohibiting child labor, and in 1904, she and Florence Kelley, who was also a Henry Street resident, founded the National Child Labor Committee. Wald's suggestion to President Theodore Roosevelt of the need for a government agency to protect the rights of children led in 1912 to the establishment of the Federal Children's Bureau, headed by Julia Lathrop.

The outbreak of World War I in 1914 was a blow to Wald's pacifist convictions. Together with Kelley and Jane Addams, she helped found the American Union Against Militarism, which had as its goal ending the war by mediation. When the

United States did enter the war, Wald served as head of the Council of National Defense's committee on home nursing. She also chaired the Nurses' Emergency Council, recruiting volunteer nurses and coordinating nursing agencies during the influenza epidemic of 1918.

The war over, Wald helped found the League of Free Nations Association, a forerunner of the Foreign Policy Association. She had expanded the Henry Street Settlement to include a neighborhood playhouse in 1915, and in the 1920s, she added an experimental theater and a playground. Her health deteriorating, Wald stepped down as head of the settlement in 1933. She retired to Westport, Connecticut, where after a long illness she died at the age of 73 on September 1, 1940.

James M. McPherson and Gary Gerstle

See also: Anderson, Elizabeth Milbank; Baker, Sara Josephine; Children's Health; Immigrant Health; Kelley, Florence; Maternal Health; *Controversies in Public Health:* Controversy 5

Further Reading

Buhler-Wilkerson, K. (1993). Bringing care to the people: Lillian Wald's legacy to public health nursing. *American Journal of Public Health*, *83*(12), 1778.

Eisemann, A., (1976). *Rebels and reformers: Biographies of four Jewish Americans: Uriah Phillips Levy, Ernesteine L. Rose, Louis D. Brandeis, Lillian Wald.* New York: Doubleday.

Miss Wald and Henry Street settlement have birthdays. (1933). *American Journal of Public Health*, *23*(5), 521–522.

Reverby, S. M. (1993, December). From Lillian Wald to Hillary Rodham Clinton: What will happen to public health nursing? *American Journal of Public Health, 83*(12), 1662.

Wald, L. (1915). *The house on Henry Street.* New York: Henry Holt & Co.

Wald, L. D. (1934). *Windows on Henry Street.* Boston: Little, Brown, and Company.

Williams, B. (1948). *Lillian Wald: Angel of Henry Street.* New York: Julian Messner.

WATERBORNE DISEASES

Waterborne diseases are physical problems and diseases caused by bacterial, viral, or parasitic agents in drinking or recreational water. The pathogens often originate from animal or human waste, which is ingested by drinking, food preparation, washing utensils, household cleaning, or during recreational activities, such as swimming. Examples include *campylobacter*, *Vibrio cholera*, hepatitis A and E, *Legionella*, *Salmonella*, and *Shigella*. The body attempts to rid itself of the pathogen through vomiting or diarrhea. However, this response can be life threatening to infants, children, elderly, and people with preexisting health conditions. Severe diarrhea can result in dehydration or malnutrition. Diarrhea is the second leading cause of death among children exposed to waterborne disease, and the World Health Organization estimates more than 1.7 billion cases of diarrhea each year (WHO, 2013). Waterborne diseases are distinct from water-related illnesses.

Water-related illnesses, such as malaria, yellow fever, West Nile fever, and encephalitis occur in areas where stagnant water provides a good breeding place for mosquitoes and the mosquitoes transmit the pathogenic organisms to humans. To control water-related illnesses, health officers recommend reducing sources of standing water or chemicals to reduce mosquito breeding (Moeller, 2005). Waterborne diseases are controlled by protecting sources of drinking water from contamination and following good sanitary practices during food storage, preparation, and serving. Compared to other areas of the world, the United States has low levels of waterborne diseases. Storms, heavy rain fall, and floods increase risk of waterborne diseases. Federal, state, and local public health systems are designed to identify pathogens and take preventive action. The Centers for Disease Control and Prevention (CDC) relies on collaboration of local public health agencies and state agencies to investigate and report cases of bacterial, viral, or parasitic contamination.

Campylobacter is a bacterial pathogen found in contaminated surface and rain water, infected cattle, contaminated foods, meat, and unpasteurized milk. Contamination occurs when fecal droplets from wild birds enters drinking water sources and water treatments fail to adequately clean the water. *Campylobacter jejuni* (*C. jejuni*) is the most infective species. Human transmission occurs by ingestion of contaminated food or drink. Symptoms include abdominal pain and acute diarrhea. In severe situations, the symptoms may progress to vomiting, chills, fever, arthritis, meningitis, or Guillain-Barre syndrome, a demyelinating disease of the peripheral nerves. *C. jejuni* infection is prevented by protecting drinking and surface water from contamination, and adequate water purification and treatment is essential.

Escherichia coli (*E. coli*) is a gram-negative bacteria. Different strains are classified by virulence. The most common strains are *Enterohaemorrhagic E. coli*, *Enterotoxigenic E. coli*, *Enteropathogenic E. coli*, and *Enteroinvasive E. coli*. The microorganism is found in drinking and recreational water contaminated by animal or human feces. Infection causes abdominal discomfort, cramps, nausea, and mild diarrhea. Severe infection could progress to bloody diarrhea, vomiting, headache, fever, hemolytic colitis, hemolytic anemia, or acute renal failure. In 1999, *E. coli* serotype 0157:H7 contaminated water at a New York county fair sickened 16,000 people, including 10 children who were hospitalized (Moeller, 2005). Exposure to *E. coli* can be prevented by protecting drinking water from animal and human waste and by effective treatment and protection of water prior to distribution for human use.

Legionella bacteria are found in a variety of water sources that include rivers, streams, ponds, recreational water systems, and man-made water environments such as cooling and heating systems or spas. The species *L. pneumophila* is associated with legionellosis, a respiratory disease with two clinical manifestations in humans: Legionnaire's disease and Pontiac fever. Legionnaire's disease can result in severe pneumonia. Pontiac fever is a mild illness with influenza-like symptoms, such as coughing, muscles ache, headache, nausea, and vomiting. Prevention of *Legionella* pathogens focuses on eliminating an environment where bacteria thrive. Reducing cold water systems to less than 20°C and raising hot water systems above 50°C effectively kills *Legionella*. Other strategies to control human exposure include use of disinfections in recreational water systems, preventing the accumulation of standing water, preventing biofilm development on water systems, and creating water distribution systems that are free of dead-end loops.

Waterborne viral pathogens include hepatitis A and Norwalk-like viruses (NLVs). Hepatitis A is an infectious disease that primarily affects school-aged children and young adults (Moeller, 2005). The route of entry is oral-fecal. The virus is found in contaminated salads, sandwiches, lettuce, strawberries, and drinking water. Symptoms range from abdominal pain to jaundice. Prevention efforts focus on protecting food from fecal contamination, disinfection, and chlorination of water. NLVs are the major cause of gastroenteritis outbreaks in the United States. An estimated 23 million cases occur annually, resulting in 50,000 hospitalizations and 300 deaths (Moeller, 2005). Outbreaks occur easily in crowded and unsanitary environments. Passenger cruise ships take special precautions to avoid outbreaks (National Center for Environmental Health Vessel Sanitation program, 2013).

Waterborne parasites include *Giardia* and *Cryptosporidium*. *Giardia* is the most common drinking water parasite in the United States and is often seen in summer camps and day care centers due to contaminated water, shallow wells, or untreated water (Moeller, 2005). Human exposure causes giardiasis, a disease characterized by diarrhea, abdominal pain, and bloating. Prevention includes protecting water sources, such as groundwater, ponds, shallow wells, rivers, and streams from animal or human wastes. Water purification treatments also reduce infection. *Cryptosporidium parvum* is a waterborne parasite transmitted by swimming pools, water parks, fountains, hot tubs, or spas. The pathogen is transmitted through feces in the water. Preventive measures include protecting the water, boiling water, or filtration (National Center for Environmental Health Vessel Sanitation Program, 2013). The CDC also recommends clearing everyone out of the water when solid feces is observed in a pool, water park, or hot tub (Moeller, 2005).

Waterborne diseases are very common health problems, which can be particularly fatal for the very young, very old, or incapacitated. Fortunately, such diseases are easily preventable through individual and public health surveillance with rapid response.

Victor Okparaeke

See also: Association of Public Health Laboratories; Bioterrorism; Centers for Disease Control and Prevention; Cholera; Epidemic; Food Insecurity; Food Safety; Infectious Diseases; Snow, John; World Health Organization

Further Reading

Moeller, D. W. (2005). *Environmental health* (3rd ed.). Cambridge, MA: Harvard University Press.

National Center for Environmental Health Vessel Sanitation program. (2013). *Health practices on cruise ships: Training for employees*. Centers for Disease Control and Prevention. Retrieved from https://www.cdc.gov/nceh/vsp/training/videos/transcripts/water.pdf.

Weiss, T. C. (2015). *Water-borne diseases: Types and information*. Retrieved from https://www.disabled-world.com/health/water-diseases.php.

World Health Organization. (2017). *Microbial fact sheets*. Retrieved from http://www.who.int/mediacentre/factsheets/en/.

WEGMAN, MYRON EZRA (1908–2004)

Through his work as the secretary general of the Pan-American Health Organization (1956–1960) and as dean of the School of Public Health at the University of Michigan (1960–1974), Dr. Myron Ezra Wegman navigated the field of maternal and child health into a scientific discipline that uses biostatistics and social indexes to reduce deaths and improve health and well-being for infants, children, and mothers in developing and advanced countries. Myron Wegman was born in Brooklyn, New York, to Nettie (Finkelstein) and Max Wegman. The Polish/Lithuanian couple had six children, two of which died during infancy. Myron earned a BA in classics from the City College of New York in 1928. While deciding on a career, he was influenced by Upton Sinclair's 1925 novel, *Arrowsmith*. The book follows the main character, Dr. Martin Arrowsmith, through medical training, clinical practice, and a career in scientific research. The novel was highly acclaimed for its accuracy and for shedding light on scientific misconduct, institutional pressure, professional jealousy, greed, ignorance, and negligence in research and medicine. The concerns raised by Sinclair highlight the need for qualified, ethical practitioners in medicine and health care.

In 1932, Wegman graduated cum laude from Yale University School of Medicine. He intended to go into pediatrics. Pediatric care was shifting from treating deadly infectious diseases, such as smallpox and diphtheria, to tackling complex social and behavioral health issues. Wegman's first job was as a circuit rider for the state of Maryland. Circuit riders provided on-site technical advice and medical expertise to doctors practicing in isolated areas. Wegman covered the Eastern Shore of Maryland where he shared the latest advancements in prenatal and pediatric care. He continued his own studies by earning a master of public health degree at Johns Hopkins University and was invited to teach courses at Hopkins.

In 1940, Wegman moved to develop maternal child health in Puerto Rico. He did not stay long as the outbreak of World War II (1939–1945) increased the demand for doctors in the states. He returned to New York and accepted a position as director of school health while also teaching at Columbia University and Cornell University. In 1946, Wegman moved to Louisiana where he became chief of pediatrics at Louisiana State University and New Orleans Charity Hospital. The South was not a good fit for him. He protested the segregation of black and white infants in the neonatal ward and resisted the paranoid efforts of the McCarthy Era. In 1949, Wegman started publishing the first *Annual Review of Vital Statistics in Pediatrics*.

The report summarized national statistics on births, fertility rates, infant mortality rates, and other vital data. He translated complex, difficult to understand statistics into an understandable format. These reports were published every year in the December issue of *Pediatrics*. The data helped pediatricians to guide practices based on national data and patient needs. Wegman was a stickler for grammar. He continued to author the annual report for the next 40 years. In 1952, Wegman moved to the Pan American Sanitary Bureau, working to improve care of children and mothers in Latin America. Eight years later, he returned to education as the dean of the University of Michigan, School of Public Health.

Throughout his lifetime, Wegman published more than 200 articles. His work encompassed pediatrics, health policy, public health and nursing, international health, biomedical research, occupational lung disease, school health, and his vision for a national system of health. In 1972, Wegman served as president of the American Public Health Association (APHA). He guided the professional organization through its 100th annual meeting, focusing on the need for a national health policy. In his presidential address, Wegman said:

> The country has many accomplishments that are a source of pride, yet in other areas there are gaps, duplication, confusion or protection of special interest. Some say we have no health policy, whether it is explicit or, more often, implicit in the sum total of national action, or inaction, related to the health of its citizens. The United States clearly falls into the latter category; what we have lacks coordination, often lacks rationality and frequently has shortcomings of performance. (Wegman, 1973, p. 98)

He called on APHA members to influence policy makers by expressing the need for a national health policy that would create life, liberty, and the pursuit of happiness. In 1974, Wegman was awarded the Sedgwick Memorial Medal for distinguished service in public health. He died on April 14, 2004, at the age of 95.

Myron Ezra Wegman was a pediatrician, faculty member, and public health leader who helped move maternal and child health from infectious disease treatment to evidence-based practices in behavioral and social health. As an academic, he was known for supporting the success of students and junior faculty members, and he helped to kick-start the careers of many notable public health leaders. His ideas of using data and statistics to develop policies and practices are applicable to public health in all countries.

Sally Kuykendall

See also: American Public Health Association; Biostatistics; Children's Health; Eliot, Martha May; Infant Mortality; Maternal Health; School Health

Further Reading

Brown, V. J. (2005). Myron Ezra Wegman. *American Journal of Public Health*, 95(8), 1309–1311. doi:10.2105/AJPH.2005.066555

Wallis, A. B., & Guyer, B. (2006). Myron Wegman: Early days, lasting influence. *Maternal & Child Health Journal*, *10*(1), 5–11. doi:10.1007/s10995-005–0033-3
Wegman, M. E. (1973). Centennial presidential address policy, priority, and the power to act. *American Journal of Public Health*, *63*(2), 98–101.
Wegman, M. E. (1996). Infant mortality: Some international comparisons. *Pediatrics*, *98*(6), 1020.
Wegman, M. E. (1999). Foreign aid, international organizations, and the world's children. *Pediatrics*, *103*(3), 646.

WINSLOW, CHARLES-EDWARD AMORY (1877–1957)

Charles-Edward Amory (C.-E. A.) Winslow is a historical figure in American public health for numerous reasons. As an academic, administrator, and social activist, he advanced the fields of bacteriology, industrial hygiene, home health, public health nursing, and health education. Throughout his lifetime, he wrote over 600 articles and books. Topics ranged widely with articles on garbage disposal in urban inner cities, sex education for teachers and parents, and the influence of odor on appetite. Students of public health recognize him as the author of the commonly cited and all-encompassing definition of public health. Winslow's drive, determination, and vision for public health is best captured by his description of Lemuel Shattuck, "If we pursue our vocation with Shattuck's zeal and courage and vision and faith, the second hundred years of public health may be even harder than the first; but they will certainly be even more glorious" (Winslow, 1949). Winslow created a niche for public health as a multidisciplinary profession that uses natural science, social science, political science, and clinical practice to improve the human condition (Rosner & Markowitz, 1998).

C.-E. A. Winslow was born in 1877 in Boston as the only child of Catherine Mary (Reignolds) and Erving Winslow. At the time, the nation was changing from an agricultural society to an industrial power. Thousands of farmworkers moved to the inner cities in search of employment, joining millions of non-English-speaking immigrants. The poor working class toiled long hours in coal mines, steel mills, assembly lines, and arduous trades. The massive population movement, overcrowding, and poor living conditions bred frequent outbreaks of cholera, typhus, smallpox, and tuberculosis. Industrial toxins of lead, mercury, arsenic, and silica dust silently poisoned workers and their families. Young children worked in dangerous occupations, attaining calories from beer because it was less contaminated than milk. Health professionals debated the underlying causes and solutions to the problems of the inner cities. Some blamed the poor and immigrant workers, purporting that communicable diseases were due to immorality and ignorance. Others emerged as social reformers working to reduce the exploitation of low income workers and educate the public on sanitation and hygiene. Winslow's mother was an English actress who acted in plays featuring social controversies. His father was a vocal anti-imperialist who opposed U.S. expansion. Young Winslow was privileged to attend Boston's English High School and the Massachusetts Institute of Technology (MIT).

He planned to study biology and ultimately pursue a career in medicine until he encountered Professor William H. Sedgwick. Sedgwick stood on the side of social reform, studying the relationships between contaminated water, sewage, and disease. However, he did live in an ivory tower of simply studying the problem. He used research to identify sanitary measures and prevent water pollution. Sedgwick introduced his students to the field of practical biology, inspiring Winslow to change majors from medicine to public health. After graduation with a bachelor's degree in 1898, Winslow continued at MIT as a graduate student. He conducted research on sewage and sanitary practices where he met Anne Rogers, his future wife and scientific partner. As a student, Winslow coauthored the first textbook on water bacteriology. In 1905, he offered the first university course on industrial hygiene. The course explored factory ventilation, industrial toxins, working conditions, and the need for factory inspections. The course would have been very controversial for the time period, confronting and seeking to control powerful private industries.

After graduation, Winslow worked for the New York State Department of Health establishing health education services. In 1914, the family of Anna M. Lauder, wife of George Lauder, donated $400,000 to Yale University Medical School to fund a Department of Public Health. George Lauder was the cousin and adviser of Andrew Carnegie. A condition of the funding was that the new chair should be a physician with experience in sanitary medicine. Yale disregarded the family's request for a physician and instead hired Winslow. From the start, Winslow embraced the opportunity to inspire others. He taught undergraduates, graduate students, nursing students, and medical students. A highlight of the semester was evening lectures at Winslow's home where faculty and students discussed international cultures and philosophies. Despite his blueblood upbringing and prestigious position as chair, Winslow held firmly to his sense of empathy. Former student A. Pharo Gagge recalls attending his first Sunday dinner at Winslow's house. Dressed in a sports coat and slacks, Gagge arrived to find the other male guests and Winslow in formal dinner jackets. As Mrs. Winslow introduced the new graduate student to other guests, Winslow changed into a sports coat and slacks and reappeared among his guests (Kemper, 2015).

Winslow's influence extended beyond Yale. He advocated for public health education, serving as a consultant for the Accreditation of Schools of Public Health. To this end, he created the definition of public health, which is still used today:

> The science and art of preventing disease, prolonging life, and promoting health and efficiency through organized community efforts for the sanitation of the environment, the control of communicable infections, the education of the individual in personal hygiene, the organization of medical and nursing services for the early diagnosis and preventive treatment of disease, and for the development of the social machinery to insure everyone a standard of living adequate for the maintenance of health, so organizing these benefits as to enable every citizen to realize his birthright of health and longevity. (Winslow, 1920, p. 183)

The definition reflects Winslow's belief and experiences in public health. The phrase "science and art of preventing disease" refers to public health's role and partnership in medicine. "Organized community efforts" reflects public health as a collaborative practice with many different facets. Ending with the phrase "to enable every citizen to realize his birthright" highlights the mission of public health in social justice.

Winslow was a prolific writer, active in the American Public Health Association (APHA) and public health education. Among his numerous accomplishments are:

- Editor of the *Journal of Bacteriology* (1916–1944)
- Chair of the New Haven Demonstration Health Center (1919–1923)
- Helped establish the Connecticut Department of Public Health
- Chairman of the APHA Laboratory Section (1920–1935)
- Helped establish Yale University School of Nursing (1923)
- Vice-chairman of the Committee on the Costs of Medical Care (1928–1932)
- Chairman of the APHA Committee on Hygiene of Housing (1936–1956)
- Helped establish the APHA Public Health Nursing Section
- Helped establish the APHA Medical Care Section
- Editor of the *American Journal of Public Health* (1944–1954)

Throughout all of his accomplishments, Winslow maintained direct and honest communication and staunch advocacy for public health. On numerous occasions, he was pressured to withhold research findings, particularly information on occupational hazards. Winslow refused to bow to political pressure and stood by objective scientific data.

Winslow helped to define public health as a professional field unique from but in partnership with medicine, nursing, biology, sanitation, public policy, and mental health. He helped to craft public health practice and responsibilities.

Sally Kuykendall

See also: American Public Health Association; Council on Education for Public Health; Kelley, Florence; *Nation's Health, The*; Shattuck, Lemuel

Further Reading

Fulton, J. F. (1957). C.-E. A. Winslow, leader in public health. *Science*, *125*(3260), 1236.

Kemper, S. (2015). C-E.A. *Winslow, who launched public health at Yale a century ago, still influential today.* Retrieved from https://news.yale.edu/2015/06/02/public-health-giant-c-ea-winslow-who-launched-public-health-yale-century-ago-still-influe.

Rosner, D., & Markowitz, G. (1998). C.-E. A. Winslow: Scientist, activist, and theoretician of the American public health movement throughout the first half of the twentieth century: Commentaries. *Journal of Public Health Policy*, *19*(2), 147. doi:10.2307/3343295

Terris, M. (1998). C.-E. A. Winslow: Scientist, activist, and theoretician of the American public health movement throughout the first half of the twentieth century. *Journal of Public Health Policy*, *19*(2), 135. doi:10.2307/3343294

Winslow, C. (1951). International co-operation in the service of health. *Annals of the American Academy of Political & Social Science*, *273*(1), 192. doi:10.1177/000271625127300126

Winslow, C.-E. A. (1920). The untilled field of public health. *Modern Medicine*, *2*, 183–191.

Winslow, C.-E. A. (1944). Who killed Cock Robin? *American Journal of Public Health*, *34*, 658–659.

Winslow, C.-E. A. (1949). Lemuel Shattuck: Still a prophet. *American Journal of Public Health*, *39*, 156–162.

Winslow, C.-E. A. (1952). The cost of sickness and the price of health. World Health Organization monograph series. *Tubercle*, *33*, 119. doi:10.1016/S0041-3879(52)80053-4

WOMEN'S HEALTH

Women's health refers to the physical and mental state of a woman, regardless of the presence of disease. The women's health movement started in the early 1900s with a focus on reproductive freedom. The field now covers issues that are unique to women, such as menstruation, menopause, and gynecological wellness, as well as how certain diseases or health issues affect women differently than men. In the United States, the leading causes of death for both genders are heart disease, cancer, lower respiratory diseases, stroke, Alzheimer's disease, injuries, and diabetes. Although the diseases are similar, the level of risk, symptoms, or social implications may be vastly different for females. For example, the classic sign of heart attack is chest pain that radiates to the neck, jaw, shoulder, or arm. Although men tend to report the discomfort as a dull ache concentrated on the right side, women report the discomfort as a pressing sensation affecting the throat. Men are much more likely to recognize the symptoms of a heart attack and seek immediate treatment whereas women will go home, make dinner for their family, help the children with homework, and pack their suitcase before heading to the emergency room. This delay in recognition and treatment costs lives. Other disorders, such as depression, eating disorders, and some types of cancer are more prevalent among females. Women are more likely to be diagnosed with depression and anxiety than men and are more likely to attempt suicide. Reproductive health, sexually transmitted infections, and sexual violence are also major public health concerns. Women in developing countries are more likely to die from childbirth or pregnancy complications than women in developed countries and also are at a greater risk for HIV/AIDS. Women's health is examined across the life stages of adolescence (aged 10–19), middle adulthood (aged 20–59), and older adulthood (aged 60 and older). Each stage presents unique health needs for public health services.

The major health concerns of adolescent girls in the United States are mental health, injuries, successful transition to adulthood, adolescent pregnancy, and nutrition. Half of all mental health conditions develop by age 14. The most common brain disorders among girls are depressive disorders, schizophrenia, mood disorders, anxiety disorders, eating disorders, ADHD, and autism. The period of puberty marks the transition from childhood to womanhood. Onset can occur as young as 7 years old or as late as 17. During this time, breasts and pubic hair develop, changes in fat distribution create curves in the body frame, skin becomes oily, and menstruation begins. Regular hormonal cycles produce the menstrual period with regular shedding of blood and other materials from the lining of the uterus. Except during pregnancy or during times of starvation or severe stress, this process occurs at regular intervals starting about one lunar month from puberty until menopause. Before and during menstruation, the female may experience mood swings, headaches, cramps, difficulty concentrating, or upset stomach. As soon as puberty begins, females are able to become pregnant. Adolescents who become pregnant are at greater risk for complications during the pregnancy or birth. Internationally, more than 15 million live births every year are by girls between the ages of 15 to 19 (WHO, 2013). Complications from pregnancy and childbirth are a leading cause of death in adolescent girls in developing countries. Adolescent girls are also more likely to have unsafe abortions, which can lead to health problems such as hemorrhage, infertility, infections, and death.

Adequate nutrition is another special consideration during adolescence. Approximately one out of five adolescent girls in the United States is obese (Fryer, Carroll, & Ogden, 2012). Overweight and obesity are related to premature puberty, asthma, heart disease, breast cancer, social and emotional problems, and increased wear and tear on joints leading to total knee or hip replacements as young adults. The

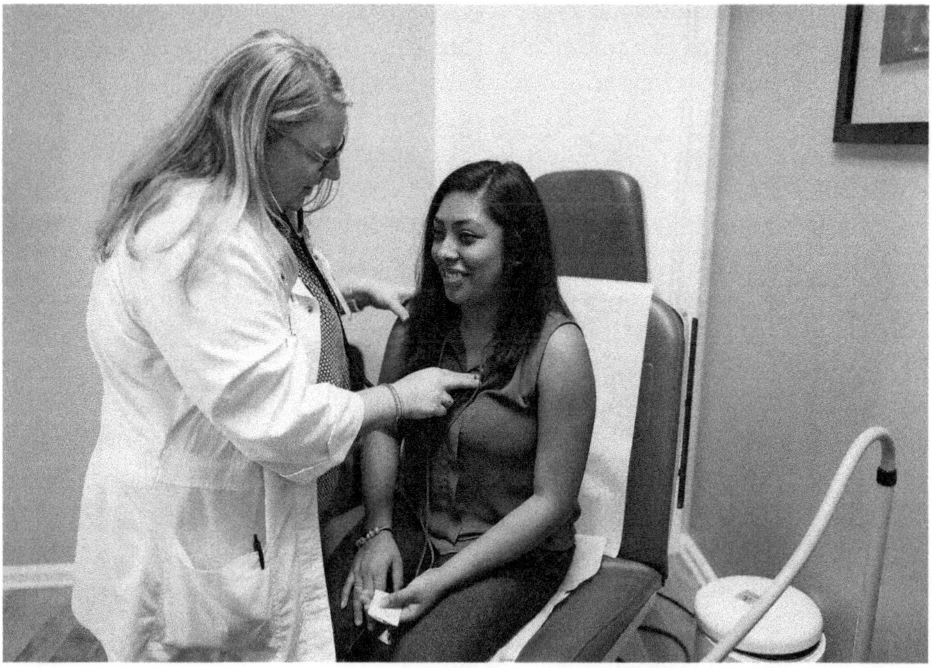

Nurse practitioner Rachel Eisenberg checks Natalia Reyes's heart during a routine physical exam at Planned Parenthood in West Palm Beach, Florida. Heart disease is the leading cause of death for women in America. (Joe Raedle/Getty Images)

physical and psychological events of adolescence generate unique nutritional needs in females. Young girls need macronutrients and micronutrients to compensate for growth spurts and blood loss during menstruation. Pregnancy further complicates the demand for a healthy diet. More than one-third of adolescent girls worldwide are anemic (WHO, 2013). Approximately 17 percent of adolescent girls in the United States are considered obese (Fryer, Carroll, & Ogden, 2012).

In middle adulthood, women's health encompasses maternal health, cardiovascular disease, cancer, sexually transmitted diseases, mental health, violence, and disabilities. Maternal health is the period of time from before a woman is pregnant to the postpartum period. There are several complications that can occur during pregnancy. These can range from mild discomfort to life-threatening. Common complications are hypertension, urinary tract infections, postpartum depression, gestational diabetes mellitus, infections, and hyperemesis gravidarum, a condition where the mother suffers from severe nausea and vomiting. Postpartum depression, which occurs after giving birth, affects 8 to 19 percent of women (Centers for Disease Control and Prevention Division of Reproductive Health, 2017). Symptoms include trouble sleeping, not feeling connected to the baby, exaggerated or excessive concerns for the safety of the baby, and worrying that the mother could harm the baby.

The female anatomy and physiology predisposes women who have unprotected sex with men to sexually transmitted diseases. In the United States, one in four people with HIV are female (CDC, 2017). Women account for 19 percent of new HIV infections (CDC, 2017). African American women carry a disproportionate share of the disease. African American women account for 60 percent of females living with HIV. White and Hispanic/Latina women account for 17 percent each (CDC, 2017). Sexually transmitted diseases weaken the body's protection against other infections and related diseases. Cervical cancer, the second most common type of cancer for women, is linked to the sexually transmitted disease human papillomavirus (HPV) (WHO, 2013).

Power imbalances promote the physical, sexual, psychological, and economic abuse of females in some societies. Worldwide, 38 percent of female murders are committed by intimate partners (WHO, 2013). Thirty-five percent of women have experienced physical or sexual violence at some point in their life (WHO, 2013). In some areas of the world, sexual violence is used as a weapon of war and ethnic elimination. In the United States, 44 percent of women have experienced sexual violence (Breiding, 2015). Victims are more likely to experience depression, sexually transmitted diseases, asthma, irritable bowel syndrome, headaches, chronic pain, and insomnia. Economic violence presents as a spectrum of abuse and is characterized by someone with power taking advantage of those with lesser power. For women, this could take the form of human trafficking or as less noticeable gender disparities in pay. Women are more likely to live longer than men. The world population above 90 years of age is 70 percent women (WHO, 2013). The primary causes of death in women over 60 is cardiovascular disease and cancer. Senior women may experience disabilities, chronic diseases, and decreased physical and cognitive functioning. Disabilities are more common among women. If a woman has a disability, she is less likely to have positive health outcomes, educational achievements, and high income compared to able-bodied women. One of the reasons women may be more likely to have a disability than men is due to the partner violence they are more likely to experience. Age-related issues may include loss of vision or hearing, arthritis, depression, and dementia. In many countries, women are less likely to receive treatment than men. Women begin menopause in their forties or fifties and become postmenopausal in their sixties. Women going through menopause may experience irregular periods, vaginal dryness, hot flashes, night sweats, sleeping problems, mood changes, weight gain, thinning hair, and loss of breast fullness. Women may go into early menopause if they have a hysterectomy (surgery that removes both the uterus and ovaries), chemotherapy and radiation, or primary ovarian insufficiency (a condition where ovaries fail to produce normal levels of reproductive hormones).

Research into women's health problems lags behind men. In 1977, the Food and Drug Administration (FDA) refused to allow women of child-bearing age to participate in early phases of clinical research. Women were not included in many large-scale studies such as how aspirin affects cardiovascular health. Furthermore, many researchers believed that women's health was similar to men's health. Women's health advocates worked for a more extensive definition of women's health. In 1983, the United States Public Health Service expanded the definition of women's health to include social issues and the biological differences between men and women. In 1993, the National Institutes of Health created a mandate that stated women and other minority groups should be included in all human participant research. In 2001, the FDA began monitoring how sex differences may account for drug safety and effectiveness. Future directions of research in women's health contain six goals (NIH, 2010). The first goal is to increase gender differences in basic scientific studies. This goal includes, but is not limited to, genetic and epigenetic studies, gender differences in the structure of male and female cells, and increasing basic research on gender differences in the prevention and treatment of diseases. The second goal is to use these findings to influence the design and application of new devices and medication such as the development of computational models and developing minimally invasive technologies for accurate screening, diagnosis, and treatment of diseases. The third goal is to personalize prevention, diagnostics, and therapies for females. This means studying gender differences in the aging process and expanding research on pregnancy-related conditions. The fourth goal is to create global alliances to increase the impact of women's health research. This includes reaching out to world class scientists in many different fields to create a plan for implementing strategies for women's health research. The fifth goal is to create and put in place new social networking media to further understanding and appreciation of women's health. This includes serving as a central resource for information for federal and state agencies, elected officials, media, health organizations, and the public on women's health research issues. The sixth goal is to utilize creative strategies to recruit an impressive women's health research workforce. Addressing the many different factors that affect women's advancement in the sciences, including organizational, institutional, and systemic factors can enhance the well-being of women, children, men, families, and communities throughout the globe.

Alison C. Walensky and Sally Kuykendall

See also: Addictions; Cancer; Eating Disorders; Ellertson, Charlotte Ehrengard; Family Planning; Heart Truth® (Red Dress) Campaign, The; Human Immunodeficiency Virus and Acquired Immune Deficiency Syndrome; Human Trafficking; Intimate Partner Violence; Kelley, Florence; Lesbian, Gay, Bisexual, and Transgender Health; Maternal Health; Mental Health; Nutrition; Planned Parenthood; Sanger, Margaret Louise Higgins

Further Reading

Breiding, M. J. (2015). Prevalence and characteristics of sexual violence, stalking, and intimate partner violence victimization: National Intimate Partner and Sexual Violence Survey, United States, 2011. *American Journal of Public Health*, *105*(4), e11–e12.

Centers for Disease Control and Prevention. (2017). *HIV among women*. Retrieved from https://www.cdc.gov/hiv/group/gender/women/index.html.

Centers for Disease Control and Prevention Division of Reproductive Health. (2017). *Depression among women of reproductive age*. Retrieved from http://www.cdc.gov/reproductivehealth/depression/.

Centers for Disease Control and Prevention Office of Women's Health. (2017). *Women's health*. Retrieved from https://www.cdc.gov/women/index.htm.

Fryer, C. D., Carroll, M. D., & Ogden, C. L. (2012, September 12). *Prevalence of obesity among children and adolescents: United States, trends 1963–1965 through 2009–2010*. Centers for Disease Control. Retrieved from http://www.cdc.gov/nchs/data/hestat/obesity_child_07_08/obesity_child_07_08.htm.

HIV among women. (2015, June 23). Centers for Disease Control and Prevention. Retrieved from http://www.cdc.gov/hiv/group/gender/women/.

Menopause. (2015). *Mayo Clinic*. Retrieved from http://www.mayoclinic.org/diseases-conditions/menopause/basics/definition/con-20019726.

National Institutes of Health. (2010). Moving into the future with new dimensions and strategies: A vision for 2020 for women's health research. Retrieved from http://orwh.od.nih.gov/research/strategicplan/ORWH_StrategicPlan2020_Vol1.pdf.

Women's health. (2013, September 1). World Health Organization. Retrieved from http://www.who.int/topics/womens_health/en/.

WORLD HEALTH ORGANIZATION (WHO)

The World Health Organization (WHO) is an international humanitarian agency with the mission of promoting health for all people throughout the globe. The WHO is an agency of the United Nations (UN) supported and managed by UN member governments. The agency collects global health data and shares the information through their website and special reports. Examples of WHO work includes publishing the *World Health Report*, working to control sexually transmitted diseases, environmental problems, epidemic and endemic diseases, and promoting maternal and child health and equitable access to care. Major health achievements are the eradication of smallpox and the control of measles, yellow fever, cholera, tuberculosis, and malaria.

The first international effort to coordinate national public health started in 1851 with the International Sanitary Conference in Paris. The conference focused on preventing the transmission of cholera and the high costs of fighting infectious diseases by standardizing rules for quarantine and minimizing redundant efforts at ports of entry. The International Sanitary Conference continued to meet annually, evolving into the Office International d'Hygiène Publique (OIHP), a permanent committee of health officials headquartered in Paris. World War I (1914–1918) disrupted OIHP's work. After the war, the agency was supposed to join the League of Nations. However, the United States objected and the League of Nations established a new international health organization. The Health Organization of the League of Nations, OIHP, the Pan American Sanitary Organization, and other agencies worked together to promote world health until efforts were again stymied by world war. After World War II, officials met to establish the UN. Delegates from Brazil and China advocated for combining the multinational health organizations into one agency. Fifty-one UN members and delegates from 10 nations drafted a Constitution of the WHO. U.S. surgeon general Thomas Parran (serving from 1936 to 1948) referred to the WHO Constitution as the "Magna Carta for world health." The Constitution was formally ratified by 26 members of the UN on April 7, 1948, a date that is now celebrated as World Health Day. The first director general was Canadian psychiatrist Dr. Brock Chisholm, a highly respected doctor and a World War I veteran.

The WHO currently employs over 7,000 people from 150 countries. Public health objectives are:

- Providing public health leadership and engaging partners.
- Identifying areas for research and translating research findings into public health practice.
- Defining standards for public health practice.
- Determining evidence-based policies that adhere to ethical principles.
- Building institutional capacity.
- Disease surveillance and monitoring.

Staff include public health professionals, medical doctors, scientists, epidemiologists, health administrators, biostatisticians, financial experts, and health economists. The organization is headquartered in Geneva, Switzerland, with regional offices in Africa, the Americas, South-East Asia, Europe, Eastern Mediterranean, and the Western Pacific. The Global Service Centre is located in Malaysia. Offices are multilingual to ensure that information is clearly communicated and effectively addresses pressing health issues. The WHO is governed by the World Health Assembly, which is composed of health ministers from member states.

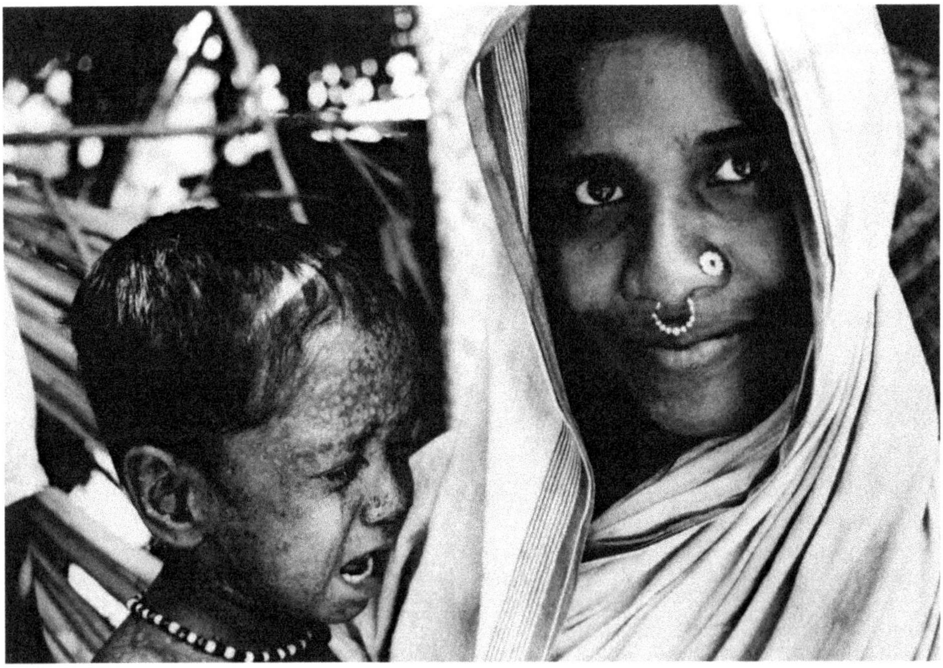

Toddler Rahima Banu shows classic signs of smallpox infection with a distinctive, bumpy rash, and blistering of the skin, mouth, and throat. World Health Organization workers responded to the outbreak by vaccinating all people who came in contact with Rahima and cared for the little girl until she recovered physically. (National Library of Medicine)

Major efforts involve monitoring trends in diseases and health problems and sharing information and best practices with nations. The WHO sends emergency responders to manage disease outbreaks at the source, containing and controlling deadly diseases, such as Ebola; manages mass immunization campaigns to ensure the safety of children around the world; ensures that prescription medicines have a single international name so that people traveling abroad can attain the drug that their doctor prescribed; and sets standards for environmental health issues, such as air pollution. Major achievements include the control of the disabling disease yaws (1952–1964), eradication of smallpox (1979), identification of the virus that causes AIDS (1983), control of severe acute respiratory syndrome (2003), the global public health treaty to reduce tobacco-related deaths (2003), and a 99 percent reduction in cases of polio (1988–2006). The Health Action in Crisis team manages responses to man-made and natural disasters, helping communities to strengthen internal capacity and to recover from disasters while minimizing threats to public health. Future priorities are global eradication of polio, advocating for disadvantaged groups living in poverty, and reducing the 500,000 maternal deaths each year caused by complications of pregnancy. The WHO works with partners around the world addressing the most pressing emerging and remerging health issues.

Sally Kuykendall

See also: Air Pollution; Alcohol; Bioterrorism; Child Maltreatment; Cholera; Disability; Disability Movement; Dunham, Ethel Collins; Eliot, Martha May; Environmental Health; Epidemic; Family Planning; Global Health; Health; Healthy Places; Immigrant Health; Infant Mortality; Intimate Partner Violence; Maternal Health; Measles; Mental Health; Pandemic; Polio; Salk, Jonas; Smallpox; Social Determinants of Health; Vaccines; Waterborne Diseases; Winslow, Charles-Edward Amory; *Controversies in Public Health:* Controversy 5

Further Reading

Parran, T., & Boudreau, F. G. (1946). World Health Organization. *American Journal of Public Health, 36,* 1267–1272.

World Health Organization. (2007). *Working for health: An introduction to the World Health Organization.* Retrieved from http://www.who.int/about/brochure_en.pdf.

World Health Organization. (2017). Retrieved from http://www.who.int/en.

The World Health Organization and Its Work. (2008). *American Journal of Public Health, 98*(9), 1594–1597.

WYNDER, ERNST LUDWIG (1922–1999)

Ernst Ludwig Wynder was a German American physician, surgeon, researcher, and public health advocate who worked diligently to create awareness of smoking as a health hazard. Between 1850 and 1900, lung cancer increased over fourfold in the United States, from 9 cases per 100,000 people to 43 cases per 100,000 (Adler, 1912). Similar increases were seen throughout the world. Some scientists suspected air pollution. Few suspected smoking because cigarettes were marketed as health enhancing. Doctors, famous athletes, and movie stars featured prominently in advertisements claiming that smoking cleared the lungs, soothed the throat, or relieved asthma. As lung cancer cases increased, medical researchers focused on treatments. Wynder focused on naming and preventing the cause. His body of research and public advocacy is a model of interdisciplinary, translational research in public health. Wynder combined aspects of epidemiology, biology, pathology, biochemistry, and health behavior to study smoking and cancer. Despite dismissal by colleagues and pressure from tobacco companies, Wynder persevered and his research saved and continues to save many lives.

Ernst Ludwig Wynder was born on April 30, 1922, in Herford, Germany, the son of Therese (Godfrey) and Alfred Wynder. In 1938, the family fled Nazi persecution to the United States. Ernst earned a bachelor of arts degree from New York University. In 1943, he became a naturalized citizen and joined the U.S. Army Intelligence Corps. After two years of army service, he attended Washington University Medical School in St. Louis, Missouri. During a summer internship at New York University, Ernst observed an autopsy of a 42-year-old man. The man died of lung cancer after smoking two packages of cigarettes per day over 30 years. After the autopsy, Wynder questioned patients about their smoking. Noticing that many patients smoked, Wynder devised a study. He returned to Washington University and convinced faculty mentor Dr. Evarts Graham to allow him to interview Graham's patients.

The idea that smoking was harmful to health was not new. In 1912, Dr. Isaac A. Adler of the New York Polyclinic and the German, Beth-Israel, Har Moriah, and Peoples Hospitals and the Montefiore Home and Hospital published the landmark report *Primary Malignant Growths of the Lung and Bronchi.* The report summarized worldwide increases in lung cancer. Much of the data came from doctors in Europe. In the 1920s, cancer specialist and director of the Instituto de Medicina Experimental in Buenos Aires, Argentina, Dr. Ángel Roffo tested the effects of tobacco tar on rabbits. Dr. Roffo concluded that "this product is highly carcinogenic; it causes carcinomas which are invasive, metastatic and aggressive" (Roffo, 2006, p. 502). Roffo recommended an aggressive public campaign against smoking. The Nazi Party was the first to organize national anti-smoking efforts. Posters discouraged smoking. Cigarettes were rationed. Smoking was banned on public transportation. Adolf Hitler, a former smoker himself, encouraged friends and colleagues to quit the habit. The campaign was consistent with the Nazi goal of creating a physically perfect and genetically pure race (Proctor, 1996). German doctors believed that smoking caused birth defects. Messages and rationing were frequently aimed at German women in an effort to promote fertility and children's health. Roffo died in 1947, and the anti-smoking movement was dismissed as Nazi propaganda.

In May 1950, Wynder published his first study on smoking and health while in his fourth year as a medical student. Gathering the smoking histories of 605 men with bronchiogenic carcinoma and 780 men with other diseases, Wynder and Graham (1950) discovered that patients with lung cancer reported higher rates of smoking, longer smoking histories, and heavier smoking than patients with other diseases. The study provided epidemiological analysis by mathematicians at the University of Washington. The statisticians rejected the null hypothesis that smoking was *not* related to lung cancer. The odds that the differences in smoking between the two groups was due to chance alone was less than one in 10,000. Wynder and Graham surmised that smoking was related to lung cancer and, based on patient report, cigarette smoking posed higher risk than pipes or cigars. Experts criticized the study because it only proved that the two variables, smoking and lung cancer, existed together (a cross-sectional, correlational study). The study did not prove that smoking caused lung cancer. Dr. Charles S. Cameron, medical director of the American Cancer Society, told the press:

> The evidence that has been adduced does not justify an indictment of smoking as a cause of lung cancer, in our opinion. We believe that the methods of collecting this evidence have all had certain inadequacies, and we are now initiating another study which we hope will put us in a better position to answer this question in five years. (Spencer, 1950, p. 136)

Cameron believed that cancer was due to hormonal factors.

Meanwhile, in England and Wales, deaths due to lung cancer increased from 612 in 1922 to 9,287 in 1947 (Doll & Hill, 1950). Within several months of Wynder and Graham's report, Drs. Richard Doll and Bradford Hill of the British Medical Council published a similar hospital-based study. Doll's 1,732 patients with carcinoma and 743 general medical and surgical patients confirmed Wynder's analysis. By 1954, Doll and Hill published their landmark study "The Mortality of Doctors in Relation to Their Smoking Habits" in the *British Medical Journal*. The study followed 40,564 male and female physicians over 29 months. All deaths due to lung cancer were among smokers and the more one smoked, the greater the risk of lung cancer. This prospective study of a highly reliable, healthy population was a critical step in showing that smoking causes lung cancer.

Wynder completed his medical internship at Georgetown University Hospital in Washington, DC, and residency at the Memorial Hospital for Cancer and Allied Diseases. He continued his quest to discover the cause of lung cancer at Sloan-Kettering Institute in New York. His research was stymied by big tobacco, office politics, and comparisons with bench science. Tobacco companies pressured Sloan-Kettering director Frank Horsfall financially. They asked him to stop Wynder's research and his anti-tobacco press announcements. Wynder's research was saved by world famous virologist Dr. Peyton Rous. Rous cautioned Horsfall against interfering with science. Inside and outside of Sloan-Kettering, Wynder's frequent requests for press interviews aroused professional jealousy. He was the target of criticism for the quality of his work and his personal life as a bachelor.

In 1960, Clarence Cook Little, an expert in tumors in mice, held a public debate with Wynder. Little argued that cancer was caused by viruses, and Wynder's research simply showed a correlation between smoking and lung cancer, not that smoking caused lung cancer. By the standards of bench science, Little was correct. To prove that smoking caused lung cancer, Wynder would have to take a group of healthy nonsmokers, randomly assign them to smoking or nonsmoking groups and then follow them over a period of time to see if lung cancer developed. Of course, such a study would be highly unethical. Retrospective studies (comparing past smoking history with disease) or quasi-experimental studies (using nonrandomized groups) were scientifically weak but ethical. Wynder's hands were tied by the limitations of translational research. Wynder recruited Dietrich Hoffmann from the Max Planck Institute of Biochemistry in Munich, Germany. The researchers used animal testing to discover the carcinogenic ingredients in tobacco tar, benzo(a)pyrene, and polynuclear aromatic hydrocarbons. Although tobacco companies dismissed the science, few experts dared disagree with the idea that smoking causes cancer. In 1969, the new director of Sloan-Kettering admonished Wynder. He claimed that Wynder's research was irresponsible, and all future publications had to be reviewed and cleared by the director's office (Doll, 1999). Again, Rous came to Wynder's defense. The reprieve was only temporary. Wynder's research budget was cut.

In Framingham, Massachusetts, 5,209 men and women were participating in a large cohort study investigating lifestyle and cardiovascular disease. With motivation from the Framingham Heart Study and the philosophy that "common diseases have common causes," Wynder established the American Health Foundation (AHF) as a research institute (Stellman, 2006, p. 14). Knowing that the federal government would provide limited support for nontraditional, interdisciplinary, translational research, Wynder developed funding partnerships with the American Cancer Society, Eastman Kodak Co., Northwestern Mutual Life Insurance Co., Time, Inc., and several other large benefactors. The AHF researchers studied novel topics, such as saccharin and bladder cancer; cell phones and brain cancer; low fat diet and low incidence of breast cancer in Japan; and rye bread and low incidence of intestinal cancer in Finland. The organization recruited participants for the Multiple Risk Factor Intervention Trial (MRFIT, pronounced Mr. Fit). Male participants of MRFIT received counseling on cigarette smoking, diet, and health care in the community. Wynder was very active in prevention medicine, setting public policies against smoking, and advocating for comprehensive school health education programs. In 1972, he started *Preventive Medicine,* the peer-reviewed, quality research journal.

Dr. Ernst L. Wynder died on July 14, 1999, at the age of 77. Throughout his lifetime, he made landmark discoveries in cancer research. He noticed characteristics and patterns among patients that suggested common causal factors and developed the best possible ways to study the issue and test his hypotheses. Colleagues describe Wynder as someone who was always one step ahead, able to predict the next area of research. However, Wynder was not content with novel discoveries. He was very clear in his responsibility as a doctor and a scientist. He worked to get the message out that smoking causes cancer. He stood solidly against public opinion, big business, and ivory tower politics to ensure that the public understood the real price of cigarette smoking. Even as the field of oncology evolved, Wynder continued to look for ways to enhance human health.

Sally Kuykendall

See also: Addictions; Birth Defects; Cancer; Causality; Epidemiology; Men's Health; Surgeon General; Truth Campaign, The; *Controversies in Public Health:* Controversy 2; Controversy 4

Further Reading

Adler, I. A. (1912). *Primary malignant growths of the lung and bronchi.* New York: Longmans, Green and Company. Retrieved from https://archive.org/details/primarymalignant00adle.

Doll, R. (1999, December). Ernst Wynder, 1923–1999. *American Journal of Public Health,* 89(12), 1798–1799.

Doll, R., & Hill, A. B. (1950). Smoking and carcinoma of the lung. *British Medical Journal,* 2(4682), 739.

Doll, R., & Hill, A. B. (1954). The mortality of doctors in relation to their smoking habits. *British Medical Journal,* 1(4877), 1451.

Johnson, J. A. (1998). Ernst Wynder, M.D., president, American Health Foundation. *Journal of Healthcare Management,* 43(2), 107.

Proctor, R. N. (1996). The anti-tobacco campaign of the Nazis: A little known aspect of public health in Germany, 1933–45. *British Medical Journal, 313*(7070), 1450–1453.

Roffo, A. H. (2006). The carcinogenic effects of tobacco. *Bulletin of the World Health Organization, 84*(6), 500–502.

Spencer, S. M. (1950). Can we check the rising toll of lung cancer? *Saturday Evening Post, 222*(41), 36–136.

Stellman, S. D. (2006). Ernst Wynder: A remembrance. *Preventive Medicine: An International Journal Devoted to Practice and Theory, 43*(4), 239–245. doi:10.1016/j.ypmed.2006.08.007

Weinberg, R. (1999). Ernst Ludwig Wynder, 1922–99. *Nature, 401*(6752), 442.

Wynder, E. L. (1959). Laboratory contributions to the tobacco-cancer problem. *British Medical Journal, 1*(5118), 317.

Wynder, E. L., & Graham, E. A. (1950). Tobacco smoking as a possible etiologic factor in bronchogenic carcinoma. *Journal of the American Medical Association, 143*(4), 329–336.

Z

ZOMBIE PREPAREDNESS

In 2011, the Centers for Disease Control and Prevention (CDC) surprised pop culture fans by publishing a blog entitled *Preparedness 101: Zombie Apocalypse*. What began as a tongue-in-cheek campaign to educate the public on emergency preparedness has become one of the CDC's most amusing and popular public health programs. The blog post uses the example of a zombie apocalypse to expound on the CDC's preparedness strategies and outline specific ways readers could prepare for an emergency. The website provides a list of items to keep available in case of natural, man-made, or supernatural disasters and offers suggestions for a personalized safety plan.

The idea of the dead returning to life traces back to the earliest civilizations. In the *Epic of Gilgamesh*, King Gilgamesh searches for the secret to eternal life in hope of bringing his friend Enkidu back to life. The word "zombie" derives from the West African words *nzambi* (god) and *zumbi* (fetish). The term was brought to Haiti and the new world by enslaved Africans and would have embodied the spirit of enslaved people as lifeless, apathetic, emaciated corpse-like figures. According to Haitain folklore, the dead are reanimated by a voodoo god. Those who please the god are taken to heaven while others are enslaved for eternity. Over time, horror genre adopted the image of the zombie as mindless and soulless and reanimated by magic, virus, or radiation. George Romero's 1968 hit movie *Night of the Living Dead* is credited with introducing zombies into pop culture. In 2011, Dr. Stephen Schlozman, Harvard medical school physician and professor, appeared on a late night weekend radio show mimicking the famous H. G. Wells *War of the Worlds* radio show dramatic adaptation. Schlozman described the transmission and physiology of the (fictional) disease ataxic neurodegenerative satiety deficiency syndrome (ANSD). Public reaction was stunning. Some people continued the hoax by submitting medical questions on how to prevent zombie infection. Over 1,000 people complained to the network about the "irresponsible" journalism. The F.C.C. received more than 600 letters of complaint, and Schlozman reports that Harvard administrators were not amused by the hoax. One complainant expressed concerns that the doctor violated the Hippocratic Oath. Regardless of what one thinks of Schlozman's interview, it is clear that people are fascinated by outlandish stories.

In 2011, Ali S. Kahn created a blog for the CDC that applies the basic concepts of public health response and emergency preparedness to a zombie apocalypse.

Zombie Preparedness guidelines describe essential supplies needed to survive man-made, natural, or supernatural disasters. (Centers for Disease Control and Prevention)

The blog provides a comprehensive list for items necessary for a public health emergency:

- Water
- Medications and health supplies
- Food
- Tools
- Cleaning and personal care items
- Safety supplies
- Clothing
- Copies of important documents
- Electronics

Specific sections describe additional supplies for children and pets. The CDC also published a digital graphic novella, detailing the events of a zombie outbreak, available as a PDF on the CDC's website. In case of an emergency, the CDC would conduct an investigation, provide technical assistance, consult with local authorities, manage cases, and control spread. Disease surveillance, investigation, and control are part of the typical CDC responsibilities with any critical disease outbreak or public health emergency. What makes the zombie preparedness campaign so special is the public's response. Normally, people don't get too excited over preparing for a hurricane, tornado, or snowstorm. A zombie apocalypse draws people's attention. "Lisa" commented "That is soooooo awesome!!!! Thanks, CDC." Shelabella writes:

> I think this is an excellent campaign for the CDC to breathe life back into disaster preparedness. I love the zombie theme & think it's timely, unique, and has plenty of shock factor to make it memorable and highly effective.
>
> The levity behind this is something that will interest my teenage boys . . . something that is so hard to do in this day and age (unless you're a pixel, perhaps). Anyway, I really like this campaign, because it presents a disaster in a manner that I can actually entice my family into discussion; and it will provide some assistance for any potential disaster as well. Awesome job!

Solega of the Zombie Outbreak Response Team (ZORT) of Helena, MT, responds to the conversation of adding a weapon to the emergency response kit:

> I notice quite a few people posting about the usefulness of a baseball bat in the event of a zombie apocalypse. If you read the Zombie Survival Guide, it explains with gruesome detail exactly what happens to the guy with the baseball bat. It wasn't pretty and now there's a zombie with a baseball bat. In all seriousness, though, I think the biggest reason that weapons weren't addressed in this particular post was largely because it's designed to be an all encompassing emergency plan, not JUST for zombies. You're not going to need a shotgun in a hurricane. You specifically. Yea, you, I see you reading this post. You definitely don't need a shotgun. Ever.

Some comments complain about the public resources used to develop and maintain the website. One reader notes that garnering this amount of interest and attention would be very expensive and saves significant advertising dollars.

The CDC's Zombie Preparedness campaign highlights how health educators strive to create imaginative and informative programs to prevent health crises and to promote well-being. As public health educators compete with big businesses for public attention, campaigns such as the Zombie Preparedness campaign will become a model for other public health programs.

Mark Black

See also: Bioterrorism; Centers for Disease Control and Prevention; Emergency Preparedness and Response; Epidemic; Health Communication; Influenza; Pandemic; State, Local, and Territorial Health Departments

Further Reading

Centers for Disease Control and Prevention. *Zombie preparedness.* Retrieved from https://www.cdc.gov/phpr/zombies.htm.

Preparedness 101: Zombie pandemic. Retrieved from https://www.cdc.gov/phpr/zombies_novella.htm.

Schlozman, S. (2013). The Harvard doctor who accidentally unleashed a zombie invasion. *The New York Times.* Retrieved from http://www.nytimes.com/2013/10/27/magazine/the-harvard-doctor-who-accidentally-unleashed-a-zombie-invasion.html.

Controversies in Public Health

CONTROVERSY 1: SHOULD DRUG PRICES BE REGULATED IN THE UNITED STATES?

Introduction

In 2015, U.S. pharmaceutical companies spent over $58 billion on drug discovery, research, and development (R&D). To protect pharmaceutical industry investment, the federal government awards exclusive rights of marketing the drug for a period of up to seven years. Drug patents allow the company time to recover the cost of R&D from the consumer. However, recent cases of extraordinarily high price increases well after product development raise concerns of price gouging by pharmaceutical companies. A study published in the *Journal of the American Medical Association* compared the cost of R&D to drug prices and concluded, "Although prices are often justified by the high cost of drug development, there is no evidence of an association between research and development costs and prices; rather, prescription drugs are priced in the United States primarily on the basis of what the market will bear" (Kesselheim, Avorn, & Sarpatwari, 2016). People with chronic or acute illnesses are highly vulnerable to price gouging. Prescription medications account for up to 17 percent of all health care costs. A significant portion of Medicare and Medicaid expenses are prescription medications. To protect consumers and government-funded health care programs, many other countries regulate drug prices. The United States is one of the only nations that does not regulate prices. This raises the question of whether drug prices should be regulated in the United States.

The Tufts Center for the Study of Drug Development estimates that pharmaceutical R&D can cost up to $2.6 billion per drug. Yet, recent cases suggest that development does not always justify price. In 2001, Questcor purchased the rights to Acthar Gel, an adrenocorticotrophic hormone analogue used to treat infantile spasms, systemic lupus erythematosus, and multiple sclerosis in relapse. The drug was developed by researchers at the Mayo Clinic in 1950. Questcor increased the price from $40 to $23,000. In 2015, Valeant acquired rights to the drug Isuprel, a drug used to support blood pressure in patients with heart problems. Valeant raised the price from $440 per vial to $2,700 per vial. The explanation given for the increase was to maximize shareholder profit. Hospitals had to remove the life-saving drug from crash carts because they could no longer afford it. Before Turing Pharmaceuticals bought the rights to Daraprim, a drug used to treat parasitic infections among people with immunosuppression due to AIDS or cancer, the drug cost $13.50 per pill. Turing increased the price 5,000 percent to $750 per pill. In 2016, Mylan Pharmaceuticals increased the cost of EpiPen from $57 (in 2007) to over $500. Unexplainable price increases are particularly common with drugs used to treat rare diseases. When Marathon Pharmaceuticals received approval to sell deflazacort, a drug to alleviate the symptoms of Duchenne muscular dystrophy, the drug price increased from $1,200 per year to $89,000 per year. Not all increases are so egregious. Pfizer and Allergan employed a different strategy by raising the price of almost all of their drugs by 10 percent. Pharmaceutical companies argue that price increases are absorbed by insurance companies and patients rarely have to pay the actual cost of the drug.

Some experts argue that the culprit behind higher drug prices is a business model that values profit over people. Money clouds one's ability to discriminate between right and wrong. In short, money corrupts ethics. The case of Johnson and Johnson and Massachusetts General Hospital and Harvard University professor Dr. Joseph Beiderman demonstrates the dangers of applying the business model to pharmaceutical research and marketing. In 2002, Johnson and Johnson donated $700,000 to Biederman's Center for the Study of Pediatric Psychopathology. The highly regarded child psychologist performed a research study comparing Johnson and Johnson's drug Risperdal to placebo. The study found no difference in treatment effectiveness. Johnson and Johnson executive Dr. Gahan Padina substituted the original report with a new report indicating that Risperdal was significantly better than placebo. Beiderman agreed to "support the safety and effectiveness of risperidone [Risperdal]." Later investigation by Congress revealed that Beiderman failed to report $1.4 million in consulting fees from Johnson and Johnson (Gardner, 2008). The Alliance for Human Research Protection explains:

> The real scandal perpetrated by Biederman has nothing to do with his consulting fee shenanigans and everything to do with the real life (and death) consequences . . . Many remember Rebecca Riley, the Hull, MA, toddler whose death in 2004 made headlines. But she is merely the tip of the iceberg. According to the New York Times from 1993 through 2008, 1,207 children who were given Risperdal suffered serious problems, including 31 who died. Among the deaths was a nine-year-old who suffered a fatal stroke 12 days after starting therapy with Risperdal. (Azerrad, 2011)

The case shows that higher drug prices do not necessarily mean better research or better health care. In fact, higher drug prices mean that people on limited incomes will look for ways to reduce costs. Fourteen percent of Americans skip doses, take less medicine than prescribed, or delay filling prescriptions in order to reduce drug costs (CDC, n.d.).

Drug patents protect the company's intellectual property. By providing exclusive rights to manufacturing and marketing, drug companies are able to recoup the costs of R&D from consumers. Drug companies also employ strategies of *evergreening* or *hard switching* to extend market exclusivity. Evergreening is patenting a slightly different version of the medicine by making minor, insignificant changes to the drug. Hard switching is removing a drug that is about to go generic and replacing it with a higher priced product. Orphan drugs present a special challenge to drug companies and therefore consumers. Orphan diseases are diseases that are not related to other, more common diseases and affect less than 200,000 Americans. To encourage R&D into the treatment of orphan diseases, the federal government passed the Orphan Drug Act of 1983. The law offers special incentives, tax breaks, and exclusive rights to market in exchange for the development and manufacture of orphan drugs. Despite additional incentives, the cost of orphan drugs is extraordinarily high. The average annual cost of a nonorphan drug is $27,756 per patient. The average cost of an orphan drug is $140,443 per patient.

Discovering and developing new drugs is an expensive business, driven by high patient demand and aggressive market competition. Unfortunately, high prices can make drugs unaffordable and inaccessible to many people who need the medicine to survive. Furthermore, the federal government may be paying twice for the drug, the first time through grants or subsidies for R&D and a second time through publicly funded health care services. Salini Iniganti and Alex Black debate whether drug prices should be regulated in the United States.

Sally Kuykendall

Further Reading

Azerrad, J. (2011). *The real Beiderman scandal.* Alliance for Human Research Protection. Retrieved from http://ahrp.org/the-real-biederman-scandal.

CDC. (n.d.). *Percentage of U.S. adults not taking medication as prescribed to reduce prescription drug costs in 2013, by age group.* In Statista—The Statistics Portal. Retrieved July 19, 2017, from https://www-statista-com.ezproxy.sju.edu/statistics/397724/adults-not-taking-medication-as-prescribed-to-lower-prescription-drug-costs-by-age.

Daniel, H. (2016). Stemming the escalating cost of prescription drugs: A position paper of the American College of Physicians. *Annals of Internal Medicine, 165*(1), 50–52. doi:10.7326/M15-2768. Retrieved from http://annals.org/aim/article/2506848/stemming-escalating-cost-prescription-drugs-position-paper-american-college-physicians.

Gardner, H. (2008, November 25). In documents, ties between child psychiatry center and drug maker. *The New York Times,* p. 22.

Kesselheim, A. S., Avorn, J., & Sarpatwari, A. (2016). The high cost of prescription drugs in the United States: Origins and prospects for reform. *Journal of the American Medical Association, 316*(8), 858. doi:10.1001/jama.2016.11237

PhRMA. (n.d.). *Spending of the U.S. pharmaceutical industry on research and development at home and abroad from 1990 to 2015 (in million U.S. dollars).* In Statista—The Statistics Portal. Retrieved July 19, 2017, from https://www-statista-com.ezproxy.sju.edu/statistics/265090/us-pharmaceutical-industry-spending-on-research-and-development.

Smith, A. G. (2016). Price gouging and the dangerous new breed of pharma companies. *Harvard Business Review Digital Articles,* 2.

Yes, Drug Prices Should Be Regulated by the Government

The United States spends more per capita on health care than any other developed nation. National spending on health care exceeded $10,000 per person in 2016. In comparison, Canada's national health care spending was estimated to be $4,608 per person, and the United Kingdom's spending was only $4,003 per person in 2015 (OECD, 2015). One of the major factors that is increasing U.S. health care spending is the rising cost of prescription drugs. It is estimated that prescription drug spending will increase by 4 to 7 percent through 2021, creating a $580 billion to $610 billion market (Aitken et al., 2016). In 2013, per capita spending on prescription drugs was $858 compared with an average of $400 for 19 other industrialized nations (Kesselheim, Avorn, & Sarpatwari, 2016). Part of the reason that consumers in the United States pay a much higher price for their drugs is because pharmaceutical companies are free to establish their own prices without regulation.

American consumers have no bargaining power when it comes to prescription drugs. There is no single entity that can bargain on behalf of consumers due to the complexity of the health care system with its various insurers, employers, and federal/state programs. All of these different entities negotiate their own contracts and drug prices for their individual consumers. Due to a lack of regulation in pricing, Americans pay anywhere from two to six times more than the rest of the world for brand-name prescription drugs according to the International Federation of Health Plans. In other countries with national health care systems, the government is the main purchaser of prescription drugs. As such, they are able to effectively negotiate with drug companies to get the lowest drug prices possible for consumers.

Despite being one of the largest providers of health care in the United States, Medicare cannot negotiate with pharmaceutical companies. In 2003, Congress expanded the program to include Part D prescription drug coverage but prohibited Medicare, the largest single-payer health care system in the United States, from setting drug prices. In the same expansion, Congress required eligible Medicare Part D plans to cover all drugs in certain disease categories (e.g. cancer, depression). This left the determination of drug prices under these categories at the discretion of the pharmaceutical manufacturing companies, who are free to establish whatever price that they believe the market will bear. If Medicare were able to negotiate with pharmaceutical companies directly, the price of drugs for everyone could be driven down. Since this is not the case, American consumers are left without much bargaining power and much higher drug prices.

Americans also deal with the effects of direct-to-consumer marking of prescription drugs. Unlike most Western nations, the U.S. has not banned the direct advertising of pharmaceuticals to consumers. Many suggest that this type of marketing encourages consumers to take medications unnecessarily, or choose more expensive brand-name drugs. When drugs that are newly on the market are advertised to consumers, the purchase and use of those drugs accelerate despite unknown long-term outcomes for the drug (Lyles, 2002). Due to the lack of regulation in advertising, many drug commercials contain emotional testimonials but lack actual scientific data (Woloshin, Schwartz, Tremmel, & Welch, 2001). In addition to potentially misleading drug consumers, the added costs of production for advertising (e.g, television commercials, magazines, billboards) are ultimately passed on to the consumer.

At this time, the government is trying to find a balance between (1) giving pharmaceutical companies financial incentives to innovate and produce breakthrough drugs and (2) keeping drug prices as low as possible. The current system for incentivizing drug research involves patents that cover an innovative drug for approximately 20 years. In addition to patents, the Food and Drug Administration (FDA) can grant temporarily market exclusivity rights, which would ensure that the FDA would not approve a generic version of a particular drug for a set amount of time. Together, the patents and market exclusivity rights guarantee that new, brand-name drugs get an average of 13 years of sales before a generic, more affordable, alternative medication enters the market (Grabowski, Long, & Mortimer, 2014). Once a generic drug is able to be introduced to the drug market, there is an increase in competition and a decrease in costs for both the brand-name and generic versions of the drug.

Unfortunately, many people do not have the ability to wait for an affordable generic to come to market when they are dealing with a life-threatening illness, and they cannot afford what is available. According to a survey by *Consumer Reports*, many respondents took "potentially dangerous" steps due to high drug costs: not filling a prescription (17 percent), skipping a scheduled dose (14 percent), or taking an expired medication (14 percent). The survey also found that 19 percent of respondents spent less on groceries, and 15 percent postponed paying other bills so they could afford their prescription drugs (Consumer Reports, 2014).

Unchecked by the government, pharmaceutical companies are making large profits at the expense of Americans' health and well-being. Drug companies attempt to justify the high prices they set by arguing that they need to offset the high costs of research and development (R&D). However, drug companies spend much more on marketing their drugs to consumers than they spend on R&D. For example, Johnson and Johnson spent $17.5 billion on sales and marketing, but spent a mere $8.2 billion on R&D while making $71.3 billion in revenue in 2016. Furthermore, the premiums that pharmaceutical companies earn from charging substantially higher prices for their medications in the United States compared to other Western countries generate substantially more than they spend globally on their R&D (Yu, Helms, & Bach, 2017).

Without government regulation of drug prices, an increasing number of Americans will be unable to access the medications that they need to maintain their quality of life. This will lead to poorer health outcomes and higher health care costs. Higher spending on prescriptions drugs is not only a burden for those who are sick or needing medication. These costs are ultimately passed on to everyone who has health coverage in the form of premiums, deductibles, and other forms of cost sharing. Furthermore, drug spending increases costs for taxpayer-funded programs like Medicare and Medicaid, resulting in higher taxes and cuts to public funding. There needs to be some form of government regulation of drug prices so that the financial and physical health and well-being of Americans is not at the mercy of pharmaceutical companies' bottom line.

Salini Inaganti

Further Reading

Aitken, M., Kleinrock, M., Pennente, K., Lyle, J., Nass, D., & Caskey, L. (2016). Medicines use and spending in the US: A review of 2015 and outlook to 2020. Parsippany, NJ: IMS Institute for Healthcare Informatics.

Grabowski, H., Long, G., & Mortimer, R. (2014). Recent trends in brand-name and generic drug competition. *Journal of Medical Economics*, *17*(3), 207–214.

Kesselheim, A. S., Avorn, J., & Sarpatwari, A. (2016). The high cost of prescription drugs in the United States: Origins and prospects for reform. *Journal of the American Medical Association*, *316*(8), 858–871. Retrieved from http://doi.org/10.1001/jama.2016.11237.

Lyles, A. (2002). Direct marketing of pharmaceuticals to consumers. *Annual Review of Public Health*, *23*(1), 73–91.

OECD. (2015). *Health at a glance 2015*. OECD Publishing. Retrieved from http://doi.org/10.1787/health_glance-2015-en.

Some Americans take risks with needed drugs due to high costs. (2014). *Consumer Reports*. Retrieved from http://www.consumerreports.org/cro/2014/09/some-americans-take-risks-with-needed-drugs-due-to-high-costs/index.htm.

Woloshin, S., Schwartz, L. M., Tremmel, J., & Welch, H. G. (2001). Direct-to-consumer advertisements for prescription drugs: What are Americans being sold? *The Lancet*, *358*(9288), 1141–1146.

Yu, N., Helms, Z., & Bach, P. (2017). R&D costs for pharmaceutical companies do not explain elevated US drug prices. *Health Affairs*. Retrieved from http://www.healthaffairs.org/do/10.1377/hblog20170307.059036/full/.

No, Drug Prices Should Not Be Regulated by the Government

The federal government should not regulate drug prices. In order to develop a drug, pharmaceutical companies must discover, develop, manufacture, and market products. The costs of these processes are much higher than other consumer products. After discovering a drug, the company has exclusive rights to market. In many cases, consumers do not actually pay the listed drug price. Many people are covered by insurance or health maintenance organizations who barter for discounted drug prices. Members pay copay or reduced price, not the full price of the drug. Once the drug goes off patent or exclusive rights to market, it can be manufactured by a generic drug company. The generic company does not have to pay for research and development (R&D). Generic drugs actually drive up prices. Customers have no loyalty to the original manufacturer. Consumers will opt for less expensive generic brands. The pharmaceutical industry is a high-risk business with responsibility to shareholders. If shareholders do not benefit from their financial investment, they will find other businesses to invest in. Restricting drug prices would limit future R&D and impair the discovery of new pharmaceutical treatments.

Pharmaceutical R&D is a risky investment. Many potential formulations fail either in the laboratory or when tested in humans. Clinical trials for novel drugs are large, complex operations that follow strict study protocols. Paid study participants are closely monitored by highly trained medical professionals and scientists using advanced medical technology. In order to obtain Food and Drug Administration (FDA) approval, the pharmaceutical company must test the formulation, dosages, and regimens and monitor adverse effects and long-term consequences. The process of discovering a new drug begins with researching the basic physiological process causing the disease. Potential treatments are selected by either studying current therapies or by random selection of biological products. The new formula may be extracted from plants, minerals, or animals or may be artificially synthesized. Variations of the compound of interest are tested through computer models, on cells or tissues, or on animals to determine pharmacologic activity, therapeutic value, and potentially harmful effects. The preferred compound is then formulated into a pill, capsule, ointment, liquid, spray, or patch. Chemists, pharmacists, doctors, and other scientists determine and test possible dosages and forms of administration. Other compounds may be added to delay absorption or to stabilize the compound to prevent it from deteriorating too quickly. Before the drug is tested in humans, it must undergo toxicology testing on animals, cells, or tissues. When the drug is considered safe for human consumption, the pharmaceutical company files an Investigational New Drug (IND) Application. The IND describes all of the results of the research to date and provides a detailed plan for testing the drug in humans. Unless the FDA decides to stop the clinical evaluation, drugs are automatically approved for the next stages of testing. Phase I clinical evaluations investigate how the healthy body absorbs, metabolizes, and excretes different amounts of the drug. Phase II studies investigate effectiveness and adverse effects in the healthy body. Phase III studies investigate safety and effectiveness among the intended consumer, hospital patients, or outpatients. After Phase III studies, the pharmaceutical company must determine the most effective way to manufacture large batches of the drug without altering the formulation. The product may be tested again in bioavailability studies to ensure that the manufactured product matches the original compound. The pharmaceutical company will then file a New Drug Application (NDA) with the FDA. The NDA summarizes all of the research from laboratory and clinical testing. After the drug is approved for marketing, the pharmaceutical company will continue to study the long-term effects of the drug or effects of the drug in special populations such as children or pregnant women. Bringing one new drug to market is a 10- to 12-year process costing approximately $2.6 billion (Tufts Center for the Study of Drug Development, 2014). Pharmaceutical R&D costs more than other industries. In 2009, the pharmaceutical industry spent $32,610 million on R&D while medical technology companies spent $9,047 million (Research!America, n.d.). The good news is that this level of expenditure allows pharmaceutical companies to develop over 1,000 new drugs each year, advancing treatments for cancer, heart disease, and other causes of death and disability. Price control would restrict new drug development.

A second factor that drives up drug prices is the pressure to recoup expenses before exclusive rights to market end. Pharmaceutical companies can patent a novel drug for 14 years from the NDA approval date. After that time, the drug may be manufactured and sold in generic form. Generic drugs are drugs that are chemically the same as the branded drug but less expensive because the generic company does not have to pay for R&D. Generic drugs are very attractive to consumers paying out of pocket, insurance companies, and pharmacy benefit programs. With limited time before a drug goes off patent, pharmaceutical companies are under pressure to market the drug and recoup expenses. In 1997, the FDA permitted pharmaceutical companies to advertise directly to consumers. Direct-to-consumer marketing further drives up costs. In 2016, the pharmaceutical industry spent $23,333.95 million on advertising (Schonfeld & Associates, n.d.). Among the top 10 pharmaceutical companies, marketing accounts for 17.9 percent (Roche) to 28.4 percent (AstraZeneca) of sales (BBC, n.d.). In addition to consumer marketing, pharmaceutical companies must educate prescribing physicians. One-on-one physician education, journal publications, and conference presentations add to drug cost.

A third factor that increases drug prices is consumer demand. Drugs improve quality of life and keep people in the workforce and functioning in communities. The average person over age 65 fills 9 to 12 prescriptions per year (Burton, 1998). Half of all drug expenditures are by people with chronic disease. As baby boomers age, demand for pharmaceuticals increase. More people are taking drugs for longer periods of time, and managed care has made prescription drugs more affordable. Drugs also offer an affordable alternative to other treatments. For example, pharmaceutical treatment for hepatitis C is less expensive than liver transplant surgery. Health insurance increases demand by making drugs more affordable. Insurance companies develop lists of drug formularies, medications that have been shown to be effective in treating a disease and medications that are cost effective. Pharmaceutical companies give large discounts to pharmacy benefit plans in order to ensure that their drug is listed on the formulary. Consumers on pharmacy benefit plans only pay the copay. Patients and insurance companies rarely pay the list price of a drug.

There are other solutions to the rising cost of pharmaceutical products other than government price regulation. Pharmaceutical companies take a major risk in developing new drugs. To minimize risk, the government could subsidize pharmaceutical research. Alternatively, allowing pharmaceutical companies longer periods of time to recoup R&D costs or requiring insurance companies to pay what the drug is worth to develop and market are a few ways to reduce price while still ensuring that pharmaceutical companies produce novel drugs to treat disease.

Alex Black

Further Reading

BBC. (n.d.). *Top pharmaceutical companies' expenditure on marketing as a percentage of sales in 2013.* In Statista—The Statistics Portal. Retrieved August 7, 2017, from https://www-statista-com.ezproxy.sju.edu/statistics/271784/marketing-expenditure-of-pharmaceutical-companies-in-2009.

Burton, T. M. (1998, November 16). Hard to swallow: America's soaring drug costs, *Wall Street Journal,* p. A1.

Consumer Reports. (2014). Some Americans take risks with needed drugs due to high costs but they remain leery of low-cost generics, Consumer Reports poll finds. Retrieved from https://www.consumerreports.org/cro/2014/09/some-americans-take-risks-with-needed-drugs-due-to-high-costs/index.htm.

Paul, D. P., III, Chandra, A., & Lambrinos, F. (2006). Global pharmaceutical costs: Evaluating the American approach. *Journal of Medical Marketing,* 6(1), 38–48.

Pharmaceutical R&D [microform]: Costs, risks, and rewards. (1993). Washington, DC: Office of Technology Assessment, Congress of the U.S. For sale by the U.S. Government Printing Office, Superintendent of Documents.

Research!America. (n.d.). *Expenditure on research and development in U.S. health care 2009 by industry (in million U.S. dollars).* In Statista—The Statistics Portal. Retrieved August 7, 2017, from https://www-statista-com.ezproxy.sju.edu/statistics/272020/research-and-development-expenditure-by-health-care-industry.

Schonfeld & Associates. (n.d.). *Advertising spending in the pharmaceutical preparations industry in the United States from 2010 to 2017 (in million U.S. dollars).* In Statista—The Statistics Portal. Retrieved August 7, 2017, from https://www-statista-com.ezproxy.sju.edu/statistics/470460/pharmaceutical-preparations-industry-ad-spend-usa.

Sloan, F. A., & Hsieh, C. (2007). *Pharmaceutical innovation: Incentives, competition, and cost-benefit analysis in international perspective.* Cambridge, UK; New York: Cambridge University Press.

Statista Survey. (n.d.). *How high do you think the pressure on physicians is from the pharma industry to prescribe certain drugs?* In Statista—The Statistics Portal. Retrieved August 7, 2017, from https://www-statista-com.ezproxy.sju.edu/statistics/694566/us-adults-that-believe-physicians-are-under-pressure-from-pharma.

Tufts Center for the Study of Drug Development. (2014). *Cost to develop and win marketing approval for a new drug is $2.6 billion.* Retrieved from http://csdd.tufts.edu/news/complete_story/pr_tufts_csdd_2014_cost_study.

CONTROVERSY 2: SHOULD THE FEDERAL GOVERNMENT RESTRICT ADVERTISING OF PRODUCTS THAT HAVE AN IMPACT ON PUBLIC HEALTH?

Introduction

The history of cigarette advertising, fast food advertising, and prescription drug marketing shows how business competition for consumer dollars presents challenges for public health and raises questions regarding the federal government's role and responsibility in policing advertising of products that impact public health. Tensions between product marketing, public health, and personal responsibility garnered popular interest with the tobacco industry Master Settlement Agreement. The multibillion dollar lawsuit uncovered incriminating internal documents from big tobacco companies. Despite an earlier agreement that restricted marketing to young people, tobacco companies were intentionally targeting 14- to 18-year-olds with cigarette advertising. Middle-aged and older smokers were dying, and cigarette makers needed new customers. Young smokers promised high returns on advertising expenditures. Using brand imprinting, tobacco companies hoped to establish a new generation of smokers with the public health programs of Medicare and Medicaid picking up the bill.

The classic example of the conflict between advertising and public health is Joe Camel, the cartoon character developed by the marketing team of R. J. Reynolds Tobacco (RJR-T). For many decades, cigarettes were advertised as health enhancing. Doctors, nurses, and dentists endorsed cigarettes as an effective treatment for relieving tension, asthma, hay fever, or bronchial irritation. Popular sports figures pronounced that smoking helped to clear the throat, improving athletic performance. Movie and radio stars presented smoking as fashionable, dignified, and sexually attractive. When studies showed that smoking was actually harmful to health, tobacco companies entered a voluntary agreement to self-regulate marketing. The Cigarette Advertising Code of 1964 banned advertising to young people and prohibited false health claims. By the early 1970s, RJR-T executives were looking for ways to compete with Marlboro and Winston cigarettes. Secret planning documents reported that young people offered the greatest opportunity for long-term cigarette sales growth:

> The brands which these beginning smokers accept and use will become the dominant brands in future years. Evidence is now available to indicate that the 14 to 18 year old group is an increasing segment of the smoking population. RJR-T must soon establish a successful new brand in this market if our position in the industry is to be maintained over the long term. (R. J. Reynolds Research Department, 1976)

One executive suggested using a comic strip–type character, and a plan was developed "to contemporize the Brand [Camel cigarettes] thus making it more relevant and appealing." The "Heroic Camel Mascot" Joe Camel was developed to "generate excitement, awareness and appeal for the Brand" (Macfarlane, 1988). With a development cost of $4,500 and advertising budget of $5.6 million, Joe Camel was rolled out in 1988. Within three years, nearly as many children recognized Joe Camel as recognized Mickey Mouse. The campaign to brand imprint was extremely successful. Among a sample of six-year-old preschool children, 91 percent recognized the mascot's association with cigarettes (Fischer et al., 1991). Before the Joe Camel campaign, teenage smokers accounted for $6 million of Camel cigarette sales. By 1992, teenage smokers accounted for $476 million of Camel cigarette sales. With smoking-related medical expenditures reaching $50 billion per year, Medicare and Medicaid bore most of the brunt of the cost. State governments successfully sued the tobacco industry and were awarded complex settlement payments through the Master Settlement Agreement. The agreement strictly prohibits tobacco advertising to youth.

The fast food industry faced similar accusations of advertising unhealthy products. In 2003, two youth sued McDonald's alleging that eating McDonald's fast food made them overweight. The plaintiffs lost the lawsuit. However, their concerns were examined through the film *Super Size Me* (2004). The documentary follows director and producer Morgan Spurlock over a 30-day period in which he only eats at McDonald's restaurants and investigates the fast food industry. The film points out that in 2001 McDonald's spent $1.4 billion on worldwide advertising, Pepsi spent over one billion dollars, and Hershey Foods spent $200 million. The highest annual budget for the public health program, Five-a-Day, was $2 million, one one-hundredth of Hershey Foods. In 2004, Congress passed H. R. 339 Personal Responsibility in Food Consumption Act, making it illegal to sue any food manufacturer or business on the grounds of causing obesity or obesity-related diseases. Nevertheless, the film had an impact. Within six weeks, McDonald's started offering healthier food items and stopped supersized servings.

In 1998, Purdue Pharma distributed 15,000 copies of a video advertising OxyContin. Intended for use as patient education in the doctors' waiting rooms, the video advertised that opioids do not have serious side effects and should be prescribed more often. Within a year, the number of opioid prescriptions increased by 11 million. By 2010, doctors wrote enough prescriptions to medicate every adult in the United States for one month. Today, over 4 million people abuse pain killers. The estimated cost of prescription drug abuse in the United States in 2006 was $53.4 billion, including $42 billion in lost productivity (Hansen, Oster, Edelsberg, Woody, & Sullivan, 2011).

The United States believes in a free market economy where the federal government does not interfere with business in any way. Toward this end, businesses spend $183 billion each year on product advertising. In 2015, McDonald's spent $802.1 billion on advertising, cigarette companies spent $763.1 million, and Perdue Pharma spent $3.9 million. In the same year, the Centers for Disease Prevention and Control were allocated $1.1 billion for chronic disease prevention and health promotion, a decrease of $110 million from 2014.

In the following arguments, Dr. Shayan Waseh and A. J. Smuskiewicz explore the issues of federal government restrictions on advertising for two industries that impact public health: advertising for the tobacco industry and pharmaceutical advertising.

Sally Kuykendall

Further Reading

Campaign for Tobacco-Free Kids. (2013). *Camel cigarettes: A long history of targeting kids.* Retrieved from https://www.tobaccofreekids.org/microsites/camel/Camel_History.pdf.

Fischer, P. M., Schwartz, M. P., Richards, J. W., Goldstein, A. O., & Rojas, T. H. (1991). Brand logo recognition by children aged 3 to 6 years. *Journal of the American Medical Association, 266*(22), 3145.

Hansen, R. N., Oster, G., Edelsberg, J., Woody, G. E., & Sullivan, S. D. (2011). Economic costs of nonmedical use of prescription opioids. *The Clinical Journal of Pain, 27,* 194–202.

Macfarlane, H. B. (1988). *Camel mascot.* Truth tobacco industry documents. Retrieved from https://www.industrydocumentslibrary.ucsf.edu/tobacco/docs/#id=qxhv0090.

R. J. Reynolds Research Department. (1976). *Planning assumptions and forecast for the period 1977–1986+ for R. J. Reynolds Tobacco Company.* Retrieved from https://www.industrydocumentslibrary.ucsf.edu/tobacco/docs/#id=fldw0098.

Schonfeld & Associates. (n.d.). *Advertising spending in the cigarettes industry in the United States from 2010 to 2016 (in million U.S. dollars).* In Statista—The Statistics Portal. Retrieved July 8, 2017, from https://www-statista-com.ezproxy.sju.edu/statistics/470438/cigarettes-industry-ad-spend-usa.

Statista. (n.d.). *Food advertising in the United States.* Retrieved from https://www.statista.com.

Yes, the Federal Government Should Restrict Advertising

Pharmaceutical advertising in the United States has become a topic of great public health interest in contemporary times. Pharmaceutical companies, which are responsible for discovering, developing, and manufacturing many of the medications that are in common usage today, spend a large proportion of their expenditures on advertising. This marketing of medications can have a significant impact on the decision-making process that patients and physicians use when choosing which medication to use. Therefore, there are a series of ethical and public health considerations that necessitate the restriction of such pharmaceutical advertising.

Pharmaceutical companies utilize a diverse range of marketing strategies to inform physicians, pharmacists, and patients about their medications. Some of these different approaches include hosting educational and promotional meetings, distributing free samples for patients to physician's offices, sending promotional mailings, and publishing print advertisements.

There are, however, two main forms of pharmaceutical advertising that form the bulk of pharmaceutical marketing expenditures. The first is direct-to-physician detailing, which is face-to-face promotion with physicians. This type of advertising constitutes over $15 billion of annual pharmaceutical marketing expenditure (Mack, 2013). Pharmaceutical sales representatives meet with physicians to encourage them to prescribe more of a certain medication, through sales techniques or by giving incentives to the prescribers.

The second main form of pharmaceutical marketing is direct-to-consumer advertising. This kind of advertising is often seen on billboards or television and radio advertisements, and is meant to raise awareness of name-brand medications in patients to encourage them to ask their physician for certain medications. The costs of direct-to-consumer advertising are more than $3 billion of annual pharmaceutical marketing expenditure (Mack, 2013).

These two forms of pharmaceutical advertising have significant effects on the choices that physicians and patients make when deciding what medication regimes to begin. Physicians that receive more money from pharmaceutical companies are also more likely to prescribe that company's brand of medication. For example, ophthalmologists who received more than $5,000 in payments from pharmaceutical companies prescribed almost 20 percent more name-brand prescriptions than their colleagues who did not receive any money from pharmaceutical companies (Ornstein et al., 2016). A similar trend was seen across fields and specialties. This increase of name-brand prescribing is significant because name-brand medications often carry a much higher cost than equally effective generic medications. Additionally, direct-to-consumer advertising has similar negative effects by causing patients to ask for medications that are inappropriate or even harmful (Mintzes et al., 2003). This can lead to medication overutilization or suboptimal patient management.

Although pharmaceutical advertising is an important and effective form of marketing for pharmaceutical companies, the potential harmful impacts of such marketing warrant governmental restrictions and regulations. Pharmaceutical advertising must be restricted in order to avoid inappropriate prescribing habits, reduce misinformation, and prevent the promotion of new drugs before their safety is fully determined.

A 2006 study found that while over 80 percent of direct-to-consumer advertisements made factual claims and arguments supporting the use of their advertised drug, only a quarter of such advertisements mentioned any relevant risk factors or disease prevalence (Almasi et al., 2006). By omitting such information, pharmaceutical companies misinform patients and may encourage them to ask for medications that they are not eligible for or are unlikely to need. The federal government can restrict this practice by mandating that pharmaceutical advertisements include disease prevalence or risk factor information. This regulatory strategy is likely to face opposition and be considered as overly burdensome by pharmaceutical companies.

Additionally, due to the expensive investments required to develop novel classes of medications, many new drugs receive heavy direct-to-consumer promotion early in their life cycle, even prior to the medication's full safety profile being known. Vioxx, a brand-name medication marketed by Merck, is an example of the detrimental impact that this can have on patients. Merck invested over $500 million to advertise Vioxx, leading to over $1 billion in annual sales in the United States (Ventola, 2011). By extensive advertising, patients were led to believe that taking Vioxx was better for their health. However, it was not revealed until later that Vioxx elevated the risk for myocardial infarctions and stroke in many of these patients. It was only after five years of being advertised and sold on the market that Vioxx was voluntarily withdrawn because of its negative health effects.

Although the claim by pharmaceutical companies that such extensive advertising is required to maximize profits to offset their large research and development costs, it would be dangerous to leave their advertising strategies unregulated or unrestricted. In this regard, the United States is one of only three countries in the world, along with New Zealand and Brazil, to permit pharmaceutical companies to advertise directly to consumers. In every other country in the world, this practice is banned. Therefore, extensive experience around the world has been generated showing that the restriction of pharmaceutical advertising practices does not overly interfere with the functioning of the pharmaceutical industry and the overall health care system. In fact, it allows physicians greater opportunity to exercise their expertise in prescribing the appropriate medications for their patients, while protecting patients from the challenges and negative health effects of misinformation and inappropriate medication use.

The government should carry out its regulatory functions and restrict the advertising employed by the pharmaceutical industry for marketing its medications. It is particularly important that certain forms of pharmaceutical advertising that have the greatest opportunity for negative health ramifications, such as direct-to-physician and direct-to-consumer advertising, be regulated and restricted for the benefit of patients. The United States should change its policies to reflect the worldwide consensus regarding direct-to-consumer advertising. This will serve to protect patients, empower physicians, and ensure that the decision-making process behind patient medication regimes is ethical and effective.

Shayan Waseh

Further Reading

Almasi, E. A., Stafford, R. S., Kravitz, R. L. & Mansfield, P. R. (2006). *PLOS Medicine, 3*(3), e145.

Mack, J. (2013). Pharma promotional spending in 2013. *Pharma Marketing News, 13*(5), 1–6.

Mintzes, B., Barer, M. L., Kravitz, R. L., Bassett, K., Joel, L., Kazanjian, A. . . . Marion, S. A. (2003). How does direct-to-consumer advertising (DTCA) affect prescribing? A survey in primary care environments with and without legal DTCA. *Canadian Medical Association Journal, 169*(5), 405–412.

Ornstein, C., Groeger, L., Tigas, M., & Jones, R. G. (2016). *Dollars for docs*. New York: ProPublica. Retrieved from https://projects.propublica.org/docdollars.

Ventola, C. L. (2011). Direct-to-consumer pharmaceutical advertising: Therapeutic or toxic? *Pharmacy and Therapeutics, 36*(10), 669–684.

No, the Federal Government Should Not Restrict Advertising

The federal government's main stated goal in restricting the advertising of tobacco products is to prevent people, especially children and adolescents, from purchasing and using these products, thereby protecting public health. Related goals are to help tobacco users quit using these products and to generally reduce the harmful effects of tobacco (BeTobaccoFree.gov, 2017). It is the intention of the present essay to argue that tobacco advertising restrictions are not only an infringement on personal freedom by the government, but also supremely hypocritical of the government.

Arguments against restrictions

Standard arguments that are made against tobacco ad restrictions include the following (Debate.org, 2017):

- Restrictions violate the First Amendment, because they restrict the free speech of tobacco product manufacturers (Langvardt, 2014).
- Restrictions violate the Fourteenth Amendment, because they abridge the rights of thousands of tobacco farmers, cigarette factory workers, and other people in the tobacco industry.
- Since tobacco is a legal product for people above a certain age, banning its advertisement is unreasonable.
- Advertisements for alcohol, an addictive substance with adverse health consequences, are ubiquitous on television, so it is unfair to discriminate against tobacco products that are associated with comparable health problems.
- Advertisements do not force anyone to smoke. They merely help make people aware of particular brands of a product that they are going to use anyway.
- Advertisements are not as important in influencing the smoking behavior of young people as are their parents, other family members, teachers, friends, and other people in their lives. Thus, the focus of anti-tobacco efforts should be on those people rather than ads.

Each of these points has been widely debated in the public realm (Debate.org, 2017). However, to better understand this controversial issue, it is beneficial to review the history of government restrictions on tobacco ads.

Ever-expanding restrictions

The road to the government's advertising restrictions on tobacco began in 1964, when the U.S. surgeon general declared smoking to be a cause of increased mortality, followed the next year by the first required health warning on cigarette packages (BeTobaccoFree.gov, 2017). This warning gave official sanction to something that had long been common knowledge—cigarettes are bad for smokers' health. Many decades before the surgeon general's proclamation, people had referred to cigarettes as "coffin nails"—as is evident in a 1906 short story by O. Henry titled "The Higher Abdication," in which a character asks, "Say, sport, have you got a coffin nail on you?" (Will, 1999)

The first U.S. law targeting advertising was the 1970 Public Health Cigarette Smoking Act, which prohibited the advertising of cigarettes on television and radio (Be Tobacco Free.gov, 2017). No longer could the Marlboro Man, the iconic representation of American smoking and freedom developed by the Leo Burnett agency in 1955, be seen riding across TV screens (The Marlboro Man, 1999). But he would still frequently be found in magazines, on signs in convenience stores and gas stations, and on highway billboards.

Further, broader, and stricter restrictions were instituted over subsequent decades—with each new law expanding government power over citizens in the names of "public health" and "children." In 1986, smokeless tobacco advertisements on television and radio were banned. In 1992, Congress passed the Synar Amendment to force states to restrict cigarette sales to people aged 18 and older. The 1998 Master Settlement Agreement between most states and the four largest tobacco companies led to several new restrictions, including limits on billboard ads and public transit ads (BeTobaccoFree.gov, 2017).

Several new regulations were included in the Family Smoking Prevention and Tobacco Control Act of 2009. This act gave the Food and Drug Administration (FDA) the authority to regulate the manufacture, distribution, and marketing of tobacco products, similar the way the FDA has long regulated pharmaceuticals. After the act went into effect in June 2010, tobacco companies could no longer sponsor sports, music, or other entertainment events, nor could they display their logos on hats, shirts, or other apparel (BeTobaccoFree.gov, 2017; Tobacco Control Legal Consortium, 2009). The act also prohibited the use of "light," "low," "mild," and other moderating adjectives in ads and labels; banned outdoor ads within 1,000 feet of schools; limited ads in publications with "significant teen readership" to simple black text on white backgrounds; and required disturbing graphics to be added to label warnings (BeTobaccoFree.gov, 2017). Moreover, the act gave the FDA broad authority to impose additional restrictions on marketing as it deemed appropriate to "promote overall public health" (Tobacco Control Legal Consortium, 2009).

The few remaining permitted venues for cigarette ads as of 2017 include the Internet, magazines, and signs inside stores. A number of tobacco restrictions have been legally challenged, usually on grounds that they violate the First Amendment, but few have been overturned by the courts.

Increasing tax revenues

This history review shows how U.S. government restrictions and regulations over tobacco advertising and marketing have expanded enormously for more than half a century. The motivation for these laws has apparently been an attempt to hide two facts from Americans that all cognitive and sentient citizens already know—that cigarettes exist and that they are bad for your health. As cigarette ads have become rarer, government pronouncements about the evils of smoking have become louder. Simultaneously, taxes on cigarettes have become higher (Face the Facts, 2012). In 2015, federal tax revenues from tobacco sales in the United States totaled about $14 billion, compared with about $7 billion in 2000. State and local tax revenues from tobacco sales were even higher. Annual federal tobacco tax revenues are projected to spike to more than $30 billion by the 2020s (Statista, 2016).

Tax revenues increased despite a decline in U.S. cigarette and tobacco sales in the early 2000s, and they continued to increase as sales began to rise again in 2015 (Yang & Rosenberg, 2015), when 36.5 million American adults were cigarette smokers (CDC, 2016a). About 25 percent of U.S. middle and high school students used tobacco products in 2015—roughly the same percentage as in 2011 (CDC, 2017). It is obvious that vast numbers of people still want to smoke even without seeing advertisements, and that they are willing to pay higher taxes, which now make up more than 40 percent of the price of a pack of cigarettes (CDC, 2017).

Hypocrisy

In summary, the government is demonizing a product that Americans already know is bad for their health, but they continue to want it anyway, for whatever reasons they may have for wanting it . . . it makes them happy, it satisfies a craving or addiction, it calms them down, it helps them focus, whatever the case may be. Each individual has his or her own reasons for smoking tobacco, just as he or she does for smoking marijuana, drinking alcohol, eating tasty but fatty foods, gambling, texting all day on cell phones, driving fast cars, having multiple sexual relations, or engaging in any other behaviors that can be described as satisfying in some ways and risky in other ways. In a "free country," citizens should be allowed to engage in risky behaviors, and they should be expected to deal with the consequences. And, although tobacco products are demonized by the government, these products and the massive amount of tax revenue generated by their sales remain legal. Thus, it is clear to any thinking citizen that, despite the ad bans and the scary warnings, the government *really does not want them to stop smoking!* The money is too good to give up. The hypocrisy of the government's advertising and marketing restrictions is obvious.

It is time to stop the charade. If people are going to smoke anyway and if smoking is going to remain legal, manufacturers should be allowed the same freedom to promote and sell their products that manufacturers of other legal products have. And public health officials should respect the rights and the intelligence of citizens to weigh the adverse consequences of smoking against the perceived benefits by allowing them to view ads for these products, just as they can view ads for any other legal product they may want to purchase.

A. J. Smuskiewicz

Further Reading

BeTobaccoFree.gov. (2017). U.S. Department of Health & Human Services. *Laws/policies.* Retrieved from https://betobaccofree.hhs.gov/laws.

Centers for Disease Control and Prevention (CDC). (2016a). *Smoking & tobacco use: Current cigarette smoking among adults in the United States.* Retrieved from https://www.cdc.gov/tobacco/data_statistics/fact_sheets/adult_data/cig_smoking.

Centers for Disease Control and Prevention (CDC). (2016b). *Tobacco use among middle and high school students—United States, 2011–2015.* Retrieved from https://www.cdc.gov/tobacco/infographics/youth/pdfs/youth-tobacco-use.pdf?s_cid=bb-osh-youth-graphic-008.

Centers for Disease Control and Prevention (CDC). (2017). *Smoking & tobacco use: Economic trends in tobacco.* Retrieved from https://www.cdc.gov/tobacco/data_statistics/fact_sheets/economics/econ_facts.

Debate.org. (2017). *Should advertising tobacco products be banned in all forms?* Retrieved from http://www.debate.org/opinions/should-advertising-tobacco-products-be-banned-in-all-forms.

Face the Facts. (2012, September 23). *A tax revenue source that's just smokin'.* Retrieved from http://www.facethefactsusa.org/facts/a-tax-revenue-source-thats-just-smokin.

Langvardt, A. W. (2014). Tobacco advertising and the First Amendment: Striking the right balance. *William & Mary Business Law Review*, *5*(2). Retrieved from http://scholarship.law.wm.edu/wmblr/vol5/iss2/2.

The Marlboro Man. (1999, March 29). *Advertising Age.* Retrieved from http://adage.com/article/special-report-the-advertising-century/marlboro-man/140170.

Statista. (2016). *Tobacco tax revenue and forecast in the United States from 2000 to 2021 (in billion U.S. dollars).* Retrieved from https://www.statista.com/statistics/248964/revenues-from-tobacco-tax-and-forecast-in-the-us.

Tobacco Control Legal Consortium. (2009). *Fact sheet 5: Tobacco product marketing restrictions.* Retrieved from http://www.publichealthlawcenter.org/sites/default/files/fda-5.pdf.

Will, G. (1999, October 3). From "coffin nails" of old days: Cigarettes' health threat well-known. *Sun Sentinel.* Retrieved from http://articles.sun-sentinel.com/1999-10-03/features/9910010840_1_tobacco-companies-tobacco-industry-coffin-nail.

Yang, S., & Rosenberg, A. (2015, October 7). *Why cigarette sales are rising in America.* CNBC. Retrieved from http://www.cnbc.com/2015/10/06/why-cigarette-sales-are-rising-in-america.html.

CONTROVERSY 3: SHOULD PARENTS HAVE THE RIGHT TO REFUSE VACCINATIONS FOR THEIR CHILDREN?

Introduction

Vaccinations are one of the greatest public health accomplishments of the 20th century, saving millions of children from premature death or disability. Despite overwhelming medical evidence in support of childhood immunizations, a public debate continues of whether parents should have the right to refuse vaccinations for their children. At the heart of the controversy is the question of individual rights versus common good. Individual rights are the ability to think, act, and behave without retribution by the government. The right to life, liberty, and the pursuit of happiness are the principles on which the original 13 colonies were founded. Common good is a concept from political science, economics, philosophy, and ethics that holds several meanings. One meaning of common good refers to a resource that is owned by all members of the community, such as public roads or parks. The second meaning refers to social justice. Common good considers the needs of individual members of a group and acts according to what is best for most or all of the members. Common good is also one of the founding principles of the nation. "We hold these truths to be self-evident, that all men are created equal" assumes that the desires or needs of one person do not supersede the rights of others. Thus, we have a nation founded on the right to individual freedoms (the right to refuse vaccinations) and the right to common good (the right to ensure health within the community). Controversies arise when these two rights come in conflict with each other.

Until the advent of the sanitation movement, microbiology, immunology, and antibiotics, infectious diseases were the leading cause of death. The most notable example of destruction and devastation due to infectious disease was the Black Death pandemic of 1346–1353. An estimated 100 million people died. The bacterium *Yersinia pestis* wreaked havoc with death rates of up to 80 percent in heavily populated areas. The plague permanently impacted social structures and economies. Early Americans constantly struggled against infectious diseases. In 1837, smallpox spread across the Great Plains. Those who had been vaccinated, primarily white people, were immune. Over 15,000 Native Americans died. Entire tribes were wiped out along with valuable early American history and culture. Into the 20th century, smallpox, measles, diphtheria, typhoid, polio, and pertussis claimed thousands of lives each year. In 1900, there were 21,064 cases of smallpox resulting in 894 deaths. In 1920, there were 469,924 cases of measles with 7,575 deaths and 147,991 cases of diphtheria with 13,170 deaths. In 1922, there were 107,473 cases of pertussis with 5,099 deaths (U.S. Department of Health, Education, and Welfare, 1953). By 1998, vaccination was routinely practiced. The annual number of deaths due to smallpox was zero; measles caused 89 deaths; diphtheria accounted for 1 death; and 6,279 people died of pertussis (Impact of Vaccines Universally Recommended for Children—United States, 1999). Many of the infectious diseases that killed thousands of young children are almost unheard of today.

There are many different public health methods of preventing the spread of infectious diseases. Good handwashing, sanitation, antivirals, and antibiotics reduce transmission and therefore infectious diseases. Immunizations work by triggering the body to create immunity to the pathogen. Weakened or dead bacteria or viruses are introduced into the body. These antigens stimulate the immune system to create antibodies. When and if the immunized person comes in contact with the pathogen again, the body uses the antibodies to fight the infection. Vaccines do have adverse effects. Very few people enjoy getting stuck with a needle. Side effects include redness, pain, or irritation at the injection site. To ensure that vaccines are given at the appropriate time and spacing, the American Academy of Pediatrics developed an immunization schedule for children. Public health and medical professionals administer vaccines according to the schedule. Most parents agree that vaccines are necessary and safe. Only 3 percent of parents believe that vaccines are not necessary and not safe (Gust et al., 2005).

From a public health perspective, vaccinations work in two ways. They protect immunized individuals and they protect unimmunized individuals. When the majority of people are vaccinated against a disease, it is harder for the microorganism to spread and infect. Based on past epidemics and mathematical modeling, scientists can predict the percentage of a population that must be vaccinated in order to inhibit transmission. Measles, an airborne disease, is effectively inhibited when over 92 to 95 percent of individuals are immunized. The more people who are immunized, the harder it is for the germ to move from person to person. This concept, known as herd immunity, is particularly important because not every individual is able to get vaccinated. Some people may be allergic to vaccine ingredients. Other people have compromised immunity and rather than developing antibodies, they become infected with the pathogen. Some vaccines are contraindicated during pregnancy or among the very young. Herd immunity protects people who are unable to be vaccinated. The concept also creates opportunity for parents not to immunize believing that if everyone else's child is immunized, their child does not need immunizations.

The threat of losing loved ones to cholera, smallpox, polio, pneumonia, influenza, or typhoid is unfamiliar to today's generation of parents and children. In the following essays, A.J. Smuskiewicz discusses why parents should be able to opt out of vaccinations for their children, and Dr. Nooshin Asadpour discusses why parents should not be able to opt out.

Sally Kuykendall

Further Reading

American Academy of Pediatrics. *Immunizations.* Retrieved from https://www.aap.org/en-us/advocacy-and-policy/aap-health-initiatives/immunizations/Pages/Immunizations-home.aspx.

Centers for Disease Control and Prevention. *Vaccines and immunizations.* Retrieved from https://www.cdc.gov/vaccines/index.html.

Gust, D., Brown, C., Sheedy, K., Hibbs, B., Weaver, D., & Nowak, G. (2005). Immunization attitudes and beliefs among parents: Beyond a dichotomous perspective. *American Journal of Health Behavior*, *29*(1), 81–92.

Impact of Vaccines Universally Recommended for Children—United States, 1990–1998. (1999). *Morbidity and Mortality Weekly Report*, *48*(12), 243.

U.S. Department of Health, Education, and Welfare. (1953). *Vital statistics—special report, national summaries: Reported incidence of selected notifiable diseases. United States, each division and state, 1920–50* (p. 37). Washington, DC: U.S. Department of Health, Education, and Welfare, Public Health Service, National Office of Vital Statistics.

World Health Organization. *Immunization.* Retrieved from http://www.who.int/topics/immunization/en.

Yes, Parents Should Have the Right to Refuse Vaccinations for Their Children

Approximately two centuries of clinical experience and scientific research have proven that vaccinations have generally been beneficial to the health of individuals and the public as a whole. They are responsible for dramatic progress in fighting some of the world's most disabling and deadly diseases, perhaps most notably the eradication of smallpox and the prevention of poliomyelitis. Ongoing research continues to develop new vaccines to slow the spread of newly emerging diseases, as well as to battle long-known but ever-evolving pathologic viruses.

Despite the great advances in human health that are widely attributed to vaccines, controversy continues to surround these prophylactic substances—and, in fact, public resistance in the United States is increasingly pushing back against government, medical, and media demands to vaccinate (Blaszczak-Boxe, 2016; Hotez, 2017; W. W., 2015). A survey conducted by the Pew Research Center in 2014 found that 30 percent of Americans believed that the vaccination of children should be a matter for parents to decide rather than being required by government. Among poll respondents aged 18 to 29, 41 percent believed that parents should have the right to make vaccination decisions (Mackey, 2017).

The reasons for this substantial public resistance are multiple, including rebellion against what some view as the increasingly excessive power of government, doubts about the honesty and integrity of the medical and scientific establishment, the influence of popular anti-vaccine celebrities, religious motivations, libertarian political motivations, and other factors. And it doesn't matter what respected medical experts and powerful government officials say—some Americans simply do not believe these authorities. Rather, they prefer to follow their own instincts and beliefs and to put trust in their own experiences or in anecdotal evidence that they may have heard from friends, family, or famous people.

So the question arises, should individuals have the right to opt out of medically recommended and legally required vaccination regimens for themselves and their children—for whatever reasons they may have for doing so? Should they be allowed to refuse vaccinations for their children even when to do so might reduce the effectiveness of efforts to protect the overall public health, including the health of other children in school? Moreover, should they be allowed to reject vaccinations even if their rejections are based on scientifically incorrect or questionable ideas?

People opposed to vaccinating their children are widely ridiculed as ignorant "anti-vaxxers." Yet, various legitimate arguments can be put forth that the answers to the above questions are "Yes." The goal of the present essay is to argue that such a position can be viewed as legitimate, logical, reasonable, and respectable—not necessarily that it is the "correct" position. One can personally support the use of vaccines, while also supporting the rights of other people to decide if they want to use vaccines for themselves and their children. Such is the stated position of Senator (and ophthalmologist) Rand Paul (W. W., 2015).

Freedom of choice, Freedom from risk

Perhaps the most important arguments in favor of the right to refuse vaccinations are based on the concept of individual freedom of choice concerning life, liberty, and the pursuit of happiness—a concept enshrined in the U.S. Declaration of Independence. Part of freedom of choice is freedom to avoid potential risks for oneself and one's children—no matter how vanishingly small those risks may apparently be. Each of us has a different tolerance for risk. Some people jump out of airplanes wearing artificial wings on their arms and legs; other people refuse to even get into an airplane. The risk of flying on a five-mile-high jumbo jet might be easier for an individual to judge than the risk of an invisible microbe and the mysterious substance injected into the body to fight it. Nevertheless, pharmaceutical companies must admit that any vaccine and any other pharmaceutical product does indeed carry *some* risk of adverse health effects, though they usually make those admissions in tiny lettering or rapidly spoken dialogue. It is not entirely illogical for a mother to decide she does not want to take a chance that her child will be one of those tiny statistics of serious adverse effects.

Adding to the logic and legitimacy of such a decision is the fact that government officials recommend about twice as many vaccines today, in 2017, as they did three decades ago. The greater number of vaccines means a greater chance of rare, adverse vaccine reactions actually happening. The recommended childhood vaccine schedule advocated by the U.S. Centers for Disease Control and Prevention (CDC) in 2017 includes 16 different vaccines administered in 69 doses through age 18 (Parpia, 2016). More shots are surely to come eventually. No physician or scientist can predict with accuracy which individual will be the unlucky rarity who becomes harmed by a vaccine, so how can an individual legitimately give his or her informed consent to turn his or her child over to the state for vaccination?

The risk-to-benefit ratio of vaccines is diluted if vaccines are not 100 percent effective, which they are not. No vaccine can be fully guaranteed to prevent the designated disease, because vaccines are imperfect products as soon as they leave the pharmaceutical manufacturing facility. Furthermore, research published in the *Journal of the American Medical Association* in 2012 found an association between reduced childhood vaccine efficacy and exposure to the environmental chemicals known as perfluorinated compounds (PFCs), which are in nonstick pans, waterproof clothing, stain-proof carpeting, and many other commonly encountered materials (Grandjean et al., 2012). The efficacy of vaccines is also weakened by their widespread use, because the more they are used, the more evolutionary pressure is placed on the targeted viruses to develop genetic mutations that render the vaccines useless and possibly make the microbes more dangerous. This situation is similar to the antibiotic resistance currently creating serious problems for the medical community (Mercola.com, 2014).

Personal experience versus scientific evidence

Although it is quite reasonable that all people deserve to exercise their freedom of choice regarding manufactured chemical combinations that are put into their bodies and their children's bodies, perhaps the most deserving of having their views respected are parents who have observed their children experiencing adverse effects after vaccination. No amount of expert testimony denying any link between the diphtheria, tetanus, and pertussis (DPT) vaccine and encephalopathy or the measles, mumps, and rubella (MMR) vaccine and autism is going to convince a mother who personally observed such a link that it didn't happen. It doesn't help the medical establishment's argument that numerous pharmaceuticals approved for use by the government later had to be withdrawn from the market because of safety or efficacy problems that ultimately became apparent during clinical use. Examples of vaccines withdrawn from the U.S. market include Wyeth Laboratories' rotavirus vaccine in 1999 and GlaxoSmithKline's Lyme disease vaccine in 2002 (CDC, 1999; Nigrovic & Thompson, 2007).

The CDC acknowledges vaccine withdrawals with the following wording, which is probably not going to reassure many vaccine skeptics:

> There have been only a few vaccine recalls or withdrawals due to concerns about either how well the vaccine was working or about its safety. Several vaccine lots have been recalled in recent years because of a possible safety concern before anyone reported any injury. (Centers for Disease Control and Prevention, 2015)

Although vaccine advocates frequently belittle parents who are outspoken vaccine skeptics, such as actress and activist Jenny McCarthy (Frontline, 2015), what is more logical and understandable for a mother to believe? Her own eyes and her own personal experience, or profit-conscious pharmaceutical companies and government regulators who have been proven wrong before?

Solution to dilemma?

The most obvious argument against allowing personal choice on childhood vaccines is that the threat to other students' health is increased when unvaccinated children are present in school. Surgeon Jeffrey A. Singer, who supports parent choice, has proposed a solution to this dilemma:

> . . . allow a public school to require that parents keep their children out of school in the event of an outbreak of a contagious disease for which they refused vaccination, and not allow the children back into school until the threat has been deemed to have ended by public health authorities. (Singer, 2015)

That idea would strike a reasonable balance between protecting public health and preserving freedom of choice.

Populist rebellion

The current popular rebellion against vaccines might be viewed as part of the general populist trend against big government, big business, big media, big authority, and big establishment, which has been evident in such developments as the United Kingdom's Brexit referendum in June 2016 and the U.S. election of Donald Trump as president in November 2016. Trump himself has often expressed skepticism about vaccines (Mackey, 2017). These developments seem to be reactions against giant government establishments that are always expanding their own power and that of their corporate donors, while reducing the personal choices of regular, common people. Authorities in Brussels set economic rules that people in England had to follow even though they had no say about it. Authorities in Washington ruled that all Americans had to purchase certain types of health insurance and use only certain doctors or else pay a tax penalty.

State laws requiring Americans to inject numerous laboratory-made chemicals into their children in order for their children to attend school—and recent moves by states to clamp down on personal belief waivers to those requirements (Fisher, 2017; Mercola.com, 2014)—are seen by many people as yet more excessive, undemocratic, and even tyrannical rules. They resent these rules being foisted on them by faceless and distant bureaucrats, so-called "experts," and corporate profiteers who they feel cannot be trusted. In the times we live in today, such a view is not illogical.

The rejection of vaccines might also be considered part of another trend—that of seizing control of one's own health and body, rather than automatically obeying establishment medical dogma. Other aspects of this trend include moves to drink raw milk, remove fluoride from public drinking water, eat GMO-free foods, and use drug-free holistic and alternative modes of health care. All such efforts to increase personal health care freedom are deserving of respect rather than ridicule.

A. J. Smuskiewicz

Further Reading

Blaszczak-Boxe, A. (2016, August 29). More parents are refusing vaccinations, but their reasons are changing. *LiveScience*. Retrieved from http://www.livescience.com/about.

CBS News. (2015, January 23). *Should parents be allowed to choose whether to vaccinate their kids?* Retrieved from http://www.cbsnews.com/news/should-parents-be-allowed-to-choose-whether-to-vaccinate-their-kids.

Centers for Disease Control and Prevention (CDC). (1999, November 5). Withdrawal of rotavirus vaccine recommendation. *Morbidity and Mortality Weekly Report*, 48(43), 1007. Retrieved from https://www.cdc.gov/mmwr/preview/mmwrhtml/mm4843a5.htm.

Centers for Disease Control and Prevention (CDC). (2015). *Vaccine recalls.* Retrieved from https://www.cdc.gov/vaccinesafety/concerns/recalls.html.

Fisher, B. L. (2017, February 8). *Take action in 2017 to protect vaccine freedom of choice.* National Vaccine Information Center. Retrieved from http://www.nvic.org/nvic-vaccine-news/february-2017/take-action-2017-protect-vaccine-freedom-of-choice.aspx.

Frontline. (2015, March 23). *Jenny McCarthy: We're not an anti-vaccine movement . . . we're pro-safe vaccine.* Public Broadcasting Service. Retrieved from http://www.pbs.org/wgbh/frontline/article/jenny-mccarthy-were-not-an-anti-vaccine-movement-were-pro-safe-vaccine.

Grandjean, P., Andersen, E. W., & Budtz-Jorgensen, E. (2012). Serum vaccine antibody concentrations in children exposed to perfluorinated compounds. *Journal of the American Medical Association, 307*(4), 391–397. doi:10.1001/jama.2011.2034. Retrieved from http://jamanetwork.com/journals/jama/fullarticle/1104903.

Hotez, P. J. (2017, February 8). How the anti-vaxxers are winning. *New York Times.* Retrieved from https://www.nytimes.com/2017/02/08/opinion/how-the-anti-vaxxers-are-winning.html?_r=0.

Mackey, R. (2017, January 10). Trump asks anti-vaccine activist Robert Kennedy Jr. to lead panel on vaccine safety. *The Intercept.* Retrieved from https://theintercept.com/2017/01/10/trump-names-anti-vaccine-activist-robert-kennedy-jr-lead-panel-vaccine-safety.

Mercola.com. (2014, April 29). *Should parents be allowed to decide about vaccines?* Retrieved from http://articles.mercola.com/sites/articles/archive/2014/04/29/children-vaccines.aspx.

Nigrovic, L. E., & Thompson, K. M. (2007). The Lyme vaccine: A cautionary tale. *Epidemiology and Infection, 135*(1), 1–8. doi:10.1017/S0950268806007096. Retrieved from https://www.ncbi.nlm.nih.gov/pmc/articles/PMC2870557.

Parpia, R. (2016, February 17). Questioning the safety of the CDC's childhood vaccine schedule. *Vaccine Impact.* Retrieved from https://vaccineimpact.com/2016/questioning-the-cdcs-childhood-vaccine-schedule-vaccine-combinations-never-tested-for-safety.

Singer, J. A. (2015). *Seeking balance in vaccination laws.* CATO Institute. Originally published by Reason.com. Retrieved from https://www.cato.org/publications/commentary/seeking-balance-vaccination-laws.

W. W. (2015, February 4). Resorting to freedom. *The Economist.* Retrieved from http://www.economist.com/blogs/democracyinamerica/2015/02/rand-paul-vaccination.

No, Parents Should Not Have the Right to Refuse Vaccinations for Their Children

The choice to vaccinate a child is one of the first important decisions that a parent makes. This decision can be particularly challenging in a world with conflicting messages about the benefits and risks of vaccination. It is therefore imperative that all parents are armed with the information they need to appreciate fully the importance of vaccination.

Prior to the advent of immunization, many children from around the world died from diseases that are easily preventable today, such as polio, smallpox, whooping cough, and measles. The immunization of children against childhood infectious diseases represents one of the greatest public health achievements of the 20th century (Diekema, 2005). The Centers for Disease Control and Prevention (CDC) estimated that over 300 million illnesses and 700,000 deaths were prevented between 1994 and 2013 in the United States due to vaccination alone (Whitney et al., 2014). The World Health Organization (WHO) reports that vaccinations save about 2.5 million lives each year. However, this success has also led to many young parents never having seen or heard of the detrimental effects that vaccine-preventable diseases can have on a family or community (CDC, 2016). It is important that parents remain aware that these diseases do exist and that not vaccinating puts their children, as well as others, at risk for illness and death. It is estimated that more than 3 million people die each year from diseases that are preventable through vaccination (WHO, 2016). It is thus evident that children all over the world, including in the United States, can be and still are susceptible to these diseases. Therefore, parents should not have the right to refuse the most well-established form of protection against serious infectious diseases.

The role that vaccination can play in the development of a healthy immune system is another fundamental reason it should be mandated. When a child becomes infected with a given disease, the child's immune system produces antibodies against it. However, it takes time for the immune system to stop the disease from causing illness, so the child still gets sick. After this initial encounter, the immune system "remembers" the disease, and if it ever enters the body again, the body can produce antibodies fast enough to prevent a second illness. Vaccines are a safer substitute for a child's first exposure to a disease, since vaccines contain a tiny amount of a weakened or killed germ, thereby imitating a given infection without causing illness (CDC, 2014). The vaccination schedule is thus designed to protect young children before they are likely to be exposed to potentially serious diseases, particularly when they are most vulnerable to infections (CDC, 2017). Although some parents view illnesses as a natural part of the development of a child's immune system, subjecting a child to a vaccine-preventable disease that is known to cause significant suffering and even death, places both the child and those around him or her at far greater risk.

The risks of not vaccinating, in fact, outweigh the potential side effects of vaccinating. For example, measles vaccinations decreased deaths due to measles 79 percent worldwide, preventing an estimated 20.3 million deaths (WHO, 2017). The most common side effects of vaccination are mild and include redness, soreness, and swelling where the shot was administered. Serious side effects, such as severe allergic reaction, are very rare. The ingredients contained within a given vaccine, such as preservatives, stabilizers, and residual substances, are safe in the amounts used, and each play a necessary role in either making the vaccine or ensuring that it is safe and effective (CDC, 2017). Safety monitoring continues after a vaccine has been approved through a vaccine safety system that serves to assess the frequency and severity of these effects while considering the epidemiology of natural disease. The rates of adverse outcomes following natural measles infection are high, with encephalitis in 1 in 1,000 and death in 1 in 1,000. In comparison, the risk of MMR-associated immune thrombocytopenia purpura is 1 in 40,000 doses and is transient (Smith, 2015). Therefore, compared to the significant risks associated with natural infection, vaccines appear to be the obvious choice. Physicians can serve to educate parents about the risks of vaccination in a properly contextualized way that stresses the fundamental value of vaccination.

Although there are many evidence-based resources available for both physicians and parents, distinguishing between reliable and unreliable information is a challenge. This is yet another reason to mandate universal vaccination, thereby preventing misinformation from negatively affecting parental decision making. For example, the belief that vaccines are linked to autism is a classic fear of parents and one that often leads them to choose not to vaccinate their child. This concern arose from a controversial and significantly flawed 1998 case series that provided weak proof of causal association. In fact, the study was later discredited when it was discovered that the results were fraudulent. Over the years, several large epidemiologic studies have found no association between MMR and autism, which has been repeatedly affirmed by the Institute of Medicine (IOM) in 2001, 2004, and 2011. Yet, many parents continue to believe that vaccination causes more harm than good. Requiring parents to vaccinate their child can allow health care providers who are better informed and more up to date on the scientific literature to drive the decision-making process.

Even when parents appreciate the tremendous benefits of vaccination, care must be taken to avoid allowing parents to dictate the approach to vaccination. This is particularly important with regard to adherence to the current immunization schedule. This schedule is designed to protect children against diseases when they are most susceptible, and thus any delay in the schedule may increase risk for infection. Parents may also find it difficult to watch their children receive a shot, but they must remember that the short-term pain does not even begin to compare to the suffering that may result from contracting a potentially deadly disease such as measles, pertussis, or diphtheria. Requiring parents to follow the standardized and evidence-based immunization schedule can contribute to the more effective protection of all children.

Vaccinations are vital in protecting children from potentially deadly infectious diseases and maintaining generations of healthy children. It is important to remember that one parent's choice not to vaccinate their child does not only put their own child at a greater risk for illness and even death, but also increases the susceptibility of other children to a host of diseases. Keeping all children safe and healthy is the primary goal of vaccination, a fact that lies at the heart of why vaccination should be a mandatory part of children's health care.

Nooshin Asadpour

Further Reading

Ben-Joseph, E. P. (2015). *Frequently asked questions about immunizations.* Johns Hopkins All Children's Hospital. *KidsHealth®*. Retrieved from https://www.hopkinsallchildrens.org/patients-families/health-library/healthdoc/frequently-asked-questions-about-immunizations?id=20785.

Centers for Disease Control and Prevention. (2014). *Why are childhood vaccines so important? Vaccines and immunizations.* National Center for Immunization and Respiratory Diseases. Retrieved from https://www.cdc.gov/vaccines/vac-gen/howvpd.htm.

Centers for Disease Control and Prevention. (2016). *What are the reasons to vaccinate my baby?* CDC features. National Center for Immunizations and Respiratory Diseases. Retrieved from https://www.cdc.gov/features/reasonstovaccinate/index.html.

Centers for Disease Control and Prevention. (2017). *Making the vaccine decision.* For parents: vaccines for your children. National Center for Immunizations and Respiratory Diseases. Retrieved from https://www.cdc.gov/vaccines/parents/vaccine-decision/index.html.

Diekema, D. S. (2005). Responding to parental refusals of immunization of children. *Pediatrics*, *115*(5), 1428–1431. doi:10.1542/peds.2005-0316

Smith, M. (2015). Vaccine safety: Medical contraindications, myths, and risk communication. *Pediatrics in Review*, *36*(6), 227–238. doi:10.1542/pir.36-6-227

Whitney, C. G., Zhou, F., Singleton, J., & Schuchat, A. (2014). Benefits from immunization during the vaccines for children program era—United States, 1994–2013. *Morbidity and Mortality Weekly Report*, *63*(16), 352–355.

World Health Organization (WHO). (2016). *Children: Reducing mortality.* Fact sheet. WHO Media Centre. Retrieved from http://www.who.int/mediacentre/factsheets/fs178/en.

World Health Organization (WHO). (2017). *Measles.* Fact sheet. WHO Media Centre. Retrieved from http://www.who.int/mediacentre/factsheets/fs286/en.

CONTROVERSY 4: SHOULD PUBLIC HEALTH PROFESSIONALS ADVISE PEOPLE OF A HEALTH RISK WHEN THEY ARE UNCERTAIN ABOUT THE LEVEL OF THE RISK?

Introduction

Threats to public health occur frequently and communicating such risks is a core responsibility of public health. Unfortunately, in many cases, time is of the essence and public health departments must decide whether to warn people of a potential risk before the cause, mode of transmission, or treatment is known. The problem is that communicating partial information, inaccurate information, or inadequately communicating information can cause confusion or undermine public trust in the profession. For example, the myth that vaccines cause autism came from a poorly devised but highly publicized study. Although the doctor who did the study lost his medical license and numerous subsequent studies have discredited the original research findings, the myth continues. The controversy—should public health professionals advise people of a health risk when they are uncertain about the level of risk?—more often pits the individual's right to know against business interests. The two main public health principles underlying this controversy are the *precautionary principle* and *health risk communication*. The precautionary principle states that if an action is suspected of causing harm, the burden of proof that it does not cause harm is on the person, organization, or government committing the action, rather than the person or community being acted on. This means that if a business is exhausting chemicals into air and residents believe that the chemicals are causing breathing problems, the business is responsible for proving that the chemicals are safe. The precautionary principle is standard practice in many countries around the world. The controversy becomes more complicated in the United States where personal injury law has different rules. Toxic torts require the injured party to provide the burden of proof. With the potential for hundreds of millions of dollars in legal settlements, the stakes are very high and tend to overshadow public health practices.

The precautionary principle was created as the result of several large-scale environmental disasters. Love Canal, Times Beach, Seveso, Minamata, and Chernobyl helped people to realize that prevention or early control of environmental disasters is easier than cleanup. The precautionary principle originated in Germany and was adopted by the United Nations General Assembly in the 1982 World Charter for Nature. The principle puts the burden of proof on the person or organization doing the action. This means that the person or organization must stop the action and prove that the action does not cause harm before proceeding with the action. The most common uses are in occupational and environmental health. The U.S. Chamber of Commerce objects to the precautionary principle on the grounds that the assumption of risk limits businesses and restricts the economy. Any government regulation on business should be based in science, not suspicions of harm. Instead, businesses propose using a more detailed risk-benefit analysis, which weighs the potential risks of the action against social and economic benefits. Thus, using the precautionary principle, warning people of potential risks could unnecessarily restrict businesses.

Risk communication is a branch of public health that constructs and transmits thoughtfully managed messages to citizens so that they may take action to protect their health. The basic steps of risk communication are gathering accurate information from reliable sources; identifying the goals or objectives of the communication; identifying the target audience; identifying the channel or medium to transmit the message; creating and piloting the message; developing a plan for promotion; implementing the strategy; and evaluating the process, impact, or outcome. During health emergencies, this process must be done very quickly, effectively, and accurately. A good example of risk communication in action is the evacuation warnings prior to Hurricane Katrina (2005). The health communicator needs to tailor the message to the audience, be honest and open, empower the public with information, use credible and reputable sources of information, work with the media, listen carefully to the audience's response and concerns, and avoid dismissing or minimizing the listener's concerns (Covello & Allen, 1988). It is important to recognize that not every health warning will result in action. After a message is communicated, the listener judges the risk and decides whether to take action. Many people stayed in their homes during Hurricane Katrina because they had stayed through previous hurricanes. Factors that influence risk perception are the nature of the risk, level of control, possible benefits from the risk, and type of risk. People are more likely to accept risks if the risk is voluntary, natural (as opposed to man-made), within their control, or has some perceived benefits. They are less likely to take risks if the risk is catastrophic, unfamiliar, or affects children (Fischhoff et al., 1981). Health communication is a very complex practice, and the health communicator must anticipate reactions and respond appropriately. After the devastation of Hurricane Katrina, many changes were made in subsequent disaster warnings, such as alerting people as to where to go for safe shelter and which shelters allowed pets.

Knowing what to announce and when is critical. Many more lives could have been saved if the warnings used prior to Hurricane Sandy had been used prior to Hurricane Katrina. On the other hand, there are times when public health warnings may be misguided or misinformed. Announcements regarding cell phone use and brain cancer, vaccines and autism, or saccharin and cancer create a loss of trust in scientists and health professionals. In the following essays, Dr. Dave Reynolds and

Dr. Shayan Waseh explore whether public health professionals should advise people of a health risk when they are unsure of the level of risk.

Sally Kuykendall

Further Reading

Berthoud, B. (2015). *The precautionary principle in EU risk regulation: A matter of priorities.* Hamburg, Germany: Diplomica Publishing GmbH. Retrieved from https://www.anchor-publishing.com/document/277346.

Centers for Disease Control and Prevention. *Risk communication.* Retrieved from https://www.cdc.gov/healthcommunication/risks/index.html.

Covello, V., & Allen, F. (1988). *Seven cardinal rules of risk communication.* Washington, DC: U.S. Environmental Protection Agency, Office of Policy Analysis.

Elder, K., Xirasagar, S., Miller, N., Bowen, S.A., Glover, S., & Piper, C. (2007). African Americans' decision not to evacuate New Orleans before Hurricane Katrina: A qualitative study. *American Journal of Public Health, 97*(1), S124–S129.

Fentiman, L. C. (2014). Are mothers hazardous to their children's health? Law, culture, and the framing of risk. *Virginia Journal of Social Policy & the Law, 21*(2), 295–340.

Fischhoff, B., Lichtenstein, S., Slovic, P., & Keeney, D. (1981). *Acceptable risk.* Cambridge, UK: Cambridge University Press.

Goldstein, B. D. (2001). The precautionary principle also applies to public health actions. *American Journal of Public Health, 91*(9), 1358–1361.

Goldstein, B. D. (2005). Advances in risk assessment and communication. *Annual Review of Public Health, 26,* 141–163. doi:10.1146/annurev.publhealth.26.021304.144410

Myers, N. (2004). The rise of the precautionary principle. *Multinational Monitor, 25*(9), 9–15.

Rosner, D., & Markowitz, G. (2002). Industry challenges to the principle of prevention in public health: The precautionary principle in historical perspective. *Public Health Reports, 117*(6), 501–512.

Wiedemann, P. M., & Schütz, H. (2005). The precautionary principle and risk perception: Experimental studies in the EMF area. *Environmental Health Perspectives, 113*(4), 402–405. doi:10.1289/chp.7538

Yes, Public Health Professionals Should Advise People of a Health Risk When They Are Uncertain about the Level of the Risk

Public health officials should advise people of health risks, regardless of the degree of uncertainty. The primary reasons to support informing the public are as follows: it is what the public wants and expects; it is what ethical guidelines require; failure to do so may be punishable by law; and the uncertainty inherent in every risk assessment can be clearly communicated, empowering individuals to make their own decisions. Concerns that the public will become confused and panic in the midst of uncertain risk levels are largely unjustified.

The American public expects local, state, and federal authorities to protect them from health hazards, such as air and water pollution, by frequently testing numerous samples to ensure they are safe. If they cannot be protected, then the public wants information about how they can protect themselves, such as by staying indoors or drinking only bottled water. Surveys have shown that half of all Americans want more information, including what they can do to protect themselves (Princeton Survey Research, 2000). Ninety percent said it would be "somewhat" or "very important" to them that information on hazards be made public. Indeed, to protect and inform are among the duties of the Environmental Protection Agency, and the Centers for Disease Control and Prevention, two of the most well-recognized federal agencies involved in public health risk assessment and reduction.

Public health institutions and officials must adhere to ethical principles and guidelines. This includes valuing the community. According to the Public Health Leadership Society (PHLS), corresponding ethical actions include: "communication; truth telling; transparency (i.e., not concealing information); accountability; reliability; and reciprocity" (PHLS, 2002, p. 5). The society considers it an essential public health service, "to inform, educate, and empower people about health issues" (PHLS, 2002, p. 12), and states, "there is a moral obligation in some instances to share what is known" (PHLS, 2002, p. 6). The only exception would be when such information is confidential or could, "bring harm to an individual or community if made public (Thomas, 2004, p. 11). An example might be that a given individual or community has been the source of a sexually transmitted disease outbreak. Public health ethics also address uncertainty: "Action is not based on information alone. In many instances, action is required in the absence of all the information one would like" (PHLS, 2002).

Although the ethical principles are intended primarily for institutions with a decidedly public health mission, individual public health personnel are bound to the society's *core competencies* (Thomas, 2004). Specific to providing communities with information, an ethical core competency is listed as, "Effectively presents accurate demographic, statistical, programmatic, and scientific information for professionals and lay audiences" (Thomas, 2004, p. 10). Since the mid-1970s, numerous states have enacted laws that require companies that could expose the public to hazards to disclose this information. Other laws allow those who might be put at risk, such as through employment, use of a product, or living in proximity to the known hazard, to obtain health risk information, even if this information is privately held (Baram, 1984). Failure to abide by such "duty-to-disclose" or "right-to-know" laws has resulted in class action lawsuits and large payouts to injured parties. Some states' right-to-know laws apply to every company and organization that collects—or should collect—"hazard information" relevant to employees, politicians, and citizens, in general (Baram, 1984). Colorado's regulations on epidemics are but one example (see Codes 1009-1 and 1009-5). American society places a high value on the public's need-to-know health and safety risk information, even when privately held, and many state and local laws support this view. Withholding health risk information simply because a public health professional believes the degree of uncertainty about the finding is too great, likely would subject the individual or his or her employer to punitive damages resulting from personal injury. And applicable laws do not appear to include any exemption to disclose health risk information simply due to a high degree of uncertainty.

Every health risk assessment conducted involves some degree of statistical uncertainty due to such things as measurement error. This is true whether measuring opinions, behaviors, or the physical properties of things. Uncertainty is also a component of risk levels obtained through modeling or estimation. For example, the health risks associated with pesticide exposure involves uncertainty because lab animals serve as surrogates (stand-ins) for humans. The risk to humans is estimated based on what happens to the exposed animals. It is standard practice in many scientific fields to report potential sources of error for any given result, along with the degree of uncertainty.

One objection to health officials publicizing uncertain health risk information is that people will not modify their behavior due to a lack of confidence. However, research from the field of risk communication suggests that several other factors influence the adoption of protective health behaviors. These include anxiety, risk severity, susceptibility, duration, trust of source, degree of individual control over risk, degree to which advised behaviors are deemed actionable, and likelihood they will be effective (Rubin et al., 2009). Furthermore, the public recognizes the existence of uncertainties and incomplete information within health risk messaging, such as in the early stages of a disease outbreak.

Although the perception among many public health professionals may be that the public will panic during a health crisis, in actuality, the public is more likely to respond with skepticism and apathy, regardless of the level of uncertainty reported (Rubin et al., 2015). For example, in the face of bovine spongiform encephalopathy (mad cow disease), which had contaminated some of the beef supply, even in the face of unknowns and uncertainty, of which the public was readily aware, they did not panic (Millstone et al., 2006). In fact, the general public held more sophisticated assumptions about health risks than either public policy makers or the general media outlets gave them credit. For example, whereas it was assumed the public would see the risk in all-or-none terms, they instead took a nuanced approach to the crisis.

The field of public health risk communication (Bennett et al., 2010), as well as guidance from the World Health Organization (2013), suggests that the question is not *whether* public health officials should communicate health risk levels of which they are uncertain, but rather how to communicate this information. The degree of uncertainty can be accurately conveyed to both expert and lay audiences, along with various recommendations so as to motivate health protective behaviors, the ultimate goal.

David J. Reynolds

Further Reading

Baram, M. S. (1984). The right to know and the duty to disclose hazard information. *American Journal of Public Health*, 74(4), 385–390.

Bennett, P., Calman, K., Curtis, S., and Fishbacher-Smith, D. (Eds.). (2010). *Risk communication and public health* (2nd ed.). Oxford, UK: Oxford University Press.

Colorado Department of Public Health and Environment, Disease Control and Environmental Epidemiology Division. (2007). *State board of health rules and regulations pertaining to preparations for a bioterrorist event, pandemic influenza, or an outbreak by a novel and highly fatal infectious agent or biological toxin*, CO Code Regs. § 1009-5, reg. 1. Retrieved from https://www.sos.state.co.us/CCR/GenerateRulePdf.do?ruleVersionId=1588.

Colorado Department of Public Health and Environment, Disease Control and Environmental Epidemiology Division. (2017). *Epidemic and communicable disease control*, CO Code Regs. § 1009-1, reg. 6. Retrieved from http://www.sos.state.co.us/CCR/GenerateRulePdf.do?ruleVersionId=7134&fileName=6%20CCR%201009-1.

EPA. (2017). *About EPA: Our mission and what we do.* Retrieved from https://www.epa.gov/aboutepa/our-mission-and-what-we-do.

Millstone, E., van Zwanenberg, P., Bauer, M., Dora, C., Dowler, E., Draper, A., Dressel, K., Gasperoni, G., Green, J., Koivusalo, M., & Ollila, E. (2006). Improving communication strategies and engaging with public concerns. In C. Dora (Ed.), *Health, hazards and public debate: Lessons for risk communication from the BSE/CJD saga.* Copenhagen, Denmark: World Health Organization Regional Office for Europe.

Princeton Survey Research Associates. (2000). *National survey of public perceptions of environmental health risks.* Princeton, NJ: Topline Results. Retrieved from http://healthyamericans.org/reports/files/survey0620.pdf.

Public Health Leadership Society. (2002). *The principles of the ethical practice of public health* (Version 2.2). Retrieved July 4, 2017, from https://www.apha.org/~/media/files/pdf/membergroups/ethics_brochure.ashx.

Rubin, G., Finn, Y., Potts, H., & Michie, S. (2015). Who is sceptical about emerging public health threats? Results from 39 national surveys in the United Kingdom. *Public Health, 129*(12), 1553–1562. doi:10.1016/j.puhe.2015.09.004

Rubin, G. J., Amlôt, R., Page, L., & Wessely, S. (2009). Public perceptions, anxiety, and behaviour change in relation to the swine flu outbreak: Cross sectional telephone survey. *British Medical Journal, 339*(7713), 156.

Thomas, J. (2004). *Skills for the ethical practice of public health.* Public Health Leadership Society. Retrieved from https://nnphi.org/wp-content/uploads/2015/08/ph-code-of-ethics-skills-and-competencies-booklet.original.pdf.

Wester, M. (2011). Fight, flight or freeze: Assumed reactions of the public during a crisis. *Journal of Contingencies & Crisis Management, 19*(4), 207–214. doi:10.1111/j.1468-5973.2011.00646.x

World Health Organization, Regional Office for Europe. (2013). *Health and environment: Communicating the risks.* Copenhagen, Denmark: WHO. Retrieved from http://www.euro.who.int/en/publications/abstracts/health-and-environment-communicating-the-risks-2013.

No, Public Health Professionals Should Not Advise People of a Health Risk When They Are Uncertain about the Level of Risk

The purpose of public health is to contribute to the health and well-being of entire populations. This broad aim is accomplished through a variety of mechanisms, such as promotion of healthy lifestyles, infectious disease control, biomedical research, injury prevention, and environmental health. Public health professionals are responsible for creating and maintaining systems that promote the health of the population in a multitude of ways. They are likewise responsible for protecting and safeguarding the population from a variety of harmful influences, whether it be negative lifestyle behaviors, dangerous toxins and pollutants, or contagious diseases.

Many times, however, public health professionals are faced with situations where the risk to the population is uncertain and the decision to act or not act becomes of paramount importance. An example of a circumstance where public health professionals are forced to act on limited evidence to make highly impactful decisions can be seen in hydrofracturing in the United States, particularly in states like Pennsylvania that rely heavily on hydrofracturing.

Hydrofracturing is the use of high-pressure water to cause cracks in the ground to release natural gas. This process provides an immense amount of natural gas to the nation and is responsible for many tens of billions of dollars of energy, business, and jobs (Dows, 2015). However, environmental impact analysis has shown that the chemicals used in hydrofracturing can sometimes find their way into the drinking water of nearby towns and localities (Howarth, Ingraffea, & Engelder, 2011). Many of these chemicals have unknown effects on human health and human reproduction. Therefore, public health professionals are forced to balance the real and immense socioeconomic benefits of hydrofracturing with the potential for a yet to be determined level of risk to people's health.

By showing precaution about the risk of harm to human health and recommending that hydrofracturing be halted until further research is carried out, many people would lose their jobs, and the price of consumer gas and goods would increase across the nation. This would harm many people who require their income from working in the hydrofracturing industry to support their families. Additionally, households across the United States would have to spend more on their gas bills and for products that rely on cheap natural gas to be affordable. This would prevent people from being able to save more money and spend money on things like healthy food, exercise, and recreation—all of which are definitively associated with better health. Thus, acting on an uncertain level of risk, public health professionals can often hastily make decisions that cause real and measurable harms to society. They can cause harm to the public health in order to possibly prevent a future harm.

Although the prevailing view in the public health field is that of the "precautionary principle," it is clear that the precautionary principle has many serious drawbacks that warrant further consideration. The precautionary principle states that when there is the risk for a serious and irreversible harm, regulatory action and preventative measures should be undertaken even if the exact level or potential for risk is not fully understood (Applegate, 2000). Simply stated, the precautionary principle recommends that public health professionals err on the safe side of concern and act on any potentials for risk. Although this is an effective paradigm for preventing major public health problems, it does have serious drawbacks.

One example is with genetically modified organisms, also known as GMOs. Plant GMOs are engineered by agricultural scientists by inserting different codes into their DNA. This allows the plant GMOs to show a variety of very desirable traits such as exhibiting pest resistance, having a longer shelf life, holding more nutrients, and producing much larger yields. Overall, the creation of plant GMOs has been a tremendous benefit for humanity and has prevented many people from starvation and allowed better access to higher nutrient foods for many others.

Due to the man-made nature of genetic engineering in plant GMOs, however, some public health professionals are concerned about the potential for health side effects from eating GMO foods. There has been a recent push for state and federal governments to mandate that different food companies label their packaging to indicate whether or not their food contains any GMOs. They pose that such labeling would allow consumers to decide whether or not they want to expose themselves to the risk of whatever unknown health effects GMOs may have. However, the agricultural and food industries have fought against these regulations by stating that such labeling would unnecessarily cause consumers to think that GMOs might be unhealthy and therefore not purchase GMO products. Additionally, evidence shows that GMO products for the most part are not associated with any evidence of harm to human health (Panchin & Tuzhikov, 2016).

Therefore, the question becomes: should public health advise people about the health risk of GMOs through food package labeling, even when the likelihood of the health risk of GMOs is unknown or minute? If the decision is guided by the precautionary principle, then a public health professional may recommend package labeling, at least until further and more extensive research concludes that GMOs are fully safe. This would be more harmful, however, because doing so would cause an immediate harm. For example, while labeling GMO foods may reduce the amount of GMOs ingested, it is unclear how beneficial this would actually be. On the other hand, many of the affordable fruits and vegetables in supermarkets and grocery stores are GMOs, and people may eat less of these healthy foods. Unlike the health risk of GMOs, having a poor diet is strongly and definitively associated with the risk of harm to health. Additionally, GMOs allow for foods to be more affordable and accessible to people. Requiring package labeling may cause the price of foods to increase, also leading to less healthy eating habits. Therefore, by informing the public about potential (and unlikely) health risks, they may be driven by fear to act in even more unhealthy ways. Therefore, it is important that public health professionals show wisdom and consideration in making decisions to inform the public regarding potential and unknown health risks.

Shayan Waseh

Further Reading

Applegate, J. S. (2000). The precautionary preference: An American perspective on the precautionary principle. *Human & Ecological Risk Assessment*, 6(3), 413. doi:10.1080/10807030091124554

Dows, F. (2015). *The economic benefit of fracking*. Washington, DC: Brookings Institution. Retrieved from https://www.brookings.edu/blog/brookings-now/2015/03/23/the-economic-benefits-of-fracking.

Howarth, R. W., Ingraffea, A., & Engelder, T. (2011). Natural gas: Should fracking stop? *Nature*, *477*, 271–275.

Panchin, A. Y., & Tuzhikov, A. I. (2017). Published GMO studies find no evidence of harm when corrected for multiple comparisons. *Critical Reviews in Biotechnology*, *37*(2), 213–217. doi:10.3109/07388551.2015.1130684

Sandin, P., Peterson, M., Hansson, S. O., Ruden, C., & Juthe, A. Five charges against the precautionary principle. *Journal of Risk Research*, *5*(4), 287–299.

CONTROVERSY 5: SHOULD UNDOCUMENTED IMMIGRANTS HAVE ACCESS TO HEALTH CARE?

Introduction

Soon after I moved to England, I developed a urinary tract infection. It was the weekend. It was painful and I did not know what to do. When I could no longer take the discomfort, I went to the local emergency room. The nurses and doctors were rude. I felt like a second class citizen, abusing national health resources on a nonemergent problem. Thankfully, they did treat me and gave me instructions on how to register with the National Health Service. For the next five years, I worked as a nurse and paid taxes in the United Kingdom. I don't know what it is like to be an undocumented immigrant in need of health care. I know what it is like to become suddenly and unexpectedly ill in a foreign country where one does not know how to navigate the health care system. An estimated 12 million undocumented immigrants live in the United States. Many do not seek care due to language barriers, documentation status, or other fears. Failure to seek medical care jeopardizes individual and public health. Tuberculosis or HIV/AIDS may be transmitted to others. Untreated mental health problems can impact coworkers, neighbors, and communities. These issues raise the question of whether undocumented immigrants should have access to health care.

People immigrate for a wide variety of reasons, seeking better opportunities, love, adventure, or escape from violence. The United States is a nation of immigrants, people who were searching for a better life. Yet, the country's health care system cannot sustain unrestricted immigration and access to care. The United States spends more on health care than many other countries, $9,403 per person per year (World Bank Group, 2017). The Affordable Care Act restricts undocumented immigrants from seeking health care. Beyond this legal restriction, undocumented immigrants are less likely to seek health care. Reasons given are fears of inability to pay for care, discrimination, language barriers, bureaucracy, deportation, shame and stigma, and inability to navigate the health care system. Safety net services, such as emergent care centers, free clinics, food banks, and maternal and child health care organizations, provide short-term care but are typically insufficient for demand. As a result, undocumented immigrants are at increased risk for serious complications or putting others at risk.

As the world becomes a global community, migration is likely to increase and infectious diseases do not discriminate by nativity. Those who migrate will be at greater risk for endemic diseases or may transmit endemic diseases from their country of origin to the new country. Experts from the University of Pittsburgh and Harvard University recommend expanding access for undocumented immigrants, education and outreach to undocumented immigrants, and enhancing safety net services as well as developing novel insurance programs for immigrant populations. A comprehensive approach to immigrant care (documented or undocumented) trains health care providers on how to work with diverse populations and teaches immigrants how to navigate the U.S. health care system (Hacker, Anies, Folb, & Zallman, 2015). In the following essays, Matthew Black and Dr. Shayan Waseh present the controversy of should undocumented immigrants have access to health care.

Sally Kuykendall

Further Reading

Hacker, K., Anies, M., Folb, B., & Zallman, L. (2015). Barriers to health care for undocumented immigrants: A literature review. *Risk Management and Healthcare Policy, 8*, 175–183.

Philbin, M. M., Flake, M., Hatzenbuehler, M. L., & Hirsch, J. S. (2017). State-level immigration and immigrant-focused policies as drivers of Latino health disparities in the United States. *Social Science & Medicine*. doi:10.1016/j.socscimed.2017.04.007

Torres, J. M., & Waldinger, R. (2015). Civic stratification and the exclusion of undocumented immigrants from cross-border health care. *Journal of Health & Social Behavior*, *56*(4), 438–459. doi:10.1177/0022146515610617

World Bank Group. (2017). *Health expenditures per capita (current US$)*. Retrieved from http://data.worldbank.org/indicator/SH.XPD.PCAP?end=2014&start=1995&view=chart&year_high_desc=true.

Yes, Undocumented Immigrants Should Have Access to Health Care

Undocumented immigrants should have access to health care in the United States. Although the Affordable Care Act brought health insurance coverage to millions of uninsured Americans, undocumented immigrants were excluded from federal requirements. Undocumented immigrants do not currently have access to publicly funded health care. This is done to protect public resources and to deter illegal immigration. The problem is that when a large population inside the country goes unmonitored and untreated by health officials, problems arise. Preventative care such as STD testing or vaccinations are not available to unauthorized immigrants, risking disease outbreak among legal residents. Unauthorized immigrants are in constant contact with other U.S. residents and citizens. Many unauthorized immigrants work in the agricultural and food service industries (Kullgren, 2003). Any infection or disease can potentially spread to others, regardless of passport or immigration status. Such an outbreak could potentially lead to massive spending on treatment for U.S.

citizens. Unauthorized immigrants may turn to self-medication or unlicensed medical care. Partial treatment or mistreatment could lead to drug-resistant disease. Many public health professionals advocate for health care for unauthorized immigrants from a prevention standpoint and from a human rights perspective. By not treating people who require help, the United States is turning a blind eye to people in need, including children (Biswas, Toebes, Hjern, Ascher, & Norredam, 2012). If the CDC and NHS are expected to protect the country from illnesses, it is in the best interests of everyone in the country that unauthorized immigrants have access to public health care.

People migrate for numerous reasons. Some flee political or religious persecution, others migrate voluntarily. Human population movement through air, sea, and land travel helped to shape world culture, the global economy, health, and lifestyle. Despite the many benefits of global travel, historically, human migration created opportunities for pathogens to spread from one area to another. Migrants carried communicable diseases endemic in their country of origin to new areas, as the early European settlers brought smallpox to Native Americans. Conversely, migrants new to an area may be susceptible to communicable diseases common in the arriving country. Today, screenings, vaccinations, food safety, and border protection regulations provide a high level of biosecurity. Tourists and business travelers are just as likely to transmit communicable diseases as migrants. In fact, the World Health Organization lists the most frequent health problems of new refugees and migrants as unintentional injuries, hypothermia, burns, gastrointestinal illnesses, cardiovascular diseases, birth and pregnancy complications, diabetes and hypertension, similar problems as might be seen among ordinary U.S. citizens. Infectious diseases are actually associated with poverty, inadequate sanitation, and limited access to vaccinations or health care. The underlying problem is not the migrants but the conditions that they are leaving. The risk of exotic illnesses being brought into the country by migrants or refugees is fairly low.

Traumatic, forced migration creates monumental health problems of mental disorders, high infant mortality, substance abuse, malnutrition, post-traumatic stress disorder, and vulnerability to infection and higher risk of noncommunicable diseases. Diseases are further compounded by overcrowded living conditions, limited access to personal hygiene facilities, malnutrition, conflict, or economic crisis. Female refugees and migrants may have experienced physical or sexual violence leading to emotional and reproductive health problems. Children, especially, are prone to respiratory and gastrointestinal infections. From a humanitarian perspective, depriving vulnerable populations of health care is malicious and uncivilized.

The public arguments against providing health care to unauthorized immigrants purport that the cost would be prohibitive and that the nation should not support illegal immigration. The Pew Research Center estimates that there are currently 11 million unauthorized immigrants in the United States (Passel & Cohn, 2016). The majority of unauthorized immigrants are from countries other than Mexico, primarily from Asian and Central American countries. Many of these are middle to high income countries. In the United States, 8 million undocumented immigrants are employed. At least two-thirds have lived in the United States for at least a decade. The Center for Immigration Studies estimates that the cost of treating undocumented immigrants is approximately $4.3 billion per year. The American Hospital Association reports losses due to all uninsured patients are approximately $41.1 billion per year. Providing health care for undocumented immigrants may not significantly reduce unreimbursed costs to hospitals. However, it would divert undocumented patients from seeking the expensive care of emergency rooms or untreated, complicated illnesses, to more preventive services.

Beyond economics, there is a social benefit to providing health care to undocumented immigrants. For many years, the United States enjoyed the status of a world power, respected as the world's social conscience. The plaque at the base of the Statue of Liberty welcomed struggling immigrants with the message, "Give me your tired, your poor, your huddled masses yearning to breathe free, the wretched refuse of your teeming shore. Send these the homeless, tempest-tossed to me, I lift my lamp beside the golden door." The United States is a nation of immigrants. To dismiss or diminish people in need contradicts the values on which the nation was established. Consistent with American values, undocumented immigrants should have access to health care services.

Matthew Black

Further Reading

Biswas, D., Toebes, B., Hjern, A., Ascher, H., & Norredam, M. (2012). Access to health care for undocumented migrants from a human rights perspective: A comparative study of Denmark, Sweden, and the Netherlands. *Health & Human Rights, 14*(2), 49–60.

Johns, K. A. (1998). The tuberculosis crisis: The deadly consequence of immigration policies and welfare reform. *Journal of Contemporary Health Law & Policy, 15,* 101.

Krogstad, J. M., Passel, J. S., & Cohn, D. (2017). *5 facts about illegal immigration in the U.S.* Retrieved from http://www.pewresearch.org/fact-tank/2017/04/27/5-facts-about-illegal-immigration-in-the-u-s.

Kullgren, J. T. (2003). Restrictions on undocumented immigrants' access to health services: The public health implications of welfare reform. *American Journal of Public Health, 93*(10), 1630–1633.

Passel, J. S., & Cohn, D. (2016, September). *Overall number of U.S. unauthorized immigrants holds steady since 2009.* Pew Research Center. Retrieved from http://assets.pewresearch.org/wp-content/uploads/sites/7/2016/09/31170303/PH_2016.09.20_Unauthorized_FINAL.pdf.

Portes, A., Fernández-Kelly, P., & Light, D. (2012). Life on the edge: Immigrants confront the American health system. *Ethnic & Racial Studies, 35*(1), 3–22. doi:10.1080/01419870.2011.594173

Sanchez, G. R., Sanchez-Youngman, S., Murphy, A. A., Goodin, A. S., Santos, R., & Valdez, R. B. (2011). Explaining public support (or lack thereof) for extending health coverage to undocumented immigrants. *Journal of Health Care for the Poor and Underserved, 22*(2), 683.

World Health Organization. (2017). *Migration and health: Key issues*. Retrieved from http://www.euro.who.int/en/health-topics/health-determinants/migration-and-health/migrant-health-in-the-european-region/migration-and-health-key-issues.

No, Undocumented Immigrants Should Not Have Access to Health Care

The flow of undocumented immigrants into the United States rapidly increased throughout the 1990s and reached a plateau over the past decade. There are currently an estimated 11 million unauthorized immigrants in the United States. Although half of these undocumented immigrants originate from Mexico, immigration from Asia and Central America has constituted a rising share of the undocumented immigrant population throughout the last 10 years. Although many of these undocumented immigrants live throughout the nation, there are a group of six states that host the concentrated majority of unauthorized immigrants: California, Texas, Florida, New York, New Jersey, and Illinois account for 59 percent of all unauthorized immigrants in the United States (Krogstad, Passel, & Cohn, 2017).

The emergence of undocumented immigration, also referred to as illegal immigration, has been responsible for significant cultural, financial, and labor contributions between the United States and Mexico as well as other countries. Over 8 million unauthorized immigrants are in the U.S. civilian workforce, and 1 out of every 20 people working or looking for work is an undocumented immigrant (Krogstad et al., 2017). Although the policy and approach that is being taken toward undocumented immigration is a highly polarized political topic, the impact and cost of undocumented immigration are well studied.

Undocumented immigrants and their families, similar to any average American family, rely on the federal and state governments for a variety of services and support in accessing health care, enrolling in education and university, and utilizing public works in their communities. Since many undocumented immigrants are forced to work in occupations that do not report their incomes to the Internal Revenue Service, they are often unable to pay income tax to offset their usage of government services and funding.

Therefore, the question of whether or not to allow undocumented immigrants to have access to health care is a vital one. A study carried out by RAND was able to extrapolate that the total medical spending for the adult undocumented immigrant population across the nation was likely to be more than $6 billion a year (Goldman, Smith, & Sood, 2006). At least $1 billion of this was paid for by state and federal government funds.

The United States already spends more than any other country in the world on health care by a large margin. In 2015 alone, U.S. health care spending exceeded $3 trillion and accounted for almost $10,000 per person. Although the cost of health care for undocumented immigrants may not seem like a large expenditure, it would be one more additional cost to drive up runaway health care spending.

Additionally, studies have shown that undocumented immigrants currently utilize significantly less health care than their counterparts who have legal status in the United States (Pourat, Wallace, Hadler, & Ponce, 2014). This is often attributed to lack of insurance coverage and fear regarding their illegal immigration status. By expanding health coverage to include health care for undocumented immigrants, health care utilization would likely increase and lead to exponentially higher health care costs, which would then be an added burden on taxpayers and the government. Although annual per capita expenses for health care were 86 percent lower for uninsured immigrant children than for uninsured U.S-born children (presumably because of lack of coverage and fear of their illegal immigration status), their emergency department utilization rates were nearly three times as high (Mohanty, Woolhandler, Himmelstein, Pati, Carrasquillo, & Bor, 2005). Emergency departments are likely more utilized because they are prohibited from asking about income, insurance, or citizenship status before rendering care. If access to non-emergency department care were opened to all undocumented immigrants, then those health care costs might show similar patterns of use as the currently highly utilized emergency departments.

Another issue that is vital to considering whether or not undocumented immigrants should have access to health care is that implementing subsidized health care for undocumented immigrants would create incentives for citizens of other countries such as Mexico to illegally immigrate into the United States. Many people already illegally immigrate into the United States seeking opportunities to work and sustain a family. Adding the ability to receive health care would create an even more enticing attraction to coming to the United States. The legal immigration process exists to serve the function of facilitating legal and regulated immigration into the United States, but by incentivizing illegal immigration through the expansion of services offered to undocumented immigrants, the function and efficacy of the legal immigration system would be undermined.

If health care is accessible by undocumented immigrants in the United States, then there may also be a surge of illegal immigration for the purpose of receiving health care in the United States. Since immigrants who would enter the United States for the purpose of receiving health care would often be sick, this would drive up health care costs in the United States and add an increased tax burden on U.S. citizens as well as on immigrants who followed legal processes to enter the country and find jobs.

A final consideration is that many fully legal U.S. citizens already suffer from a lack of insurance or suffer from underinsurance. Even with the expansion of Medicaid through the Affordable Care Act, many people in the United States still are effectively unable to access non-emergency health care services in an affordable and timely manner. A study in 2017 showed that 10 percent of primary care visits in community health centers in states that chose to expand Medicaid coverage were still uninsured (Huguet, Hoopes, Angier, Marino, Holderness, & DeVoe, 2017). There would therefore be an ethical concern in providing health care access to immigrants who illegally enter the country before providing health care for all American citizens and legal immigrants. Therefore, undocumented immigrants should not receive access to health care unless they are able to follow the legal and regulated immigration process when entering the country.

Shayan Waseh

Further Reading

Center for Medicare and Medicaid Services. (2016). *National health expenditures 2015 highlights*. Washington, DC: Author. Retrieved from https://www.cms.gov/Research-Statistics-Data-and-Systems/Statistics-Trends-and-Reports/NationalHealthExpendData/downloads/highlights.pdf.

Goldman, D. P., Smith, J. P., & Sood, N. (2006). Immigrants and the cost of medical care. *Health Affairs*, *25*(6), 1700–1711.

Huguet, N., Hoopes, M. J, Angier, H., Marino, M., Holderness, H., & DeVoe, J. E. (2017). Medicaid expansion produces long-term impact on insurance coverage rates in community health centers. *Journal of Primary Care & Community Health.* Retrieved from http://journals.sagepub.com/doi/abs/10.1177/2150131917709403?url_ver=Z39.88-2003&rfr_id=ori:rid:crossref.org&rfr_dat=cr_pub%3dpubmed.

Krogstad, J. M., Passel J. S., & Cohn, D. (2017). 5 facts about illegal immigration in the U.S. *Pew Research Center*. Retrieved from http://www.pewresearch.org/fact-tank/2017/04/27/5-facts-about-illegal-immigration-in-the-u-s.

Mohanty, S. A., Woolhandler, S., Himmelstein, D. U., Pati, S., Carrasquillo, O., & Bor, D. H. (2005). Health care expenditures of immigrants in the United States: A nationally representative analysis. *American Journal of Public Health*, *5*(8), 1431–1438.

Pourat, N., Wallace, S. P., Hadler, M. W., & Ponce, N. (2014). Assessing health care services used by California's undocumented immigrant population in 2010. *Health Affairs*, *33*(5), 840–847.

Directory of Organizations

American Public Health Association (APHA)
800 I Street, NW
Washington, DC 20001
202-777-2742
https://apha.org
The APHA is the primary professional organization of public health practitioners, administrators, researchers, and educators in the United States.

Association of Public Health Laboratories (APHL)
8515 Georgia Avenue, Suite 700
Silver Spring, MD 20910
240-485-2745
https://www.aphl.org
The APHL is the national organization networking state and local government health laboratories, companies, laboratory professionals, and students interested in the laboratory sciences.

Association of State and Territorial Health Officials (ASTHO)
2231 Crystal Drive, Suite 450
Arlington, VA 22202
202-371-9090
http://www.astho.org
The ASTHO is a national nonprofit network of current and past public health officers in the United States, U.S. territories, District of Columbia, Mexico, and Canada.

Centers for Disease Control and Prevention (CDC)
1600 Clifton Road
Atlanta, GA 30329-4027
800-CDC-INFO (800-232-4636), TTY: 888-232-6348
https://www.cdc.gov
The CDC is a unit of the U.S. Department of Health and Human Services (DHHS) responsible for disease surveillance, treatment, and prevention and response to man-made and natural disasters.

Centers for Medicare and Medicaid Services (CMS)
7500 Security Boulevard
Baltimore, MD 21244
https://www.cms.gov
The CMS is a division of the DHHS responsible for managing programs that finance health services for the elderly, people with special health needs, people with limited income, and those who are not covered by employer-sponsored health plans.

Council on Education for Public Health (CEPH)
1010 Wayne Avenue, Suite 220
Silver Spring, MD 20910
https://ceph.org
The CEPH is an agency that reviews the teaching, research, and service efforts of schools and programs in public health and accredits those schools and programs that meet the documented standards.

Health and Medicine Division of the National Academies of Sciences, Engineering, and Medicine
2101 Constitution Avenue, NW
Washington, DC 20418
202-334-2352
http://www.nationalacademies.org/hmd
Formerly known as the Institute of Medicine (IOM), the Health and Medicine Division (HMD) of the National Academies of Sciences, Engineering, and Medicine (the National Academies) provides independent, nonpartisan advice to Congress and the White House to ensure that each new or revised policy has a valid scientific basis.

Health Resources and Services Administration (HRSA)
5600 Fishers Lane
Rockville, MD 20857
https://www.hrsa.gov
The HRSA is the federal agency responsible for ensuring that people who are geographically isolated, economically disadvantaged, or medically vulnerable are able to access quality health care.

Indian Health Service
5600 Fishers Lane
Rockville, MD 20857
https://www.ihs.gov
The IHS is an agency within the DHHS responsible for fulfilling the nation's obligation to provide community health services and primary health care to 2.2 million indigenous Americans from 567 tribes.

National Association of County and City Health Officials (NACCHO)
1201 Eye Street, NW
4th Floor
Washington, DC 20005
202-783-5550
http://www.naccho.org
The NACCHO is a nonprofit organization serving local health departments, health department administrators, and practitioners by providing professional skill-building resources and networking opportunities.

National Cancer Institute (NCI)
BG 9609 MSC 9760
9609 Medical Center Drive
Bethesda, MD 20892-9760
800-4-CANCER (800-422-6237)
https://www.cancer.gov
The NCI is an institute within the National Institutes of Health (NIH) responsible for coordinating and supporting cancer research and treatment.

National Heart, Lung, and Blood Institute (NHLBI)
P.O. Box 30105
Bethesda, MD 20824-0105
301-592-8573
https://www.nhlbi.nih.gov
The NHLBI is a federal agency responsible for advancing knowledge of the causes, treatment, and prevention of heart, lung, and blood disorders.

National Institute on Drug Abuse (NIDA)
Office of Science Policy and Communications
Public Information and Liaison Branch
6001 Executive Boulevard
Room 5213, MSC 9561
Bethesda, MD 20892
301-443-1124
https://www.drugabuse.gov
The NIDA conducts and supports research on the causes and consequences of addictive substance use and translates this science into practical advice for policies, programs, and practices in public health.

National Institutes of Health (NIH)
9000 Rockville Pike
Bethesda, MD 20892
301-496-4000, TTY: 301-402-9612

https://www.nih.gov
The NIH is the federal agency responsible for advancing scientific knowledge of the causes, treatment, and prevention of human diseases in order to promote well-being of the nation.

Office of the Surgeon General
200 Independence Avenue, SW
Washington, DC 20201
https://www.surgeongeneral.gov
The surgeon general is the country's senior medical officer responsible for communicating important health information to the nation and managing the U.S. Public Health Service.

Society of Public Health Educators (SOPHE)
10 G Street NE, Suite 605
Washington, DC 20002
202-408-9804
http://www.sophe.org
The SOPHE is the primary professional association of public health educators with the mission of identifying and addressing the challenges and needs of community-based and clinical health professionals.

Substance Abuse and Mental Health Services Administration (SAMHSA)
5600 Fishers Lane
Rockville, MD 20857
877-SAMHSA-7 (877-726-4727)
https://www.samhsa.gov
The SAMHSA is the federal agency responsible for leading national efforts in prevention, treatment, and recovery of substance abuse, mental illness, and behavioral health problems.

U.S. Department of Agriculture (USDA)
1400 Independence Ave., SW
Washington, DC 20250
202-720-2791
https://www.usda.gov
The USDA is a federal agency that protects and promotes the health of farmworkers, the public, and the environment through food safety, nutrition education, food policies, land management, rural development, research, and education.

U.S. Department of Health and Human Services (DHHS)
200 Independence Avenue, SW
Washington, DC 20201

877-696-6775
https://www.hhs.gov
The DHHS is the federal agency responsible for managing medical, public health, and social services.

U.S. Environmental Protection Agency (EPA)
1200 Pennsylvania Avenue, NW
Washington, DC 20460
202-564-4700
https://www.epa.gov
The EPA is the federal agency responsible for supporting public health by protecting the air, water, and land.

U.S. Food and Drug Administration (FDA)
10903 New Hampshire Avenue
Silver Spring, MD 20993
888-INFO-FDA (888-463-6332)
https://www.fda.gov
The FDA is an agency of the DHHS responsible for protecting and promoting public health through the regulation and supervision of a variety of types of food and drug products.

U.S. Public Health Service (USPHS)
800-279-1605
https://www.usphs.gov
The USPHS is one of the seven uniformed services under the direction of the executive branch of the federal government composed of health professionals serving throughout the nation to promote health, prevent disease, and advance public health science.

World Health Organization (WHO)
http://www.who.int/en
The WHO is an international humanitarian agency of the United Nations (UN) with the mission of promoting health for all people throughout the globe.

Glossary

Access to health care: The ability to locate and use medical services in a timely manner in order to promote the best possible health outcomes.

Acute illness: A temporary health problem that comes on suddenly and resolves within a few days to weeks.

Anatomy: The science of the structure of the body parts and organ systems.

Anticipatory guidance: A form of pediatric counseling that predicts the next stage of physical or social development of a child in order to educate and advise parents in effective parenting techniques.

Beneficence: Acting with goodness or kindness.

Best practices: Actions, programs, or treatments that are accepted and recommended by the majority of experts in the field.

Biopsychosocial: A perspective of care and prevention that considers the role and interaction of biological, psychological, and social factors in disease occurrence or prevention.

Biostatistics: A field of statistics applied to biological or health data.

Birth defect: A physical, structural, or functional abnormality present at birth.

Case study: A type of research study that details the life experiences of one person or group of people.

Causal factor: A factor or condition that determines whether a specific disease, event, or outcome will occur.

Causality: An action, condition, or factor that brings about a specific outcome.

Chronic illness: A long-term or permanent health problem.

Cohort study: A type of research study that follows the diet or activities of a large group of people for a long period of time, in some cases for their entire life.

Collaboration: A style of working with other people that brings together people of different strengths and backgrounds in order to achieve a common goal.

Communicable disease: An illness that spreads from one person to another through direct or indirect contact.

Community: A geographic area or a group of people with shared characteristics or interests.

Comorbid: An additional disease or diseases that are commonly seen at the same time as a primary disorder. For example, cardiovascular disease and diabetes mellitus are comorbid diseases, often seen with obesity.

Construct: Conceptual elements that interface to form a health theory.

Copayment: A nominal fee charged to customers of health insurance for medical services or prescription medication.

Data: Ideas or numbers that provide information.

Demographics: Data that describes a specific population.

Diagnosis: The act of investigating signs or symptoms in order to identify the cause or disease.

Disease: A condition that interferes with normal functioning of the human body.

Efficacy: The power to achieve the intended outcome.

Emerging disease: A disease that appears in a population for the first time.

Empowerment: To give power or authority to someone who traditionally lacks or is deprived of such power.

Endemic: Native or natural to a particular geographic region or group of people.

Epidemic: Rapid outbreak or growth of a health condition in a specific geographic area or within a specific group of people.

Epidemiology: The study of the distribution and determinants of disease within human populations.

Eradicate: To put an end to or destroy.

Evidence-based: Actions, programs, or treatments that have been proven to work through rigorous research.

Health promotion: Any planned set of educational, political, or regulatory activities intended to support individual or population health.

Hemorrhage: A life-threatening emergency of profuse, uncontrolled bleeding.

Herd immunity: A strategy of preventing communicable disease by increasing the immunity of enough individuals so that pathogens cannot infect susceptible hosts and achieve transmission to others.

Homicide: The death of a human being caused by the action or inaction of another person.

Host: A person, animal, or plant on which a pathogen lives.

Hygiene: A set of practices to prevent the spread of communicable diseases and promote health.

Hypertension: High blood pressure.

Hypochondriac: A person who is overly anxious about disease.

Iatrogenic: Illness caused by medical procedures.

Incidence: The number of new cases of disease in a given population at a given time period.

Infectious disease: Illness caused by a microorganism.

Injury: Damage to the human body caused by exposure to mechanical, thermal, electrical, chemical, or radiant energy.

Intentional injury: Purposeful damage to the body.

Intervene: To alter a problem, condition, or disease while it is occurring in order to minimize the adverse outcomes.

Intervention: Actions, programs, strategies, or behaviors that alleviate a health problem after it has started.

Jaundice: A yellowish tinge of the skin or whites of the eyes caused by excess bilirubin in the blood, a telltale sign of liver problems.

Justice: To treat fairly and equally.

Key stakeholder: An influential person or group with an interest in the project or problem.

Life expectancy: The number of years of life anticipated at a specific age.

Means of transmission: How an agent or pathogen moves from one host to another host.

Metabolite: An intermediate product of metabolism.

Metabolize: The chemical process of changing food, medication, or chemicals brought into the body into a form that can be used by the body.

Model: A symbol representing a larger or more complex idea.

Moderating factor: A factor or condition that affects an individual's potential for disease.

Morbidity: Illness or disease.

Mortality: Death.

Needs assessment: A systematic investigation of a health problem within a specific population. Needs assessments are used to identify the next steps toward alleviating the problem.

Pandemic: A rapid, widespread outbreak of an infectious disease, affecting multiple human populations across geographical countries or continents at a particular point in time.

Paradigm: A clear example, pattern, or model that represents a larger concept.

Pathogen: A bacterium, virus, helminth, or other microorganism that causes disease.

Pathology: A branch of medicine that deals with how a disease causes structural or functional abnormality.

Pediatrics: A branch of medicine that deals with children and diseases of children.

Physiology: The study of normal functions of cells, organs, tissues, or body systems and related chemical activities.

Positive reinforcement: Giving a reward in order to increase the likelihood of a certain behavior.

Postpartum: After childbirth.

Post-Traumatic Stress Disorder: A mental health disorder that is triggered by a traumatic or stressful event.

Practice: The application of ideas or methods to perform a particular function.

Prevalence: The number of people affected by a disease or condition in a particular population at a given point in time.

Prevention: Programs, people, or behaviors that stop an anticipated event, condition, or disease from occurring.

Process: A series of actions or operations in order to achieve a particular outcome.

Program planning: A field of public health that plans, develops, implements, and evaluates health promotion or disease prevention activities.

Protective factor: A condition that promotes optimal health.

Protocol: A set of rules that outlines procedures and conduct of scientific research or medical care.

Public: Ordinary people living or working in the community.

Quality of life: A standard of health, comfort, and satisfaction of an individual or population.

Racial segregation: The practice of restricting certain people from public facilities or benefits on the basis of race or perceived race.

Racism: Prejudice or discrimination against someone due to the misconception that one race is superior to another.

Reassortant virus: The mixing of genetic material from two or more viruses to create a new virus with properties of each of the parent viruses.

Reemerging disease: A disease that was once a major health problem, declined, and is becoming a major health problem again.

Research: A planned, systematic investigation.

Research participant: A person who participates in an experiment or study trial.

Respect for persons: The bioethical principle that describes treating others with dignity, kindness, and honor.

Reward: An incentive, praise, or gift that is given in return for desired behavior.

Ring vaccination: A strategy of preventing communicable disease by building a buffer against transmission by vaccinating a circle of individuals around the infected person.

Risk factor: A condition that increases the potential for injury or disease.

Sanitation: A term in public health that refers to cleanliness, adequate sewage disposal, and ensuring a safe water and food supply.

Screening: A medical strategy that checks for disease regardless of the presence of symptoms.

Shoe leather epidemiology: Epidemiological investigation that involves direct inquiries with the affected individuals.

Socioeconomic status: The combination of education, income, and occupation that determine one's standing in society.

Sociologist: A scientist who studies the nature and behaviors of people in groups.

Stillborn: An infant born dead.

Suicide: The intentional act of killing oneself.

Surveillance: Close and continuous observation.

Symptom: A sign that indicates disease or disorder of the body.

Teratogen: An agent that causes malformation of the embryo.

Theory: A hypothetical set of concepts that provide an explanation of complex behaviors, events, or situations.

Toxin: A substance that is harmful to the body.

Treatment: The pharmaceutical, medical, or surgical remedy of a disease or health problem.

Unintentional injury: Unexpected hurt or damage to the body resulting from neglect or carelessness.

Universal population: People who are unaffected or marginally affected by a health problem.

Universal prevention: A form of treatment that targets all people in the population, including those who do not suffer from a health problem, and aim to prevent the problem in the population.

Violence: The use of physical force or power that either results in physical or emotional injury or has a high likelihood of resulting in injury, death, or psychological harm.

About the Editor and Contributors

Editor

Sally Kuykendall, RN, PhD (CHES), is a professor in health services and a program evaluator of community-based public health programs. She earned a diploma in nursing, a BSc (hons) in chemistry and biology, an MS in health education, and a PhD in health sciences. Kuykendall worked as a critical care nurse in England and the United States before authoring numerous articles and reports on bullying and violence prevention. She wrote the book *Bullying: Health and Medical Issues Today* and served as content consultant on the public television movie *Beyond the Bully* (2014) by KSMQ in Rochester, MN. Her current research investigates scientific and scholarly misconduct.

Contributors

Nadav Antebi-Gruszka, MA, MPhil, is a doctoral candidate in the departments of Sociomedical Sciences and Psychology at Columbia University. His research focuses on LGBT health, HIV and substance use prevention, and technology.

Nooshin Asadpour, MD, is a pediatric resident physician at St. Christopher's Hospital for Children in Philadelphia, PA. Dr. Asadpour earned her bachelor's degree in biochemistry from Temple University and her medical degree from the Lewis Katz School of Medicine. Her love of children has led her to pursue a career in pediatric medicine. She plans to work as a general pediatrician in an urban setting where she can empower children and youth to build a strong foundation for a healthy existence in all domains of their life.

Elizabeth Y. Barnett is a postdoctoral fellow at Harvard Medical School and Brigham and Women's Hospital. She specializes in the development, implementation, and evaluation of health promotion programs, particularly in workplaces, communities, and schools.

Diana Bertorelli graduated from Saint Joseph's University with a master of health administration. Her research interests include the prevention and management of chronic diseases, particularly diabetes.

Alex Black holds a bachelor's degree in computer science and is studying for a master of business administration. His research interests include automotive maintenance and safety.

Mark Black is a consultant with Center City Film & Video and volunteer with EvoXLabs. Black designs digital images for medical continuing education and assistive technologies for people with disabilities.

Matthew Black holds a dual bachelor's degree in mathematics and chemistry and a master's degree in education. His area of expertise is math education for inner-city youth. He is currently pursuing a PhD in mathematics education at Pennsylvania State University.

Georgiana Bostean, PhD, is an assistant professor of sociology and environmental science and policy at Chapman University. Her research focuses on the social determinants of health and has been published in journals including the *American Journal of Public Health*, *Social Science and Medicine*, and *Journal of Immigrant and Minority Health*.

Rochelle Caviness is an independent scholar whose main area of interest is the history of science, technology, and medicine.

George W. Dowdall, PhD, is professor emeritus of sociology at Saint Joseph's University and an adjunct fellow at the Center for Public Health Initiatives of the University of Pennsylvania. His most recent book is *College Drinking: Reframing a Social Problem/Changing the Culture* (Sterling, VA: Stylus, 2013).

Leapolda Figueroa is a graduate of the College of Professional and Liberal Studies, majoring in healthcare administration at Saint Joseph's University. Ms. Figueroa works as a health administrator and is currently applying to law school to work in healthcare law.

Ariel A. Friedman, BA, is an MEd candidate in the Department of Clinical and Counseling Psychology at Teacher's College, Columbia University. Her research interests include LGBT health, sex positivity, gender nonconformity, and alternative family planning methods.

Sarah R. Green, MD, is a pediatric resident at Saint Christopher's Hospital for Children in Philadelphia. She plans to pursue a career in adolescent medicine. Her current research focuses on depression screening in adolescents.

Julia Hanes, LSW, MSW, is the intimate partner violence (IPV) specialist at St. Christopher's Hospital for Children through Lutheran Settlement House (LSH). Through this work, Julia responds to crisis consults for victims and survivors of IPV and trafficking. In addition, Julia trains the hospital staff about IPV and trafficking and how to talk to caregivers and patients about those topics. Outside of the hospital system Julia has presented at the Trans Health Conference on IPV and trans-related issues. Julia received a master's degree in social Work from New York University.

Salini Inaganti is project manager at Public Health Management Corporation (PHMC). Her research interests include health communication, decision making, organ donation, and health disparities.

Amy Jessop, PhD, MPH, is founder and director of Hepatitis Treatment, Research and Education Center (HepTREC). Dr. Jessop's work focuses on the prevention, screening, and treatment of infectious diseases, particularly vaccine-preventable infections and viral hepatitis.

Jennie Jacobs Kronenfeld is professor emerita in the Sociology Program, Sanford School of Social and Family Dynamics, Arizona State University. Her research areas are medical sociology and aging and the life course with special focus on health policy, health care utilization, and health behavior. She serves as editor of the annual *Research in the Sociology of Health Care* published each year by Emerald Press. She is coeditor of Health and associate editor in chief of the *American Journal of Health Promotion.* She has served in many roles with the American Sociological Association (ASA) including as chair of the Medical Sociology Section and other positions in this group. She is currently serving as a council member with the Retired Sociologist Interest Group of the ASA. She has served as secretary-treasurer of the Medical Care section of the American Public Health Association. She is a past president of Sociologists for Women in Society.

Louis Kuykendall Jr., DMin, is an ordained clergyperson in the United Church of Christ (UCC) and a volunteer hospice chaplain. His research focuses on the spiritual care of hospice patients. He is pastor and teacher in a local UCC parish and trains hospice and church volunteers regarding end-of-life issues and spiritual care.

Marvin J. H. Lee, PhD, is editor of *The Journal of Healthcare Ethics & Administration*, published by The Institute of Clinical Bioethics at Saint Joseph's University. He is also a bioethics consultant at the institute. His research primarily focuses on ethical issues concerning medicine, culture/tradition, and health administration. Dr. Lee majored in philosophy as an undergraduate, and took his interest in medical ethics and health care administration during his graduate years; he earned his master's at Yale University and completed a PhD at Cambridge University, England.

Susana Leong earned her doctorate and master's degrees in health and behavior studies from Columbia University, and her bachelor's degree from the University of

California, Berkeley. Dr. Leong is an adjunct assistant professor in the Department of Physiological Nursing at the University of California, San Francisco.

Kristie Lowery is a health care professional with more than 40 years of experience in the industry. Half of her career has been focused on quality, risk management, regulations, and patient safety. She has participated in the development of 12 professional posters on patient safety interventions and contributed multiple articles on patient safety concerns. She has experienced the evolution of patient safety since the Institute of Medicine issued the "To Err is Human" report in 1999. She continues to communicate with consumers to inform them of patient safety concerns and their role and responsibilities while navigating the health care system.

Noora F. Majid is a master of public health graduate from the Mailman School of Public Health at Columbia University. Her interests include intervention design, evaluation, and health communication, specifically related to the prevention and management of chronic diseases.

Erin Mathews is a premed student at Ursinus College in Collegeville, PA, majoring in biology and French. She intends to pursue a career in dermatology.

Neil Mathews, MD, is a family and sports medicine physician at Lehigh Valley Hospital in Allentown, PA, and assistant professor in the Department of Family Medicine. He also serves as head team physician for a professional hockey team and has extensive experience in the diagnosis and management of concussions.

Maria DiGiorgio McColgan, MD, MSEd, FAAP, is a board certified child abuse pediatrician, medical director of the Child Protection Program at St. Christopher's Hospital for Children, and an associate professor at Drexel University College of Medicine. Dr. McColgan is the founding advisory board chair and pediatric advisor of Prevent Child Abuse Pennsylvania.

Caitlin Monahan is a BA candidate in the psychology department in the College of Arts and Sciences at New York University. Her research focuses on intersectionality, power relations, and stigma of marginalized social groups.

Autumn Nanassy, MA, is the trauma research coordinator for St. Christopher's Hospital for Children. Her research primarily focuses on pediatric trauma and burns.

Kim L. Nguyen earned her bachelor of science in biology with minors in health care ethics and business administration from Saint Joseph's University. She explored the topic of telemedicine in her publication titled "Obstacles and Solutions in the Implementation Telestroke: Billing, Licensing, and Legislation." She is currently an MD candidate at Drexel University College of Medicine pursuing pediatrics.

Victor Okparaeke, PhD, is a graduate of Walden University School of Public Health, and the University of Health Sciences, School of Medicine, Antigua, WI. His interests include community and environmental health issues, as well as the prevention and management of hypertensive disease and diabetes in rural communities.

Godyson Orji, DHA, is a visiting assistant professor of Health Services at Saint Joseph University. Dr. Orji's research and interest are in health informatics, health information management, health care analytics, and health economics and outcome research.

Sean P. Phillips is a doctoral candidate in modern European history at the University of Notre Dame, where he is a past Annese fellow of the Nanovic Institute for European Studies. He is a recipient of the Francis A. Countway Library Fellowship in the history of medicine and a Wood Institute Grant from The College of Physicians of Philadelphia. His dissertation explores the role of Catholic clergy in the propagation of the smallpox vaccine in 19th-century France.

David J. Reynolds, PhD, health psychologist at Joint Base Andrews, trains and supervises residents in behavioral medicine. His main interests are PTSD, chronic pain, and insomnia. He is a veteran of the Persian Gulf War and Operation Enduring Freedom, having served 4 years in the Marines and 16 years in the Air Force.

Staceyann Smith is a pediatric resident at Saint Christopher's Hospital for Children in Philadelphia, PA. She earned her BS in human science from Georgetown University. In 2015, she earned a dual MD/MPH degree from the University of Connecticut School of Medicine and School of Public Health. Her professional interests include childhood obesity and child advocacy.

A. J. Smuskiewicz is a freelance writer and editor with more than 25 years of professional experience. He specializes in science, health and medicine, sexuality issues, music, and current events.

Timur Suhail-Sindhu, MD, is currently a resident in psychiatry at Dartmouth Hitchcock Medical Center. His clinical and research interests include addiction, trauma-related disorders, and psychotherapy.

Eileen L. Sullivan is licensed pharmacist and an assistant professor in the Department of Health Services at Saint Joseph's University. Sullivan teaches courses in chronic illness, health and society, medical terminology, and global health initiatives. Her research focuses on nonpharmacologic interventions to improve quality of life for people living with Alzheimer's disease.

Christine M. Thomas completed a bachelor's degree in Interdisciplinary Health Services at Saint Joseph's University in Philadelphia, PA. Christine intends to expand her knowledge of the health care field in the branch of physical therapy, specializing in neurology. Throughout her studies, Christine focused on prenatal care, developing a promotional video on public health for Mercy Health System clients.

Rochelle Thompson, MS, is the injury prevention coordinator at St. Christopher's Hospital for Children. Her primary focus is providing education and tools to help save lives and reduce preventable unintentional injuries.

Tenille J. Torres is a health researcher particularly interested in the development of community-based participatory research to eliminate racial gaps in health and equity. She received her MPH at Boston University School of Public Health in maternal and child health.

Stephen K. Trapp, PhD, is a research associate at the University of South Florida. He has a particular interest in positive psychology constructs as they relate to chronic health conditions and physical rehabilitation.

Jason S. Ulsperger is an associate professor of sociology at Arkansas Tech University, where he teaches gerontology. He has published on a wide variety of elder care topics, including aging, nursing home reform, and abuse in long-term care facilities. He is currently studying ritualized practices related to volunteerism among the aged.

Catherine van de Ruit, PhD, is an assistant professor of health and exercise physiology at Ursinus College. Her scholarship focuses on public health responses to the AIDS epidemic in Southern Africa and on quality improvement in clinical settings in South Africa and the United States.

Simon Waldbaum, PhD, has spent over a decade conducting biomedical science research, most recently at the University of Colorado Anschutz Medical Campus. His primary research focus and areas of publication have been in the field of neurology, illuminating the link between neuronal mitochondrial oxidative stress and the development of acquired epilepsy.

Alison C. Walensky is an independent scholar with a master of special education, grades 1–6. She has taught over 500 students in her past three years of teaching, including 125 students with Individualized Education Plans.

Shayan Waseh is an MD/MPH candidate at Thomas Jefferson University in Philadelphia, PA. His past research has included telemedicine training curricula and diagnostic tools for detecting Alzheimer's disease. He is interested in applying population health approaches to solving contemporary health care challenges in patient access, health care quality, and medical costs.

Index

Page locators in **boldface** indicate main entries in the encyclopedia.